METTERNICH

(1773–1859)

METTERNICH IN 1805

From the portrait by François Gerard in the Portrait Gallery of the National Library of Vienna.

Reproduced by kind permission of the Director of the Vienna State Collections and Messrs. F. Bruckmann of Munich.

METTERNICH

1773–1859

A Study of his Period and Personality

by
ALGERNON
CECIL

EYRE AND SPOTTISWOODE
LONDON

First published January 1933
Reprinted February 1933
Second Edition April 1943
Third Edition January 1947

*This Book is produced in complete conformity
with the Authorized Economy Standards
and is printed in Great Britain for
Eyre and Spottiswoode (Publishers) Limited
15, Bedford Street, Strand, London, W.C.2
by Jarrold and Sons, Limited, Norwich*

CONTENTS

LIST OF ILLUSTRATIONS

PREFACE TO THE 1947 EDITION

A REISSUE of this book appears to invite a few additional observations. Since it was last published the world has had an even clearer vision of the self-wise reformer than was afforded by the Peace of Versailles. The exhibition of startling varieties of democracy, displayed of late both at Potsdam and Paris has been eloquent with the language of flowers—not excluding *fleurs du mal*; whilst, on adjoining lawns, to continue the pleasing metaphor, Mr. Bevin or others might be seen exchanging buff and rebuff with M. Molotov and his team in a hearty game of blind man's buff, played according to the rules of the new diplomacy. Meantime the blunder, which some 'reactionary' persons might have styled a crime, of letting Austria disintegrate has been further illustrated by the lapse under Russian influence, if not into Russian hands, of the Czecho-Slovaks and the Jugo-Slavs—composite states constructed, not in the grand manner of the Habsburg tradition, but in the sentimental fashion of nationality, and of a nationality ill-defined. At home as well as abroad the decline of the Liberal Party whose resurrection in Britain its prophets had falsely foretold, may have caused some onlookers to reflect that Sir Archibald Sinclair's comparison of it, in his General Election broadcast, to Cordelia battling with the Gonerils and Regans of Labour and Conservatism (as represented presumably by his late colleagues in the Coalition Government) achieved exactitude at any rate in one respect. For Cordelia was presently hung; however lamentable the circumstances.

All these matters bear obliquely upon the case of Metternich who had perceived the worth of Austria, the weakness of the Liberal foundation and the way to work, if only for a few momentous years, a concert of Europe. Far too many persons have committed themselves to his condemnation to expect that the minor works of history should for the present take any adequate measure of his accomplishments or achievement. Should human civilization, however, survive the means of wholesale destruction it is now busy fashioning, intellectually as well as physically, it may, perhaps, be recognised that to Metternich, more than to most people, it owed a century of comparative peace, in which to recover its strength after the first onset of "the Revolution", to set its house in order, and to repair and replace what moth and rust had corrupted. This work was in fact begun; and the Victorian era is proof of it. But we did not know how to finish.

Of any such understanding of past events, we cannot, as I said, expect to find the reflection in the minor works of history. But in history like the late Sir Adolphus Ward's volumes on Germany, through which such wide learning filters, and in Taine's *Origines de la France Contemporaine*, which of all great histories is, I venture to say, at the present time the most worth reading, the apologia of Metternich is made. He saw, like Taine, the virtue of the *ancien régime*, no less than its defects; he perceived, like Joseph de Maistre, that the answer to a Revolution is not as was earlier urged, a counter-Revolution, but the contrary of a Revolution; he understood, like Bacon, that change in politics to be healthy should come, like change in Nature, almost unperceived, so that we know neither the day nor the hour. Like a thief in the night a new era should slip in; like a sunset fading a dead epoch be gone. All statesmanship worthy of the name must emulate such moving from precedent to precedent, shunning all noise of agitation, cultivating above all graces patience. Ideas should sleep long before they stir us and fall again placidly to sleep before they leave us.

Beside all the lamentable nonsense that has done duty for wisdom in our time; beside the praise of social systems that turn into menacing despotisms; beside leagues of nations that engage us in vast commitments and think to save their reputation by changing their name—it is wholesome to place some of Taine's dispassionate conclusions; for they are as much to the point in regard to this latter phase of the Revolution as in respect to that former one which England fought with Metternich as her ally.

Take, for example, first of all, Taine's considered judgment on the French aristocracy before the Revolution and compare it with the portrait of M. le Marquis in *A Tale of Two Cities*, from which, I suspect, most Englishmen derive their conception of a noble of the *ancien régime*. Here, then, in succession are Taine's comments on the French aristocracy as seen on the eve of the Revolution, at its outbreak, and as it reached its consummation. I select what are to my mind the significant sentences. Take first his judgment on the hot-house plants confined and cultivated at Versailles:

"Une culture mal entendue les avait détournés de leur emploi naturel, pour en faire des arbres de luxe et d'agrément, souvent creux, étiolés, faibles de sève, trop émondés, trop coûteux d'ailleurs:...; et le jardinage savant, qui les contournait, les groupait, les alignait en formes et en

bosquets factices, faisait avorter leurs fruits, pour multiplier leurs fleurs—
Mais les fleurs étaient exquises, et même aux yeux du moraliste, c'est
quelque chose qu'une telle floraison. Du côté de la politesse, du bon ton et
du savoir-vivre, les moeurs et les manières avaient alors atteint dans le
grand monde un degré de perfection que jamais en France ni ailleurs, elles
n'ont eu auparavant ou n'ont regagné depuis, et, de tous les arts par
lesquels les hommes se sont dégagés de la brutalité primitive, celui qui
leur enseigne les égards mutuels est peut-être le plus précieux...".[1]

Then consider Taine's judgment on the provincial Noblesse:

"J'ai eu beau lire, je n'ai point trouvé en eux les tyrans ruraux
que dépeignent les déclamateurs de la Révolution."[2]

From that conclusion pass on to the great historian's witness to the
general capacity of the nobles as they gathered at the States-General:

"J'ai lu vingt volumes de leurs procés-verbaux: on ne peut voir de
meilleurs citoyens, des administrateurs plus intègres, plus appliqués, et qui
se donnent plus de peine sans autre objet que le bien public. La bonne
volonté est complète. Jamais l'aristocratie n'a été si digne du pouvoir
qu'au moment où elle allait le perdre; les privilégiés, tirés de leur désoeuvre-
ment, redevenaient des hommes publics et rendus à leur fonction, reve-
naient à leur devoir."[3]

Finally, consider this verdict on the conduct of those who have not
merely been deprived of privilege but of protection for life and
property:

"J'ai lu en original plusieurs centaines d'enquêtes manuscrites; presque
toujours j'y ai admiré l'humanité des nobles, leur longanimité, leur
horreur du sang. Non seulement beaucoup d'entre eux ont du coeur et
tous ont de l'honneur, mais encore, élevés dans la philosophie du dix-
huitième siècle, ils sont doux, sensibles; ils répugnent aux voies de fait.
Surtout les officiers sont exemplaires; leur seul défaut est la faiblesse:
plutot que de tirer sur l'émeute, ils rendent les forts qu'ils commandent,
ils se laissent insulter, lapider par le peuple...Leur courage est de l'espèce
la plus rare, puisqu'il consiste à rester en faction, impassibles sous les
affronts et sous les coups.—Par une injustice énorme, une classe entière qui
n'avait point de part aux faveurs de la cour et qui subissait autant de
passe-droits que les roturiers ordinaires, la noblesse provinciale, est con-
fondue avex les parasites titrés qui assiégeaient les antichambres de
Versailles."[4]

The real aristocracy in England, as Metternich said, was the
squirearchy; and for Taine the same is true in France, *mutatis mutandis*.
But the Revolution in its blindness warred precisely against the class
which on the whole has had a better conception of political liberty
and public duty than any other, just as it warred also against the

---

[1] Les Origines de la France Contempte., Vol. VIII, p. 138
[2] *Ibid.*, I, 51   [3] *Ibid.* II., p. 154   [4] *Ibid.*, III., p. 245

institution which first threw wide open the doors of a "career open to talent"—the Church.

I conclude with some apposite words of Disraeli's, written, apparently, under the influence of parting with Metternich and, certainly, during the passage of Europe through the second phase in 1849 of that Revolution which is now far advanced into its third:

"I think," Disraeli writes to a friend, "I told you of my farewell with Metternich. Though nobody talks of foreign affairs I hear, among the initiated, that there are odd whispers, and the general state of things is anything but satisfactory. The fact is the elements of government do not exist in the greater part of Europe, and we are destroying them pretty quickly in England. Russia alone develops herself, and will develop herself still more in the great struggle which is perhaps nearer than we imagine. Once destroy the English aristocracy, and enthrone the commercial principle as omnipotent in this island, and there will be no repelling force which will prevent the Slavonians conquering the whole of the South of Europe."†

Hebrew prophets sometimes saw very far ahead.

August, 1946   ALGERNON CECIL

---

†Monypenny and Buckle, "Life of Benjamin Disraeli." III, p. 195.

I

INTRODUCTION

THE republication of this book has seemed to its Publishers to invite or even require some introductory discussion of its bearing upon recent political developments; and this opinion has the more cogency that at the date of its first appearance it was described by an eminent reviewer as being in the nature of a challenge. If that charge was justified, it is important to consider in what way.

So far as I can see the book might be termed a challenge because its historical outlook was in general contradiction with the views and valuations, moral and political, in contemporary use; or because its inescapable background of the Habsburg Empire was inacceptable to modern sentiment; or finally, because its special subject, viz. the work and personality of Metternich, was paradoxically praised. It may, then, be pertinent to reconsider these matters, not in any abstract way as if we had to choose between the world of the nineteenth century and a perfect society, between the Austrian Empire and an ideal state, between Metternich and an impeccable statesman, but rather as offering a critical alternative to the great "Liberal experiment" which was actually made in 1919, to the sound of trumpets proclaiming a new earth and indeed a new heaven, if any heaven at all, but which ended so catastrophically in 1939 with the drums of war, like so many tom-toms, beating in the advent of more savage hostilities and more ferocious hatreds than ever before.

Comparisons are said to be odious, and the comparisons of history are particularly odious to those whose politics are derived from Utopian theories and not from the study of facts. But, though in deference to one of my critics who complained of a comparison drawn between the shortcomings in public finance of ministers in Metternich's time and country and in our own I have suppressed a footnote, I must still insist that the comparative method in history offers the only method of getting our estimates either of forms of government or the merits of statesmen even approximately correct. The "use of history," observes a sagacious writer,[1] "is to light the present hour to its duty." It is misused, then, if it be treated as an exhausted torch or an extinguished luminary. Somewhere, although, maybe, beyond our puny vision, it ever flames and flashes; and

[1] Abbott, "Thucydides," p. 7.

7

never was its distant radiance better calculated to be a beacon-light than in the Egyptian darkness of the present hour. The child and hero of the Revolution, with whom at every stage of Metternich's career we have to deal, knew its value well. "Let my son," said Napoleon, "read and meditate upon the lessons of history, which is the only true philosophy."

Let the student, then, shed all pre-dispositions as he starts to survey the *ancien régime* or fixes his eye upon the figure of Metternich. Since this book was first published we have had time to consider a Europe "liberated" from the rule of priests and kings, and dominated by an Austrian house-painter, an Italian schoolmaster and a Georgian "kinto" from Tiflis. These are all in the descent, not hereditary but intellectual, from the Corsican adventurer, and much more truly sons of the people than he could claim to be. That alone affords some food for reflection. But, after it is digested, let the student remind himself of some opinions derived from eminent, but none too friendly sources, regarding Metternich, or rather the services rendered by Metternich to Europe. Let him consider, for example, Dr. Gooch's remark that Metternich was "the brain of the victorious alliance" which liberated Europe from Napoleon;[1] or Albert Sorel's conclusion that "the work of Vienna (that is, of course, of the Congress of Vienna) . . . obtained for Europe the most fruitful period of peace it has ever enjoyed;"[2] or again Mr. Woodward's rather grudging admission that "in the dark century which has followed the Vienna treaties there is a magnificence about a policy conceived in terms of general European interest."[3] Let the student mark these tributes and ask himself whether the subject to whom they relate had not a title to political greatness which most men might envy and to which few attain. By such considerations are old prejudices dispelled and good—that is detached—dispositions fostered.

I recall with the greater satisfaction after what has been said that my own interest in Metternich was first excited by a reference to him, slight yet significant, in a book by a Liberal Prime Minister who had made contact with the Continent—with its thought and more particularly with contemporary leaders of public opinion in Germany. In Rosebery's monograph on Pitt, Metternich is mentioned as saying that each day was of value to him only as the eve of

---

[1] G. P. Gooch, "Studies in Diplomacy and Statecraft," p. 254.

[2] Sorel, "L'Europe et La Révolution Française", VIII, p. 502 and I, p. 10 note.

[3] Woodward, "Three Studies in Conservatism," Metternich, p. 75.

its morrow—a sentiment so pregnant with the notion of intelligent advance as to make it seem strange that its author should ever have been decried as the soul of "reaction." Later, as my interest in Europe grew, so did my interest in Metternich increase; and, when I was invited to contribute this study of him to a series concerned with the careers of some eminent Europeans, the chance of gratifying my curiosity to the full seemed to have come. In one respect at least I might confidently hope that I was qualified for the work. Early contact with Conservatives had so tempered my understanding of politics—and of past politics, which is history—that not even the fortunate chance which gave me one of the most distinguished Liberals of his time as my tutor at Oxford deprived me of the inclination to ask myself questions, and not least among them the question upon what first principles or basic premises Liberalism rested its latent claim to have proved all things and to have detected that which was true. Everywhere a deep assurance of finality seemed to underlie its pleasing profession of the open mind; yet there was reason enough to wonder whether it was really in any position to provide the rock-bottom required for an enduring, and, much more, for an everlasting mansion of thought. Time at any rate was needed to test the value of this revolutionary style in building; for Gladstone's powerful personality, so long as it remained dominant, rendered experiment valueless. The greatest Liberal in Britain had been formed in a school of theology and politics highly conservative and even in some respects mediæval. The question to be tried was, then, whether Liberalism could stand without the sustaining genius of a master dependent, like England itself, upon distant and deeper influences than either was ready to recognise.

This question was put to the test in circumstances peculiarly favourable. Seldom can a British Administration have surpassed in political talent or European dispositions that which Asquith formed in 1908. Yet neither Morley's French models nor Haldane's spiritual home in German philosophy,[1] though both men towered as thinkers above the politicians of their time, sufficed to renovate the crumbling fabric of Liberal opinion. It fell; and great was the fall of it. Britain had not exhausted her interest in the Continental Revolutions of 1789 and 1848; but it was the Socialist and no longer the Liberal element in modern political architecture that was engaging her attention. Haldane's secession from the Liberal to the

[1] I need hardly say that I have no sort of intention of associating myself with the scurrilous use that has been made of this expression to discredit one of the greatest of our Secretaries for War.

Labour Party was symptomatic of the change; and, if they are right who identify the League of Nations as the last refuge of Liberalism, then a tale of which Voltaire and Madame de Staël began the telling on the banks of Lac Léman may not inappropriately be said to have closed in that fine palace of peace at Geneva whence the representatives of collective security have had to retreat since the return of war.

These matters are, however, only important here in so far as they reflect upon the writing of history and in especial upon that of recent times. Liberalism to so many distinguished men of the last century seemed the last word of wisdom that it is hardly surprising if its old valuations of thought and things are still widely accepted by historians without challenge or inquiry. Yet that which demonstrably no longer secures allegiance in practical politics has *ipso facto* been dislodged from any compelling authority in the sphere of history. The congregation of the faithful is indeed still to be found and deserves to be honoured for its faithfulness in adversity, but its premises are too commonly denied in practice to leave any of its conclusions conclusive. Metternich merits the benefit, therefore, of corresponding doubts; and the verdict upon him of careful reconsideration.

I say so with the more confidence as I look again at the generous words which Herbert Fisher prefixed to the original edition of this book and which are reproduced here with no waning gratitude or weakened affection on my part for him who first wrote them. His Liberal principles were, so far as I know, never shaken; yet his wider mind, if I rightly understood some words he once said to me, recognised to a rare degree the strength of the case upon the other side. Not for nothing had he tasted the society of Taine, nor for nothing recorded the dark forebodings of Renan regarding the fate of France! *"La France se meurt: ne troublez pas son agonie"* —he is the English chronicler of that poignant *cri de coeur* from one whose mentality had made, as it used to seem to me, a rare impression upon his own. The words were prophetic when this book appeared: they have now been fulfilled within the measure of their meaning.

It seems difficult to exaggerate the consequence of the catastrophe of France to the study of European history. The birthplace of the Revolution has fallen in Paris with a more resounding crash than the last home of the *ancien régime* at Vienna; and every argument that was once drawn from the disintegration of Austria to confuse the Conservative can now be derived from the collapse of France to confound the nationalist and the democrat. The Revolution, to judge by the test of time, has not proved so sound a preservative of the integrity of the state as the *ancien régime*. But, more than that, it can now be seen clearly that France and Austria were as necessary to each other as to European solidarity. The reconstruction of the Continent has produced no coherence even where the changes gave us the best right to expect it. Liberalism has not been justified of all its children, or even of the most part of them.

Among the Liberals of the last century Acton was perhaps alone in recognising both the value of Austria and the perils of the principle of nationality to the genius of European civilisation; and I should like to think that this study of Metternich had proceeded along lines not altogether inconsistent with the vision of one who could write in 1862, three years after Metternich's death, that "those States are substantially the most perfect which, like the British and Austrian Empires, include various distinct nationalities without oppressing them."[1] Metternich, if it comes to that, boasted to Varnhagen von Ense that, in the best acceptation of the term, he was himself a Liberal: and, if some words he addressed to Marmont be any index to his mind, then he was surely convinced that his own part in the history of his age would be able to bear the fierce scrutiny of Time, no less than the urgent eyes of Rostand's *L'Aiglon*. "I make one simple condition," he said, when Marmont asked what he should tell the duc de Reichstadt regarding Napoleon, "that you tell him the whole truth without disguising the good or the evil."

These two slight colloquies alone should serve to disturb, if not dispel the notion that Metternich was a blind reactionary or an unscrupulous partisan. But there is more than that to be said. The charge of reaction, even if it could be brought home to him, as perhaps it might be, say, to Eldon (himself, however, with his brother Stowell, a notable instance of talent rising unassisted to the top in a time supposedly overlaid with privilege) would form no valid indictment. An age which has seen the Liberal Party shelve the classical doctrine of *laissez-faire* and, in a vain attempt to keep abreast of Labour, substitute the mediæval idea of welfare for that of wealth, has no title to regard reaction as an evil. The philosophy of Vico, which conceives the world as moving in cycles, has more claim upon attention to-day than the assumption of continuous, almost auto-

---

[1] "The History of Freedom and other Essays," p. 298.

matic progress. But, however that may be, Metternich, on his own showing, was so little of a reactionary as to desiderate the designation of a reluctant stationary. "My life," he wrote in 1820, "has coincided with a hateful time. I came into the world too soon or too late; I feel good for nothing. Earlier I should have had my share of the pleasures of the period; later I should have helped in reconstruction; now I pass my life in propping up worm-eaten buildings. I ought to have been born in 1900 and to have the twentieth century before me."

The words of sagacious politicians are as those of good physicians who know that the human body must be made ready before an operation can be wisely performed. The passage just quoted enables one to understand how it was that after he had fallen in 1848 and was an exile in Brighton—at a time, in fact, when his fortunes were at their lowest ebb—Metternich could prove such an inspiration to Disraeli, then at work upon the evolution of Tory-Democracy. "You are the only philosophical statesman I ever encountered," Disraeli wrote to him after a visit . . . "I catch wisdom from your lips and inspiration from your example." The writer was confessedly a flatterer; but a letter of the same date to Mrs. Disraeli, from which a quotation is given in the text, removes any suspicion of compliment from these expressions. Thus, so far from Metternich being just "*un homme d'autrefois*," he showed himself, even in old age and exile, capable of inspiring one of the most brilliant and constructive minds of the coming period. What could a man do more to prove himself alert, intelligent, evolutionary?

The truth is that the legends of publicists, writing under the influence of contemporary prepossessions, deserve quite as close a scrutiny as the legends of saints propagated by enthusiastic admirers; and, when a strong personality is, like Metternich's, capable of evoking more hatred than affection, then the scrutiny needs to be closer still. How much misplaced political energy has gone into the creation of the legend of the Bastille and the celebration of the fourteenth of July! How few people know yet that the capture of the famous fortress was in fact a savage attack upon the forces of order by a horde of vagrant banditti, whose exploits in the way of plundering shops and assaulting peaceful citizens had so much alarmed the resident Parisians of the time that the tocsin was rung, not, as generally asserted, to sound the knell of the *ancien régime*, but just as an alarm bell to summon all men of good-will to defend the common right of honest citizens to be protected against ruffians.[1] It is high time some trouble were taken to correct that popular delusion and the yet more popular inference. Still, as a distinguished Liberal historian of our own day has courteously remarked, "We historians are a fallible folk and must be charitable to one another."[2]

The legend of Metternich as a reactionary is not likely to be revised by any mind that remains incarcerated in the legend of the Revolution as evolved by Girondin ideologues and propagated by political idealists. It needs a temperament cool and detached as that of Thucydides to take the just measure of a man who fought the Revolution in the person of its foremost representative, and yet had the presence of mind to recognise that Napoleon had become its master, as well as being its incarnation, and, that, in so far as he was the former, he merited the consideration of such as aimed (to borrow Joseph de Maistre's phraseology) not at a counter-revolution, but at 'the contrary of a revolution'—at the reconditioning, that is, if the simile be any help, rather than at any immediate reconstruction of the dilapidated house of Christendom.

It may be of assistance to the argument, so as to get both a distant and a nearer view of the subject, to interject at this point some observations of Thucydides regarding revolutions in general, and of Pitt regarding the French Revolution in particular.

"And so," observes the Greek historian, "there fell upon the cities on account of revolutions many grievous calamities, such as happen and always will happen while human nature is the same, but which are severer or milder, and different in their manifestations, according as the variations in circumstance present themselves in each case. For in peace and prosperity both states and individuals have gentler feelings, because men are not then forced to face conditions of dire necessity; but war, which robs men of the easy supply of their daily wants, is a rough schoolmaster and creates in most people a temper that matches their condition. . . . So it was that every form of depravity showed itself in Hellas in consequence of its revolutions, and that simplicity, which is the chief element of a noble nature, was laughed to scorn and disappeared, while mutual antagonism of feeling, combined with mistrust, prevailed far and wide."[3]

Turn the page and consider the climax:

"At this crisis, when the life of the city had been thrown into utter confusion, human nature, now triumphant over the laws and accustomed even in spite of the laws to do wrong, took delight in showing that its

[1] The true story can be conveniently read in Louis Madelin's "The French Revolution," pp. 71–78.
[2] G. M. Trevelyan, "England under Queen Anne," III, p. xii.
[3] Thucydides, III, cc. 82-84 (Loeb translation).

B

passions were ungovernable, that it was stronger than justice and an
enemy to all superiority."

So much for a classical judgment of history upon the general
subject of wars and revolutions. Now let Pitt be briefly heard, as he
was once actually heard and at length in February 1793, on the
international aspect of the Revolution in France:

"Such a violation of rights as France has been guilty of," he said,
"it would be difficult to find in the history of the world." Then again,
nearly two years later, "I have no idea of any peace being secure, unless
France return to the monarchical system. . . . That there may, however,
be intermediate changes that may give the probability of peace with that
country, even should it continue a republic, I am ready to allow, though I
certainly think that the monarchical form of constitution is best for all
the countries of Europe and most calculated to ensure to each of them
general and individual happiness."[1]

Such echoes from Pitt and Thucydides should serve to compel
even the most prejudiced student to consider whether opposition
to the Revolution in France was not aligned with the best opinion,
not merely of the time, but of all time. For, as time itself has shown,
it was not the lyrics of the enthusiastic young Poet but the dooms of
the sagacious old Statesman which discovered the coming course of
events; and Wordsworth lived to recognise, by implication at least,
the far-sighted wisdom of Burke. The very children of the Revolution
rose in judgment against it. Condorcet, by his suicide, and Madame
Roland, by her familiar apostrophe, testified to the crushing misery
of a deception the completeness of which has been admirably and
dramatically rendered in Laharpe's "Souper de Cazotte." The
apologetic of Metternich between 1814 and 1848 is thus to be found
on every page of European history between 1792 and 1815. For
though the apologists of the Revolution have been many, its apology
is still to seek. Patience, which Pitt reckoned to be the first quality
of a statesman, would have given the Royal Government time to put
its programme into effect. Doubtless the *ancien régime* had moved
too slow; yet more people have starved, and longer, in Europe to-
day, whilst the slumbering Democracies, so-called, have been trying
to put their houses in order, than ever starved in France whilst the
honest Necker and the well-meaning Louis sought to make good
their promises. But passion, not patience, has been the cardinal virtue
of the Revolution from the beginning; and the result can be read in
the record of the crescendo of crime that ensued—in the September
massacre of helpless prisoners that was, by just so much that they

[1] December 30th, 1794.

were already prisoners and helpless, worse than the massacre of suspected enemies on St. Bartholomew's Day; in the militarism that gave Europe its first taste of conscription; in the military dictatorship that drenched all Europe in blood and tears for fifteen years. It is a remarkable testimony to the hold of the "progressive fallacy" upon the human mind that these things, and not the opposition to them, should be credited with the relative peace, freedom and eventual prosperity that followed the return to historical tradition in France and its maintenance in England. Metternich, though he could not be blind to the essential falsity of a movement which raised a new autocracy upon professions of liberty, developed the new military caste behind the smoke-screen of equality, and inaugurated incessant war with shouts of fraternity, never to all appearance lost his temper like the *emigrés* or his sense of humour like the Whigs. He was essentially a political physician, and showed himself so at every turn. If his observations to Guizot and Thiers deserve to be treated as sincere estimates of his own powers of diagnosis and not as amusing "leg-pulls," he must have been not a little vain of his powers of diagnosis; but he had at least the saving grace of a deep sense of responsibility. "Every mistake which I make affects nearly thirty million human beings,"[1] he declares. His sentiment had even then an old-fashioned sound; since Napoleon had openly enquired of him, what a number of totalitarians have since secretly wondered, whether the lives of a million of men mattered at all to such supermen as themselves. The Revolution and its Contrary were at issue in that matter; for, if the *ancien régime* had troubled little enough about the lives of men, the Revolution had troubled still less; and conscription, not for home defence but for foreign warfare, became at once its most characteristic mark and from a Christian standpoint its clearest condemnation.

The French Revolution was in fact symptomatic of a much deeper malady in the spirit of man than monarchy was in a position to dispel or than Liberalism has, in general, been ready to recognise. It was not, like the English Revolution of 1688, the assertion of a local preference for aristocratic as against autocratic government or for a national as against a universal Church: nor was it, like the American Revolution, analogous to the revolt of a strong-willed daughter against a domineering mother. On the contrary it reached to the root of matters which were matters for all mankind. "Men," as Dr. Gooch observes, "like Burke and Tom Paine, Immanuel

[1] Woodward, "Three Studies in Conservatism," p. 17.

Kant and Joseph de Maistre, who agreed in nothing else, were convinced that the problems it raised concerned humanity as a whole."[1] These four, though contemporary spectators, were variously remote from the scene of action. The sagacious Mallet du Pan, however, who though a working journalist had abandoned the charged atmosphere of his native Geneva in 1782 to enjoy the more congenial air of Paris under the *ancien régime*, reached the same conclusion and recorded it in a trenchant warning to the effect that anyone who regarded the Revolution as exclusively French was disqualified from judging it. It should then, on this evidence, be treated as an international event. To what a full extent this was true can, however, be more fully appreciated now than it could be at the time.

The wars of religion, so-called, were over; yet the student of the French Revolution will, to probe its depths and appraise its significance, find himself forced into the sphere of theological thought and Christian doctrine. "Our heart is restless until it rests in Thee," St. Augustine had written in the last days of the Western Empire and on the eve of those Dark Ages which preceded the coronation of Charlemagne by the Pope and the rising again in Rome of an imperialism that was to be styled Holy as well as Roman, to endure almost to a year for a millenium, and, despite all the mockery that in its latter days its grand name provoked, to leave upon the soil of Europe the outline, misty and spectral, yet never completely blotted out, of a city or commonwealth of God. The great phrase of Augustine not only sank deep into the mind of Christendom but stretches still, like a scroll spread out, across the horizon of the Middle Age, so that keen students of the period, as for instance Professor Powicke in his "Christian Life in the Middle Age,"[2] testify constantly to the presence there of a rare sense of quietness, confidence and stability behind all the turmoil of the time. A beauty, not of this world, breaks through, shedding its restful radiance over the whole field of thought and urging men to recognise that to act rightly one must first think truly, and that to think truly one must first seek to put oneself in a state of grace.

Between this singular light, which, as some might be found to declare, "never was on sea or land," and the eyes of Humanity the Revolution interposed itself; and, in the confusion that followed, restlessness of mind in respect to all things in heaven and earth increased and multiplied. The Revolution, indeed, at the beginning was still content to provide mankind with some sort of a

---

[1] "Studies in Modern History," p. 118.   [2] p. 21.

deity—with a Supreme Being conceived in the style of the eighteenth century as arguable, remote, and frigid. So arguable that in France, even when the Revolution was well on its way, he cannot be said to have been disproved to the satisfaction of the finer intelligences; so remote, that in Russia he has lately become lost in the snows; so frigid that, neither in France nor in Russia nor anywhere else, could such a Being, however arguably supreme, be loved by anyone in his right senses! Such was the Revolution's God. Its goddess was Reason—Reason impersonated at her inaugural feast by a prostitute. One can hardly be surprised that within a time religion was declared by some revolutionists to have been no more than an opiate by means of which the masses of the people were drugged into dull repose.

It was in these circumstances that tranquillity, which is as much a condition of wise politics as of great art, was largely lost to Christendom. Emotion must always be latent, if not patent, in finished statesmanship, for without some movement of sympathy or antipathy who dare hope to govern a world of pain? But it needs for the best results to be emotion recollected in tranquillity, reconsidered in marmoreal calm, and recalling, like sculpture itself, the thought of frozen music. Reduce it to the mere notion of sympathy for the under-dog, and society becomes, as the Revolution has given the world only too much occasion to remark, no better than a dog-fight.

Under such limitations "La belle France," who had been hitherto *frondeuse* and a Gallican, now led the riot of human unrest. The gay vesture of her cities and the sunlit smile of her fields veiled, but could not hide her secret suffering. She might have been the lovely Io tormented by a gad-fly; and even still her voice rises above the sound of her poets complaining with the tragic grandeur of a Phèdre:

> Me nourrissant de fiel, de larmes abreuvée
> Encor, dans mon malheur de trop près observée,
> Je n'osois dans mes pleurs me noyer à loisir,
> Je goûtais en tremblant ce funeste plaisir;
> Et, sous un front serein déguisant mes alarmes,
> Il fallait bien souvent me priver de mes larmes.[1]

The history of France in the nineteenth century, and so far in our own, has, if we interrogate it, been one long search to find a cure for this passion of unrest. Every remedy that politics suggests has been tried in turn, and in turn found wanting. Every doctor has been called in, and in turn dismissed. Neither the great administrative

[1] "Phèdre," Act IV, sc. 6.

genius of Napoleon, nor the genial good-nature of Henri Quatre, invoked, if not recalled by the restoration of the Bourbons; neither the philosophy of Guizot nor the poetry of Lamartine; neither the autocratic nor the Liberal imperialism of Napoleon III; neither the clericalism of the Second Empire nor the anti-clericalism of the Third Republic; neither the nationalism of Poincaré nor the socialism of Blum has availed anything. The Revolution far from producing the regeneration that 'progressive' publicists have grown into the habit of assuming, has been the precursor of a mortal malady with many complications—of a declining birth-rate, of a distracted and discredited Chamber, and at last of a moral *débâcle*, beside which the "*Débâcle*" of which Zola wrote was as nothing. That was a true voice which cried "La France se meurt; ne troublez pas son agonie."

Let the English reader, then, who, with the merits of a Liberal constitution as a panacea for all ills impressed upon his mind, is disposed to believe that an opportune grant of free institutions on the part of the *ancien régime* at the assembling of the States-General in 1789, or a little before, could have averted the catastrophe of Europe which followed, or that any similar medicine would have operated infallibly in other countries at other dates, review and reconsider his opinion. Let him reflect that in fact the points which Necker's government was, as we know, prepared to concede as part of the royal programme—taxation by consent, for instance, regular meetings of the States-General, the abolition of lettres-de-cachet, freedom of the Press and local government—met and matched very fairly the more important and intelligent demands in the cahiers, or memorials, which the deputies brought up with them.[1] Let him reflect that the parties were to all intents and purposes agreed and that no more than a little commonsense was wanting to give effect to their respective cogitations. Let him reflect that, to quote from Madelin's dispassionate survey, the Royal Government was "the most honest, perhaps, that France ever possessed"[2] and that "at Versailles the favourite reading was not Machiavelli but Rousseau;"[3] and he may learn that he must breathe no more the phlegmatic, compromising air of English politics, if he is to understand the world of the Continent either at that time or after. Upon the similitude of the British Constitution which the French enjoyed under the Orleans Monarchy the country pronounced sentence of

---

[1] A convenient summary of both of these may be found in Madelin's "French Revolution," pp. 38 and 45.   [2] *Ibid.*, p. 37.   [3] *Ibid.*, p. 39.

death in terms that have become historic: *"La France s'ennuie."* And into that casual witticism a very world of wisdom may be read.

A disagreeable malady, fatal to vitality and even to congenital vitality, went at the time of the Renaissance by the name of "the French disease." Now for the second time France had begun to propagate a European sickness, but this time it was a sickness of the soul, and deadly in proportion. Bossuet had said something to the point when he indicated boredom as a significant taint or train communicated to the mind of man by original sin. The germ thus generated passed very definitely into the sphere of political ideas at the date of the Revolution. "Change for change's sake" became as engaging a sophistry in the senate as "art for art's sake" in the studio; and it had the power, and indeed the purpose, to undermine the best administration in the world. Metternich saw no value in it; nor has it any. It poses as a divine discontent; but it promotes a revolution of destruction.

Was Metternich's diagnosis at fault? Or was "the Spirit of the Time" taking a deeper plunge into the abyss of man's mystery than Liberal eyes had vision to follow? Were Edmund Burke and Joseph de Maistre prophets of the True God, or would Bentham and Mill suffice to meet the crisis and remove the danger? The stage was set in Paris and, if the Liberals were right, the problem-play should have been solved there by the close of its fifth, if not of its third act. But the tired actors were still acting, when Bodley, about 1900, wrote his book on "France," and are acting still, now that Dr. Brogan[1] has arrived to chronicle their futilities and follies. The spirit of France has disintegrated under the influence of the spirit of the Revolution; her decline was evident, her fall delayed, yet still impending. And what happened to France yesterday may happen to Europe to-morrow; for the spirit of Revolution has spread, not as once from capital to capital, but from country to country. Doubtless it is no more than a time-spirit and in time will pass. Always one can hear, if one listens for it, "the laughter of gods!"—of false gods—"in the background." Yet no man has been able to cast it out. Volatile as the spirit of unrest may be, its presence can sometimes be detected as if it corresponded rather to the contagion of a human body than to an infection in the air. The Germans at a certain date that can be named enclosed Lenin in a railway-carriage and deposited him in Russia like a microbe enclosed in a phial. There he worked industriously, and according to the very type and pattern of the French

[1] "The Development of Modern France" (1870-1939).

Revolution. He deserves to be classed with Robespierre; nor will
the disciples of Mathiez perceive any insult in the comparison. But
in what might perhaps be called the classic conception of revolutionary drama, a Robespierre brings a Napoleon in his wake; and
for that greater part M. Stalin seems cast.

Though a book has been published with not unimpressive statis-
tics to prove that a large development of Russian resources was
already in operation under the Russian *ancien régime*, M. Stalin gave
to economic change an impetus, a scope and an acceleration that
might fairly be called Napoleonic. He may be credited, as his
invasion of Finland, not to speak of his penetration of the Baltic
Republics, indicates, and as his collaboration with Germany in a
new partition of Poland, even whilst his representative was presiding
at Geneva, had previously foreshadowed, with emulating Napoleon
likewise by the magnitude and the astuteness of his designs. But
of this full demonstration is wanting; for Providence, resolved,
apparently, upon the destruction of Herr Hitler, who was himself
in all likelihood meditating an exchange of the ambitions of Frederick
the Great for those of Napoleon, drove the German Führer into the
madness of attacking Russia before the mutual exhaustion of the
British and German Empires was complete and a broad way opened
for Russian ambition toward Istanbul or India.

The Revolution, as was observed, passed through Germany
in the keeping of a human body—passed, only, however, to return
and, like the spirit it was, take possession of the soul of the
German people. There are those—and they constitute not the
least important and influential element in modern Germany—
who recognise its passage, its power and its persistence. Few passages in Dr. Rauschning's record of conversations, not imaginary,
with the leaders and adherents of the Nazi movement are more
worth attention than that in which he describes the reaction of
the German staff-officer "down to the junior Captain" to the
European situation a little before the present war. The words that
follow are taken from the mouth of a typical representative of
the German military caste. "Our feeling," he says, "is that we
have reached much the same stage as when the French armies came
under Napoleon's command. We are the heirs and defenders of the
Revolution. The Revolution runs in the blood of all of us down to
the junior Captain on the staff. We were all on the wrong track.
Scharnhorst and Gneisenau are no models for us to-day; nor are
any of the other men who try to unite the ideas of the Revolution

with the traditions and ideas of other times. To-day we are simply
'children of the Revolution' . . . Our patterns to-day are the young
generals of the French Revolution. Our model is Napoleon with his
pace and change in tactics. It is logical that we should seek in our
armies the revolutionary fanaticism of the *sans-culottes*."[1]

It is the same reporter of conversations with the Nazis and their
adherents who warns us that "the revolution of dynamism is nothing
but a permanent *coup d'état*."[2] It was so, as we have seen, in France
from the beginning; but in Germany it might have been expected
to produce yet more catastrophic effects, for there the fire kindled
by Rousseau first reached the prairie recovered by Luther from the
domain of Latin civilization. Goethe, who was no friend to the
French Revolution, had been, as he explained to Eckermann,[3] a still
greater foe to the attempt to bring about a similar event in Germany
where it would not even have had the merit of being indigenous.
Revolutions based upon artifice, he observes with quiet sarcasm,
have no countenance from God, Who, as he phrases it, "keeps aloof
from such bungling (*der sich von solchen Pfuschereien zurückhält*)."
From such upheavals his catholicity of thought led him to distinguish the work of Christ, in whose gospel of love he perceives the
response to and consummation of Jewish aspirations.

This is, possibly, the place to say a word in passing upon a
matter which involves a digression but hardly, in dealing with the
foundations of a Christian society, an irrelevance. Much revolutionary doctrine of French origin is now being smuggled into the
current thought of this country under cover of labels ostenta-
tiously described as Galilean; and not a few "chaplains of King
Demos" (to borrow Dr. Inge's phraseology) are aiding and abet-
ting the illicit traffic. *Episcopi in Anglia semper pavidi!* Bishops in
England, according to the adage, are always timid; and it appears
more than once to have been left to the more courageous Deans
—Dean Swift in his day, and Dean Inge in ours—to remind
the world, if only obliquely, of the benediction pronounced upon
peace-makers. The historian may perhaps play a modest part in
assisting these caustic controversialists to rescue the Sermon on
the Mount from the rough handling it habitually receives from
the belligerent apostles of peace and philanthropy. A change of
heart, a regeneration of spirit is all with which Christ appears to
concern himself; and the value of any gift, from a cup of cold water

---

[1] Rauschning, "Makers of Destruction," p. 78.   [2] *Ibid.*, p. 273.
[3] January 4th, 1824.

upwards, is in his eyes measured only by its weight in loving-kindness. The modern reformer, who proposes to do his charities chiefly or entirely through the distribution of other men's goods, must consequently seem to the historian as surprising an exponent of the Christian Gospel as the Good Samaritan who to his oil and wine adds an abundant provision of guns and bombs. It is impossible to conceive St. Francis of Assisi in either rôle; and, when one has said that, one has said, perhaps, all that is necessary. Yet since it is safest to be specific and clearest to be concrete, illustration may do a little more to distinguish the evolution inaugurated by Christ from the revolution according to Rousseau and Robespierre.

About the date that Metternich had indicated as right for undertaking the work of reconstruction—at the beginning that is of the twentieth century—two outstanding opportunities presented themselves for dealing with class feeling and national feeling on Christian lines. What became of them we know; what might have been done with them it is worth while to consider.

It fell to the lot of Mr. Lloyd George to play the star-part in respect of the problems of wealth and poverty in 1909 and of peace and war in 1919. There is a saying of Gladstone's that the difference between the Christian and the Socialist is to be found in this— that the Christian says "What is mine is thine," whilst the Socialist says "What is thine is mine;" and the saying is entirely consonant with the most admirable thing in the earlier Liberal tradition, which perceived that force is no remedy for a certain sort of wrongs and consequently threw the greater stress on persuasion. It was open, then, to Mr. Lloyd George, not just to have observed that some men in this country were exceedingly rich and others desperately poor; but to have appealed to rich and poor alike to raise their thoughts and hearts beyond avarice and envy, and, subject to Parliamentary assent, to agree to abide by the recommendations of a permanent body representative of all interests and required by its terms of reference to emulate the impartiality of judges of the High Court of Justice. That might have been; and since, even in the days of the Regency, Rush, the then representative of the United States of America in London, had noted the rare generosity of the well-to-do in England, there is no safe ground for suggesting that it could not have succeeded. Passion, however, and not Christianity, was in the ascendant on both sides; and Revolution won the day, with results still waiting to be fully ascertained.

Much the same sort of thing happened with international relations in 1919. If the blessing on the peace-makers has any sense or significance, it must surely be operative most of all in time of war. But the democratic sentiment of the country was so well-satisfied with the idea of a "fight to the finish" that, by the time it came to the peace-making, no one knew how to make the peace. The value of Lord Lansdowne's proposal that the possibilities of peace should be earlier explored remains a matter of opinion; the failure of the policy of fighting-to-the-finish is a matter of fact. If, indeed, General Smuts's recent version of history be correct, there never was any peace at all but the War went on for twenty years longer, like a smouldering fire, and then, in 1939, burst again into flame. The wisdom of this world is confined to its generation and, when that generation happens to be unusually slow of understanding, the worst is always to be feared. The Germans had never learnt either from Luther's Bible or Hegel's philosophy to be good neighbours, but they could not reasonably be expected to learn to become better ones from experiencing the provisions of the Peace of Versailles.

Such matters as these bear closely upon the standard by which Metternich has to be tried. There is no saying what a religion, which in its pristine energy had the power to seat the Pope upon the throne of the Cæsars and, with no military force at its disposal, to impose the Canon Law upon European Society, may not be able to achieve whenever it renews its strength at the Altar of God; and the historian who feels bound to ridicule some modern Friends of Humanity, may well raise his hat, even if he does not choose to bend his knee, when, like Gibbon sitting on the Capitol and listening to the chant of the monks in the church adjoining, he considers the decline and fall of the Roman Empire and the rise and exaltation of the Christian Church. But there was no hope in Metternich's time, as his observation of things in Rome sufficiently shows, of rebuilding the spiritual temple of Christendom upon the old and only site; nor is to be supposed that the utmost piety in the precincts of the Eternal City would have provoked any response in the London of the Regency or the Paris of the Restoration. Even, however, had the waters of human regeneration stood at a higher level—had the Tiber, so to say, been in flood and the Thames freighted with such souls as Thomas More's on its way from Chelsea to its trial at Westminster—the modesty of David might well have caused states-men, whose hands, however involuntarily, were stained with twenty years of bloodshed, to pause before attempting a political reconstruction upon the only catholic foundation still left standing by time. For anything like that a Solomon was needed; and Metternich, to give him his due, never aspired to the rôle so lightly assumed in later times by the so-called "Big Three" at the Paris Peace Conference of 1919 and with such dire results. It is much to his credit that he tried rather to recondition than to reconstruct and that, in the thirty critical years that followed Napoleon's downfall, he held Europe together so well as he did. He was neither the minister of the *ancien régime* nor of a counter-revolution but the minister of a transitional generation feeling after and finding that contrary-of-a-revolution which deserves in such circumstances to appeal to every historic eye and enlist the services of every sagacious mind. Interested as he was in physical science to a greater degree probably than any statesman of his time, he might have been expected to demonstrate that pressure of physics upon politics which first came under consideration in the Victorian era: and this in fact he does. His policy is evolutionary as opposed to revolutionary. Mutations, perhaps one might say, needed in his eyes to be born and not made.

Nothing discovers Metternich's freedom from the sort of conservatism that at a later date made the Comte de Chambord refuse the throne of France, ostensibly at least for the sake of the white flag of the Bourbons, than his readiness to deal with Napoleon. Pitt might declare that the Jacobinism of Robespierre and Barère, of the Directory and the Triumvirate, had "centred and condensed" in Bonaparte, who was "at once the child and the champion of all its atrocities and horrors;" but Metternich was content with cool objectivity. No regard for hereditary monarchy rendered him irreconcilable. He was always willing to come to terms with Napoleon, if Napoleon would come to terms with Europe. Not only, so far as he was concerned, might the French keep the new dynasty as the guarantor of the revolutionary changes in France, but the Hapsburgs might make a virtue of necessity and give a daughter in marriage to the Bonapartes, as formerly to the Bourbons. This attitude he maintained even when the tide turned. In 1813 at Frankfurt, as later at Châtillon, he was ready to negotiate, and to negotiate on the basis of good terms for France. "Anything," Fyffe declares, "was welcomed by Metternich that seemed likely to avert or even postpone a struggle with Napoleon for life or death." Among the statesmen of the Allies he was the least intransigent. His proposals anticipated the canons of nineteenth-century justice by offering to France, first her natural (or, as one might say, her philosophic) frontier, then her historic one, and by leaving her in either case the ruler whom she had both chosen and deserved. Had they taken effect, the slightest aggressive move on the part of the French government would presumably have acted like an alarm bell and set all Europe arming; Napoleon's power, already sensibly diminished as the Hundred Days were to show, would have further declined; the Napoleonic legend would never have taken shape; and the Napoleonic régime, having tamed the revolution, would in its turn have been tamed by it. But Napoleon was not the man to accept the fate of an extinct volcano; and Metternich knew him better than to suppose that he would. Neither perhaps would the Allies, if it had come to the point, have agreed to a solution demanding almost as much political subtlety and sensibility as if the Allied Nations of to-day were to offer the Germans peace-negotiations on the condition of withdrawing their armies behind pre-war boundaries as a symbol of defeat and of receiving the reward of their iniquities in the shape of Herr Hitler as their ruler for the rest of his natural existence. Yet, though the negotiation failed, Metternich obtained very substantial benefit from it; for he was able to show the French clearly that what stood between them and peace was not a denial of their natural or at least historic frontiers, but the character of their sovereign.

Metternich's management of the preliminaries of peace compares, indeed, no less favourably with the British approach to the Peace of Utrecht than does his management of the peace-making with that over two hundred years later at Versailles. He did not, like the Englishmen of Queen Anne's time, reject the excellent terms that might have been had in 1709 only to accept worse ones—and that at the expense and behind the back of their Allies—three years later. It cannot be said of him and Wellington, as it has been lately said of Eugene and Marlborough, that "neither of them made an effort to alter the preposterous character of the Preliminaries, yet both, immediately after the failure of the negotiation, privately confessed how preposterous they were."[1] He had no megalomania to live down, no strong words to elude, no need of some pen bitter as Swift's to recommend the claims of what Prof. Trevelyan calls "the forbidden word of common sense"[2]—the word, that is, of peace. To read the opening sentences of Swift's "Conduct of the Allies" is to recall to what degree the Whig politicians of

[1] Trevelyan, "England under Queen Anne," vol. II., p. 401.
[2] Ibid., p. 388.

Anne's time had been selling the peace of Europe for the sake of saving their faces. "I lay it down for a maxim," observes the author of that famous pamphlet, "that no reasonable man, whether Whig or Tory (since it is necessary to use those foolish terms), can be of opinion for continuing the war upon the footing it now is, unless he be a gainer by it, or hopes it may occasion some new turn of affairs at home to the advantage of his party; or, lastly, unless he be very ignorant of the kingdom's condition, and by what means we have been reduced to it. Upon the two first cases, where interest is concerned, I have nothing to say; but, as to the last, I think it highly necessary that the public should be freely and impartially told what circumstances they are in, after what manner they have been treated by those whom they trusted so many years with the disposal of their blood and treasure, and what the consequences of this management are likely to be upon themselves and their posterity."

The abortive peace negotiation of 1709 was never, perhaps, more worth study than at the present time; nor any conduct of his distant ancestor better deserving of Mr. Churchill's close attention than in that matter. Enough, however, here, if Metternich's diplomacy is recognised by virtue of its consistent moderation to have avoided all needless bloodshed and any such shame as that into which Britain fell by refusing anything less than complete victory, represented by the cry of "no peace without Spain," and afterwards coming to a secret understanding with the enemy which left her Allies in the lurch and Spain in the hands of the Bourbons.

Metternich's peace settlement emerges equally well from a comparison with the negotiations which led up to and eventuated in the Peace of Versailles a little over two hundred years after the Peace of Utrecht. No reproach lies against him and his colleagues for assenting to an armistice on one set of assumptions and concluding a peace upon another. He did not, to be specific, first agree that covenants of peace should be "openly" arrived at and then impose terms separately determined: he did not first arrange that disarmament should be mutual, even if not simultaneous, and then reach the opinion that it would be best left one-sided: he did not pledge himself to the equivalent of an absolutely impartial adjustment of colonial claims and then leave the beaten foe without a single colony. The historian is confronted with no assurance in the name of the Governments allied against Napoleon comparable with that of President Wilson on November 5th, 1918, when he affirmed

that the Allies were prepared "to conclude peace with the German
Government on the conditions laid down in the President's address
to Congress on January 8th,"—that is on the basis of the Fourteen
Points; the German government, let it be added, having previously
taken up the position in October, 1918 that "the aim of the transactions to be entered into would thus be only to seek an agreement
on the practical details of the enforcement of these points." Metternich, in other words, allowed himself no lie in the soul, such as led
the French and British Governments to bamboozle the Germans
with the shadow of a peace of conciliation and almost in the same
breath to gratify their own peoples with the substance of a peace
scarcely distinguishable from one of revenge. As in private life he
showed himself one of the least vindictive of men, so in public
affairs he proved himself one of the most pacific of statesmen. Had
the claims of justice, conceived as rendering to every nation its
due, weighed with him more than considerations of the future
tranquillity of Europe, the settlement might have been very different
from what it was. Entertaining, however, a low opinion of mankind,
he was neither too hard upon sinners nor too expectant of saints.

"He saw men," says one of the great historians of the Napoleonic
period, "as they were, gauged their characters, flattered their
vanities, and in his political calculus allowed for vulgar foibles as
well as for science and good sense. He had the strong dash of cynicism which the enthusiasts lacked, and this . . . was valuable in an age
of hyperbolic expectations."[1] The writer of that sentence was not
thinking of Metternich, though he well might have been. He was in
fact speaking of the man whom Metternich defeated—of Napoleon
in his most statesmanlike hour—of Bonaparte during the Consulate.
Some measure of the cynicism here commended, at any rate if a
reservation be made in respect to flattery, is a condition at almost
all times of any intelligent conduct of political, and more particularly
of foreign affairs. It is in line with the conclusions of the wisest
and greatest of Greek historians—of that Thucydides of whom
Abbott has remarked justly enough that "without a doubt" if he
were writing to-day, he would be reckoned "a cynical pessimist."[2]
It is not out of line with the arresting admonition to Christian men
to be wise as serpents, no less than harmless as doves, nor with the
subtle consideration that the light of the Christian character requires
the complement of salt, rather than of sweetness. Is it then altogether

[1] H. A. L. Fisher, "Napoleonic Statesmanship," p. 374.
[2] G. F. Abbott, "Thucydides," p. 159.

out of place to recall that a certain cynicism of outlook and judgment seemed, if contemporary opinion be consulted, profoundly characteristic of the personality of the last, and possibly the greatest British foreign secretary of the nineteenth century? Had such cynicism as Salisbury's remained in fashion, we might not have had so much reason to remark in recent times that it is the business of the wise to undo the mistakes of the good. Not, of course, that the good are invariably or necessarily devoid of understanding! "We must deal with our enemies," wrote Albert, designated "the Good," to Stockmar in 1853, "as honourable men, and deal honourably with them, but that is no reason why we should think them so."

The Victorians, take them for all in all, were abler men than the Edwardians, as the Edwardians in their turn were abler than the unfortunate Georgians who lost the flower of their youth on the battlefield. The Prince Consort's information regarding human nature was by so much in advance of that of the well-intentioned amateurs who in our time have concerned themselves with the conduct of foreign affairs; and this is true whether we look to the Right or to the Left. Mr. Chamberlain and Lord Halifax, attempting to carry on a highly ambitious foreign policy with no weapons, to speak of, in their hands, furnish a fitting pendent to the figures of the late Mr. Arthur Henderson and Mr. Philip Noel Baker, of whom two German writers,[1] with a good title to be heard, have lately remarked that they "were, with great respect, led by the nose in what concerned the actual condition of German armament and re-armament."

The engaging simplicity of these good men is doubtless responsible for their political insufficiency; they confuse the modern fashion of optimism with the theological virtue of hope, and, though things remain always as they are and their consequences will be always what they will be, desire, quite innocently and unconsciously, to be deceived. From this defect of vision have followed many tears of things in our time. Metternich, however, like Wellington and the most part of his colleagues, was so far fortunate as to entertain pretty nearly as cynical a view of human nature as Talleyrand or as Napoleon himself. There lies the explanation of what might otherwise be puzzling—the close association of good men and bad in the liquidation of the Napoleonic Empire. Castlereagh and Wellington, some of the most straightforward statesmen

[1] Curt Geyer (formerly Chief Editor of the "Neuer Vorwärts" in Prague and in Paris) and Walter Loeb (formerly President of the State Bank in Thuringia and in Saxony), "Gollancz in German Wonderland," p. 46.

of the time, get easily into touch at the critical juncture with two of the most crooked, Talleyrand and Fouché. Once the hurly-burly was done and the battle lost and won, they proved able to swallow venom of toad and fillet of fenny-snake in a manner that puts to shame the more delicate stomachs of our time, revolted as these are when they perceive the component parts of jackals, hyenas or guttersnipes seething together in the world's cauldron. The fact is that the modern doctrine of progress has produced many delicate digestions and that our politicians, whose own acrobatics sometimes make our heads turn queer, can show themselves on occasion very nice in their feeding. Every allowance should, of course, be made for men whose digestive juices operate in this way. Statecraft, which raised Hamlet's irony to fever pitch, provoked Coriolanus to a noble scorn, and drove Prospero to the isolation of an enchanted isle, offers after all, as Shakespeare's last words upon life seem to suggest, no other ending than despair—unless, indeed, as he adds, it be relieved by prayer.

However all that may be, it is the very genius of revolutionary tactics to bring honest thought under the spell of vain imaginations. Under its pressure well-meaning men turn into tireless busybodies who, not content with their legitimate occupation of paving hell with good intentions, must seek a market on earth also for their cheap cement. The consideration of their activities, it need hardly be added, is well calculated to complete and confirm a cynic's survey of the world and to provide the concluding paragraph of his apologia. "No people do such harm as those who go about doing good,"[1] observed one whose qualifications for giving an opinion included, not only such knowledge of mankind as falls to a deep student of human history, but also that which is the daily portion of an occupant of the See of London. Not without some hesitation, it is said, was the Book of Ecclesiastes added to the Hebrew Canon; yet the Sacred Scriptures would surely have seemed inadequate in the eyes of those who have marked the world and its ways, had that great work been omitted. Few books in the collection discover a greater beauty of thought and diction; but none takes a more ruthless measure of the vanity of human wishes and the worth of political endeavour. It may well be that he should be called a statesman who knows its meaning and that he should be called a politician who knows it not.

[1] Mandell Creighton quoted under the heading of "A wise bishop" in Daily Telegraph Misc. II, p. 277.

C

Among the merits of perceiving the world we live in as no more than an enlargement of "Vanity Fair" is the fact that it enables a man to approach political problems with a considerable degree of detachment. The most part of men and women have an unfortunate habit of venting their whole moral indignation, not upon the ideas that lead mankind astray, but upon the individuals or classes of individuals who stand to ideas in the relation of foster-parents. In the last great war it was the Kaiser and the military clique about him who were held to be responsible for all the evil; in the present one it is Herr Hitler and his Nazi followers who are regarded as the incarnation of evil things. Modern Democracy, when it goes heretic-hunting, lacks nothing of the fervour of the Middle-Age, but retains not so much as the ghost of an idea that the heresy is the better for being hated and the heretic for being loved. Upon the wickedness of Herr Hitler our Government and Nation are alike agreed: about the responsibility of Lutheranism or Hegelianism or the doctrines of race and nationality for what has come into the minds of the German people it must be doubtful whether any three persons in this country selected at random, would be able to decide, even though Lord Vansittart and Mr. Gollancz and Mr. Butler were all present to assist them with information.

The more or less cynical gentlemen who assembled at Vienna in 1814 to give a peace to Europe had to reckon with the presence of one political idealist; but he, though the master of many legions, was not very formidable as a doctor of morals. Alexander is said to have been reminded by Talleyrand that treachery is a matter of dates; and the remark, if made, was not uncalled for. He had betrayed the cause of Europe in 1807, just as another great Russian autocrat betrayed it in 1939; and his Holy Alliance, whilst it emphasised the ultimate need of some organic spiritual foundation for Europe, served to show, by the derision which it excited, that Moscow was not yet qualified to give the law to Europe in place of Rome. Castlereagh, as is well known, praised the Holy Alliance as sublime, but dismissed it as ridiculous; and it seems probable that he voiced, if rather more crudely and rudely, the cynicism of the most part of his colleagues. As he saw things, the business in hand was to get Europe back to work and to avert any recurrence of trouble by the employment of common-sense. It was, in the circumstances, perhaps a little injudicious of Professor Webster, some twenty years ago, to use the authority of his great learning to inveigle us into the belief that an idealistic creation of a much later date—viz., that League of Nations,

small and great, which assembled at Geneva—was in the direct line
of descent from Castlereagh's practical concept of a standing alliance
of the Great Powers, for the repression of Napoleon or any Bonapartist restoration. Rather than to the alliance of Chaumont or to
Metternich's working hypothesis of a "Moral Pentarchy," it is
to the Romanovs, with the eirenicon of Nicholas II as well as
the Holy Alliance of Alexander I to their credit, that we might
justly ascribe the ancestry of the recent attempt to refit Europe with
a soul. Metternich and Castlereagh aimed at little more than pro-
viding Europe with a principle and a procedure. Talleyrand had
quickly seen that in France this principle must be hereditary
monarchy; and his associates in the settlement extended the idea to
the management of Europe. There was in point of fact none other
available or, failing the restoration of the Bonapartes, even thinkable.
The Great Powers of the Continent, all of them monarchies and all
of them absolute, were alone in a position to assert "le droit par
la force," and imposed of necessity their political dispositions upon
the general shape of things in being or in process of becoming.

"Le droit par la force"—that, as Dr. Gooch has lately reminded
us,[1] was the formula appropriate to Metternich's so-called system.
The words furnish an instructive contrast to the legend which Time,
in letters as mystical yet as prophetic as those that once sealed the
doom of Belshazzar in the Halls of Babylon, has inscribed upon the
Palace of Peace at Geneva—"l'espérance sans le pouvoir." Metternich's system relied upon the effective collaboration of the Great
Powers of Europe, President Wilson's idea upon the ineffective
concurrence of the small. Neither was the equal of the nation-state
in sentimental appeal; but Metternich's Congresses held Europe
together during the decade after Waterloo, exercised some influence
upon the whole nineteenth century, reappeared towards its close in
a Concert of European Powers which, both in the Near and in the
Far East, averted any violent clash of interests, and raised an echo
in Grey of Fallodon's regretful remark that no man had been found
wise enough to make the Ambassadors' Conference of 1912–13
into a permanent machine for the maintenance of European peace.[2]
Metternich in his time had been wise enough to see that the
Congress idea should be kept alive and to develop it in the shape of
a cabinet of the Great Powers where diplomatic effort would bear
the closest possible relation to military strength. Neither parliament

[1] G. P. Gooch, "Studies in Diplomacy and Statecraft," p. 253.
[2] Grey, "Twenty-five Years," I, p. 276.

of man nor federation of the world, neither whispering-gallery nor talking-shop made any appeal to him. Yet no other statesman of modern times has had perhaps so great a sentiment about Europe. "For a long while," he told Wellington after 1815, "Europe has had for me the value of a country."[1]

The words were addressed to one whose co-operation in preserving the foundations of the Treaty of Vienna during the critical days that immediately followed Waterloo cannot well be exaggerated. The return from Elba, to which, contrary to Metternich's and Talleyrand's advice, Napoleon had been relegated by Alexander's wish, had given the Allied Governments a tempting excuse for reversing their policy of reconciliation. At that crucial juncture Wellington showed himself as great a statesman as ever Marlborough had shown himself a diplomatist; and to Wellington's unfailing regard for the essential facts of a situation (which is perhaps responsible for Sir Archibald Wavell's choice of him as "the soundest of all great generals")[2] Metternich owed much. Even before Waterloo, in a despatch of May 20th, Wellington's endeavour to make contact with the Austrian Minister is apparent. In the meeting of these two minds, however, there is nothing to be astonished at; for Metternich, as Mr. Woodward is constrained to confess, could be "in a sense . . . more practical than Napoleon himself,"[3] and the Duke was at all times and in all circumstances the embodiment of practicality and of the dry cynicism that practicality demands. They knew what idealists can never understand, that—to borrow a phrase of John Morley's—politics is one long second-best. Wellington's despatches to Castlereagh of August 11th and August 31st, 1815, consequently deserve the attention of all Englishmen who still take the trouble to reckon with human nature and other disagreeable circumstances. They constitute in other words a good manual for peace-makers in an evil world. They recognise at the outset that the Revolution and the Treaty of Paris have left France too strong for the comfort of Europe. In spite, however, of the stress he lays upon this fact, the Duke submits considerations that in his opinion outweigh the advantage of trying to reverse or circumvent it. The foremost of these is that it is neither morally just nor militarily wise to vary the settlement already arrived at in the Treaty of Paris. Though Napoleon, as he elsewhere points out,[4] had placed himself "hors la loi" by breaking the provisions of Fontainebleau, the Allies had in

---

[1] Quoted by Woodward, "Three Studies in European Conservatism," p. 18.
[2] "The Times," October 24th, 1942.   [3] Woodward, *op. cit.*, p. 17.
[4] Desp. XII, p. 352.

his opinion no just right to deprive the French people of the irregular guarantee given them by the negotiations with Louis XVIII[1]. But; however that might be, the military situation dominated and enforced the moral obligation.

"The French people," he observed, "submitted to Bonaparte; but it would be ridiculous to suppose that the Allies would have been in possession of Paris in a fortnight after one battle fought, if the French people in general had not been favourably disposed to the cause which the Allies were supposed to favour."

"The result," he reiterates, "of the operations of the Allies has been very different from what it would have been, if the disposition of the inhabitants of the country had led them to oppose the Allies. . . . My objection to the demand of a great cession from France upon this occasion is that it will defeat the object which the Allies have held out to themselves in the present and the preceding wars. That which has been their object has been to put an end to the French Revolution, to obtain peace for themselves and their people, to have the power of reducing their over-grown military establishments and the leisure to attend to the internal concerns of their several nations and to improve the situation of their people. . . . There is no statesman who, . . . with the knowledge that the justice of the demand of a great cession from France under existing circumstances is at least doubtful and that the cession would be made against the inclination of the Sovereign and all descriptions of his people, would venture to recommend to his Sovereign to consider himself at peace and to place his armies upon a peace establishment. We must, on the contrary, if we take this large cession, consider the operations of the war as deferred till France shall find a suitable opportunity of endeavour-ing to regain what she has lost; and, after having wasted our resources in the maintenance of overgrown military establishments in time of peace, we shall find how little useful the cessions we have acquired will be against a national effort to regain them. In my opinion, then, we ought to continue to keep our great object, the genuine peace and tranquillity of the world, in our view, and shape our arrangement so as to provide for it. Revolu-tionary France is more likely to distress the world than France, however strong in her frontier, under a regular Government; and that is the situation in which we ought to endeavour to place her".

These were Wellington's views, but he does not neglect to consider the only efficacious alternative.

"If the policy of the united powers of Europe is to weaken France," he writes, "let them do so in reality. Let them take from that country its population and resources as well as a few fortresses. If they are not pre-pared for that decisive measure, if peace and tranquillity for a few years is their object, they must make an arrangement which will suit the interests of all the parties to it and of which the justice and expediency will be so evident that they will tend to carry it into execution."[2]

[1] Desp. XII, p. 596.

[2] *Ibid.*, p. 623.

Such sentiments have been echoed, if not attended to, in our time. "A satisfactory settlement," wrote one who in his day had a great reputation within the walls of the Foreign Office and a high position to match it, "means that both sides are satisfied as to the general justice of the solution agreed. Failing this, the issue is not settled; it is only postponed."[1] The Whigs, as we have seen, had not understood this in 1709; nor in 1919 did the American idealist, the Welsh opportunist and the French realist who were responsible for the peace of Versailles, show themselves alive to it. It was, however, apparent to the peace-makers of 1814. The *ancien régime* had its defects; but its worst enemy could hardly accuse it of not inculcating by precept and example that manners are the making of man. The gentlemen who, at the Congress of Vienna were accused of dancing when the Congress should have been marching, attained their aim with remarkable success by avoiding hard words and harsh measures. If their code was not Christianity, it was at least not impatient of it; and, if their justice lacked the rigour of the law, it possessed the graces of good nature and good business.

"Wasn't a gentleman!" observed Wellington to some busybody who was trying to draw him on the subject of Napoleon; and that terse, trenchant reply pointed an accusing finger at that ruthless inhumanity of the Revolution against which all Europe had revolted as against something immeasurably more callous than the privileges of a grand seigneur under the *ancien régime*. Revolution of the type generated in France, it is hardly too much to say, falls automatically into the hands of fanatics, bullies and humbugs who operate and thrive on it and are as much more menacing to the citizenship of a free people than the superfine gentlemen of Versailles as is a herd of bulls in comparison with a swarm of midges to the peace of a summer's evening.

Wellington embodies the genius of the British tradition broadening down from precedent to precedent by the loyal carrying-on of the King's Government as certainly as Napoleon does that of the French Revolution with its love of violence and its legacy of unrest; and the historian who cares to deal faithfully with popular legends and too Liberal estimates will draw his conclusions. He will detect in those outstanding figures the true protagonists of the Old Order and the New; he will see exactly what the education of each type was capable of producing; and he will discover his own taste and his own moral sentiment in the process.

[1] Sir Eyre Crowe; quoted in D. Lloyd-George's War Memoirs, p. 1794.

Mr. Arthur Bryant in one of those charming books, full of patriotism and knowledge, that he has provided for the reading of a
bewildered generation, has suggested that the personality of
Charles II dethroned that of the Black Prince as the model of an
English gentleman. So in its turn and time did the Iron Duke,
made as he was of sterner stuff, dispossess the Merry Monarch,
with his easy nonchalant ways, from the place to which his French
grandfather's bonhomie and his own French mother-wit had
done so much to raise him. The French *ancien régime*, whatever
hold it may have gained in English aristocratic circles after the
English Restoration, yielded at the date of the French Restoration
to the pressure of forces essentially English and admirably calculated to effect that contrary-of-a-revolution which, as we have seen,
is the proper answer of statesmanship to all revolution of the
French kind. Wellington illustrates what Maistre and Metternich
were recommending; and not Maistre and Metternich alone. With
what animation does Goethe, himself at one time the victim of
Napoleon's blandishments, enquire of Eckermann[1] how Wellington
looked as he passed through Weimar on his mission to Russia in
1826! With what confidence does the savant warn his disciple that
he has beheld a hero!

In England, needless to say, Wellington towered high above the
rest of his contemporaries and was the idol of the time. For those
who themselves knew the Victorians, his name is written in letters
of gold on the tablets of reminiscence. I never heard my father, who
in the course of a long life had seen service in the Army, in Parliament and in the City with their various opportunities of observing
the ways of men, speak of any man that he had known, as he would
speak of the Duke. And I never found in the course of historical
research any more eloquent testimony than came under my eye in
the shape of a pair of gloves belonging to a young lady—young, that
is, in Wellington's latter days—and inscribed with the legend 'gloves
I was wearing when I shook hands with the Duke of Wellington on
such and such a date.' But, for those who did not know the Victorians,
there is the evidence of Queen Victoria's journal with its outstanding tribute to the greatness of her greatest subject; and there is, of
course, Tennyson's ode to confirm the representative truth of it.
To his contemporaries, some of them just ordinary people with eyes
to see, others of great talent or in great place, the Duke seemed to
command much more than the suffrages commonly accorded to the

[1] Conversation of February 6th, 1826.

happy or the fortunate warrior. As he anticipated the fifteenth
Lord Derby, in saying that peace was the first of British interests[1];
so he may properly be said to have shown himself in dignity of
character and devotion to duty, in sterling sense and repressed
sensibility, in indifference to criticism and contempt for flattery,
what every man of peace would wish to be and every "compleat
gentleman" really is. By the close of his life he carried such a load
of honours as it can seldom have fallen to any grand seigneur to
receive; yet his supreme distinction lay in the simplicity with which
he bore them. All that he was and did and said went to prove the
justice of Metternich's acute observation that in England the real
aristocrat was the country gentleman and that the spirit of the
country gentleman had communicated itself to all classes. "Titles,"
Metternich continues in his striking analysis of English society,
"are the equivalent of functions, and everyone can by personal
merit cut his way through to them. There is here an equality useful
in its results—an equality that raises, instead of lowering like that
of misery."

To read these observations is to rend the veil that conceals the
real Metternich from view and to perceive, if only for an instant,
that his portrait of a gentleman desiderates rather the towers of
Westminster than the pavilions of Versailles for a background.
Neither Castlereagh nor Wellington would have been able to work
with him so well as they did, had it been otherwise; nor, perhaps,
would the brilliant rejoinder which the Victorian era made at home
to the Continental Revolution have been feasible without the delay-
ing policy of Metternich abroad. Mr. Woodward, indeed, on the
strength of a remark of Princess Lieven's,[2] has led his readers to
suppose that Wellington did not regard Metternich as a great
statesman; and it is quite probable that the Duke did not place him
among the greatest. Yet there are other observations of Princess
Lieven's that have to be taken into account. "The Duke of Wellington is Prime Minister. The Duke of Wellington is Austrian. He
prefers the trickiness of M. de Metternich to the straightforwardness
of the Emperor Nicholas."[3] In such terms did the great *intrigante*
testify to Wellington's association with her old lover—to his
resumption, that is, at the height of his political career of a collaboration which circumstances had imposed at the height of his military
success. Perhaps he thought more of Metternich than Madame de

[1] Speech : 6th April, 1840.
[2] See Woodward's "Three Essays in Conservatism," p. 23.
[3] Quoted in Lady M. Wellesley's "Wellington in Civil Life," p. 95.

Lieven found it agreeable to admit to herself or expedient to say to others. Certainly, if fidelity to a man after his fall be any test of affection, Wellington must have liked Metternich well. During the Ex-Chancellor's exile in London after the revolution in 1848, the Duke called upon him daily; and in the frequency of these visits there is surely proof of something more than pity. Be that as it may, there is a peculiar interest, at a time so charged with possibilities of a European upheaval as the "year of revolution," in this simultaneous intercourse of Metternich's with the old champion of squire-conservatism and the young champion of Tory-Democracy. Stripped of all that is local and national, Metternich, from the stand-point of psychology at least, never appears more truly Prime Minister of Europe, never more really representative of the forces resisting European disintegration than when, deprived of all adventitious greatness, he has his feet on English soil, and looks back with Wellington over the past or forward with Disraeli into the future. It is no wonder that Ranke, who was introduced to him by Gentz, derived from his society "an immensely enlarged knowledge of European politics and a vivid realisation of the essential units of the European system."[1]

It may be of some interest, especially at the present time, to illustrate from Wellington's despatches and procedure in 1815 the manner in which the code of a gentleman met and mingled with the kind of cynicism so agreeably epitomised in Talleyrand's famous advice "surtout pas trop de zèle." Within a week or so of Waterloo the Duke had placed on record his attitude towards the arch-criminal in whom the revolution had become incarnate and by whom it had been rendered catastrophic. Wellington, so he told Castlereagh's half-brother, Stuart, who was assisting in the peace negotiations, had played, as he put it, too distinguished a part in recent transactions to become a minister of vengeance and was resolved, if the Allied Sovereigns wished to put Bonaparte to death, they should appoint an executioner who, as he added significantly, should not be himself.[2] The Allies, as he reminded Castlereagh, had taken up arms against Bonaparte for the second time because it was certain that the world could not be at peace so long as Bona-parte should possess, or should be in a situation to attain supreme power in France.[3] This purpose achieved, he had no use for ven-geance. On the contrary! "If the Allies will only be a little moderate,"

---

[1] Gooch, "History and Historians," p. 82 [2] Desp., XII, p. 516.
[3] *Ibid.*, p. 597.

he wrote to his brother, "that is, if they will prevent plunder by their troops, and take only what is necessary for their own security, we may hope for permanent peace. But I confess that I am a little afraid of them. They are all behaving exceedingly ill."[1]

The absence in the great soldier of all those transports of moral indignation with which we have become familiar in our politicians may be with difficulty understood. The pleasures of reprobation are great. Allowance, however, must be made for Wellington's dislike of cant and his unconsciously platonic conception of justice, not as the interest of the stronger, as revolutionaries like Napoleon and Herr Hitler believe it to be, nor as the rendering to every man his due, as many worthy apostles of retribution, not feeling disposed to leave vengeance to God, are in the habit of inculcating, but as a minding of one's own business, which, in the case under consideration, signified a doing of just what was necessary to restore, and, if possible, preserve peace. Had it been in Wellington's philosophy to thank God daily that he was not as other men are, he must evidently have declined to have any dealings with the butcher of Lyons, the odious Fouché, or even with Talleyrand who had been grievously involved in the judicial murder of the duc d'Enghien. Like Napoleon, both these men on their merits (or demerits) should rightly have been hung. Under the pressure of circumstances, and under the ægis of the Allies, they became in broken succession virtually prime ministers of France. The Duke was not the man to waste time in a wicked world by turning ruffians into martyrs. He knew enough about revolutionaries to recognise that, like the traditional *père de famille*, they were mostly "capables de tout." Thus he comments on the conduct of the Provisional Government of France in publishing a perverted account of his negotiation with Fouché in 1815 with a detachment worthy of Thucydides. It could, he writes to Bathurst, "be accounted for only by a recollection that at all periods of the French Revolution the actors in it have not scrupled to resort to falsehood, either to give a colour to, or palliate their adoption or abandonment of any line of policy; and that they think that, provided the falsehood answers the purpose of the moment, it is fully justified."[2]   As in 1814 the co-operation of Talleyrand, so in 1815 that of Fouché was in practice necessary to the restoration of the Bourbons. In like manner, no doubt, did an alliance with M. Stalin, who, regardless of his obligations as a Member of the League of Nations, had emulated, connived at, and

---

[1] Desp., XII, p. 566.   [2] *Ibid.*, pp. 551-52.

hoped to profit by the aggressions of Herr Hitler, appear necessary to Mr. Churchill's Administration; and the Prime Minister did wisely to bow, without blushing too much, to the necessities of a situation not of his making.

Some distinction must nevertheless be drawn between the two cases. The counsels of Talleyrand and Fouché were invited and received as the trustees of a projected settlement might be supposed to invite and receive the opinions of lawyers briefed by another party to the business in hand. The alliance with M. Stalin desiderates a different simile. It might be compared to a marriage very much *de convenance*, by virtue of which the heraldic shield of some family, ancient as the crusades, adds to its cross and thorny crown, new quarterings carrying the more modern devices of the hammer and sickle. It was, in fact, an alliance that had so much a look of a *mésalliance* as to lay the elder party open to such uncomplimentary comments as mésalliances are apt to provoke. It was so sudden, this exchange of the beau rôle of the champion of Christian society for the companionship of a state both totalitarian and pagan. To a perfectly detached observer it might perhaps have seemed that cynicism was winning all along the line—not merely cynicism of judgment, in face of circumstances, but cynicism embraced by the soul. But the British political idealist has an elasticity of virtue beyond compare. Politicians and publicists soon got to work to make up in vociferation what was now altogether lacking in verisimilitude; and M. Stalin, though lately decried as a *chevalier d'industrie*, was quickly exalted into a *chevalier sans peur et sans reproche*. Such are the canonizations of the world; after this manner do they come about; and with such simplicity are its faithful persuaded to adore what they have lately burnt.

Aristocracy (I do not say oligarchy) is impatient of humbug. Had Wellington—to suppose the proverbial case—set a thief to catch a thief, he would have been incapable of supposing or letting others suppose that he had set a saint to catch a sinner. He trod the stony path of realism without wincing or wishful thinking; and the advice "not to be a damned fool," administered to an officious old gentleman who with fulsome compliments had attempted to assist him across a crowded thoroughfare, would doubtless have been addressed with appropriate bowdlerizations to the "court chaplains," both ecclesiastical and lay, of King Demos. To carry on the King's government, whatever may be the case with republics, it should not be necessary to fool all the people some of the time, or some of the people all the time, or indeed any of the people any part of the time. The guardians of such a state as England might be expected to deal with the people as gentlemen do with gentlemen, neither fearing them nor fooling them. But they show at present no very active disposition of the kind.

A gentleman, for the rest, as Newman has indicated in the famous passage in his Idea of a University, falls short in many respects of the Christian idea of a complete man. But at any rate he is not an actor, a hypocrite, a Pharisee making broad his phylacteries or a Puritan intoning his cant. Froude somewhere recalls a meeting with Newman, all aglow with an enthusiasm aroused by the perusal of Wellington's despatches. It is an interesting little anecdote. Some subtle chord in the character of the great man of action had, as it appeared, broken into and harmonised with the celestial oratorio forever advancing in the soul of the great theologian. If we are so fortunate as to be able to catch any echo of that music, we shall understand better what it was that makes the rejoinder of the *ancien régime* so much more interesting and, it is not too much to say, so much deeper a criticism of life than the comparatively superficial and sometimes self-contradictory doctrine of the Revolution; what it was, in fact, that Metternich, with a keener critical insight than his critics, was attempting to preserve for Europe and for the world. Johnson and Burke before him, and Scott contemporaneously with him, all taught, in their various ways, that no inheritance of Christian civilisation was latent in the loins of the Revolution and were respectively representative, as few others have been, of all that is best in the English, the Irish and the Lowland Scottish. So much so indeed that what they uttered in thunderings and voices or to the sound of minstrelsy should be within the hearing of their countrymen still!

If, however, we are not so fortunate as to catch these echoes, there is still no reason to be misled by the novelists. Eighteenth century furniture, eighteenth century literature, eighteenth century art with its palaces and its pictures, its music and its minuets, speak for themselves and are eternal reminders of what the *ancien régime* was capable, even in its later years; and they who weep over the sunset of the Venetian Republic, struck down by the Revolution in its gorgeous autumn glory, should let a similar sensibility inform their sense so as to see clearly what it was that the bandits who broke into the Bastille had really started to destroy. The sensibility, however, of certain novelists has prevailed over the sensibility to the grace of a great period of which Burke was so profoundly aware. One might almost suppose that the powder which elegant young gentlemen of the late eighteenth century were substituting for the wigs of their fathers had, not merely been transferred to the heads of the footmen of the nineteenth, but gone to the heads of the novelists, so systematically does Thackeray, and to some degree Dickens plaster the whole genius of the *ancien régime* with the reproach of flunkeydom. Yet powder, if it had its rights, might quite as well be taken for a revolutionary as a reactionary decoration. The great ladies, who wore it at Versailles on the eve of the Revolution, were after all enthusiastically reading their Rousseau; and Robespierre had his hair in powder when in due course he sent them on to the guillotine. Wordsworth, too, in those Cambridge days of his, when the Revolution made it seem good to be alive, was, as De Quincey tells us, wearing powder and presumably finding it not incongruous with his thoughts. Let the revolutionary mind then reconsider its significance and disregard its supposed connotations; let wigs resume their rights as symbolic of the reign of Louis Quatorze and all that came of it; let powdered flunkeys be supposed the torch-bearers of "progress"; let historians emancipate themselves from the false traditions of their elders; and let that contrary-of-a-revolution which came in after Waterloo and of which the Victorians, all things considered, made such a striking success, be grasped henceforth by its head and not by its hair. So may we regain our powers of discrimination. The "hungry forties" are not pleasant to think about, and yet are nothing to the hunger and distress upon the Continent for which the Peace of 1919 is now responsible. The ignorant disregard of child welfare after the Industrial Revolution cannot easily be condoned; and yet beside the horror of the fate that has now overtaken the youth of Europe, it seems but a very little thing. The classical economists of the nineteenth century taught, we are told, a dismal science; yet it compares favourably enough with the meretricious nescience of revolutionary idealists.

Contemporary historians could see the peril which Metternich's much-abused policy was designed to meet. "If God does not miraculously aid," wrote Niebuhr in 1830, "a destruction is in store for us such as the Roman world underwent in the middle of the last century—destruction of prosperity, of freedom, of civilisation and of literature." "The Revolution," wrote Döllinger about 1860, "is a permanent, chronic disease, breaking out now in one place, now in another, sometimes seizing several members together."[1] We deceive ourselves, then, if we refuse to regard the legacy of the Revolution as a new burden laid upon civilisation. We deceive ourselves, too, if we suppose that democracy—whatever interpretation we put upon that fluid phrase—is any real answer to the problem that the Revolution raises. For one thing—and it is not so trivial a thing as it seems at first sight—democracy is ultimately dull; and all the evidence seems to show that human beings want the world to be dramatic. If one could be bored under the bourgeois Monarchy, one will in all probability be still more bored in a world delivered over to rows of stream-lined residences, even though so-called "bungalow poets" should be heard singing like canary-birds from every open window. It is in the nature of things that presently our restless intelligentsia should fall upon democracy and rend it limb from limb. The Greeks, they will say, had aristocracy, and the Hebrews hierarchy, but what in the world can be made of a society of Beveridge men, with forty-odd shillings a week, all dressed in utility suits? They are sure to say something unkind like that—the *jeunesse*, no longer *dorée* but copper-clad, of the future, yet pining as ever for the golden age. For equality will not always look so pleasing as it does just now, any more than Shakespeare will always appear an agreeable novelty if presented in modern dress.

It was interesting to notice how popular the Habsburg Monarchy immediately became with the general public so soon as the politicians had pulled it down—how "Lilac Time" took the stage and the story of Strauss engaged the films, and how for a while all the world seemed to be dancing to the old Vienna waltz, though Austria had been suppressed by the Slavs—or was it the Vandals? Twenty years later when the Germans, as was said, 'raped' what was left of Austria, there was to be heard even in Liberal circles lamentation and mourning over the once great city that, sitting solitary without her provinces and tiring of her desolation, had sold herself for gain. Yet Vienna had been undone by the Revolutionary Idealists before ever it was prostituted by the Prussians.

"The old world of culture and quality, of hierarchies and traditions, of values and decorum," observes Mr. Churchill in a study of a great Liberal in whom the pure milk of the word of Mill had become associated with the meat of political experience, "deserved its champions. Morley," he continues, "had risen to eminence and to old age in a brilliant, hopeful world. He lived to see that fair world shattered, its hopes broken, its

---

[1] Quoted from Acton, "Essays on Liberty," p. 305.

wealth squandered. . . . He lived to see . . . the nations hurled against each other in the largest, the most devastating and nearly the most ferocious of all human quarrels. He lived to see almost all he toiled for and believed in dashed to pieces."

The preservation of that fair old world of culture and quality in which a gracious Liberalism had delighted, though without acknow-ledgments, the Liberals owed more to Metternich perhaps than to any other man. Austria, however, the last legatee of the *ancien régime*, was sacrificed to the revolutionary idea of nationality and at length dismissed in Mr. Lloyd George's elegant language as nothing better than a ramshackle empire. To this general, though not quite universal defect of perception in the Liberal Party Acton must be reckoned an eminent exception. His German education, his Conti-nental connections, his Catholic faith, all tended to show him that Austria had a place and even a very distinguished place in the European community of nations; whilst his close acquaintance with French revolutionary thought enabled him to trace by what steps and why this had come to be contested by the Revolution. Among the three great revolutionary principles of which the Revolution made use that of Nationality, as he observes, was "the richest in promise of future power"—richer that is, than equality or com-munism. Upon nationality therefore the Revolution concentrated. "The France of history," Acton observes, "fell together with the French State, which was the growth of centuries. . . . The state of nature, which was the ideal of society, was made the basis of the nation; descent was put in the place of tradition; and the French people was regarded as a physical product; an ethnological, not historic unit. It was assumed that a unity existed separate from the representation and the government, wholly independent of the past, and capable at any moment of expressing or of changing its mind. In the words of Sieyès, it was no longer France but to some unknown country to which the nation was transported."[1]

In this manner the principle of nationality was exalted to the heights of idealism; and from that unreal elevation have flowed many past discontents and present disasters. Nationality was a good thing when it roused the people against Napoleon's aggression in Spain and elsewhere and voiced the will of a nation to recover its historic independence. In this capacity it served the purposes of civilisation and secured the sympathy of England. But it was a different matter when it came to be used or abused to promote the ambition of a

[1] Acton, "History of Freedom," p. 277.

State to improve its strategic frontiers or of a people to domineer over its neighbours. It had been so conceived by the French revolutionaries; and it was in such sheep's clothing that aggression worked its way into the councils of a good many European and Liberal minds. Acton was not its dupe. With cogent reasoning and concealed passion he showed how dangerous and how disintegrating the principle of nationality could thus become. "The greatest adversary of the rights of nationality," he wrote, "is the modern theory of nationality. By making the state and the nation commensurate with each other in theory, it reduces practically to a subject condition all other nationalities that may be within the boundary."[1] Already he had shown that freedom lay in quite another direction. "The co-existence of several nations under the same state is a test as well as the best security of its freedom. It is also one of the chief instruments of civilisation; and, as such, it is in the natural and providential order and indicates a state of greater advancement than the national unity which is the ideal of modern Liberalism. The combination of different nations in one state is as necessary a condition of civilised life as the combination of men in society. . . . Christianity rejoices at the mixture of races, as paganism identifies itself with their differences, because truth is universal, and errors various and particular. In the ancient world idolatry and nationality went together, and the same term is applied in scripture to both. It was the mission of the Church to overcome national differences."[2]

From these large considerations Acton's argument narrowed again to its Anglo-Austrian conclusion. "If we take the establishment of liberty for the realisation of moral duties to be the end of civil society, we must conclude that those states are substantially the most perfect which, like the British and Austrian Empires, include various distinct nationalities without oppressing them. Those in which no mixture of races has occurred are imperfect; and those in which its effects have disappeared are decrepit . . . The theory of nationality is therefore a retrograde step in history. It is the most advanced form of the Revolution and must retain its power to the end of the revolutionary period, of which it announces the approach."[3]

"Nationality," continues the historian as if driven forward by the very force of his reasoning to a prophetic vision of national socialism, "does not aim either at liberty or prosperity, both of which it sacrifices to the imperative necessity of making the nation the mould and measure of the state. Its course will be marked with

[1] Acton, "History of Freedom," p. 297.   [2] Ibid., pp. 290–91.   [3] Ibid., p. 298.

material as well as moral ruin, in order that a new invention may prevail over the works of God and the interests of mankind. . . . It is a confutation of democracy, because it sets limits to the exercise of the popular will. . . . Thus, after surrendering the individual to the collective will, the revolutionary system makes the collective will subject to conditions which are independent of it, and rejects all law, only to be controlled by an accident. Although, therefore, the theory of nationality is more absurd and more criminal than the theory of socialism, it has an important mission in the world and marks the final conflict, and therefore the end, of two forces which are the worst enemies of civil freedom—the absolute monarchy and the revolution."[1]

In the contrast that appears in the foregoing passages between the old composite conception of the state and what may with increasing justice be styled the totalitarian, revolutionary mis-conception of it we reach the philosophical antithesis behind the present European distress just as in the contrast that has been stressed between the characters of Wellington and Napoleon we touch its psychological antithesis. Politicians and publicists are constantly trying by something very near akin to sophistry to throw mankind off the trail and will explain, for example, one day that Russia is an aggressor power and the next that she is a bulwark of liberty. Honest thought must indignantly repudiate such patent inconsistency. The Austria of Metternich, like the England of Wellington or the America of Washington and Lincoln had, as Acton's argument shows, more potential freedom in its little finger than the Revolution, as propagated by France under the influence of Rousseau and Robespierre with Napoleon to help them, has got in its loins. There were doubtless in Metternich's Austria repressions of opinion that laid him open to criticism, as there have been in Mr. Churchill's England confinements in prison which have invited the strictures of a judge of the High Court. But, granting so much, both countries have enjoyed on the whole a freedom of opinion and a recognition of liberty that never brought either within measurable distance of the impact of Acton's profound remark that "the Reign of Terror was nothing else than the reign of those who conceive that liberty and equality can co-exist."[2]

[1] Acton, "History of Freedom," p. 300.
[2] "History of Freedom, and Other Essays," p. 267. Cp. A. J. P. Taylor—"The Habsburg Monarchy," p. 32, "Those who have seen in contemporary Europe the workings of a really repressive régime will look in vain in the Austria of Francis (II) for the concentration camp and the executioner, for the organised brutality and the propaganda of barbarism."

D

Toute vérité, we are often told, *n'est pas bonne à dire*; but that ought not to be interpreted to mean that every *sottise* should pass unchallenged. The Soviet Government has among its friends in England many who flatter and many who fawn; but no amount of flattery or sycophancy will make it plausible, or perhaps possible to believe that the Union of Soviet Republics is in love with even so much as one of President Roosevelt's four famous freedoms. The existence of an Ogpu seems inconsistent with freedom of opinion: and as for the other freedoms was not this very Russian Government that now is, publicly arraigned by an Archbishop of Canterbury for its anti-Christian persecutions, accused by so reputable a journalist as Mr. Chamberlin, after personal investigation, of causing the poor to starve—deliberately, in great numbers, and as a punishment— and finally pilloried by so witty an observer as Mr. Cholerton for substituting a "habeas cadaver" for a "habeas corpus"? But to make sure let the evidence be considered of a most benevolent critic of the Soviet Republic—Mr. Davies, the American Ambassador, writing in the year 1938. "The terror here," he says, "is a horrifying fact. There are many evidences here in Moscow that there is a fear that reaches down into and haunts all sections of the community. No household, however humble, apparently but what lives in constant fear of a nocturnal raid by the secret police (usually between one and three in the early morning.) Once the person is taken away, nothing of him or her is known for months—and many times never —thereafter. . . . It is commonly alleged that the secret police of this proletarian dictatorship are as ruthless and cruel as any during the old Czarist régime."[1]

In the course of his conversations with Stanhope, Wellington is reported to have remarked that a real democracy, could it be formed, would be the strongest of all governments; "but then, remember," he added, "the strongest is the most tyrannical." His acquaintance with the thought of the Continent was considerable; and his conception of what is meant by a finished democracy is consistent rather with what Rousseau has written of the general will than with that composite product of revolutionary sentiment and traditional sense that now goes by the name of democracy among the Anglo-Saxons. From the hands of the Revolution the French in the first place, and the Russians and Germans in our own time have derived a servile faith in the Napoleonic type of man as the true expression of the sovereign will of the people; and this in due

---

[1] Davies, "Mission to Moscow," p. 197.

course has produced precisely the efficiency and the tyranny that Wellington foresaw.

The principle of nationality as the best servant of the revolutionary idea can, it should be noted, work both with positive and negative effect. It can, as in Germany, build up by swift steps a totalitarian state with a powerful and aggressive hand raised against all that stands in its way, or it can, as in Austria and as in India, disintegrate an empire by slow degrees. The direct attack upon the Habsburg Monarchy in 1848, though it caused Metternich to fall, failed to overthrow the sovereign dynasty which proved still too strong for the Revolution to dethrone. Thenceforward the strategy of the assailants aimed, not so much at capturing the citadel of the old order at Vienna, but at undermining by means of the nationality principle its outlying defences in the provinces of the Austrian Empire. The common charge against Metternich is that he did not assist this process in its early stages. In point of fact he showed himself not unsympathetic with provincial aspirations. Yet even Acton implies that he ought to have promoted the making of Italy as an independent kingdom by abandoning the Austrian hold upon its northern provinces. It is improbable that the Emperor would have permitted him to do this even had he wished; and the issue is therefore only the academic one whether he should have done this if he could. The withdrawal of Austria from Italy would in his time almost certainly have resulted in the return there of France, for the first Napoleon had stimulated the old interest of the French monarchy in Italian affairs and the third Napoleon was to do so again later on. There was no particular reason why Austria should go out in order to let the French in. As Mr. Woodward allows, there could have been no question of the restoration of Venice; nor does he deny that "outside the territory under Austrian rule good governments scarcely existed."[1]

It is probable that most ministers of any Power, situated as Austria was, would have acted as Metternich did. And, as we look to-day at modern Italy, incapable even after a victorious war of retaining parliamentary government and, since then, thrice shamed by aggression in her craze for territorial aggrandisement, we may reasonably ask ourselves whether the old Italy of city-states and petty sovereignties, of schools of art and humanist studies and scientific research and spiritual interests, was not worth more to Europe than either the Liberal experiment or its Fascist termination.

[1] Woodward, "Three Studies in Conservatism," pp. 92–94.

British enthusiasm for Greek independence and Italian unity sadly needs to be tempered by the reflection that it was as a series of city-states that Greece first came to greatness and as a medley of duchies and republics, petty kingdoms and papal States that Italy attained her loftiest summit of intellectual beauty and spiritual greatness. The Athenians who heard Pericles' great funeral oration were of the generation which was to massacre the inoffensive, neutral Melians: the Florentines who raised Arnolfo's Baptistry and Giotto's Tower were of the same stock which exiled Dante, produced Machiavel and burnt Savonarola: the Romans who lifted the domed canopy of St. Peter's above the oecumenical church below and stretched the crossed limbs of its structure in sight of the City and the World, as if for wide embrace and endless blessing, were the same race who caused the succession to the Holy See to appear the prize of faction and the metropolis of Christianity to be compared to a harlot. Yet still in respect of these old societies does the positive achievement outlive the negative reproach. It has been otherwise with the Revolution, as Maistre perceived in his day, as Berdyaev and Rauschning have pointed out in ours. Its constructive strength for aggression is terrible, though transient; but its destructive power is elemental. It has roused Germany like a wind; but it swept away Austria like a whirlwind.

Since the ensuing pages were first printed, Mr. Taylor has published a critical study of the defunct Habsburg Monarchy. Mr. Taylor bases his criticism psychologically upon Liberal predispositions and practically on the revolutionary theory that Dr. Masaryk's striking personality made plausible at the peace of Versailles. It does not appear to me that the matter of the treatise is well calculated to recommend its argument. I doubt if any dispassionate reader could lay the book down without retaining a stronger impression of the intractability of the various nationalities contained in the Austrian Empire than of the ineptitude of the statesmen who carried on its business. In the period between the fall of Metternich and the fall of the Habsburg Monarchy the Emperor appears to have tried every sort of constitutional experiment excepting the real or virtual abandonment of sovereign power. Like Sir Stafford Cripps in a case that springs readily to mind, he had to draw the line somewhere, and in fact he drew it at much the same place. He would not give up control of the army or of foreign affairs nor yet the right to decide what was or was not constitutionally workable. Is there any serious student who does not see that abdication from these

functions would merely have opened the door to confusion or
chaos? But, if any such there be, the case of India seems there to
teach him better. Doubtless the analogy is not perfect, but it is
adequate. The Crown is in India, as it was in Austria, the source
of cohesion; and not only Disraeli, the pupil of Metternich, but
Morley, the pupil of Mill, was fully aware of it. "He repudiated,"
says Mr. Hirst in his admirable estimate of Lord Morley's administration of India, "the idea that India, with its diversities of races,
religions, languages, and castes, was fitted for a democratic constitution; but by appointing Indian members to the Viceroy's council
and to the India Council in London, as well as by enlarging the
representative element on the Viceroy's Legislative Council and
on the Provincial Councils, he associated many more Indians with
the work of government." *Mutatis mutandis*, this might stand for a
loose description of the Austrian problem and its treatment during
Francis Joseph's reign. And it is significant that amongst the motley
crowd of ministers who worked for that exigent but certainly not
indolent master, Taaffe, who came nearest perhaps to success, came
nearest also in character and method to Metternich.

"A more cynical, trivial Metternich" and "less philosophical,"
as Mr. Taylor tells us, Taaffe worked a composite parliamentary
majority with considerable skill, remained in power, with of course
the Emperor's backing, from 1879 to 1893, and fell before a coalition
of Young Czechs and German Liberals directed against an extension
of the suffrage on Tory-Democratic lines. Finality in politics (*pace*
Lord Russell and his disciples in every generation) is never attained;
but Taaffe made a good bid for temporary stability. "No one
thought," Mr. Taylor tells us, "that the problems of Austria had
been solved, but they seemed to have lost their dangerous character
and become manageable factors in Taaffe's parliamentary game." "It
is extraordinary," he adds, "how the bitterness went out of political
conflict and how easy, though futile, life in Austria now seemed.
Austria-Hungary was once more playing the part of a great European
power, firmly allied to Germany, going her own way in the Balkans
and eagerly courted by Russia and England."

That estimate of the Taaffe administration makes no bad envoi
to a study of Metternich and is none the less informing for the
presence of the little word "futile" so dexterously slipped in to
modify the praise. For what have Liberals themselves esteemed
higher than peace or prosperity or held up as happier than a
country without a history? Only to minds obsessed by the love of

change for change's sake could a cosmopolitan existence like that of old Vienna—blithe, gay, humane, decorative, pacific—seem futile, at least in comparison with the wastage of war or the drab level of the social reformer. Changes must come; but woe to those men who force them on from mere unrest of spirit. The last state of their country may well prove worse than the first.

"Ubi bene, ibi patria," said Goethe, the cosmopolitan product of a period whose despots were deemed benevolent. An age devastated by malevolent despotism may well look back and wonder whether Bacon had not got at the heart of this question when he wrote: "It were good that men in their innovations would follow the example of time itself, which indeed innovateth greatly but quietly, and by degrees scarcely to be perceived. . . . It is good also not to try experiments in states, except the necessity be urgent or the utility evident, and well to beware that it be the reformation that draweth on the change and not the desire of change that pretendeth[1] the reformation."[2]

The revolutionary event, towards which India is now tending under the pressure of the notion of nationality, is not yet reached; but in Austria it has already a quarter of a century behind it and is ripe for study. It is an obvious reflection that the new dispensation there has not prospered even so well as the old and that the realised ideals of Professor Masaryk, which Mr. Taylor highly commends, can hardly with justice be said to have produced any more fortunate result than Professor Redlich's abortive schemes for the regeneration of Austria which he sarcastically disparages. The Czechs in the new Czecho-Slovak State got on very ill with the Germans, and perhaps not too well with the Slovaks: in Jugoslavia the Serbs and the Croats apparently modelled their relationship upon that commonly associated with the companionship of cat and dog: whilst the territorial problems of Hungary and Roumania remain for him who can solve them, should there be man or angel equal to the task. Was it really worth while for such results to let the Habsburg Monarchy be broken up, to drive Vienna to sell her soul to the Germans and to add her conscripts to the army of the Reich? Professor Carr has added a final touch to the lurid confusion of the picture by pointing out that the three wise men of the peace conference of 1919 made the unfortunate mistake of assuming that the principle of nationality was identical with that of self-determination and had the same value in the east as in the west of Europe. In fact such plebiscites as have

---

[1] viz., to put forward or exhibit as a cover (Whateley).   [2] On Innovations.

been taken show that eastern Europeans often prefer to be included with other racial elements rather than with their own. "Only a proportion of people speaking Polish or southern Slav as their mother tongue (in one of these cases a negligible proportion, in none of them a proportion exceeding two-thirds) preferred to be citizens of a Polish or Southern Slav rather than a German State."[1] Some of us will doubtless still believe that the doctrine of nationality can solve the problems of Europe, but there are others who may dare to suspect that it is more capable of causing them.

It is an interesting observation of Mr. Taylor's that under Taaffe's administration, which came thirty years after Metternich fell, "Austria-Hungary was once more playing the part of a great European power." It is interesting because Mr. Woodward declares that the gravest charge against Metternich is that his foreign policy went beyond the means at the disposal of his country. That is no doubt a very grave charge against any foreign minister; and when in the suite of common rooms at All Souls' College so agreeably reminiscent, at least to the eye of a privileged visitor, of older ways of living and of more spacious days, Mr. Woodward converses with Lord Halifax respecting matters on which they are well qualified to speak either from study or experience, it must be hoped that he does the theme full justice. Megalomania is a great snare and is apt to prove a great delusion. But can Metternich be fairly convicted on this serious count? For thirty years and more he made his country the council-chamber of Europe; and thirty years is a long time. Pass on the space of another generation and consider Taaffe still enabling Austria in Mr. Taylor's words to play the part of a great European power. Taaffe, it is true, could not draw the bow of Ulysses; but neither, if it comes to that, did Lord Simon or Sir Samuel Hoare, Mr. Eden or Lord Halifax show signs of being able to draw the bow of Castlereagh or of Canning, of Clarendon or of Salisbury. The test of megalomania is landing a great power in a war to which its resources are unequal. Such a landing did a great sea-power suffer in 1940 and, had it not been for the consideration which Herr Hitler showed in attacking Russia and the Japanese in attacking the United States, she might well have gasped out her life in Continental commitments beyond her strength, even though all the tools she required had been supplied her from the other side of the Atlantic. Metternich, in fact, worked within his strength throughout his time and can hardly be held responsible for the effects of an ill-judged,

[1] Carr, "Conditions of Peace," pp. 43–45.

though well deserved[1] punitive expedition sixty and more years afterwards.

So long as Europe recollected what Palacky, the eminent Czech historian, had told the Frankfurt Vorparlament in 1848 and what Palmerston, the eminent British Foreign Secretary, had told his fellow countrymen a little afterwards, that, if the Austrian Empire did not exist, it would be necessary to invent it, so long may the Habsburg Monarchy be said to have possessed a guarantee of continuance in the very existence of Europe. In fact the problem of Austria has never been other than the problem of Europe itself seen through a microscope—the problem, that is, of holding together many races, and peoples and tongues, once fully conscious of a common heritage of faith and custom, but now, owing to the solvent action of the Revolution, reduced almost to vanishing point. Recent historians, content to assume that the principle of nationality is the proved agent of spiritual and intellectual progress, have not perceived that to sign the death warrant of Austria was to provide a formula for the destruction of Europe.

Metternich, as we have seen, was too good a physician to entertain this kind of illusions. "He was, no doubt" observes Mr. Taylor,[2] "right in seeing in German and Italian nationalism threats to the European system even greater than French imperialism or the ambitions of Russia; for German and Italian national states, lacking tradition and definition, must by their boundless ambition inevitably provoke in Europe a war both general and endless." Yet Mr. Taylor blames him with as much or as little reason as men blame doctors for mortality. "Metternich despaired of Austria," he declares, "because he was a reformer who had no faith in reform, a rationalist who doubted all reason but his own. . . . He lacked the radical's confidence in the new forces that the French Revolution had called into being and so relapsed into defending the existing system solely because there was nothing to take its place."[3]

Young doctors, it is said, kill their patients, whereas old ones let them die. It may be too sweeping to assert that Metternich despaired of the state but undoubtedly he belonged to that older school of physicians who, in default of any recuperative power on the part of the patient, resist the temptation of meeting the difficulty by

---

[1] I assume, of course, as I think is now sufficiently established, that the Serbian Government in 1914 were aware that the assassination of the Archduke Franz Ferdinand was contemplated and that by their connivance or negligence the assassins were able to cross the frontier from Serbia into Bosnia.

[2] "The Habsburg Monarchy," p. 33.

[3] *Ibid.,* p. 34.

recommending treatments that only accelerate decline. In face of the doctor's dilemma of Europe which we are confronting now in a later stage of the disease one might do worse than regard him as a kind of Sir Patrick Cullen and his critics as variations upon the types represented by Ridgeon, Cutler Walpole and the immortal "B.B." Cutler Walpole's face, it may be remembered, appeared, according to the Shavian report of it, "machine made and bees-waxed" but with "scrutinising and daring eyes that gave it life and force," so that one felt him "never at a loss and never in doubt" and felt that, "if he made a mistake, he would make it thoroughly and firmly." As for "B.B." had he not "a most musical voice," and was not his speech "a perpetual anthem" of which he never tired? Metternich cannot of course claim to vie with such charmers, or charlatans, if we prefer to think them so. All that a biographer dare suggest is that, after the blandishments of the revolutionary idealist have faded, as they have a way of doing, Metternich will be found, even in the retrospect, a good consultant, and possessed, like Cullen, of "arid common sense."

Europe lies dying; and Europe, as some of us understood the expression, will die. With it will pass away an incalculable amount of tradition, custom and convention out of which our civilisation had been formed. And if a Continent die, can it live again? Our Pharisees foretell a brave new world, as indeed they did, most unfortunately for their reputation, a quarter of a century ago. But our Sadducees say there is no resurrection; and our Sadducees may be right, so far at least as anything that politicians can do is concerned. Not without reason has Mr. Huxley[1] taken occasion to point out, in his study of that famous "Eminence Grise" who worked "under the red robe" of Richelieu, how much more power mystics really possess than statesmen to sway the fate of nations and how terrible may be the consequences to humanity of a mysticism perverted to the uses of the national state. "Gesta Dei per Francos!"—that was the working hypothesis with which Père Joseph, that strange Capuchin priest (now as it seemed to his master, best characterised by the name of Ezechiely, and then again as Tenebroso-Cavernoso), delayed the cessation of hostilities in order that France might have a victory so decisive as in his deluded vision to establish a Kingdom of God upon earth under French auspices.

Gesta Dei per Francos! Gesta Dei per Germanos! Gesta Dei per Anglos! Gesta Dei per populum! Gesta Dei per artifices! Gesta

[1] Aldous Huxley, "Grey Eminence."

Dei per opifices! How often the thought has come into the mind of divers kinds of men and in how many generations! All history is against the truth of it; and all religion, as it appears in the last prophecies of Christ or in the rising terrors of the Apocalypse, when the seals are broken and the trumpets sound and the vials pour forth the dregs of the wrath of God! Yet this great illusion of new worlds and new orders, made by the hand of man and perfected through man's many inventions, goes on, and is propagated, and is believed, in face of dire experience, in face of dread warnings, in face of horrors than which the world has known none greater since its beginning.

"The essential nature of the crisis through which we are living," observes Professor Carr in his Treaties on Conditions of Peace, "is neither military, nor political, nor economic, but moral."[1] But, though the truth of the statement is perhaps not generally called in question, the practical application of it, as Metternich might properly have pointed out, is rendered exceedingly difficult unless men are agreed in what morality consists. In fact the diagnosis carries one nowhere in particular. Professor Carr, like the Dean of Canterbury and Mr. Davies, appears to suppose that a new morality might be produced by some amalgamation of Christianity with Bolshevism. It is not evident how this could be. A characteristic doctrine of Christianity—and one which has greatly struck the imagination of mankind—is that Christians should love their enemies. But M. Stalin, if he has accepted the Atlantic Charter, does not appear to have assimilated the Sermon on the Mount. "'It is impossible," so *The Times* reports him to have said, "to vanquish the enemy unless you learn to hate him with all the strength of your heart and soul.'"[2] Now the vanquishing of the enemy is the very crux of the war; for unless he be vanquished, the war will have been fought in vain. But there is more than one way of vanquishing people. There is M. Stalin's way, which is an old way with mankind. But there has also to be considered the paradoxical conduct of One who, being born in an occupied country, where the conqueror was not indisposed to mingle the blood of the conquered with their sacrifices, and being on His own evidence a King, showed no kind of belief in force as an instrument for changing human hearts, treated it with fine irony, suffered himself the extremity of persecution, and at length shamed the very Cæsars into recognising the

[1] E. H. Carr, "Conditions of Peace," p. 110, cp. p. 125.
[2] "The Times," October 21st, 1942, p. 5, col. 5.

truth of teaching which in His lifetime had been dismissed by the representative of Cæsar with an enquiry, jesting or perhaps troubled, as to what truth might be. His victory was indeed so complete as to draw from the reluctant Julian the explicit admission that the Galilean had conquered in the struggle. Any fight for Christian civilisation, even a crusade initiated by a saint, has to reckon with this fact; and the curious amalgam of Christianity with Bolshevism, which is being recommended as the basis for a new and more progressive religion, is evidence among other things of an intellectual dilemma never thoroughly thought out. For the present the Allied Nations, like Père Joseph himself, hope to make the best of both methods. *Gesta Dei*, we might perhaps say, *per Christum et per Bolshevicos*, if only it were not for the difficulty that the Bolsheviks do not encourage and did, at any rate until recently, combat a belief in God.

In some parts of the Continent they see perhaps a little clearer intellectually than we do in England. Many there, maybe, like Christianity little, because they suspect it of being true, but Bolshevism even less, because they know it to be false. Anyhow, they perceive that Britain is in no intellectual position to lay the foundations of a new Europe, as Mr. Eden hopefully aspires to do by a twenty years' alliance with Russia. Professor Carr, if I mistake not, is aware that his moral thesis wears a little thin, for towards the close of his book he takes refuge in the comfortable thought of a "European planning authority" as "the master key to the problem of post-war settlement."[1] But, if "the fundamental issue" is "moral,"[2] the master key will have to be somehow moralised; and once more the question arises whether we are planning for a society dominated by love and freedom, or by hatred and coercion.

If Europe die, will it live again? Neither the modern Pharisee nor the modern Sadducee knows the correct answer. For Christian civilization, even in the far from faultless form in which it appears in the Middle Age, was very much of a miracle; and any resurrection of it will need to be something miraculous. But a miracle performed upon society can hardly be like a miracle performed upon a single man suddenly. It is at all events very difficult to imagine a mass-produced change of human hearts at the behest of a European peace-conference and still less of such a whispering-gallery as General Temperley supposed himself to have found at Geneva. Personal holiness and untiring patience will certainly be required if any

[1] *Op. cit.*, p. 334. [2] *Op. cit.*, p. 125.

advance is seriously intended to be made in that kind of industry. And old men in a hurry and young men in a ferment are equally to be deprecated as auxiliaries. Yet Youth must be there and active, not in word only but in power.

In an address which the late Sir James Barrie gave to the students of St. Andrews in the year 1922 on the subject of courage he raised the question how a practical advance was to be made in international politics. "The League of Nations," he observed in his rôle of Age speaking to Youth, "is a very fine thing, but it cannot save you because it will be run by us. Beware your betters bringing presents. You have more in common with the youth of other lands than youth and age can ever have with each other; even the hostile countries sent out many a son very like ours from the same sort of homes, the same sort of universities, who had as little to do as our youth had with the origin of this great adventure. . . . You ought to have a League of Youth of all countries as your beginning, ready to say to all governments, 'We will fight each other, but only when we are sure of the necessity'."

"To be sure of the necessity!" That is what it is so very difficult for youth to be in a world of half-truths, of fiery passions, of limited information, and of patriotic or pseudo-patriotic fervour. Perhaps, if in 1914, it could have been generally known that the Serbian Government which then was had countenanced the assassination of the Archduke and would in due course cause or permit a monument to be erected to the assassins on the site of the murder, the Austrian ultimatum might not have seemed so drastic as to deserve the death of eight million young men. Perhaps, if in 1939 it had been generally known to the British public that Sir Austen Chamberlain, had, as Foreign Secretary, written to Lord Crewe that "no British government ever will or ever can risk the bones of a British grenadier" for the sake of the Polish Corridor[1], his brother Neville, then Prime Minister, might not have risked not merely the fate of a British grenadier but the fate of the British Empire upon its maintenance. These issues, it will be said, were but occasions of war: the causes lie deeper. No doubt! Yet there is no finality to war—no war that will end war, except some apocalyptic, unimaginable, eschatological triumph of good over evil—and good policy consists largely in the selection of essential issues and good diplomacy in the avoidance of insufficient and inopportune occasions for fighting. A Minister should ask himself before he goes to war,

[1] Quoted in Gooch's "Studies in Diplomacy and Statecraft," p. 180.

what a man should ask himself before he goes to law, not whether a neighbour is a bad neighbour and accordingly to be disliked, but whether his own cause is so clear that no dispassionate court could do other than give judgment in his favour; and, after he has asked that and answered it in the affirmative, then again whether it be so much worth while the winning as to be worth the millions of lives, to say nothing of the millions of money that he may well have to spend upon it before it is won.

The generations drive on with such momentum that one of them is often enough unable to understand what seemed worth all the world to another; and, as Barrie implies, the gulf fixed between youth and age is greater than the gulfs that arise between nations. In every war the sins of the fathers are visited upon the children; yet the children will never willingly suffer for the faults of their forebears. The natural right of a man to expand his country by energy and adventure or to defend it with sword or pen will not seem to him to be justly impaired or rightly rescinded by the fact that his father and grandfather abused their powers. Peter Pan would still be Peter Pan, even though—to suppose the impossible—he were suddenly to discover that his father had really been Captain Hook.

The young are more capable of understanding such feelings than the old and, if fighting were not so exciting, might be more capable of giving them application. Still prime ministers of twenty-four must always be an exception and would not, even if we had them, always be as wise beyond their years as the Younger Pitt. Those whom Barrie addressed as young men are middle-aged men now and, having accomplished nothing of what he asked of them in youth, and having the great martyrdom of man and marthadom of woman that is now going forward before their eyes, have every inducement in the mean of their lives to attempt the enterprise which Barrie recommended to them in their prime. Possibly they may find the delay no total loss. It was the middle-aged men who made the Treaty of Vienna. Metternich was forty-one, Castlereagh and Wellington forty-five at the time; and that was, perhaps, part of the reason why they were able to lay the foundations of a hundred years peace, broken, however, by the Crimean and Franco-Prussian wars and the German and Italian attacks upon Austria associated with the battles of Sadowa and Solferino. They had perhaps fewer illusions than the young and fewer prejudices than the old. They were consequently better situated to see what could never be done at all, what could not be done at the time, and what might be done by taking risks and trusting to good fortune. For, unlike the Émigrés, they had learned something and forgotten something; and both these things are very necessary to the making of peace.

What are the things, we may profitably ask ourselves, that a man with so rare a grasp of international affairs as Metternich would in our time wish to see learnt and to see forgotten? First and foremost perhaps he might hope that men should learn or re-learn that, if there were not to be an Austrian Empire, its equivalent would have to be invented. The spirit of unrest has a town-house in every capital of Europe but its largest country estate lies in south-eastern Europe, where the disruption of Turkey has produced a plague of organised nationalities, quarrelsome, venal, ambitious, seemingly incapable of making union against a common foe or taking advice from a candid friend, even when aggression is patently marching eastwards down the Danube or threatening to make its way southwards towards the Straits. Austria, if France would have helped her, was just strong enough to have blocked the German drive-to-the-east, or, with Britain at her back, to have afforded some counter-poise to the weight of Russia rolling forward towards the mouth of the Danube, the Hellespont and the open sea. But France forsook her natural ally in 1866 and Britain, owing to her *entente* with France and her consequent entanglement with Russia from 1904, was powerless, even if the growing sentiment of nationality in England had allowed, to sustain her. Thus, in the event, the balance of power was rudely shaken by the dissolution of the only German state capable of working in with French and British policy in central and eastern Europe. Metternich would have understood what neither President Wilson nor Mr. Lloyd George, nor even Clemenceau had the insight to perceive, viz., that the safety of Europe desiderated the retention in one hand of Prague, Vienna and Budapest.

This is the first matter that a skilled political consultant might invite a student to remark as a theory carried to demonstration by the events of the last twenty years. But there are others. It might be rediscovered from the event that Britain's way is on the sea and that she needs no Continental alliances for her own protection. The matter has been put to the test and in circumstances as unfavourable to defence as can well be imagined with all the coast of France in German hands. England in 1940 was in the gravest danger; not, however, because she had rejected a Continental alliance but because she had concluded one. From that situation the Navy rescued her. Not only did it repatriate the army, whose defeat on the Continent had left her without her proper complement of defenders on land, but, as the eminent naval critic who writes under the name of "T.124" has shown in his book on Sea-Power, it effectively intervened to crush an attempted invasion by sea. Failing that intervention the Battle of Britian would have been fought, not over, but on British soil. Something more needs still to be added. As the same writer, whose mastery of naval affairs makes him, for that reason, an admirable critic of British foreign policy, points out, had the financial equivalent of maintaining two million men on the western front in 1917 and 1918 been invested in sea-craft we might at no greater cost to ourselves have had 625 battleships or 7500 destroyers[1] and placed our security beyond dispute. Furthermore, if the requirements of air power be now added, as they must be, to the cost of defence, it can be shown that the diversion of the money spent in sending 400,000 troops to France, with nothing but one of the greatest military disasters in British history to show for it, would have given us 6,000 aircraft—enough, if Ambassador Kennedy is right, to have forced our policy of appeasement upon Germany at Munich and so secured the peace of Europe.

Philanthropy or folly, but certainly not sound conceptions of defence nor subtle conceptions of diplomacy may dictate continental commitments; and Salisbury's summary rejection of such entanglements, so late as the beginning of the present century,[2] has been fully vindicated by the event. British interests postulate a place in Continental counsels, but military *ententes* and alliances and coalitions should follow, and not precede a decision to make war. A great seapower can achieve great things for humanity, but she will not accomplish them in the uniform of a policeman. Britain could not achieve anything decisive in the war against Napoleon, until Russia turned her coat; nor, perhaps, could he have been beaten then, unless Metternich had added his aid. What was true in Napoleon's time is, *mutatis mutandis*, true to-day. Britain has to emancipate herself from the influence of the megalomaniacs who, in the belief that they can manage the world, desire to intervene with their ineffective penalties and far-flung guarantees in every quarrel from China to Peru. *Non tali auxilio nec defensoribus istis!* By such defenders

---

[1] "Sea Power," by "T.124," p. 67.

[2] See his Memorandum printed in Gooch & Temperley, "British Documents," II, p. 68.

neither will Britain be safe nor others saved. The British guarantee of Poland gave as disastrous encouragement to the Poles as the reciprocal Polish guarantee gave futile assistance to Britain; and a compact,- born of vain imaginations, ended in equally vain disappointment. If Poland is restored in whole or in part, she will owe it to the action of Russia and be compelled in future to recognise that her independence, if it can be properly called so, rests upon Russian protection. No other guarantee, unless it be a German one, need be taken seriously. The autonomous Poland under a Russian sovereign, set up by the Vienna Congress, was in the nature of a risk, which, with a nation so proud as the Poles, did not answer; but it was a risk nevertheless rooted in realities. The independent Poland, set up by the Paris Peace Conference, was on the other hand, an essay in pure idealism, doomed (as Balfour's memorandum of 1916 had foreshadowed) to provoke a European war, so soon as Russia and Germany had renewed their strength, and destined to leave the Poles beaten, decimated, bleeding and bound to a degree hardly yet known even in their tragic history. Metternich has not this sin to his charge. The Vienna settlement probably gave the Poles their best chance of more or less autonomous government.

If there is a lesson to be learnt from the fate of Poland, there is a whole meditation to be made upon that of the Habsburg Empire. The Austrian Empire no longer exists; and a substitute has now to be invented. Had all the energy that has been wasted during the last twenty years upon the ineffectual League of Nations been expended upon bringing to birth an effective league of nationalities in the valley of the Danube, Europe would have been far better served. A strong confederation, with its foreign affairs and its military defences under common but single-minded control, would be worth all the vague projects of some new Hague tribunal or Geneva assembly that seem to tempt Mr. Hull and Mr. Eden, unable apparently to learn to forget or to remember to learn. Whilst they have been thinking, others associated with them in the present struggle have been acting; and it looks very much as if the result of their cogitations, should these ever take effect, might be a League of Nations without a law of nations to justify its existence. The development of air-power has already played havoc with the former rights of small countries, which the Allies were supposed to be defending. Neutrality has gone by the board. In any future struggle every point of vantage, no matter whether it lie in Iceland or Holland, in Iran or Iraq, will obviously and instantly be seized, so soon as war breaks out, by one or the other belligerent, if only for fear of being anticipated by its opponent. The sovereign independence of weak states is consequently gone beyond recovery. Incapable of protecting themselves, they must now either consent to become members of some larger group or expect to be over-run at or before the first outbreak of hostilities, in which, perhaps, they will have no concern. So by new considerations are we dragged from the theory of small nationalities, raised to the status of independent entities, which governed the deliberations of Paris in 1919, and recalled to that of large mixed states, like the Habsburg Monarchy, which prevailed in 1814 at Vienna and corresponded well enough with the Transatlantic Republicanism of the United States of America as re-shaped by the hand of Abraham Lincoln. The practical difficulty in Europe is now to make men into good mixers. In that respect the New World has something to teach the Old one.

If the theory of nationality deserves to be forgotten, so does an extravagance of the opposite kind that was recently very popular in the circles that look for light to Geneva. It was said, apparently on the authority of Russia, that war was one and indivisible. There is nothing more amusing than to see a theory killed by a fact which the theorist himself has unwittingly produced. After the Japanese attack at Pearl Harbour "war one and indivisible" should certainly have brought Russia into conflict with Japan. But, though more than a year has passed, Russia is not at war with Japan. War is not therefore one and indivisible any more than ever it was; and this dogma also of the League of Nations creed would seem to deserve oblivion. So is it, too, with the fond fancy that the coming dispensation of of the world cannot be half-slave and half-free. For there will as probably be totalitarianism in Moscow as a free government in Washington.

A hundred years hence, when all the passion of the present time has died into distant thunder rumbling among the eternal hills, Herr Hitler will in all likelihood have his bones brought back from whatever St. Helena they may have been buried in and exposed for veneration by the disciples of the Revolution, if any still exist, in some crypt of another Invalides. It will be said that he perceived that the time had come for a unification of the world under a single government; that he saw that the German people, with their wonderful gifts of industrial organisation, were better adapted than any other to accomplish this aim; that, had he been able to effect his purpose, international socialism would have followed close upon

E

the heels of national socialism; and that, with so great an end in view, the means—the ruthless, brutal means—must not be hardly judged.

That is a theme in the best style of the Revolution; and it will be swallowed with avidity by the spiritual descendants of those who in their time have extolled the doings of the Jacobins, the Bolsheviks and the Nazis. Totalitarianism is a very tempting creed, and even more tempting in international than national affairs; but it is not a creed for such frail creatures, mentally and morally, as ourselves. If the League of Nations, instead of illustrating the sentiments of Mrs. Jellyby and the finance of Mrs. Pardiggle, were ever to be stiffened into prepotency by ubiquitous authority and overwhelming command of force, Humanity might presently recoil from the superstate it had set up as Frankenstein from the monster he had made. Imagine for a moment—and it is no idle imagination—this highest prize of worldly power in the hands of a Russian autocrat, versed in all the despotic arts of the Ogpu, or of an American boss, familiar with all the democratic apparatus of party management and political intrigue; and the merits of a balance of power in international relations will become more obvious than its demerits, and the maintenance of individual sovereign states, or sovereign confederations of states, dear as the maintenance of liberty itself.

Such international authority as we dare dream of must rest then in spiritual minds, must exercise its power only by persuasion, recommend itself only by lovingkindness, prove itself both in word and deed to be born of the Incarnate God. Catholics, to their discomfiture, Protestants, to their satisfaction, know what happened when spiritual authorities turned too friendly an eye, as the Sons of Thunder had done before them, upon coercive methods. Doubtless the ecclesiastical position was safeguarded; doubtless the Church did not cease to abhor the shedding of blood; doubtless "extermination" retained its proper sense of exile. Still the use of force was countenanced, if only obliquely, by the stewards of the mysteries of God. Let the good pagan learn, then, from the mistakes of Christian men. It is for the kingdoms of this world that their citizens destroy one another, maim one another, wound one another, bomb one another, widow one another, cause the parent to mourn the child, and the child the parent. Lovingkindness has no part in these things.

The internationalism we seek can never come about until men have truly learnt to think internationally. Ethics, as Aristotle is at pains to show us, is properly a branch of politics; and until the best of a man's patriotism is given to the Kingdom of God instead of to the national state, we shall get no way in this direction. But the Kingdom of God is within us and demands of its leading citizens a high degree of intellectual as well as spiritual development. The eighteenth century, because it was more deeply interested in the things of the mind and, if not in "grace," at least in the graces, was more really cosmopolitan than our own: and the thirteenth, because profoundly interested in the things of the spirit, more cosmopolitan still than the eighteenth. Perhaps only if the revolution of the centuries brings such pre-occupations again into fashion, shall we behold once more the dry light of truth blending with the radiant light of vision. Europe had care of these things once, for they were to a peculiar degree committed to her keeping and from them sprang her unity and such peace as she ever possessed.

Meanwhile the World's Government, like the King's Government, has to be carried on; and Metternich's methods deserve the closer study on the part of all who are interested in the avoidance of complete European disintegration. His informal concert of Great Powers constitutes a more promising international executive than any debating society or other kind of Areopagus can now hope to produce; his unofficial type of premiership a less invidious leadership in council than the formal election of a president of the world; his respect for tradition a better pledge of continuity than any hasty pouring of new wine into old bottles. Europe does not perhaps possess the man to fill the post which he occupied so long and with, on the whole, so much distinction. But to look for such a leader, either in Britain or in Russia, though these states may be the most powerful in Europe at the close of the war, is no hopeful enterprise. Britain, whether she chooses to recognise it or not, has now her back to the Channel, her face towards the Atlantic, her future not in an orientation but an occidentation of her policy; and, where North America is not willing to accompany her, she would be mad to attempt to go. Russia, on the other hand, has her eyes wide apart; the one is fixed upon Asia and the other upon Europe; and which is the master-eye no man, even perhaps in Russia, can yet say for certain. These circumstances alone should prove enough to disqualify any Briton or Muscovite for the European premiership. No hasty reconstruction on Anglo-Saxon or Anglo-Soviet principles would in any case be likely to endure. Europe will need to be reconditioned before it can be reconstructed. Order will need to be established before liberty can live. Groups will have to grow. Justice will need to be reconceived as a minding on the part of each nation of its own business, a playing by each nation of its own part in the harmony of the whole. And to do more than produce an exhaustion and call it peace may require a long patience, even perhaps a seeming inaction. Europe must have time to regain consciousness of her lost integrity and perceive the implications of her past, if she is to feel the call of a future. England would appear already to have saved herself by her exertions. To save Europe by her example is an immeasurably more difficult undertaking; and she cannot reasonably hope to accomplish it unless Europe should give her, for some Wellington still to be found, a Metternich in exchange.

* * *

I have made some minor alterations and additions in this edition. I should like especially to express my obligation to the late Professor Temperley's "England and the Near East" and to Professor Webster's paper on "Palmerston, Metternich and the European System" published in the Proceedings of the British Academy 1934. I regret to have failed, in spite of every effort, to procure a copy of Erich Meissner's "Germany in Peril," which, I gather, contains a valuable defence of the Austrian standpoint in European affairs.

I cannot close this Introduction without some expression of gratitude, however inadequate, to Mr. Nevile Watts and Mr. W. E. Campbell for the kind help and advice they have given me in respect to it, though of course they incur no responsibility for the opinions it contains.

ALGERNON CECIL

February, 1943

I

METTERNICH

"The first year of the nineteenth century found me on the field of battle where I have fought during the last forty-nine years without deserting my flag. In this long period nothing has escaped me; I know all that forms the history of this period and also, as a result, the history of my public life. Well! I think that my own history is preferable to that of society during the first half of the century. A glance at my life brings peace to my soul, but the sight of the world does not do as much. . . ."

Metternich, to his daughter, Countess Sandor,
December 17, 1849.

THE propriety of attaching to any epoch of history the name of a single individual, though often assumed, may well be challenged. Human life is infinitely various and human nature remarkably rebellious. All our types and impersonations tend, as knowledge is increased, to dissolve into misleading phantasms, and, though we speak with some assurance of consent of the age of Dante or of Shakespeare, of Cæsar or of Napoleon, it is only, if we understand what we are about, because such giants as these tower above their time and not because they represent it. A man of Metternich's eminence, in any case, bestrides no world of imagination or action like these colossi. He rises to his height, not through immensity of genius but by capacity of understanding; and there is but a measurable increase of ability raising him above his fellows. If then he may serve to show the meaning of that stretch of history which lies between the decline and fall of Napoleon and "the year of Revolution," he does so by no blinding force of talent, but rather as the wisest of the creatures of circumstance at that time in being.

Doubtless even to this office Metternich's pretensions can be challenged. In France, for example, Chateaubriand was simultaneously investing Altar and Throne with a magic and mystery iridescent as the sea-changes that reveal and shroud again the cliff at St. Malo where he has made his everlasting mansion. In Germany for no small part of our period Goethe was moulding in stillness the talent of his race; whilst Stein, after long storm and stress of battle, forged to a yet stronger steel the character of a people, destined one distant day to wrench from France her age-long primacy in war and, as the contemporary epigram went, to cause Europe to exchange a mistress for a master. Look towards Russia, and, at those windows that give west upon Europe, there appears the face of him who had seemed able to divide two continents with

Napoleon; a master of vast legions, a dreamer of generous and grandiose dreams, a potentate whose forces no man could then measure and of whose purposes no man could long feel sure. His brother stands at his side—that same Nicholas whose figure was as that of a Greek god, whose powerful frame would quickly cause a horse to tremble[1] and to whom, as Englishmen have cause to remember, "General Février" was to play traitor in the winter of 1855. Here were principalities and powers; but also there was rising, when our period opens, another influence of much future concern to Europe. The author of the Soirées de Saint-Pétersbourg, the Savoyard eagle whose winged words were presently to brush the dust of two centuries from the palace of the Popes, was in the first decades of the century spreading his pinions beside the waters of the Neva. Berdyaev is witness in our time, as was John Morley in that of our parents, to the abiding power and interest of one who in his own view stood neither for Revolution nor Counter-Revolution but for the obverse of Revolution. To find at the advent of the Restoration a greater strategist or grander figure than Joseph de Maistre we might have to look to the masters of the sword rather than the pen. Over England throughout Metternich's day of power Wellington, selfless in victory as in defeat,[2] was keeping watch and ward.

Men of renown as all these were, there is not one of them through whose eyes a student may hope to see so much of the significance of the Restoration as through those of Metternich. Not only is their influence upon events more casual and obscure, but also they are for the most part at their greatest in elements comparatively unfamiliar to common men—seeming, as one might fancy, to live and move and have their being in frost or flood, on air or ocean or actually under fire. Metternich stands upon dry earth; no man of his time with firmer feet. Not in him is to be found that romantic sensibility of which is born the poet's dreaming eye, the prophet's distant vision, the patriot's heart, the soldier's simple faith in duty. He is of the company of more worldly men; his views are practical, is even at times opportunist; his noted "system", as he maintains, no more than common sense; his end the peace and order that plain men want. He prides himself upon his ability to see things as they really are, upon his prosaic mentality. His statesmanship is free from zeal and not devoid of a pleasing kind of cynicism. If we take our place beside him we stand as good a chance as now exists to get at the mind of his generation. Ideologues, revolutionaries,

---

[1] Vitzthum.   [2] *i.e.* political defeat.

soldiers, and *arrivistes* of all sorts had devastated its youth; and he perfectly understood its objections to them. The length of his reign is the proof of his understanding.

It was inevitable that, when his period closed in new convulsion, Metternich's reputation should have suffered an even greater eclipse than commonly befalls statesmen who are but lately dead; and we can easily attach too much consequence to the fact. The world moves with no even steps, mainly because human beings are for the most part badly balanced. One political excess is redressed by another and a sort of lopsided advance is now widely accepted as the best method to use in the progressive policing of human nature. But there is something more in the matter than this. We feel the defects of the institutions we have and perceive the advantages of those we have not. Only the fullness of education or experience can teach us that progress in one political direction involves too often regress in another; that *le mieux est l'ennemi du bien*; that forms of government are what we make them, many workable and none unexceptionable; that a political change is a prodigious speculation. To Gibbon, just as our period opens, it had seemed that on a wide survey of history the government of the Antonines and their immediate predecessors had beyond question provided the largest known measure of human happiness and prosperity;[1] yet, before he closed his eyes on time, Paris had declared for democracy in the belief that it was inaugurating the golden age.

This new adventure in optimism was not, as everyone knows, particularly successful. Liberty would not march with Equality. Fraternity, operating in cold blood, appeared to include the massacre of one's fellow-citizens, and, when its blood grew warm, the conquest of one's neighbour's territory. Metternich rose to fame and power on the strength of the disillusionment. With no diplomatic assets but a thrice-beaten, heterogeneous, half-dismembered Empire to help him, he took at the critical conjuncture the decisive step which resulted in the liberation of Europe from an insatiable tyrant battening on a false philosophy. He did more. He made Vienna, what it never before had been nor has been since, the focus of European diplomacy as well as the nucleus of an international idea. He passed by much the years of Napoleon III and of Bismarck, his diplomatic successors in an unofficial premiership or presidency in European counsels. And, largely as a result of his labours, the world had rest from war for close upon forty years.

[1] "Decline and Fall," c. III.

Metternich's achievement was so great that, when Time pushed him at last from his place, the clamour of criticism was resounding. Liberalism hastened to point a moral at his expense; and History, not certainly for the first time, became infected with propaganda. "Few statesmen, indeed few historical personages of modern times," observes, with reference to Metternich, so cautious and competent an historian as the late Master of Peterhouse,[1] "have been judged with more passion, and accordingly with a larger admixture of injustice." In point of fact there was no other moral to be drawn from his fate than the half-truth that times change and men with them. Seventy years later Liberalism itself had grown fully as old as Metternich and had aged as obviously. Its face was faded, its conversation had grown stale, its doctrine was doubted. The Peace that concluded its century of effort gave the lie to its opinions; for the assignment of Süd-Tirol to Italy by the statesmen of the victorious Entente Powers involved the same principle as the assignment of Lombardy and Venetia to Austria by Metternich and Castlereagh at Vienna. None, indeed, who make a dogma of democracy, or suppose nationality to be the last word in civilisation, or reckon liberty to be realised in an untutored choice between right and wrong, or fancy that freedom is implicit in popular government, or regard party conflict as an intelligent aid to public administration, will, perhaps, make much of Metternich's politics, just as none who take it for granted that a dictated peace is in the nature of things preferable to a negotiated one, will see the point of his diplomacy, nor any who assume that the material expropriation of the rich improves the moral—or, for the matter of that, the material—condition of the poor will find themselves in a good way to understand his economics. Such views, however, have lately a little lost their assurance, troubled by that "force of things" beside which Metternich saw good sense aligned and against which he thought mere cleverness helpless.[2] The wheel of opinion is once more slowly turning and looks as if, in time, it might come round full circle. Meanwhile Srbik's monumental volumes are there to show that the foremost opponent of the Revolution can even now be studied without personal partiality or political hypocrisy.

He hangs, then, in the picture-gallery of History—this remarkable and interesting person, of whose politico-philosophic attainments Disraeli, "his last and greatest scholar,"[3] thought so highly—not

[1] A. W. Ward, "Germany," I, p. 55.   [2] "Mémoires," VIII, p. 406.
[3] Srbik, II, p. 313.

primarily for remembrance of some past fashions in diplomacy, nor merely as the lively image of a bygone time, though he has some claim on each account, but pre-eminently as a great European. His sense of the solidarity of society was rare; his sense of the solidarity of nations quite exceptional. To him more than to Castlereagh, whose insular hesitations became by degrees apparent, is due that method of constant conference between the Greater Powers which, hard to use as the bow of Ulysses, has alone shown itself capable of discharging the Cupid's arrows of civilized intercourse and hitting the target of international need. He was, no doubt, as we say, and as others will say in turn of us, of his generation. He did what every man must set himself to do who would be more than a spectator of passing events or a shedder of idle tears—he lived in his age, submitting to its limitations, sharing its hopes and fears, entertaining its convictions, consolidating, so far as the everlasting flux of opinion will allow, its strength, and suffering its decline. He was not, however, merely a man of his world, but a man of *the* world; and his wisdom, though in some ways the wisdom of his time, was in more the wisdom of all time. We can learn as much from him, perhaps, as it is possible for one distracted century to be taught by another. For he had seen the express image of popular revolution; he had beheld Humanity all naked and shameful; he had been intimate, not only with the chief rulers of the Old Order but with the grand master of the New; and he had watched for half a century the waters of circumstance flowing beneath the bridges of time.

The hours, days, years of Metternich's period may indeed be more easily conceived than some others as moving, within the serene and luminous circle of eternity, "like a vast shadow . . . in which the world and all her train are hurled"; and there have been not a few—Bibl lending them even yet no little countenance—who, though perhaps unacquainted with the magic of Vaughan's verse, have seen in the great Austrian Chancellor precisely "the darksome statesman," obscurantist and slow-moving as a midnight-fog, busy with surreptitious intrigue, careless of perjury, and a cause, if not of blood, at least of tears. It is a fancy portrait, with as much fancy in it as in Stendhal's Comte Mosca[1] or in Landor's "imaginary conversation" where Metternich is made to talk with "Kaiser Franz" and Hofer. Here, in reality, was no autocrat nor any policy of "thorough," and, if we must imagine Metternich at all before

[1] I am assuming the truth of the popular identification.

his piece is played, let it be rather in such a guise and against such a background as a scene-painter, fully sensible of the competing forces and consummate perils of the time, might have designed for an opening tableau.

Imagine, then, a room where late Renaissance influences still linger in the decoration—the classic forms, the amoretti with their wreaths of roses, the suggestion of a palace dissolving into a *fête-champêtre*—and, in the midst of it, Metternich. Is it a mere fancy to find in the broad brow, the penetrating, clear blue eyes and aquiline nose, the gracious smile, the gently mocking mouth, the pale, fair skin, the hair so prematurely white, some suggestion of a statesmanship in which one observer has noted finesse and friendliness as the leading features. Behind the evident charm of manner, the elegant address, the intriguingly abstracted air, the exceptional dignity of bearing, we shall at any rate make no mistake in assuming the presence of cool calculation and a resolute, supple will.[1] The Chancellor seems to be explaining to a group of counsellors and kings around him the principles of statecraft much as a doctor might instruct his pupils in the science of sanitation or, as in a conversation picture, a gentleman may be seen imparting to his friends and family the common-sense of life. Notice the air of well-being and distinction which characterise the company, yet notice, too, that they are plainly by no means free from care. The cause of their apprehension can be guessed by glancing through the two windows that give upon the world without. On the one side there is to be seen Paris with the Revolution raging at its height, on the other "the sun of Austerlitz" shining in its strength upon the strewn battle-field below. The artist's execution is excellent, so much so, indeed, that, as we look, we come to share the apprehensions of the pleasing, anxious beings in the sunlit room. We hear with them the roaring of guns and the rolling of tumbrils; and we enter enough into their feelings not to wish their peace destroyed by the tramp of armies or the wine of life dashed from their lips by a crowd half-drunk with blood, even though for lack of a larger share in the loving-cup.

Into this charmed society, to which men still look back for the sake of a dramatic emphasis, now almost wholly lost to them, no less than for a certain grace in modes and manners more delicate than they any longer possess, we, if we would see Metternich as he really was, have somehow to force our way. We can no longer

---

[1] I owe not a little in this description to La Garde-Chambonas's "Souvenirs du Congrès de Vienne," p. 343.

hope to reach it by any broad staircase or lofty hall; and this although, if our latest psychic science is to be believed, the creatures of that vanished world are in some fourth-dimensional sense still somehow with us and even actually to be met with in spots hallowed by historic memories.[1] Our way into past time lies across the thick dust of the muniment-room and through the mortal stillness of the library. But, if we find and follow it, we may hope to see again, as from a masked recess, a society that lingered still in Central Europe into our day and perished actually at our hands. Its indiscriminate destruction was to many a matter of pure rejoicing; yet there have always been some few who doubted. Not even the representatives of Republics invariably make good Republicans. "We too," said a foreign observer with envious and melancholy meaning to Prince Bülow in 1905, as they watched together the progress of a court-ball in the Salon Blanc at Berlin, "we have seen and known all that, when Le Roi Soleil was enthroned at Versailles and the cynosure of all eyes."[2] It was the Ambassador of France who spoke.

The fall of the French Monarchy in 1789 had in truth initiated, as every clear-sighted critic saw, a process of European disintegration comparable only to the great cracking of Christendom under the impact of the Reformation. Another unity was little by little lost to the forces of European cohesion; loyalty as a political motive went the way of reverence; and civilisation was left to shore itself up, as best it might, with the conflicting aid of 'natural' boundaries and nationality-enthusiasms. Metternich's life was cast, as he fully appreciated, at the beginning of this era of transition ; and his life's work was directed towards holding Europe together until, sooner or later, the power of the Revolution should be spent and the real hour of reconstruction should arrive. His character and circumstance, his foes and his friends, his criticism of life, his hours of failure and success, Time's action upon his fame and fortune, Time's reaction, and Time's ultimate revenge are all in some measure the subject of this book. And the whole should be as a portrait with eyes that seem to turn, now this way, now that, over a wide field of vision, and as a portrait framed.

---

[1] Cp. Mr. J. W. Dunne's observations in the new edition of "An Adventure" (edit. E. Olivier).
[2] Bülow, "Mémoires," II, p. 146 (French edit.).

II

FIRST BEGINNINGS AND FINAL ENDS

THE greatest statesman that the Austrian Empire ever possessed did not belong to Austria nor, when he was born in 1773,[1] did any Empire of that name exist to which he could have belonged. Not the light beer of Vienna but the sparkling wine of the Rhineland ran in the veins of the Metternichs; and their orientation was less towards the Holy Roman Emperor, ensconced amidst the splendours of Schönbrunn, than towards the picturesque old dignitaries who ruled as prince-bishops over all things secular and spiritual in the cities and sees of Mainz and Trier. A Metternich had himself been Elector and Archbishop of Trier in the early seventeenth century, and partly from him and partly from his then reigning successor the subject of these pages took his Christian names of Clement, Wenceslas and Lothar. Every circumstance, indeed, of birth and origin seemed to befit the rising champion of the *ancien régime*. He was appropriately born at Coblentz, a place destined to become the starting-point of the Counter-Revolution. His father was not less in keeping with his destiny. Count Francis George Charles Metternich-Winneburg-Beilstein—to give him all his due—a man profoundly pompous and beautifully bewigged, satisfied in various capacities the requirements of an old-time courtier in *opéra-bouffe*. Starting with the office of hereditary chamberlain to the Archbishop of Mainz, this singular personage first undertook to represent the Elector of Trier at the Imperial Court at Vienna and then, after some further promotion, reversed his rôle and became Minister of the Imperial Court at Trier. A prosy babbler, an habitual liar and a glittering spendthrift, he seemed to be in no condition to endow his son with outstanding talents; but his tendencies, if they were in some measure passed on to his offspring, were, as by miracle, transmuted in the process. Chatter was turned into conversation, pointless mendacity into diplomatic finesse, idle prodigality into expenditure well calculated to obtain value for money. The alchemist, at any rate so far as one can trust surface appearances, was no other than Metternich's mother. Countess Beatrice Kagenegg—to give her her maiden name—was one of those remarkable women who are generally to be found in a family when we look up the antecedents

[1] May 15th.

of great men. Metternich's wit and charm and beauty, his light touch in talk, his lively way with ideas, his dexterous adaptability to circumstance, his finished knowledge of the French tongue— all these things were apparently derived from a parent, possessed of the graces which the old society of France and the parts of Europe adjacent had brought to perfection. In the world in which he grew up French modes were, indeed, already in vogue, the Elector of Trier being, as it chanced, the maternal uncle of King Louis XVI; and to her dying day Metternich wrote to his mother in French, a language plainly congenial to his mind and which he came to speak with the so-called "accent d'Empire." His studies were, for the rest, eclectic, for he was taught both by a priest and a Protestant. He took more kindly to the teaching of the latter, a disciple of Basedow, the German Rousseau. It is a circumstance none the less to be neglected by the student that his Protestant tutor—John Frederick Simon —was presently to afford instruction as well by example as by precept. Simon, in point of fact, like some other revolutionaries who had imbibed the teaching of Jean Jacques, exhibited in his career the underlying defects of his master's gospel. Well has John Morley observed that the "Vicaire Savoyard" is no better than "a rag of metaphysic floating in the sunshine of sentimentalism"! Nothing of Rousseau—not even these, his finest pages—stands the stress of life; and so Simon presently demonstrated. Saturated with sentiment, he concluded in crime; and the intellect that had been trained by Rousseau became comrade with Robespierre. Metternich passed in due course into the care of other tutors, but the impression of his tutor's decline from enthusiasm for freedom and equality into approval of the Terror and the guillotine remained, as Srbik observes, indelible.

At Strasbourg University, to which great qualifying school for diplomatic, not less than ecclesiastical appointments he was sent in his sixteenth year, Metternich came under the instruction of the eminent Koch. At the feet of this master of political jurisprudence others destined like himself to leave a name in history were about this time sitting—Benjamin Constant, Talleyrand, Montegelas. International law as exemplified in the Peace of Westphalia was the theme of Koch's discourses; and the Professor found in it a substitute for the loss of the old medieval foundation of community of religion and a counterweight to the growing power of the national State. But before Metternich left the University, the tenuous world of the jurist became subject to rough usage. The Revolution began to deliver up its true meaning with the attack upon the Bastille; and even in Strasburg the town-hall was wrecked by the protagonist of a better state of society. Metternich put off childish things and took sides at once with law and order. Whilst the ill-starred Simone who had been in attendance at the University, crossed into France to attach himself to Marat, his pupil moved to Frankfort to assist at the imperial coronation of perhaps the wisest of the Habsburgs.

The Emperor Leopold II is placed by the historians of the eighteenth century among the more eminent examples of that enlightened despotism upon which the frail structure of European solidarity conceived after the manner of Koch, not a little depended. He had shown good dispositions and uncommon talents as Grand-Duke of Tuscany and, though a reign both short and troubled gave him but little chance to put his qualities to the proof on the larger field of the Empire, he must be reckoned among the rare successors of the Antonines. The seventeen-year-old Metternich, participating in the high ritual pertaining to the highest of secular dignitaries in his capacity of Master of the Ceremonies to the Catholic section of the College of the Counts of Westphalia, received, like Goethe some ten years before, a majestic impression of the power of unity and tradition. The historic scene, following closely as it did and with all the effect of violent contrast upon the burning by the Jacobins of the Town Hall at Strasburg, profoundly affected his imagination. Too young to appreciate the hollow aspect of the affair, the boy may have felt the better its symbolic appeal to the thought of a European society founded upon Latin civilisation, consecrated by Christian faith and embellished by time. He had a soul that was naturally Conservative and naturally European; and his Christianity, as we shall see, grew with political experience.

It was at Frankfort, as fortune would have it, that Metternich first saw one who was presently to embody, at least for him, the ideals both of the old world and the new imperialism—the Archduke Francis, the heir to the possessions of the House of Habsburg, the coming successor of the Emperor Leopold upon the Imperial throne, Ripening with new experience and ripe for more, the boy passed on from the pageants of Frankfort to the class-rooms of Mainz, where Nicolas Vogt was enlivening the staid legalism of Koch with historic facts and political fancies. Two schools contend to this hour as to the extent of Metternich's philosophic attainments; but it is at least safe to say that he listened appreciatively to a philosophic historian who came like himself from the Rhineland and drew from the circumstance a fine energy of patriotic sentiment. One distant day, when the other was dead, he was in all solemnity to subscribe himself Vogt's grateful pupil. Out of the fogs of antithesis and the mists of time, out of oppositions of love and hatred, desire and recoil, order and freedom, supersition and unbelief, Vogt somehow extracted, with German thoroughness, the governing principles of a European society and the ideas, in particular, of a balance of power amongst sovereign states and of aristocracy as the guardian of the golden mean. The old imperialism of the Middle Age, the hegemony of Bourbon or Habsburg, the desire of racial expansion and the development of the mercantile system of national finance were alike antipathetic to this comprehensive critic; and his aspirations ended in an unreal world where his beloved Rhineland appeared as the centre of a rationalised Catholicism and the pivot of a new balance of power in Europe. Patriotic zeal, however, operated more wisely in his treatment of the young Rhinelander with whose education he was charged. In some words which Metternich never forgot he placed his pupil's character in its proper relation to the circumstances of the time and the prospect of the future. "Your intelligence and your heart," he said, "are well set in the right way; persevere also in active life; the lessons of history will be your guide. Long as your career may be, you will not see the end of the conflagration that is consuming a great State at our doors. If you do not wish to incur reproach, never leave the right road. You will see supposedly great men pass you in the race. Let them be and do not quit your intended path. You will catch them up again, if only because you will come across them as they retrace their steps."[1]

Such things, then, Metternich learnt at the University of Mainz. At its brilliant Court, where the Elector encouraged light conversation and lighter morals, he received from the lips of fair women other lessons that he liked as well or better. A French flirt—the Duchess de La-Force, née Marie Constance de Lamoignon—taught him the pleasures of flirtation; and he appreciated them so thoroughly that he renewed them perpetually, not altogether without diplomatic consequences. But, whilst learned professors were singing the praises of history and tradition in the lecture-room, and young married women were making love to budding boys in the boudoir, and dashing youths were growing ecstatic about the rights of man, whilst Metternich went dancing at Frankfort with one who was to become famous as Queen Louise of Prussia, and at Mainz the

[1] "Mémoires," I, p. 12.

Elector was celebrating the new Emperor's accession with befitting conviviality, the thunder of the French Revolution was approaching continually closer to the doomed Electorates of the Rhineland. Custine occupied Mainz with the revolutionary armies in October 1792. Songs of popular deliverance were sung in its streets; but the liberation of the people from their ancient rulers was quickly turned into enslavement by their new invaders. Revolutionary France had stretched out her hand to grasp her "natural" frontier.

The Old Order fled and was found again at Coblentz, where Metternich took stock of that piteous crowd of fugitive nobles whom the great cynic of the period was presently to stamp as incapable either of learning or forgetting. It was a survey that made him no die-hard. He has put it on record that the Frenchmen of that time did not understand the Revolution and that he doubted whether with some rare exceptions they ever did so.[1]

Old Metternich, meanwhile, was muddling away after his manner in Brussels, where under the title of imperial ambassador he fulfilled the functions of a prime-minister. He had happily more sense in regard to the affairs of his son than in regard to those of his sovereign. An opportunity occurred of sending the young man to England; and he took it.

It was thus that in the midst of commotions of mind and circumstance Metternich was thrown into transient contact with the man best qualified of all men living to confound the destructive fallacies of the hour with profound and penetrating criticism. Attached to a financial mission from the Netherlands to England and recommended to notice by the fact that his nomination as imperial envoy to the Hague was known to be likely, he became acquainted with the Prince of Wales—at that time, as he assures us, a model of good looks, good manners and good sense—with Pitt, with Fox, with Sheridan, with Grey, but above all with Burke. Sixty does not talk at ease with twenty; and Burke in 1794 was sixty-five and Metternich but twenty-one. We should be foolish to suppose that much in the way of philosophic conservatism passed from the great Irishman to the young Rhinelander by word of mouth. Yet Srbik is surely justified in his conjecture that Metternich's six months' stay in England and casual glimpse of one whose imagination seized and whose intellect displayed the deeper issues of the struggle then in progress proved no blind alley in the young man's wander-years. Just as to have seen Shelley once and been spoken to by him was

[1] "Mémoires," I, p. 15.

rightly reckoned an inspiration, so it was here with one immeasurably wiser and after his manner no less eloquent than the poet. Metternich, as he tells us himself, passed as much time as might be in the House of Commons and followed with particular attention the trial of Hastings. There was never, so Macaulay thought, a spectacle so well calculated as the latter "to strike a highly cultivated, a reflecting and an imaginative mind." But however that may be, Metternich must at any rate have become in some degree acquainted with Burke's matchless rhetoric, Burke's half-mystical reasoning, Burke's passionate faith that in an affectionate regard for national institutions and a tempered reverence for traditional authority are to be found the springs of the sublime and the beautiful in public life. Yet the appetite of the student of psychological reactions is rather whetted than satisfied by the circumstance. Did the young man, not merely hear, but understand? Was the coming champion of Conservatism aware as he sat and listened that he was in the presence of a supreme exponent of its final meaning? Did the pupil of Koch and Vogt recognise that the body of thought which had been wholly swathed in the dry legalism of the one and half-stifled in the quaint provincialism of the other had by this radiant being to whom justice was a passion, catholicity an instinct, diversity of function an æsthetic grace, history as well a sentiment as a sense, and the golden mean a mystic measure, been invested evermore with shining raiment? We cannot tell. We only know that, like the proverbial ships at night, the two men, divided originally by all the seas that race and age and temperament can fix, yet flying the same flag and associated in the same endeavour, just met and passed, whilst one was still young enough to have the east in his eyes and the other was moving swiftly westwards.

Other ships and other cargoes of a very different kind, yet in their way as well calculated to convey some idea of England's greatness, came under Metternich's eye. From a hill above Cowes he watched two great convoys of merchantmen, sailing west and east, pass out to sea under cover of the Grand Fleet and remembered it years after as the finest sight he ever saw. Greatly as the scene differed from that which he had beheld at Westminster it had provided him with a rare glimpse of England's strength to add to that of England's freedom.

The Revolutionary armies did not stay their advance on the Continent because the coming champion of the Counter-Revolution was learning political science and the meaning of sea-power in the

British Isles; and their progress was not without consequences to
his career. During the course of 1794 they concluded the conquest
of the Low Countries, tossed the princelings of the Rhineland off
their thrones and turned the *émigrés* out of Coblentz, the Metternichs
among them. Pretty well ruined by the loss of his goods on the left
bank of the Rhine—some three and a half square German miles
of territory, some six thousand two hundred vassals and some fifty
thousand florins of income, as a biographer quaintly calculates[1]—
and pretty well discredited by the failure of his policy in what was
to be the Austrian Netherlands no more, old Metternich fled to
Vienna to get what he might out of a dissatisfied master. On the
whole he did well for himself and his family. Both a place and a
pension were found for him; but for the recovery of political prestige
and the revival in new surroundings of social consideration he had
to look to his more brilliant son.

The younger Metternich had in fact his foot already on the ladder
when the fall of fortune occurred. Accredited, according to expectation, as the imperial representative at the Hague upon his return
from England, he found himself, indeed, owing to the French conquest of Holland, no better than an ambassador *in partibus*, but his
qualifications for diplomatic work had at least been admitted, and
he strengthened them at his parents' instigation by a matrimonial
alliance. That he was in love with Eleonore von Kaunitz is not to
be supposed; he had lost his heart to the little French flirt at Strasburg
and had nothing left but a *mariage-de-convenance* to offer his wife. But
the excellence of his parts to some extent supplied in the eyes of his
fiancée the absence of his affections; and the charmless girl, delighted
with his cultivated address, good intelligence and cool self-
possession, became convinced of the profundity of his mind and the
strength of his religion. She discovered in due course that his
principles were less solid than she supposed and is alleged to have
consoled herself by countervailing attachments. But she was at
least in a position to plead that she had amply satisfied the object
for which she had been chosen by the Metternichs. A grand-daughter
of the famous Minister of Maria Theresa, she had made her husband
the member of a family with as great a political tradition as any in
Vienna; and this was no mean advantage in the case of one whom
the compulsion of events was converting from a Rhinelander into a
Viennese.

Metternich's first marriage took place on September 27th, 1795,

[1] Srbik, "Metternich," I, p. 79.

in a town to be one day otherwise celebrated—in Austerlitz. For three years afterwards, whilst the falling Empire made what head it might against the strong current of Napoleon's growing genius, he lay, as the phrase is, fallow. Society, science, medicine—these were his pleasures and pursuits; and he seemed as if he wanted nothing more. But after the defeat of the Imperial armies had opened the door again to diplomatic business, he followed his father as private secretary to Rastatt, where a place was presently found for him among the negotiators as plenipotentiary of the Catholic section of the College of Westphalian Counts. The work of dissolving or as it was called mediatising the multitudinous sovereign states of the Holy Roman Empire involved all the humours of contact between the polished and sometimes pompous procedure of the *ancien régime* and the rough methods of a half-baked civilisation, at once military and democratic. Old Metternich became as usual a figure of fun; and young Metternich in all probability liked the upstart Frenchmen none the better that his father appeared to them more than commonly absurd. He had, however, occasion to make reflections upon a survival of greater consequence. His letters show that the helplessness of the worn-out institution, which Voltaire had already effectively ridiculed by observing that it was neither Holy nor Roman nor an Empire, came home to him forcibly; and we may ascribe to these hours of wasted negotiation a first beginning of those final ends which dominate his life—the re-establishment of the hegemony of the Habsburgs and the restoration of an organic civilization in Europe. He did not perhaps distinguish so clearly as we do the one aim from the other.

The Conference of Rastatt ended abortively in the March of 1799; and Thugut, who was in control of Austrian policy, once more attempted to solve on the battle-field the difficulties he could not settle in the council-chamber. For a year and over Metternich once again dawdled, illustrating, it is to be hoped, more than the reputation of his private life at Rastatt might suggest, that lifelong horror of low company to which he lays claim in his memoirs.[1] Then in 1801, with peace in prospect, the Emperor offered him a choice of diplomatic appointments. He could go as he pleased either to Copenhagen or Dresden as imperial ambassador or to the Reichstag at Regensburg as the representative of Bohemia. He chose discreetly. He had resolved to take diplomacy seriously. He never wished, as he tells us, to do anything by halves; if

[1] "Mémoires," I, p. 39.

diplomat he was to be, he would be one altogether. Saxony offered as central a post of observation as a man could desire. Here Prussian policy worked more openly than at Vienna and with more insistence and directness. Here Russian aims, at a time when the tension between Vienna and Petersburg had closed the ordinary avenues of communication, were to be gleaned from the large number of Russian residents. Here French designs in regard to Germany might be seen and studied. Dresden was the green-room whence he stepped on to the European stage.

III

THE EMPEROR AND THE EMPIRE

IT is convenient at this point in the narrative to pause and consider the sovereign whom Metternich had set himself to serve. The Emperor Francis II has been variously portrayed. Metternich maintained, with something possibly of a courtier's care, that his master had for him every requisite quality—that the Emperor was calm, prudent, high-principled, of sound judgment, and benevolent disposition. "Heaven," he declared,[1] "has placed me near a man who seems as if he had been made for me. The Emperor Francis does not lose a word. He knows what he wishes; and his wish is always good." And Aberdeen, who assures Croker that few men had had a better chance than himself of observing the Emperor's character, describes it as "simple rectitude and honesty."[2] Treitschke[3] has supplied us with a very different portrait. The Florentine in Francis, he argued, lurked beneath the bluff good-humour of the Viennese. The Emperor was that least tolerable of characters—the *faux bonhomme*. Calculation and cruelty lay behind the mask of benevolence. Intellectual apathy, love of ease, and a shrewd perception that Austria had little or nothing to gain by change, combined to make him a conservative of the narrowest type. In fine—and this is the exaggeration which betrays the artist's malice—he was spiritually as well as racially related to Philip II of Spain, to Philip, that is, as he appeared before some recent researches set him in a more favourable light. Francis II of Austria was neither so interesting nor so disagreeable as this. Sketch a typical Habsburg, and you have drawn his outline. He was, in fact, much what Charles V had been before him, and what Francis Joseph was to become after him—patient to the point of phlegm; matter-of-fact to the exclusion of enthusiasm; conservative to the destruction of enterprise; a Catholic of a secular, not to say, Febronian cast; a gentleman, if perhaps rather a clumsy one; a lover of and loiterer in ancient ways; in a word the first citizen of Vienna. Beside all this, there was, as the observant young eyes of the second Napoleon noted, a constant force of religious faith perceptibly dominating both his words and acts.[4] Like George III of England, he suffered from a poor address but, like George III also, he instinctively drew, as time went on, all the advantage that

[1] "Mémoires," III, p. 388.   [2] Croker, III, p. 229 (A. to Croker, March 10, 1851).
[3] "Deutsche Geschichte," I, p. 605.   [4] Montbel, "Le Duc de Reichstadt," p. 304.

can be derived from years and adversities, played the part of patriarch of his people to perfection, and gained continually in popular esteem without appreciable effort. Such was, so far as we can now discern his figure, the man whom Metternich had to reckon with; such were his limitations; such the dispositions that might be turned to account. It was not the least element in Metternich's statecraft that he studied his master as intelligently as a wise man will, whether that master be sovereign-lord or sovereign-people.

The confidence reposed by the Emperor in the young envoy was shown in the fact that the diplomatic instructions[1] which Metternich carried with him to Dresden were of his own composition. These included a general survey of the diplomatic situation as it appeared from the Austrian standpoint in the year 1801 when the Habsburgs, after surrendering to France as the result of two wars their interest in the Netherlands and, in northern Italy, the frontier of the Adige, and receiving from Bonaparte's hands the stolen goods of Venice, needed both to consolidate their gains and cut their losses. The occasion for forming new international relationships had evidently arrived, the difficulty of defending the Low Countries being gone with the cession of them and the old French alliance, originally concluded by Kaunitz against the Great Frederick and subsequently cemented by the marriage of Louis XVI and Marie Antoinette, being put out of date by the advent of the Revolution. Metternich dwells upon this not less than he dwells upon the natural attraction between Austria and England arising out of a total absence of conflicting interests. Yet, though in this respect his observations seem tending towards a reversal of the Diplomatic Revolution of 1756, in another they maintain as firmly as before the tradition of the great statesman into whose family he had married. For him, as for Kaunitz, Prussia is still the principal, the perpetual foe. He describes her in terms which might have satisfied the propagandists of the Entente Powers during the Great War of 1914–18. "Her whole policy," he declared, "consisted in the enlargement of her territory and the extension of her influence; to attain it she was willing to adopt any manner of means and pass over the law of nations and the universal principles of morality." He repeats himself presently with alarmed emphasis. "Sustaining her part by freeing herself from all the rules of political ethics, exploiting the misfortunes of other countries without regard for obligation or promise, strong by reason of the numerous acquisitions

[1] See "Mémoires," Vol. II, pp. 2–16.

she has made or is going to make, Prussia has latterly found a place among the Greater Powers. Thanks to the cohesion of the most powerful States of the Empire, her influence in the affairs of Germany has become of such consequence that the Imperial Government is enfeebled by it." No wonder Treitschke tried to damn Metternich as a nonentity! The Austrian Minister saw far too clear for the Prussian historian.

Prussia, or, if we prefer to call it so, Brandenburg, was in fact, as Metternich saw, neither an honest German nor a good European. The Treaty of Basel, then some five years old, stank in his nostrils. To gain a little and, as it proved, brief authority in Northern Germany Prussia had not scrupled in 1795–96 to desert her allies of the First Coalition, to infringe the Constitution of the Empire by the conclusion of a separate peace with the enemy, to hand over German nationals in her trans-Rhenane province to France and to countenance or at least connive at the extension of the French frontier to the Rhine. Such things were at variance with Metternich's conception of statesmanship; and he had no use for a Power that perpetrated them. If we turn to a later remarkable passage in his memoirs containing his cosmopolitan confession of faith, we can see the principles of his objection. "The great axioms of political science," he declares, "come from the knowledge of the true political interests of all States; upon these general interests rests the guarantee of their existence. Conversely, particular interests, which derive sometimes great importance from transient or accidental circumstances and whose care constitutes the statecraft of a restless and limited policy, have only a relative and secondary value." . . .[1]

Now Prussia, from the day when Frederick the Great avowed his reasons for the capture of Silesia to the day when in the reign of William II a German Chancellor wrote to his own and the Emperor's friend, that "the Prussian genius is hard and ruthless,"[2] has been, on her own showing, at least intermittently, sceptical of the doctrine which Metternich lays down; and there is nothing particularly remarkable in his having, even at this comparatively early stage of her history, diagnosed her character so clearly. What showed, however, incipient statesmanship of a high order was that, with the Revolution, whose terrors he was the last man to underrate, polluting all the air of Europe, he should have kept his harshest words for Prussia rather than for France. He was in truth

[1] "Mémoires," I, pp. 30–31.
[2] Haller, "Philip Eulenburg" (tr. Mayne), II, p. 132. Bülow to Eulenburg.

cool and capable observer enough to distinguish between diseases of different import. He saw that the commotion of Europe was a flux and the destructive energy of France a fever, but that in the case of Prussia he had to deal with something more self-centred and malevolent—with a carnal mind in the State that meant enduring enmity to the commonweal of nations. To the considered selfishness, the ruthless egotism of a Power, behind whose brazen face the lost soul of the Great Frederick has seemed, decade after decade even to our own time, to be working out its malignant purposes, the imperial tradition of Austria, preserving as it did the thought of a United Christendom, to say nothing of the defence against Islam of a common civilisation, was radically opposed.

Not that the Imperial Government at Vienna had never fallen! In the Polish Partition business it had, as Metternich would have been the first to confess, and in fact here confesses, stumbled into Prussian policies. The downfall of Poland, removing, as it did, the buffer between the three great Eastern Powers, was, he declares, an act "opposed to all the principles of good policy." Yet, as he indicates, the motive which was in Prussia greed, was only in Austria weakness. Unable to prevent a crime against Europe, the Imperial Government attempted to provide compensations for itself. It was an attitude, we may reflect, ignoble enough to justify to the full the caustic sarcasm, "Elle pleurait mais elle prenait toujours"; yet the tears were not so much those of the crocodile as of declining age subjected to the rude pressure of youth. Let that be, however, as it may, provided only that we recognise that Metternich made no defence of the Polish Partitions. The next thing to notice is that his concurrence in Kaunitz's opinion of Prussia was inevitably modified by recent developments in France. The fall of the Bourbons had undone, for the time at any rate, Kaunitz's great achievement in uniting the two great Catholic dynasties of Europe against the political Protestantism of the Great Frederick. Austria was without an ally, or at best without a congenial ally. A new France had arisen —a France pregnant with ideas which were subversive not only of the social order but of the international balance. If peace was to be preserved, Austria must establish fresh relationships and discover other friends.

Thugut, Colloredo and Cobenzl, who in the opening century were charged with the conduct of Imperial policy, could make nothing of the international situation. Thugut, the boldest of the three, had imagined that Austria might make head unaided against the Revolution; but his illusions were shattered at Marengo, and Cobenzl had taken his place after the Treaty of Lunéville. The new Minister, whom Metternich dismissed as a man of fashion, rested in the comfortable but inadequate expectation that Bonaparte would destroy the Revolution; and his colleague, Colloredo, whom Metternich frankly characterised as an ass, cherished the still fonder faith that the Holy Roman Empire was instinct with vitality. In point of fact that institution was all but defunct. Under Bonaparte's auspices Western Germany was being mediatised and Northern Italy republicanised. The first harvest of Revolution had been reaped; the winnowing-fan of war was at work; and in the great heritage of the Habsburgs as elsewhere the grain was being sifted from the chaff.

At the Court of Saxony, where topography and military weakness bred uncertainty and indecision, Metternich watched and pondered. It was in that hour of formative reflection that he came into contact with one who may be regarded either as his jackal or his *éminence grise* —the publicist Friedrich von Gentz, a converted revolutionary. Their minds tended to march together; and on this occasion, though it was not always so, they arrived at a common conclusion. The Revolution, they argued, was the immediate peril; the prospect of its suppression by Bonaparte was illusory; Europe could be saved only by a pan-German opposition; an alliance between Austria and Prussia was consequently urgent. In 1803 Metternich significantly left Dresden for Berlin. He had been moved at the critical juncture to the decisive point of the diplomatic battle.

Yet still Cobenzl hesitated to strike. Not the French occupation of Hanover, nor the violation of Imperial territory by the capture of the duc d'Enghien, nor yet the new imperialism of France dividing and disputing the old honours of Charlemagne's legacy, could bring him to the point. Only after Napoleon had assumed the crown of Lombardy and converted Italy into a kingdom, only when ancient principalities had been annexed and new ones created for the conqueror's kindred, did the provocation prove too great. Then at last the man of fashion was prevailed upon to countenance the aims of the war-party and to give instructions accordingly. The Emperor Francis was better served by his diplomatists than by his soldiers. In Petersburg, where Stadion represented him, an alliance was rapidly arranged with the young and impulsive Alexander. But at Berlin, where Metternich had to deal with a monarch of a different type, more time was required; and time was not upon Francis's side.

Frederick William III of Prussia is a sovereign of whom some impression is desirable, for his character was a factor in the fate of Europe and we shall meet with him perpetually in these pages. The husband of one of the great queen-consorts of history, he fell himself, for all his fine figure, into the category of cautious, insufficient, irresolute men from whom much is expected in the beginning and little obtained in the end. At the Vienna Congress he was to make so good an effect at first by his modest and sagacious bearing that even women preferred him to the showy Alexander; but, before the Congress was over, he was spoken of as the Emperor of Russia's valet-de-chambre.[1] He was, as Metternich came to know in later days, the prey of indolence and weakness, with a spirit of opposition in him upon which diplomacy might play.[2] But even in 1804, when the enchanting Queen was still at his side to raise his courage, Metternich had looked into his mind and found the greatest of his motives to be fear.[3] Fearful of mistakes in general and of France and Russia in particular, the swaying King strove to make terms with all contingencies, whilst looking to events to guide him. His Ministers reflected the instability of his mind and, on much the same principle as actuated certain Scottish Houses in the days of the Pretenders, one of them maintained good relations with France whilst another affected the Austro-Russian alliance.

As the plans of the Allies matured in the course of 1805, and as the aid of Prussia became more necessary, Metternich and Alopéus, the Russian Ambassador, strove the harder to defeat the French leanings of Haugwitz and, through the support of Hardenberg, to drag Prussia out of her neutrality into the alliance against Napoleon. They succeeded, but too late. The very violation of Prussian territory by the French at Anspach, which steadied for a moment the King's wavering resolve, contributed to bring about Mack's catastrophic capitulation at Ulm; and that catastrophe caused Frederick William's fearful mind once again to treble. The Prussian Government had no sooner signed the treaty of Potsdam with Austria and Russia than Haugwitz betook himself to the headquarters of Napoleon with proposals of mediation. Thus, whilst, like the rustic in the adage, the King of Prussia gazed expectant at the stream of circumstance, opportunity slipped past. Alexander, with impetuosity as gross as Frederick William's indecision, hastened to try conclusions at Austerlitz; and Austria paid the price of a rash

[1] Weil, "Les Dessous du Congrès de Vienne," I, pp. 207, 525.
[2] "Mémoires," III, p. 277.   [3] Ibid., II, p. 22.

young man's ambition with a crushing defeat. The King of Prussia, advised by the event, hastened to ratify Haugwitz's defensive alliance with France, which contained a mutual guarantee of the existing possessions of both Powers, and of course, effectively superseded, if it did not literally contradict, the treaty of Potsdam. Austrian diplomacy had been ruined by Prussian pusillanimity.

The Peace of Pressburg, which Francis was now driven to sign, took from him what remained of his possessions in Italy and of his influence over Germany, took from him his devoted provinces of Tirol and Vorarlberg, and took from him one-sixth of his revenue as well as three million of his subjects. So great a disaster made his vast pretensions sound absurd. The old Empire of Charlemagne had withered away, and there was a new Charlemagne in the field. Francis had prudently prepared for the event. A year or so before he had added the style of Emperor of Austria to his titles; and he now solemnly resigned the wider dignity of Roman Emperor. It was a tacit admission that to east and to west of him there reigned potentates as great as, if not greater than himself.

This extension of the name of the old Austrian Archduchy into a general name for the whole Habsburg dominions, though interesting enough to the student of international politics, did little or nothing more, so far as the State was itself concerned, than regularise a convenient custom. To Metternich, however, expatriated as he was from the Rhineland and attached hitherto by no more than a personal tie to the Emperor, it might be said to have given a country. The consolidation of Austria upon its new foundation became his care, and, if he inevitably worked for it rather as an architect than a son, this was no more than wise men and good ministers have elsewhere done before him. Designed in a style fundamentally opposed to that of the Revolution, this great central Power had always for him beyond its plainer, more immediate purpose the diplomatic value to Europe of a nucleus of moral energy.[1]

The dark days after Austerlitz gave scope enough for anxious broodings. To Metternich it seemed that civilisation was reeling and that the Second of December, when the Peace of Pressburg was signed, was a day of more dreadful omen than the Fourteenth of July when the Bastille had fallen. The alternatives had grown plainer. Either a new world must be brought to birth or the old world regenerated. He set himself to do the latter. It was the choice of a man

[1] See "Mémoires," V, p. 166.

who prized precisely those things that the Revolution was assailing—
loyalty, order, elegance, degree, a justice not fondly conceived in
terms of equality, and a peace not foolishly pursued by means of
upheavals.

Though Louis Cobenzl, and with him the asinine, or supposedly
asinine Colloredo, fell after Austerlitz, power did not immediately
pass into Metternich's hands. The impressionable Stadion, with his
clear understanding and his tendency to extremes, was recalled to
take over the department of foreign affairs from his post as Ambassador at Petersburg; and Metternich was meant to replace him in
Russia. But the diplomatic shuffle did not go through smoothly.
Philip Cobenzl, who should have gone simultaneously as Austrian
Ambassador to Paris, was not acceptable to Napoleon; and Metternich was eventually chosen in his stead. The appointment was largely
Talleyrand's doing. Metternich with his usual good manners had
made himself agreeable to a certain M. de Laforest, who was
Talleyrand's confidential agent at Berlin, and none too comfortable
in consequence. Laforest did not forget these civilities; and Talleyrand, whose diplomacy desiderated a better relationship between
France and Austria, recommended favourably to the notice of his
master one who had been thus favourably recommended by his
creature to himself. Metternich was taken completely by surprise
and shrank in diffidence from a task so difficult. Francis, however,
was insistent. The nomination was made. And thus, by virtue of an
incident to all appearance trifling and fortuitous, Metternich
obtained the chance of studying at close quarters the man whom he
desired and designed and was destined to overthrow. He made
good use of his opportunities.

IV

DIPLOMACY WASTED

"It was only at Paris," Metternich assures us in his Memoirs, "that my public life began." In Dresden he had been in the main a spectator, though placed to great advantage; in Berlin in the outstanding negotiation with Prussia he had acted more or less as an understudy to the Russian Ambassador, Alopéus; in Paris he came into his own and stepped towards the front of the stage.

In the vast pageant that was in progress there was no sign of a pause. The battle between the Old Order and the Revolution, incarnate in its strongest son, had now been fully joined and, though still far from its conclusion, was approaching a climax. All around, like vast scenic and orchestral effects, events were announcing the magnitude of the strife of change with conservatism. The Powers of Europe were plainly shaken; principalities of long standing tottered and fell; dynasties trembled; States were being stretched or dismembered with as little concern as the victims of Procrustes; and a new code of human relationships was proclaimed amidst the dust and din of circumstance with as much assurance as if it had descended like the tables of the Law from the smoke and solitude of Sinai. We can hardly exaggerate if we wish to imagine the terrors of the spectacle upon the mind of a spectator placed at the very centre of the amphitheatre—in a Paris itself at that very time stamped with many outward and visible signs of drastic, though certainly not always undesirable change. For the camp-fires of the Revolution were spreading ever farther to the east; the sombre horizon of Russia, above which the figure of Speranski was just beginning to appear, was touched with lurid and fitful light; in the Balkans the long-hidden volcanoes of the Turkish Orient were beginning to send up smoke; and from the nearer distance—between Rhine and Danube—came the intermittent sound of the drums of War with some echo of the tumbrils in their beat. The outlook over the Continent for such as Metternich was, as in the case of the prophet of old, a vision of darkness and sorrow; only in the roaring of the seas behind him were there to be heard voices of hope. In the year in which Austria fell and the dying Pitt took his ten-year measure of the extent of the catastrophe, the Ocean—not yet apprised of the bold claims of both combatants to enslave its waters—carried Nelson to his triumph at Trafalgar. Incalculable as ever, the restless waves play in the background of our drama; though perhaps neither Metternich, for all his vaunted insight, nor any man at that time alive, could have read their meaning or estimated the full influence of sea-power upon history.

In the front of the vast and memorable scene two actors towered imperially above the rest. The master of the slow, fateful hordes of Muscovy and the master of a race brilliant as the Greeks and militant as the Romans—the Emperors of Russia and of the French—dominated the stage and symbolised forces deep as Nature itself. "Napoléon," observes Vandal, tempted by the splendour of his theme into a flashing epigram, "c'est l'action; Alexandre c'est le rêve." In the days before Austerlitz Metternich had come to know the latter as in the days after Austerlitz he learnt to know the former; and he has left us studies of them both that repay attention. His estimate of Alexander is so much the more valuable that it agrees with that of Napoleon, who strove ten years with him for the possession of Alexander's wayward soul. The Emperor of Russia, as these critics saw him, was the essence of versatility with all its charm and all its inconstancy. At every turn, so Napoleon told Metternich, there was to be detected in him some deficiency, which spoilt the rest; but precisely what that deficiency would be in any particular case was not to be foreseen. And Metternich, with a longer experience, noted the strange periodicity of Alexander's moods. An idea with the Russian Emperor would take two years to germinate, and would, in the third year, bear fruit, only in the fourth to be wearied of and condemned as noxious, and in the fifth to be left to wither away. Thus his life, which abounded in purposes, had never purpose; for he neither knew how to follow a policy, when he had framed it, nor how to discount its incidental evils when he had recognised its substantial claims. As in war, so in peace his associates had always to be ready to find him gone. He was, in fact, a politician of the most pathetic school—a visionary continuously losing hope and learning fear. Having proved all things and held fast to none, having consorted first with liberals and ideologues and finally with conservatives and mystics, he, whose sovereign power was supreme and unchallenged, came at the end, as Metternich declares, to die from weariness of life.

So much for the lord of dreams; what of the lord of action? Napoleon's character, as Metternich sketched it in the light of an experience more extensive and intimate than that of any other foreigner, except possibly Alexander himself, is a penetrating study which has left a deep mark upon subsequent criticism. The Emperor of the French appears as the very antithesis of the Emperor of Russia. Though he dislikes Voltaire and approves Christianity and Catholicism as instruments of civilisation and order he disbelieves profoundly in the motives that religion inculcates. Honour and virtue are good enough for ideologues; public and practical men are guided only by interest. It was, Metternich declares, useless to argue with him on this point; and frequent attempts to do so had in the Ambassador's experience invariably failed. Only dreamers had any use for ethics; and for disinterestedness as for dreamers he had himself no use at all. He lived in fact, as Metternich warns us, outside the moral categories. He was neither good nor bad; he took merely the shortest road to his immediate end. When he came across devotion as in the case of Duroc, who was perhaps his favourite retainer, he put it down to instinct. "Il m'aime comme un chien son maître" he told Metternich.

Regarding men simply as instruments, Napoleon showed a peculiar tact in selecting them for his purposes and a total absence of generosity in rewarding them for their services. Easy and tractable in private life, indulgent, even over-indulgent towards his sisters, he was in his public capacity utterly ruthless, though without malevolence. The favoured child of the Revolution, he had no scruple in "confiscating," as Metternich puts it, the whole substance of his parent to his own profit. Domination was his deity; his political ideal a hierarchy of petty sovereigns with himself at the head of them. Hence of all conceptions of empire that of Charlemagne most appealed to him, but in a form disfigured and exaggerated, so that the Pope was required to become subservient and to fix his see, in fact if not in name, at Paris. He sought even to invest himself with such a divinity as hedged pre-Revolutionary kings, became covetous, when he heard of it, of the style of Sacred Majesty, which the Austrian Emperor retained, and in the belief that only legitimism supplied a sure foundation for authority contended that he was no usurper but had mounted a vacant throne. These aspirations and arguments discovered rather than concealed the parvenu. Metternich in fact could never forget his first view of the imperial adventurer, when he presented his credentials at St. Cloud—the short square figure in uniform, the too studied carelessness contending with the not less studied effort to look imposing, and—damning mark of the self-made monarch—upon his head a hat which he thought it magnificent to keep on. Trivialities in all conscience trifling enough, yet appearing in one form or another at critical audiences and just sufficient to destroy, at least in the mind of a man of better breeding, otherwise well-calculated effects! We gather, indeed, that in Metternich's view the rant of a player and the cant of a plebeian transferred the honours on more than one critical occasion to the representative of the older society; and we need the less to doubt this impression that it is in such close accord with a famous page in almost contemporary fiction. Who that has once read it can forget the passage in "La Canne de Jonc," where Alfred de Vigny makes the Pope counter one of Napoleon's harangues with the simple comment "Comediante!" and the next with the not less contemptuous and laconic "Tragediante!"? These simulated rages, these calculated threats might serve with those who knew no better; in Metternich, cool, distinguished and almost imperturbable, they brought out all the confidence inherent in a superior type of training.

In fact, as Talleyrand plainly told Alexander at Erfurt, Napoleon was not civilised; and Metternich is well-justified in maintaining that in his case comparisons confuse counsel. He was neither Alexander nor yet Attila, but a phenomenon unlike any seen before. Nor has all the bitter experience of our own time quite produced his equal. He stands alone at the summit of his column of fame, an Emperor with two faces—the face of a man on the one side, of a beast on the other. The man whose triumphal monuments are still the glory of the French and the pride of Paris; whose poor ashes after twenty years were brought back, with much tragic pomp, from St. Helena to the Invalides by a *bourgeois* government in search of a *beau geste*; whose legendary fame was sufficient to raise his family a second time to the throne of France; to whose memory Béranger dedicated, perhaps, his sweetest song ; and upon whose latest days an English Prime Minister lavished all the power of his prose, is the brute who shot down his prisoners in Syria after their lives had been promised them; who for fifteen long years drowned Europe in blood and tears, terrorised its peoples, occupied its capitals, seized its treasures, set up his brothers in place of its kings; who made an end of Venice and a mock of Rome; who, flouting morality, national and international at once, took and shot the duc d'Enghien; who, in a moment of revealing egotism, told Metternich without a blush,[1] when fortune turned against him, that, though he might perish, he would drag down in his fall the whole of society; and who, to conclude, found it in his soul to commit a final infamy by rewarding with a legacy

[1] "Mémoires," I, p. 288.

the would-be assassin of his conqueror. Metternich—and we shall never understand him unless we recognise it—had to deal with a monster— a monster gifted, as he particularly notes, with the charm of penetratingly lucid understanding and admirably exact expression, and capable, as we all know, of incomparable enterprise, magnificent energy and even, when as by Josephine or his army his heart was stirred, of something like a rough caress; yet still a monster, ruthless, calculating, tyrannical, the end of humane society for a generation or more if he had prevailed. To substitute an heroic saga for the old nursery tale of "Boney" is to afford ourselves the indulgence of a glittering fancy and to evade the compulsion of an ugly fact. For here in truth is no Jason with his golden fleece, but a Cretan or, if we prefer, Corsican bull.

It was in Paris and in the summer of 1806 that the *retiarius* began to walk round the victim which he was to conquer and to cage some ten years later. His prospects looked poor, yet his equipment was excellent. He was acceptable to Napoleon; he was acceptable to Talleyrand; he was acceptable in general to women, who were indeed credited with some share in his nomination and in particular, as it proved, to one woman whose influence at Court was to grow in proportion as that of Hortense Beauharnais declined—to the Emperor's sister Caroline, the wife of Murat, at that date also the mistress of Junot but soon to be his own. His relations with her, who was later Grand Duchess of Berg and afterwards Queen of Naples, were politically important as well as personally intimate. With something of calculation about them in the beginning they retained, after all passion was spent, something of friendship in the end, so that, at the crumbling of her brother's fortunes, Caroline turned again to Metternich and Metternich did not wholly turn away from her.

If the Austrian Ambassador knew how to be agreeable to women, he knew no less how not to be disagreeable to men. He made few observations and no epigrams. "You have succeeded here," Napoleon told him in 1808, "because you do not talk and people cannot quote any sayings of yours."[1] It was as flattering a testimony as in the circumstances a diplomatist could wish for. He had the other great diplomatic quality which pairs with tact—a continuous power of adjusting or readjusting his point of view to the course of events. In the days after Austerlitz he entertained an idea of effecting some kind of accommodation between the Old Order and the Revolution

[1] "Mémoires," II, pp. 158–59.

G

by virtue of a middle wall of partition running from the mouths of the Weser to the head of the Adriatic; and, when he first came to Paris in the summer of 1806, in all probability he had this still in his mind. The defeat, however, of Prussia at Jena in October 1806 and of Russia at Friedland in June 1807, followed as they were by the *volte-face* of Alexander at Tilsit and the reduction of Frederick William to something not much better than a shadow-king, turned such projects into moonshine. On the raft upon the Niemen, where the French and Russian Emperors met and made friends, the diplomatic situation was changed out of all recognition. Alexander, consenting to that which Francis had wisely refused,[1] allowed the Eastern Question to gain precedence over the Western peril. It was exactly what Napoleon wanted.

The French Emperor had for some while perceived that in the fate of Turkey was to be found an apple of discord sufficient to poison the relations of the three Christian Powers of Eastern Europe and impair their ability to make common cause against himself. Talleyrand's plan on the eve of Austerlitz had been to give Austria the Danube as far as its mouths so as to turn her head finally eastwards; and an understanding with Austria had always for Napoleon the greater attraction. But Austria had no inclination to shift her eyes. Her orientation was, in fact, then and for long afterwards occidental. She wanted her faithful Tyrolese, her hold upon Germany, her footing in Italy; and she wanted these things not less because Napoleon had taken away with them that impalpable pre-eminence in the west which had seemed the birthright of the Habsburgs. Stadion, at any rate, fresh from contact as he was with the sympathetically conservative circles of the Russian nobility, disinclined to rate the proffered gifts of the Gauls higher than the proverbial gifts of the Greeks, and, less than ever tempted by Turkish preserves when they reached him in the guise of French confections, had as little use for the scheme of Talleyrand as for Alexander's project of a new alliance against France. He wanted to avoid commitments; for his friends in Vienna were afraid—afraid as well of revolution as of war.

It was in these circumstances, then, that Napoleon tendered the insidious apple to Alexander. He did this with the utmost art, covering the fruit with silver wrappings until it seemed a very symbol of concord and progress. Alexander, young, benevolent and ambitious, was easily bewitched by the persuasive eloquence of a

[1] Vandal, "Nap. et Alex." I, p. 7.

mentor who appealed at once to his personal feelings by virtue both of soldierly achievement and reforming zeal and to his political imagination by opening the prospect of a Russia advanced without effort to the Danube—and perhaps beyond it. The magic fruit was taken and tasted; a vision of the fabled East, rich with romance and rescued from Turkish oppression, rose before Alexander's eyes; and, careless of the difficulties involved in accommodating his new obligations to Napoleon with his old ties to Francis and Frederick William, he walked in a gay garden of dreams.

"Toute alliance," says Vandal, speaking, we may hope, for his own nation rather than for all mankind, "nait de haines partagées." Such parentage the new Alliance possessed. In hatred of England the masters of France and Russia were at one; and in a general way, though not when it came to detailed discussion, their common sentiment fitted in well with Eastern projects. To invade India, or even to menace it, was to strike a blow at British prestige; and the road to India lay through Turkey. Convinced by the end of 1807 that Alexander would neither forego the acquisition of the Danubian provinces of Moldavia and Wallachia nor consent to let France take Silesia from Prussia as a set-off to their annexation by Russia, Napoleon in the January of 1808 began seriously to develop his plans for a partition of the Ottoman Empire. He spoke of them to Talleyrand and to Metternich, inviting the latter to participate in the adventure and divide the spoil. The invitation, needless to say, was not disinterested, for Austrian co-operation was required to counterbalance Russian greed. Though Metternich would have preferred to keep things as they were in the Near East, the best thing to be done in the circumstances, as Talleyrand advised him and as he advised his master, was to go in with the spoilers. "We cannot save Turkey," he wrote to Stadion in the beginning of 1808, "therefore we must help in the partition and endeavour to get as good a share of it as possible."[1] Napoleon was, in fact, actually talking about the "just and geographical claims" of Austria on the Danube.[2]

The counsels of January were dissolved, however, by the events of the following months like snow by summer. Unwilling to comply with the requirements of the Continental System, the House of Braganza—the Royal House of Portugal—was curtly deposed by Napoleon's mandate in February; Junot, whose inconvenient attentions to Caroline Murat in Paris had attracted Napoleon's displeasure, being entrusted with the business. The Spanish Government was

[1] "Mémoires," II, p. 149.   [2] *Ibid.*, p. 155.

persuaded to countenance this proceeding; and Spanish troops were dexterously abstracted to assist in it. The principle of his suzerainty thus conceded and the passage of his armies thus prepared, Napoleon went on to deal with the Royal House of Spain as he had done with its neighbour. By the end of May the younger branch of the Bourbons had, as the phrase went, "ceased to reign," and the eldest of the Bonaparte brothers assumed its style and dignities.

In face of these developments, could the Habsburgs consider themselves safe? Metternich thought not. No treaty with France, he reasoned, had the value of a peace, because no peace with revolution was possible. Whether it were Robespierre who declared eternal war upon the châteaux or Napoleon who made it upon the Powers, the tyranny was the same, the danger in the latter case only the more general. Although, therefore, there was no reason to suppose that Napoleon entertained any idea of hostilities against Austria, to adopt a policy of isolation was to misunderstand the situation. There was no room for quietness and confidence. Turkey was threatened; Austria lay across the road of the French advance. She might participate in the partition or she might refuse to let the French armies pass. She might, in other words, assist or resist; but either course involved an army ready to strike. Even if, in view of Austrian opposition, the French advance upon Turkey proceeded by way of Germany and Russia, what, he asked, was Austria to oppose to the French armies when they returned victorious?

The talk both in Paris and Germany, as Metternich emphasised in a second despatch, was only of war with Austria; and though the reasons given for this were various, the effect of them was identical. In face of this general opinion, in face of the two hundred thousand men that Napoleon had placed upon the Austrian frontier, it was a huge responsibility to maintain that French designs were peaceful. An estimate of the probabilities led to an opposite conclusion. Napoleon, Metternich said in so many words, was meditating their destruction; he was meditating it because the moral existence and geographical extent of Austria were alike incompatible with a universal French supremacy. When the attack would come was uncertain, but it was in the character and policy of Napoleon to make it at the first favourable moment. An interview with Fouché had not proved reassuring, for, though the Minister of Police declared that in his personal opinion Napoleon neither desired war nor ought to make it, he admitted that the Emperor allowed the propagation of bellicose sentiments and that all the soldiers were in sympathy with them. In the circumstances Metternich, while strongly opposed to any provocation of hostilities by Austria, recommended his Government to place the army upon a war-footing and to take the people into its confidence—"to talk to the Public, to tell it the truth, never to leave off talking to it."[1] So little, indeed, did he correspond with the common notion entertained of him that he emphasises the failure to make any popular appeal as "an immense mistake" in which the Austrian took precedence of all other Governments.[2] He was, however, without illusions. "Our chances are poor," he told Stadion, "because, according to my calculations, they rest upon Russia." To reach an understanding with Russia was, however, at least worth attempting; and he advised a diplomatic approach calculated, in return for Austrian co-operation in the partition of Turkey, to obtain the assurance of Russian support in the event of a French attack. Metternich was writing in early July. Before the month was out, his despatches grew in precision. The course, he told Stadion, that French diplomacy had for some time followed was usual with Napoleon when in search of a quarrel: "He provokes us," as Metternich puts it, "to take measures of security by putting about rumours; he asks us why we frighten our neighbours; such is his regular method of procedure."[3] In face of reports and warnings like these it might have puzzled cleverer brains than were to be found in the Austrian Cabinet to know what on earth to do; and Stadion, with half an empire to retrieve and the remaining half to defend, may be excused if he blundered.

The diplomatic tangle was indeed prodigious; and Napoleon himself was getting involved in its meshes. His plans had at this date attained their boldest development. His eye was scanning three continents and appropriating the great central sea out of which the fairest form of civilisation had risen like Venus from the deep. His hands were stretched out far both eastwards and westwards to grip and to grind. There seemed no end to the power and enterprise of that swift and sudden mind.

The torchlight of the student and the searchlight of the event have, however, long illuminated the Emperor's then cryptic and confusing motives. His dominant object is supremely plain—the consummation in a French victory of the long struggle that had raged intermittently since Crécy. The nature of the conflict with England had the effect of opening issues at a remote distance. The exigencies of the Continental System compelled him to secure the

[1] "Mémoires," II, p. 187.   [2] Ibid., p. 187.   [3] Ibid.

co-operation of Russia; and the co-operation of Russia was only to be retained by satisfying her ambitions in the Near East. The partition of Turkey had thus become an immediate possibility, and the disposal of the Imperial City where the keys of two Continents were kept an urgent and, as the conversations that took place at Petersburg in the spring of 1808 between Caulaincourt and Romanzoff showed, an insoluble problem. "The fundamental part of the great question," Napoleon wrote to the former in May, "is always this—who shall have Constantinople?" If Russia were to have that supreme prize of the partition, the acquisition, as the French Ambassador made plain, must be qualified by the presence of France at the Dardanelles. To this, however, Russia showed no sign of assenting. Yet the condition was to have been expected. For precisely at the Hellespont the dreams of Alexander and Napoleon might be said to have met. If the Black Sea, completely shielded and thoroughly possessed, was the romance of the Romanoffs, the Mediterranean, whose waters washed the shores of sea-girt Corsica, was that of the Bonapartes. Gallipoli, Egypt, Spain—here were the gates of that which Napoleon meant to turn into a Gallic lake; and he had it in his mind to hold them all. The Spanish Navy was necessary to his maritime strength in the struggle with England; and half his quarrel with Spain lay in the fact that the Spanish Government was spending upon military what he desired to see diverted to naval equipment.[1] Thus the attempt to subjugate the Peninsula, eventful as it proved, was but a detail in a project of empire covering Western Europe, compassing the Mediterranean and caressing the Orient. The Spanish insurrection shattered, at least for the moment, the visionary plan; and Dupont's capitulation at Baylen afforded some measure of coming difficulties. In Vienna, to make matters worse, the Sovereign and the complex of people under his sway took heart of grace. It was clearly impossible for Napoleon to meet Alexander at Erfurt in the autumn with the full programme of conquest that had been under discussion. Europe had to be reduced to obedience before Asia could be brought into subjection. Until France was ready to join in the scramble, the Russian advance must be limited to the Danube. Meanwhile Napoleon resolved to try the effect of a scene upon Austrian nerves.

On the Feast of the Assumption, which falls upon the 15th of August, and at the customary diplomatic reception on that day, Napoleon taxed Metternich publicly with the existence of unusual

[1] "Mémoires," II, p. 209.

military activities in Austria—the movement of troops in Bohemia
and Galicia and the mobilisation of certain militiamen in town and
country—and alluded besides to other matters in dispute between
the two Empires. According to the Ambassador's memoirs the
scene was sensational. The Emperor spoke from the first "in a
loud tone," "the conversation the longer it lasted took on Napoleon's
side more and more the character of a public manifestation," the
speaker all the while raising his voice, "as he always did when he
had the double end in view of intimidating the person he was
addressing and of making an effect on the rest of the hearers."
As Bailleu[1] has justly emphasised, this account of the interview
does not agree with that given in Metternich's contemporary
despatches. In these Napoleon is said "not to have raised his voice a
single moment" nor to have quitted the tone and expression of
"the most astonishing moderation." The discrepancy is plain, yet
not quite so damaging as might at a first glance appear. For the
despatch itself affirms that Napoleon's bearing, as he turned upon
Metternich, portended a storm; and the Ambassador's memory at
the distance of thirty years may be excused for supplying some
correspondence between the tone and the tenor of an address. Any
interview lasting as the despatch affirms an hour and a quarter, or
even over half-an-hour, as the Memoirs estimate, is apt to afford
time for different moods and material for various versions. Whether
Napoleon inaugurated it, however, with the observation "Well, and
is Austria arming on a large scale?" or with the yet more challenging
"Well! M. l'Ambassadeur, what is your Master after? Does he want
to bring me back to Vienna?" the effect is the same. He wished, it is
clear, to frighten Austria into demobilising her army and recognising
Joseph's new sovereignty in Spain and Murat's in Naples, so that
he might meet Alexander at Erfurt, where he was immediately due,
without having the Austrians on his hands as well as the Spaniards.
He failed. Metternich, with the Turkish Ambassador standing almost
at his elbow, met the charges against his Government of intriguing
in Serbia and of seeking the downfall of Turkey with calm denial,
and the complaints about Austrian mobilisation with the derisive
observation that, if the Emperor was counting the Austrian troops,
the Austrians were counting the French. A little chaff closed the
contest. The protagonists, like well-matched adversaries, did not
dislike each other.

All Paris was left talking, but Metternich kept his counsel. When

[1] See H. von Sybel, "Hist. Zeitschrift," 43, vi, "Die Memoiren Metternichs,"
pp. 245–47. Cf. Metternich's "Mémoires," I, pp. 63–4 and II, pp. 194–99.

Champagny, who had replaced Talleyrand at the Ministry of Foreign Affairs, sounded him, he replied that in diplomatic circles Europe was thought to hold a new pledge of peace. But he made it plain to his interlocutor that there must be a reciprocity of pacific endeavour, adding firmly, "If you do not want war, neither do we; if you do not fear it, we do not fear it either." And he warned Stadion that, whilst in his opinion Napoleon did not wish to engage in hostilities with Austria at the same time as with Spain, there was around the Emperor a whole circle of diplomatic agents, military adventurers and ambitious financiers, bellicose from expectation of gain and interested to see peace destroyed.

A month later and the leading actors in the great European drama—Napoleon himself, Talleyrand, Champagny, and Tolstoi, the Austrophil Russian Ambassador—accompanied, as Paris noted with a smile, by a troupe of professional actresses whose beauty was in excess of their talent, were off to play the next act at Erfurt! Metternich, had he been allowed, would have gone with them, but Napoleon would have none of him. Talleyrand, before leaving, had whispered into the Austrian Ambassador's ear that the Emperor Francis ought to break in upon his brother Emperors at Erfurt and inconvenience them by his presence. Like the other unfrocked priest who had likewise floated himself into high office on the waves of the Revolution, Talleyrand perceived that the tide was turning again and that in the future France must no longer be identified with Napoleon. He indoctrinated Metternich with this notion in Paris and Alexander just afterwards at Erfurt; and the results were important.

To all appearance, however, the sun of Austerlitz rode high as ever in the heavens. As Napoleon held high court with Alexander in those early autumn days of 1808 in the old Hanseatic town, whilst kings and sages bent before him, there was no end of his greatness. The Spanish insurrection seemed but as the rumbling of a distant volcano; the malaise of Austria no more than a cloud upon the horizon; to the east the sky remained rich with promise; and he tried once more to bewitch Alexander with the magic of the gorgeous vision. Yet in the background Talleyrand was whispering to Alexander the memorable warning which he imparted to Metternich and which Metternich placed on record:—"Sire, what are you doing here? You have to save Europe and you will not succeed in doing so except by putting yourself in opposition to Napoleon. The French People is civilised; its Sovereign is not. The Sovereign of Russia is civilised; its People is not. It is then for the Sovereign of Russia to be the ally of the People of France." Napoleon, meanwhile, was persuading Alexander to satisfy himself with the Danubian Principalities and to put off the partition of Turkey to a more convenient season.

England remained to be dealt with; and, since England could not for the moment be attacked in India, it became the more necessary to isolate her in Europe. Austria was brought thus into the midst of the discussion; for Austria was still England's friend. Napoleon wished to coerce her—to coerce her to propose to the British Government a pacification of Europe on his terms and, in the event of an English refusal, to declare war against England. For this Alexander was not prepared. The Russian Emperor was ready to support Napoleon, if attacked by Austria; he was ready to make diplomatic representations at Vienna in favour of the recognition of Joseph and Murat as kings of Spain and Naples; but he was not ready to deprive Austria of her rights as a sovereign state. He proved immovably firm. The Conference, when all was said and done, had been a failure.

Talleyrand returned to Paris and imparted this agreeable secret to Metternich. During October and November they conferred. In December Metternich, satisfied that the real France was the increasingly pacific and friendly France of Talleyrand and Fouché, that, in view of the Spanish insurrection, Napoleon's available forces for war with Austria fell short of the Austrian effectives, and that Russia would remain to all intents and purposes neutral, was back in Vienna and drafting a memorandum which pointed to an Austrian offensive. Stadion had for some while been of the same mind; and Francis had now reached a similar opinion. "If war," so ran the instructions that Metternich carried with him on his return to Paris, "does not enter into Napoleon's calculations, it ought to enter essentially into ours."[1]

Advices in February from Russia, where Schwarzenberg had been sent on a diplomatic mission, confirmed what Talleyrand had been saying. Alexander, inexperienced, well-meaning and not perhaps wholly untouched by the cheap cunning of the Levant, cherished the fond supposition that he could contain the international situation by countenancing the prospective combatants in turn. He had promised Napoleon support, if Austria attacked, and he had warned the Austrian Government that to begin hostilities

[1] Vandal, "Nap. et Alex.," II, p. 495.

was the sure road to ruin; yet he could not resist observing to Schwarzenberg that what he was really asking of Austria was to wait, to temporise, to husband her strength until occasion served, because, as he put it, "the hour of vengeance would one day strike." The sombre words betrayed the speaker's sympathies, betrayed by implication his ally, Napoleon, and betrayed also into ill-timed action his old friend Francis. It is true that he had guarded himself by expressly enjoining delay; but delay was the very thing that Austria could not afford. The maintenance of her armies was playing havoc with her revenues; the tension could not be indefinitely prolonged; and the choice between disarming at Napoleon's dictation or actively associating herself with the forces of England and Spain in the attempt to overthrow the tyrant must be quickly taken.

Certain other news told in the latter direction. Alexander's foreign minister—the aged Romanzoff—had come to Paris in the early weeks of 1809 with the object of bringing French and Russian policy into line. Dazzled though he was by Napoleon's genius, he gradually and reluctantly came to the conclusion that the Emperor was not sincerely seeking peace. Metternich's demonstration that the Austrian military measures were in their essence defensive and could not be held to threaten an Empire protected from attack on the east by the Confederation of the Rhine was not without effect upon his mind, and, as the result of a long interview with the Emperor in February, he confessed himself satisfied that Napoleon wanted war with Austria in order to raise money.

Such admissions were calculated to strengthen the statesmen at Vienna both in their belief that war was inevitable and in their wish to snatch the initiative in making it. They saw that Austria must try conclusions or fall to the rank of a subordinate Power, and they had before them Metternich's calculation of the preceding December that the Austrian forces, so inferior to the French before the Spanish insurrection, would in consequence of it be at least equal to the French numerically in the first and possibly decisive hours of hostilities. A burst of popular enthusiasm, echoing the voices of freedom to be heard in the Peninsula, encouraged a bold decision; and on the 9th April three Austrian armies, commanded respectively by the Emperor's three brothers, struck simultaneously north and south and west. An abandonment of the two subsidiary invasions of the Grand Duchy of Warsaw and Italy, and a concentration of strength upon the main attack in Bavaria, of which the Archduke Charles, the best general the Habsburgs ever produced, was in charge, might have changed the event; but, as it was, a month's fighting sufficed to bring Napoleon to the gates of Vienna. It was in vain that the Austrians fought their bravest at Aspern-Essling. The French effected the passage of the Danube and, now at last numerically preponderant through the arrival of reinforcements, brought the campaign to a close on the field of Wagram.

Metternich had his share in furthering the policy which found there its consummation, but he would not have allowed that any share of the blame, if blame there was, rested upon himself. Satisfied that the war was inevitable and indeed, as he puts it, "an absolute condition of existence" for Austria, he held that the really critical decisions were of a military character. The Austrian Government in his opinion had hoped too much from Russia and Prussia and looked too confidently to German national sentiment for effective support. He found some further weakness in a strategic change of plan at the last moment. For these mistakes, as for the moment chosen for hostilities, he could not be held responsible.

The Emperor was presumably of the same opinion. On those celebrated days in early July[1] when Wagram was fought, Metternich stood beside his master; and it was to him that in the hour of retreat Francis significantly addressed the laconic comment, "We shall have a great deal to do to repair the mischief." Though it was now three months since the war began, the Ambassador was but just returned from his three years' mission in France. His departure from Paris had not been smooth, nor his journey home free from difficulty. In the great hall of the Tuileries he had had to face Napoleon's indignant taunts after the outbreak of hostilities; and he had done so with a calm and a distinction that Alexander von Humboldt, who was present, recalled with admiration some forty years later.[2] The withdrawal of his diplomatic privileges and the restraint of his liberty had left him equally unmoved. Conveyed under surveillance to Vienna and detained there as a prisoner in the beginning of the French occupation, he had refused to gratify Napoleon's wish for an informal meeting, holding this to be inconsistent with his outraged dignity. Beyond question he had shown himself a great ambassador as well by his conduct in the hour of adversity as by the impression, soon to have its influence upon events, that he had made upon the great world of Paris; and Francis, as soon as, by an

[1] July 5th and 6th.
[2] See for the reference Srbik, I, p. 118 and note. There appears to be a difficulty here about the dates. Humboldt says that Metternich left Paris the day after the interview. But Napoleon left on the 13th April and Metternich not till the 26th May.

exchange of diplomatic representatives, he had regained the ablest of his subjects, resolved to keep him at his side. There was some affinity in their temperaments, some likeness in their cool self-possession, which we can hardly doubt brought them to a peculiar degree into sympathetic contact in the hour of disaster.

It was otherwise with the unfortunate Stadion. That not less courageous but much less serene politician had counted the situation desperate before the issue was decided; and the event completed his confusion. Two days after Wagram was fought he tendered his resignation as Foreign Minister; and Francis, holding as he did that one ought never to make a man stay in a post of public consequence which he wished to quit, accepted it. No similar conviction embarrassed the Emperor in respect of offices that a man had not previously occupied. He paid as little regard to Metternich's plea that he was inadequate to occupy Stadion's place as to Metternich's contention that the time was inopportune for a change, and in some well-chosen words insisted upon transferring the conduct of foreign policy to the ex-ambassador. "I count," he told Metternich, "upon the feeling you have of the gravity of the situation and upon your patriotism. Come to some understanding at once with Count Stadion as to the best method of effecting this change of ministry and let me know what you have agreed upon together."[1]

Stipulating only that Stadion should remain in the Administration at least until the close of the war and that he himself should be displaced the moment he failed, Metternich then took over provisionally the conduct of foreign affairs without the title of Foreign Minister. He was to retain control of them without a break for close upon four decades and to touch "the thirty-nine years of Kaunitz."[2] It was his constant belief that he had undertaken his duties without pleasure and that he discharged them without enjoyment.[3] Such sentiments about great place, if not always too noble to be believed, are unfortunately too common to be interesting.

---

[1] "Mémoires," I, p. 83.   [2] Kaunitz was Austrian Chancellor from 1753.
[3] See, for instance, his Letters to the Comtesse Lieven, pp. 88 and 172.

V

THE AMAZING MARRIAGE

THE Comte de Cessac, giving his opinion at a Grand Council held at the Tuileries in the January of 1810, is said to have taken occasion to observe that Austria was no longer a great Power and thereupon to have been interrupted by Napoleon with the caustic comment, "On voit bien, Monsieur, que vous n'étiez pas à Wagram."[1] We are, however, immediately concerned not with the opinions of the victorious but of the retreating Emperor.

As Metternich drove with his master over the Jablunka Pass on the way to Hungary, Francis opened his mind to his Minister. Together the two men reviewed a political situation well calculated to bring out their particular gifts of cool and dispassionate consideration by the choice that it compelled between the continuation of war upon uneven conditions and the conclusion of peace in unfavourable circumstances. Some reflection of their conversations and cogitations is, doubtless, to be found in the memorials which Metternich drew up on the 20th July and 10th August. The effect of the former is, in the first place, to show that the Austrian position after Wagram was worse than it had been after Austerlitz, inasmuch as, though the army remained a powerful striking force of two hundred and fifty thousand men with good morale, Austria in 1809 was neither backed by Russia nor flanked by Prussia as she had been in 1805, and, in the second place and as a result, to conclude in favour of peace as against war, provided that the price of peace were not any further or at least any indiscriminate cession of territory. The later memorial assumes that a pacific course has been adopted and discusses with calm detachment all that this must involve to prove successful. Metternich prefaces his remarks by observing that the Napoleonic system is in conflict with all principles of sound policy and that his own principles are unchanged and unchangeable. "Man, however, cannot battle against the force of things," and to fight on with diminished strength would be an act of pure folly. This uncompromising realism is followed by a passage of unblushing statecraft and penetrating insight:—"From the day that peace is made our system must be exclusively one of tacking, of obliterating ourselves, of accommodating ourselves to the victor.

[1] Vandal, "Nap. et Alex.," II, p. 245.

In this way alone shall we perhaps extend our existence *until the day of general deliverance*. Without the aid of Russia we must never again dream of shaking off the yoke which weighs upon the whole of Europe. That Court with its fluctuating spirit will awake the sooner if it is no longer the only one to congratulate itself upon its wretched political conduct. Continually in contradiction with itself and with the principles it professed the day before, it will perhaps come and offer us its aid when it sees us follow in its tracks with the zeal of a rival. We have then but one course open to us: we must *reserve our strength for better times* and *work out* our salvation *by softer means* without regard to the road we have followed hitherto."[1]

· In practice, as Metternich pointed out, this new policy of his meant the acceptance of the Continental Blockade and the recognition of Joseph Bonaparte in Spain. Just here, however, a reminiscence of legality intruded upon the new hard pattern of facts. In no circumstances, Metternich declared, would he be a party to giving assistance to the Spanish usurper against the legitimate sovereign. Nor was he willing that any specific approval should be afforded to the French seizure of the Papal States. Enough if this annexation was admitted in a general way together with other recent political developments of the same character, so as to leave the spiritual issues pertaining to the subject untouched! These, however, were but details that never in fact raised difficulties. The diplomatic significance of the memorials lay outside them—lay in the bold attempt to substitute Austria for Russia and Russia for Austria in the complex system that revolved around Napoleonic France. The Austrian Government, in other words, was to play at Vienna the same game that Alexander had played at Tilsit and to secure the privileged position as the friend of France which Russia had for two years held.

There were reasons for supposing that this policy, if the initial difficulties could be overcome, might meet with success. Alexander, owing to his constitutional likeness to a weathercock, had disgusted Napoleon as well as Francis. He had pretended to fulfil his obligations to his ally whilst intimating to the enemy that he had no intention of making them effective. Nobody could rely upon him, or at least not for long. The Prussians, the Poles, the Austrians—he had more or less, and with the best intentions, jockeyed them all; and now Napoleon's turn was coming. It was, besides, the case that the Austrian alliance had been the first love of the Emperor of the French. His overtures of 1806 had been repulsed both before and

[1] "Mémoires," II, p. 305.

after Jéna, but they showed the bent of his mind. Like many another upstart he was peculiarly susceptible to the charms of the *ancien régime*; and it required no great discernment to penetrate the strength of his sentiment for the supreme embodiment of the old order. In the very course of the ensuing negotiations for peace he was to profess himself ready to hand back to the Austrian Empire its lost provinces if Francis, whom with good reason he distrusted, were willing to abdicate in favour of one of his brothers[1]—the Grand-Duke of Würzburg or the Archduke Charles. Metternich, however, could not summarily dispose of his master; and, with Francis on the throne, a *rapprochement* between the Courts of France and Austria had to proceed more slowly.

The armistice concluded by the Archduke Charles at Znaïm had been followed by a negotiation at Altenburg between Metternich and Champagny. Both sides were in reality playing for time, for both sides wanted to know what view the versatile Alexander would take of the international situation. Would he, as Napoleon hoped, assent for a consideration to the addition of Galicia to the Grand Duchy of Warsaw—itself to all intents and purposes a vassal state of France with the King of Saxony for its sovereign—and thus enable the Emperor of the French at the same time to reward the Poles for their military assistance and secure them from the active resentment of Austria? Or would he, as Francis hoped, refuse to permit Austria to be still further dismembered or France still further strengthened?

Alexander was in no mood to discover all his mind, but in due course he wrote to both his imperial brethren. He made it clear to Napoleon, as indeed he had done before, that he was opposed to any resuscitation of Poland. He made it clear to Francis that his benevolence towards Austria fell short of beneficence. The rest he left to them to settle between themselves.

The effect of this attitude was to make the fate of Galicia the pivot of the negotiation. Unable to secure the integrity of Austria as the price of an alliance with France, Metternich pertinaciously tendered as much of the Polish province as might be necessary to satisfy the territorial demands of the French, knowing well enough that there was no part of his dominions that Francis cared about less nor any that was better calculated to drive a wedge between France and Russia. But Napoleon was too clever for him. Complaining that the diplomatists were making no progress at Altenburg he persuaded Francis to send Prince John of Liechtenstein to his

[1] Vandal, "Nap. et Alex.," II, p. 143.

headquarters at Vienna to learn his terms. The Prince was a fine
soldier but a poor diplomatist. He was first terrorised into negotiating,
which he had no authority to do, by the threat of an immediate
termination of the armistice; and he was then cajoled into signing a
draft project of peace which was subsequently assumed by the French
to represent a formal treaty. Guns were fired; the populace, more
interested in the conclusion of peace than the terms of the settlement,
acclaimed the event; Napoleon hurried away from Schönbrunn
before any protest could be lodged; and Prince John was left to
announce to his master that he had given away Salzburg, the
Innviertel and Berchtesgaden to the Confederation of the Rhine,
the Adriatic Littoral with Trieste and Fiume, Istria and Carniola
to the Kingdom of Italy, Western Galicia to the Grand Duchy of
Warsaw, and Eastern Galicia to Russia—a total loss of some three
and a half million subjects, not to speak of other conditions such
as a war-indemnity of 75,000,000 francs,[1] a reduction, anyhow
inevitable, of the army, and the adhesion of Austria to the Continental System.

Confronted with the fact of peace and sensible of the unpopularity
that any attempt to resume hostilities must now entail, Francis
accepted the work of his amateur envoy. The unscrupulous way in
which that acceptance was obtained, not less than the character of
the peace itself, has to be borne in mind in considering what
followed. Austria had fought a good fight—had done what she
might in support of the Spanish insurrection and in hope of the
liberation of Europe—but victory, in spite of certain common-
places both rash and familiar, had not waited upon right, and she
had fallen lower at the close of her effort than ever Turk and Prussian
had brought her in her long fight for civilisation. In that hour of
consummate trickery following upon catastrophic disaster the
Minister to whom her fortunes were being transferred turned
finally to craft. His proceedings are open to as much or as little
objection as those of the police; and his defence is identical with
theirs. He conceived himself to be dealing with a law-breaker, as
indeed he was, and he regarded the ordinary obligations of veracity
and good faith as overridden by those of national preservation.
Napoleon complained that he was a liar beyond the common.
"Tout le monde ment quelquefois, mais mentir toujours c'est trop,"
was said with especial reference to Metternich. Yet the very negotiations at Altenburg had sufficiently demonstrated that the criticism

[1] Vandal, "Nap. et Alex.," II, p. 161.

came none too happily from that particular quarter. In flagrant violation of a previous understanding, Champagny, upon Napoleon's instructions, had suddenly embodied the pourparlers in a protocol, and that protocol one which falsified the discussions almost beyond belief. Not two in twenty of the phrases which he claimed had, according to Metternich, ever been used, and even the modest remnant had lost their original significance.[1] Confronted with such duplicity, Metternich did not scruple to employ the methods which best served his ends; and no cynic will be surprised to learn that, in these circumstances, more than one woman was sacrificed.

It was about six weeks after Liechtenstein's diplomatic reverse at Vienna that Metternich, now at last formally established in Stadion's place as Foreign Minister, re-entered the capital in the wake of his master,[2] who had been most warmly acclaimed. The first important act of his administration was to revert to the proverbial policy of the House of Habsburg and substitute nuptials for hostilities. "Others," says the memorable adage, "wage war; you, happy Austria, marry." Within two days of his return—on November 29th—Metternich had whispered into the astonished ear of Laborde, the French representative at the Austrian Court, an offer of the hand of Marie Louise.

Such at any rate is the account that the French archives give of the beginning of the affair. Metternich, however, has himself a more sensational tale to tell. He had attached no importance to a hint of Laborde's that Napoleon's mind was moving from a Russian to an Austrian marriage until one day he received a letter from his wife in Paris. It appeared that at a masked ball given by the French Imperial Arch-Chancellor, the trusted Cambacérès[3], "the Countess Metternich, a little puzzled to account for the importance evidently attached to her presence at this particular function, had found her arm taken by one of the company, who led her to a distant apartment. She had seen through his disguise as soon as the man came up. It was Napoleon. He asked her whether she thought that the Archduchess Marie Louise would accept him, and if Francis would consent to the marriage. Greatly surprised, she told him she was unable to give an answer. Would you accept me, he pressed, in the

---

[1] "Mémoires," I, pp. 87, 88, and see Srbik, I, p. 120.
[2] His letter to his wife of November 28 (printed in "Mémoires," I, p. 233) shows that he arrived on the 27th November and some hours after his master. Vandal ("Napoléon et Alexandre," II, 203) appears, therefore, to be in error in saying that he arrived two days before the Emperor.
[3] "L'homme dans les talents administratifs duquel Napoléon avait le plus de confiance" (Metternich, "Mémoires," I, p. 71).

H

Archduchess's place? She replied that on the contrary she would certainly refuse him. "You are ill-natured (*méchante*)," Napoleon retorted; "write to your husband and ask him what he thinks about it." She declined to do this, but advised the Emperor to address himself to the new Austrian Ambassador. Her advice was followed and Eugène Beauharnais, with the intention of showing his mother's acquiescence, was sent next day to talk the matter over with Schwarzenberg. The Ambassador conveyed what was still no more than a "feeler" to Metternich; and Metternich passed it on to his master. The suggestion was startling but not, in the appalling circumstances of Austria, unattractive. No one, however—neither Francis nor Metternich nor Marie Louise, when it was put to her—welcomed the burden of decision. The Minister professed himself unable to advise one who was not less a father than a sovereign; the father declared with warmth that he would never coerce his daughter; the daughter observed that, where the interest of the Empire was concerned, her father's will and not her own must prevail. Eventually, after the manner of Bentham, the Emperor found a formula that satisfied him in the overruling obligation he was under to consult the happiness of his people. An affirmative reply was returned to Paris.

The conclusion to be drawn from these rather conflicting accounts of the origin of the marriage negotiations is that neither party was particularly anxious to claim the credit for them. Napoleon could not make them look pretty beside his offer for the hand of the Grand-Duchess Anne, nor Francis give them grace with the ink of the Peace of Schönbrunn not yet dry upon the document. The business was, as we say, "in the air." There were hints given in Vienna and feelers put out in Paris; but each side could with some plausibility say that the initiative had been taken by the other. "You should receive every overture," Metternich wrote to Schwarzenberg as late as Christmas Day 1809, "in a completely unofficial manner. Your Highness should not even charge yourself with it without emphasising your personal willingness to sound your Government on the subject." It was only when the Russian Court persistently delayed its answer and as the suspicion grew that that answer might prove unfavourable, only when 1809 had given place to 1810 and as the divorce of Josephine became a *fait accompli*, that matters really began to move. But, once set moving, they advanced with Napoleonic swiftness to their conclusion.

In the end of January a Privy Council, consisting of the royal

family, the great officers of State, the presidents of the Legislature
and the members of the Administration was officially summoned to
consider in Napoleon's presence the respective advantages of the
Russian and Austrian connections. The Emperor, prepared for
either event, showed, indeed, no clear predilection; Russia had the
advantage of his public regard, if Austria had that of his private
preference. A few days later, however—on the 5th of February—
despatches which made it sufficiently clear that Alexander, embarrassed by his mother's dislike of Napoleon as a son-in-law, was
countenancing delay to cover evasion, arrived from Petersburg.
The Emperor of the French was not a man to be mocked. He
resolved to give Austria the chance which Russia was playing with,
but to give it in such a form as to preclude procrastination. The
despatches from Russia were seen and considered before midday
on the morning after their arrival; the Austrian Ambassador, who
had gone in pursuit of game to the country, was hurriedly informed
that his presence in the capital was instantly required; and at 6 p.m.
Prince Eugène, who, as Countess Metternich reported,[1] was actively
promoting the Austrian connection, appeared at the Austrian
Embassy and asked for the hand of the Archduchess on behalf of
the Emperor but with the warning added that the slightest delay
in accepting the proposal would be taken as a refusal. The contract
must, in fact, be settled and signed within a few hours. Confronted
with a situation that hardly gave time for reflection, much less for
reference to Vienna, Schwarzenberg, the sweat pouring down his
face, took his courage in both hands—for he was exceeding the
limit of his instructions—and put his signature to the agreement.
Napoleon, when he learned the result of his high-handedness,
seemed beside himself for joy. He had, in fact, by this move parried
and returned the blow that had been aimed at him from Petersburg.
The courier who carried to Russia the news of the Archduchess's
acceptance passed upon his way a courier from Petersburg carrying
the news of the Grand Duchess's refusal. The rejection of the
French marriage by Alexander was, indeed, tempered by the plea
that Anne would not, in her mother's opinion, be old enough for
another two years to marry; but behind all polite and diplomatic
forms lay the profound hatred entertained by the Russian aristocracy,
with the Empress Dowager at their head, for the Revolution.
"Not by principle nor by sentiment," the Empress argued, "is
Napoleon attached to Russia but by a transient need of its assistance;

[1] "Mémoires," II, p. 315.

the actual alliance is no more than a thing of circumstance designed to paralyse the North whilst the South is being subdued."[1]

The failure of the family negotiation reacted upon the wider issue that divided the French and Russian Emperors. To obtain from Napoleon a guarantee that the kingdom of Poland should never be restored had been Alexander's earnest ambition; and a treaty to this effect lay ready for signature in Paris. Napoleon caused it to be drafted anew. For an open engagement he now substituted a secret pledge, and, instead of a definite undertaking to oppose a resuscitation of Polish independence, he agreed to give no aid to any movement, external or internal, in its favour. The change of terms left him free to countenance, though not to encourage, a Polish rising.

Meanwhile the Emperor's second marriage was being pushed quickly forward. Berthier hurried off to Vienna to act as proxy at the preliminaries and received from the light-hearted Viennese such a welcome as Savary and Caulaincourt had sought in vain at the height of the Franco-Russian alliance in the palaces of Petersburg. French society responded no less readily than Austrian to the new movement in politics; and Schwarzenberg and Countess Metternich, charged at the moment with the representation of Austria in the beau-monde of Paris, completely eclipsed the opulent Kouriakin in spite of his prodigious stomach and his preposterous clothes. A subtle influence, the advent of which we need to notice in passing, had begun to pervade the salons. It was as if the red of the Revolution had suddenly been bleached to pink, or as if the fleur-de-lys had been laid for a moment across the *bonnet rouge*. Talleyrand and all that was opportunist in the world from which he sprang had worked and waited for such a time as this—a time that was bringing, with something more even than its usual irony, the great-niece of Marie Antoinette to the throne of Revolutionary France. In Vienna, if anywhere, as he not less than Napoleon had rightly discerned, was to be found the subtle narcotic which lulls to sleep antagonisms and allows old and new to blend in fresh combinations of organic life.

Protected by a marriage contract, the terms of which had by some whim been copied from that drawn up for her great-aunt and Louis Seize, Marie Louise arrived some six weeks after Napoleon's offer had been made, upon the soil of France. Metternich had preceded her. Together with Schwarzenberg he, as Napoleon required in order to raise her confidence, awaited the new Empress's coming

[1] Vandal, "Nap. et Alex.," II, p. 297.

at Compiègne, accompanied her to St. Cloud, where the civil marriage was celebrated in the gallery of the Palace, and assisted at the religious ceremony at Notre Dame. Metternich had no need that day of any distinctive uniform to establish his pre-eminence in the diplomatic corps or to provide a notable contrast to the unhappy Kouriakin, whose barbaric display of gold and precious stones failed to conceal an interior mortification at the rebuff to Russian prestige. Congratulated and complimented, he was as usual completely at his ease and in one bold and sudden inspiration even more than usually happy. Invited by the minister or master of the household to breakfast with the rest of his colleagues at the Louvre, he took occasion to pass to the open window and, in full view of the vast expectant crowd below, to raise his glass and toast "the King of Rome." The intended title of the anticipated heir was already known; the jealous pride of the Habsburgs in their supposed titular descent from Cæsar not yet forgotten. The gesture might, therefore, well have seemed to those who saw it to be pregnant with meaning. It was as if the Holy Roman Empire had sunk to rest with a last grand salutation to the morrow's sun, unseen, indeed, but soon to rise in all its splendour above the Seven Hills.

Ecclesiastical Rome, with its wedding-garment of some twenty-five centuries' weaving, lent to the marriage of the pseudo-Charlemagne much in the way both of form and colour; yet one patch of customary splendour was noticeably small. There was no full complement of Roman purple. Certain Princes of the Church—to the ominous number of thirteen, as superstitiously-disposed persons doubtless noted—were conspicuously absent, uneasy at the lack of Papal consent for a step which in their view only the Pope could authorise. Metternich, indeed, when he wrote his Memoirs many years after, brushed away the marriage of Napoleon and Josephine as no more than a civil affair, dissoluble from its inception and of no interest to the Church. Of the story that there had been a religious ceremony he professed himself incredulous, alleging the authority of Consalvi for the view that it had been invented to secure the Pope's presence at the Coronation.[1] But Consalvi had himself led the revolt of the Thirteen Cardinals; and the story was true enough, and had given trouble enough at the time to all concerned, to be fully credited.

The facts were these. Afraid of being divorced, Josephine had informed the Pope on the eve of her coronation that she was only

[1] Cp. Welschinger, "Le Divorce de Napoléon," p. 177.

civilly married to Napoleon. The Pope had in consequence refused to attend the ceremony unless the defect was removed by a religious ceremony and had given Cardinal Fesch dispensations which, though couched in general terms, were plainly intended to empower him to effect a secret marriage. Accordingly at four in the afternoon on December 1st, 1804, the Cardinal had married Josephine to Napoleon in the Empress's rooms at the Tuileries. But for the dispensations this procedure must have been reckoned invalid, since the Council of Trent had required the presence at every marriage of the parish priest and two witnesses, and these conditions were not fulfilled.[1] In face of the dispensations, however, any irregularity appeared to have been fully covered; and, though the Court of Rome is commonly assumed by Protestants to relax its discipline in favour of any highly-placed petitioner, the most powerful Prince that the world has ever seen, with the Head of the Church actually at the time in his keeping, entertained no hope of bending the conscience of Pius VII to his personal ends. The matter was brought, instead, before bodies permeated by Gallican influence. An Ecclesiastical Council which had been set up for the despatch of such business as, had relations with the Papacy been unembarrassed, would in the ordinary course of things have been referred to Rome, advised that the diocesan and metropolitan authorities in Paris were competent to hear the cause and that, if any defect of consent in the parties were established, the contract of marriage was void. The case, argued by one canon lawyer after another, resulted in conclusions increasingly satisfactory from the Emperor's standpoint. The Metropolitan Court decided, not only that the absence of the parish priest and the two witnesses invalidated the ceremony, not only that Napoleon's consent, vital to the sacrament, had been wanting, but that no moral obligation rested upon the parties to have their illicit connection made regular.

The Archbishop of Vienna was by no means satisfied by findings of which no direct cognisance was afforded him and of which the import was rather conveyed than substantiated by Fesch, acting at that time, though without proper authority, as Archbishop of Paris.[2] Nor was Francis himself altogether at his ease respecting a business about which both his religious convictions and formal mentality prompted him to make sure. At the solicitation of Metternich, however, the Archbishop consented to accept the

[1] Pariset in the "Cambridge Modern History" follows a tradition in the Bonaparte family and affirms the presence of Berthier and Talleyrand. His statement is, however, in conflict with that of Fesch and Berthier, nor is it countenanced by Talleyrand.
[2] Welschinger, "Le Divorce de Napoléon," p. 176.

assurances of the French Ambassador that he had seen the judgment and that all was in order.

The point that Consalvi took remained untouched, however, by anything within the competence of French and Austrian statesmen, ecclesiastics or ecclesiastical courts to determine. Questions, the Cardinal-Secretary maintained, concerning the marriages of princes fall under the direct jurisdiction of the Holy See;[1] and in truth, as Henry VIII's matrimonial adventures all too clearly demonstrate, any other rule in the case of an absolute sovereign may be destructive of even the semblance of morality and decency. Metternich, however, at this time of his life, cared but little for these things. As he hoped to extract tangible relief for Austria from Napoleon's second marriage, so he hoped to turn all scruple and doubtfulness concerning it to diplomatic account for the material advantage of the Papacy.[2] In this he had no success. The action of the Thirteen Cardinals introduced the final phase of Napoleon's long struggle with Rome. Welschinger, indeed, has raised the whole story of the Emperor's divorce almost to the level of Hebrew story and dated—for the dates sufficiently agree—the decline and fall of the Napoleonic Empire from this final challenge to the Church. The frail old Pontiff, a worthy successor of St. Peter and of St. Peter in chains, on the one hand; the apparently invincible Cæsar on the other: the imperial sneer at the Papal thunder, "His lightnings won't make the arms drop from my soldiers' hands"; and in sequence the Retreat from Moscow—Theocratic History may well make something of that! Yet, even for those who perceive no imponderabilia but just dull force behind human destiny, there is surely audible in the background some laughter of whatever gods there be, so few were the years that went by before the leading figures of the imperial drama lay crushed beneath the wanton insolence of the imperial theme. The King of Rome, stripped of his sovereignty and reviewing soldiers in an Austrian uniform; Marie Louise living all too long for her credit as a wife; Josephine living just long enough to see her husband dethroned; Napoleon dying with the name of Josephine on his lips—what more could irony, let alone penitence, demand?

[1] Welschinger, p. 228. F. J. Sheed, "Nullity of Marriage," p. 47.
[2] "Mémoires," II, p. 321.

VI

THE DIPLOMATIC TIGHT-ROPE

THE amazing marriage which Metternich had effected between the oldest royal house in Europe and the youngest, or, if we like to put it so, between the Old Order and the Revolution, set all Europe speculating as to what would follow. The great event at Tilsit had not been more sensational, nor had even that dramatic *volte-face* rendered the diplomatic future more obscure. The Poles in Paris began again to raise their heads, the Germans to wonder whether their redemption might not be nearer than they had believed. "What you can be sure of," wrote Laborde to Metternich, "is that in less than five months we shall be on chilly terms with Russia and in less than eighteen at war."[1] He was as nearly right as amateur prophets can reasonably expect to be in a world where the unexpected so often happens.

Metternich had before long his reasons for assisting to produce the results predicted by sowing dissension between the Powers concerned. He had come to Paris with the express intention of fathoming Napoleon's mind. He wanted as much or more than anyone else to know precisely what the marriage signified—upon what calculation it had been based. Could it mean that the Emperor was contemplating a complete change of policy, that he had resolved to found a dynasty on the principles of internal order and external peace? It seemed unlikely, for he was a warrior born. Did he then intend to pursue his conquests, but with Austria as his auxiliary? This appeared more plausible, but was far from proved.[2] Only by a prolonged visit to the French metropolis could Metternich hope to settle his doubts. Yet even after a six-months stay he had but imperfectly resolved them. He was dealing with a magician who could conjure up fair visions of peace as easily as the spectral horrors of war and even turn the grim saga of his life into a golden legend.

"One would be making a great mistake," Metternich advised his master, "if one tried to infer the future of the Emperor's reign merely from its first years. In his marriage with an Archduchess there is for Austria a pledge that no other event could have taken the place of. All the same one would make as large an error if one

[1] Helfert, "Maria Louisa, Kaiserin der Franzosen," p. 357.
[2] "Mémoires," I, pp. 99, 100.

attributed to this advantageous union an influence capable of extending to the whole of Napoleon's plans or modifying entirely his views." And then there follows a sentence that explains Metternich as well as his great adversary in the years that we are about to traverse:—"The aspiration to universal dominion is in the very nature of Napoleon; it can be modified and checked, but one will never succeed in stifling it."[1] Therefore, Metternich concludes in substance, Austria, while recognising that the marriage of Marie Louise had saved it from crumbling into ruin, must go armed and ready to fight.

Ready to fight, but not only against France! A lesser danger threatened her more instantly. Russia, in accordance with the agreement at Erfurt, had possessed herself of Moldavia and Wallachia. Russian territory had thus reached the mouth of the Danube; and upon the mouth of the Danube Austria had already her eyes intent. Napoleon, as Metternich divined,[2] was not altogether ill-pleased to see his old enemies at issue, though he dropped a few crocodile's tears over the Russian advance, threw the blame of it upon Austria on account of her absence from Erfurt, and professed that it must prove the basis of a Franco-Austrian alliance.[3] Austria, he explained, might even go to war about it if she wished. Bound by his pledges to Alexander, he himself was compelled to remain neutral; but he would suffer no Russian acquisitions to be made on the right bank of the Danube and was prepared to countenance the intervention of Austria in the affairs of Serbia—a Turkish province groaning under Turkish oppression and destined, so he said,[4] at the dissolution of the Turkish Empire to fall into Austrian hands.

The Eastern Question, which served so well Napoleon's ultimate purpose, as Metternich thought it to be,[5] of maintaining differences between Austria and Russia, was not, fortunately for the Austrian Minister, by any means so burning as the issues which in 1810 were driving France and Russia always farther apart. In Poland and in Sweden there existed political crises clamorous for settlement and profoundly interesting to the ambitious Empires lying to west and east of them. The great wrong, consummated not twenty years before by the last Polish Partition, had placed the patriotic fervour of a courageous people at the disposal of the highest bidder; and both Napoleon and Alexander had some reason to fear the action

---

[1] "Mémoires," II, p. 378 (Metternich to the Emperor Francis, July 28, 1810).
[2] *Ibid.*, p. 367.   [3] *Ibid.*, p. 363.   [4] *Ibid.*, p. 370.   [5] *Ibid.*, p. 408.

of the other at the auction. Napoleon owed the Poles the price of the valour they had shown in his armies and, though he was content to give them no active aid in their struggle for freedom, was resolute in his refusal to bind himself in principle to their servitude; whilst Alexander, preferring as he did to see them in subjection, had not even in middle age wholly forgotten the dreams of a more generous youth. The recollection of early conversations with Adam Czartoryski in the gardens of the Taurida Palace, when the cause of Polish liberation had gone to his head like new wine, returned to the unstable mind of the puissant monarch, and he sent again for his boyhood's friend. His purpose indeed was no longer pure. He dreamed only of a Poland which, though invested with the forms of independence, should recognise him as its master and lord and attract into his already prodigious Empire all that had once been Polish and was as yet not his. Yet, if only as an alternative to the complete destruction of all Polish hopes, the idea of such a move was as much in his view as the peril of its consequences in that of Napoleon.

Metternich, watching the great game from Paris, but not fully informed of Alexander's thoughts, supposed that Napoleon would, if it came to war with Russia, offer their independence to the Poles and win by virtue of so doing.[1] Such an offer no doubt embodied the common-sense of the situation, since it meant, not only a new army at Napoleon's disposal, but one composed of patriots; and Metternich faced the probability of its being made with customary cool calculation. Galicia, he saw, if Poland was resuscitated, would have to go. The real question for the Austrian Government was whether it should seek compensation for the surrender of its Polish spoils or not. Compensation in population or revenue there was none to be had, but politically and commercially the recovery of Illyria, which Napoleon was willing to give back, would restore to Austria what Metternich calls her "natural line of activity"—in other words, contact with Italy and a place on the Adriatic. The matter was worth consideration.

Not only in Poland but in Sweden also, circumstances were straining the resources of French diplomacy. Through the little strip of Pomerania which represented all that was left to Sweden of the conquests of Gustavus Adolphus, contraband, in spite of Napoleon's Decrees, was pouring into the Continent under the eye of the Swedish Government, whilst the port of Gothenburg performed

[1] "Mémoires," II, p. 411.

the same service for the Scandinavian Peninsula. To stop this hole in the wall erected against British products became as necessary to the success of the Continental System as those products themselves were necessary to the sustentation of the Swedish people, and pressure was put upon the Swedish Government in this sense by Napoleon. Preoccupied as the Swedes were with the problem of the succession to the throne, the economic became in an odd way blended with the dynastic issue. It was thought that France might modify her demand for the exclusion of British goods if she were satisfied in the selection of the King's successor. Whilst the names of shadowy claimants of royal lineage were still under consideration, the professors of the University of Upsala, with a complement of officers to back them up, took the bold course of recommending a Marshal of France with the blood of an innkeeper in his veins. Bernadotte, the only one of Napoleon's captains with whom they had had much or anything to do, was perhaps also the one whom the Emperor least appreciated. The contest of wits between a Corsican and a Gascon is as the duel between Greek and Jew. Profoundly jealous of Napoleon and profoundly ambitious for himself, the Prince of Ponte Corvo—for to that dignity Bernadotte had been raised—was as ready to desert his master as to change his religion. For both these courses he found in fact good reasons within a short time of his election as Crown Prince. He embraced the Lutheran faith for the edification of the Swedes, but intimated, doubtless for communication to the Emperor of Russia, that he had no intention of gratifying his Swedish sponsors by attempting the re-conquest of Finland. This declaration, though as regards France it did little or nothing to mollify Alexander's resentment at the success of the French candidate for the Swedish throne, was followed before the year was out by a secret understanding between him and Bernadotte. The Swedish Government was to be free to consider its own interests without Russian interference—which signified the admission of British goods into Sweden—whilst the Russians might carry their arms east, west or south without fearing that the Swedes would stab them in the back. The signs of the times were to be read in this compact. It was not for nothing that a French Marshal had turned his back upon France.

The whole business involved a grave diplomatic blunder, of which the effects were presently to appear, on the part of the French Government. But it was less the material than the psychological consequences of it that fixed the eyes of Napoleon and Metternich when they talked it over in Paris in the September of 1810. While Marie Louise[1] had, it appeared, been scandalised at Bernadotte's change of religion, the two statesmen were more shocked by the damage done to royal prestige by the elevation of a private person to a throne. "You ought," Metternich told Napoleon, "to have attached importance to remaining the only one." And Napoleon, already shaped by his second marriage to the fashion of the *ancien régime*, admitted his fault, expressed his regret for having made his brothers and still more his brother-in-law into kings, and observed that one becomes wise only with prolonged experience. As regards the Swedish question in particular, his inaction had been prompted by a wish to remain perfectly neutral, his acquiescence by his satisfaction at getting rid of Bernadotte and at the thought of English discomfiture when a French Marshal ascended the throne of Gustavus Adolphus. He laughs loudest, says the familiar proverb, who laughs last. Bernadotte's conversion into a king had not only, as we have seen, widened the breach with Russia, but placed at the head of Swedish affairs a man astute enough to perceive the true interests of his country and resolute enough to pursue them.

Meanwhile at Vienna, where in Metternich's absence his father had been entrusted with the conduct of foreign affairs, more resolution than astuteness was apparent. Old Metternich's heart was always with the Old Order and he was much taken with some Russian advances, opportunely made during his tenure of the Foreign Office, for the resumption of close relations between the Courts of Vienna and Petersburg. A secret engagement on the part of each Power not to make common cause with any enemy of the other was all that was directly proposed; and, in return, the Prince hoped to bring about the evacuation of the Danubian Principalities by Russia and so to recover that eastward drive of Austrian policy for which his son had been substituting a push southwards to the Adriatic. Russia, however, had her eye on Austrian Poland; and the price of surrendering Moldavia and Wallachia, would, it was plain, have to be paid in Galicia.

The *vieux bonhomme* might, as likely as not, have given all that was asked in consideration of flatteries deftly blended with the more serious side of the negotiation, but that his son returned just in time to prevent a disaster which must have shattered the diplomatic work of the last six months in Paris. In a moment the Austrian

---

[1] Or possibly, as the context would suggest, Josephine (Metternich's "Mémoires," II, p. 391).

orientation was completely changed. With perfect courtesy and characteristic grace, the younger Metternich bowed out the Russian offer and his father's diplomacy. The time for such things, he well knew, was not yet. In the war that was threatening the plain policy of Austria was to maintain peace as long as she could, neutrality as long as she might and, if each in turn became impossible, to afford the French as little countenance as possible so long as they were winning and to take sides against them only if they turned to retreat. Russia, he saw clearly, must be kept in the forefront of the battle, not allowed as in 1805 to exploit her neighbour or as in 1807 to play her ally false.

Doubtless there was no nobility in all this; Austria had had enough of nobility the year before. There was only the instinct of self-preservation, the profound conviction that the saving of the State is the ultimate law of policy. The supreme need of the Empire was time to recover itself. Yet, as Metternich saw things, honour was by no means lost. "To consent," he wrote to Francis, "to any reunion of the military forces of Austria with those of a Power whose only end is the destruction of things as they have been till now and which aims at solitary domination, would be to make war upon sacred, immovable principles and so upon the most direct interests of Austria. The express feature of the Austrian situation is the moral height from which the most disastrous events have not dragged her down. Your Majesty is the central point, the true unique representative of an order of things consecrated by time and resting upon eternal unchangeable right. All eyes are fixed upon your Majesty; and there is in this rôle a grandeur that nothing can replace. The day that Austrian troops march side by side with French or confederate battalions and join with them in a war of destruction, that day your Majesty will lay down this noble character."[1] Even so, Metternich however, admitted that circumstances might be too many for him. To what we call *force majeure* he makes it clear that he would yield.

Thus, then, the Austrian Foreign Minister argued in the autumn of 1810 and carried his master with him. Without a neighbour he dared trust, without an army he dared put into the field, in face of a society whose influence upon the administration was so great as to have caused the Government of Austria at this time to be compared to a salon of aristocrats, elegant, corrupt, frivolous and disdainful,[2] he had no better auxiliary in the delicate diplomatic game, which for

---

[1] "Mémoires," II, p. 410.   [2] Vandal, "Nap. et Alex.," III, p. 17.

the next two years he had to play, than the commonplace, common-sense Emperor. He calculated on his return from Paris—and calculated correctly—that a Franco-Russian war must come in the beginning of 1812,[1] but might till then be averted. The essentials of his policy were, as we have seen, to delay hostilites as long as he could, to commit himself as little as he might, and to insure Austria as much as was possible. It was a policy befitting one whom Count Waldstein accused of "the presumption to think himself a good tight-rope dancer."[2]

The last day of the year 1810 had been marked by the issue of the momentous ukase in which Alexander, under the influence of a financial crisis in Russia, turned his back upon the Continental System which was supposed to have produced it and discriminated —in effect, if not in principle—against French and in favour of English imports. More than the annexation of the Hanseatic towns by Napoleon, which preceded it, and the dispossession of Alexander's relative—the Duke of Oldenburg—by Napoleon, which followed it, this move on the part of the Russian Government made war between France and Russia inevitable. Napoleon could not afford to leave the Russian Empire outside his economic system; Alexander could not afford to have it within. All that remained, then, for the estranged Powers to do before hostilities began was to close all the secondary avenues of danger, to bring pressure or persuasion to bear upon every potential ally or vacillating neutral, and to exploit each subtle advantage of place and occasion in the matter of attack. The diplomatic history of the year 1811 is in the main the history of such manœuvres.

Alexander believed more than his rival in the virtue of hastening the conflict. Across the vast European front of Russia from Riga to the Danube, and along the great line of approach from Paris his diplomacy was active, smoothing away complications for himself and stirring up trouble for Napoleon. Negotiations with Bernadotte to reconcile the Swedes for a cash consideration to the surrender of their claim upon Finland; negotiations in Constantinople, where Pozzo di Borgo went and worked in secret to reconcile the Porte to the amputation of its trans-Danubian provinces; negotiations in Paris, where Nesselrode and Tchernitchef were in fact if not in name accredited to Talleyrand, to quicken the torpid pulses of the France that was not Napoleon; negotiations with Czartoryski to test

---

[1] "Mémoires," II, p. 426.
[2] Buckland, "Metternich and the British Government from 1809–13," p. 61.

the patriotic fervour of the Poles; negotiations with Walmoden—an *émigré* officer long since forgotten—to form a German corps on Russian soil—all these were in progress; and yet all were as nothing in importance beside those which were passing at Potsdam and Schönbrunn.

On which side would Prussia be found, and on which side Austria, when the Napoleonic eagles, gathering from all the ends of Europe, began to circle above the plains of Poland and to pounce upon the sleepy, cumbrous body of the Russian Bear? That was, indeed, the question. Least of all men, perhaps, was Frederick William, turning now east now west in his agony and at the last for guidance to Vienna, in a position to answer it. But Metternich knew very well what Austria must do in the day of decision, not on her own account alone, but for the sake of Europe. It was in vain that the Russian colony at Vienna, with Razoumovski as its leader and Princess Bagration as its queen, plied him with their wiles. He dined with them, acted with them, and had them at his house to dance; but no private amenities caused him to lose his political balance. He was equally proof against more serious attractions. It was in vain that Russia offered the whole of Moldavia, the half of Wallachia and a free hand in Serbia in return for an alliance against France and the surrender of Galicia. It was equally in vain that Scharnhorst slipped into Vienna towards the end of the year with the suggestion of an Austro-Prussian treaty against France. Metternich knew better than to adopt a scheme which would have caused the French armies to concentrate upon Austria in all their strength, the sun of Austerlitz to be outshone, and the slaughter of Wagram to be exceeded. Yet for all that he kept Scharnhorst dallying. He saw that the twisting King at Potsdam was in all the throes of hesitation, for indeed Scharnhorst's mission argued as much; and he knew that Frederick William was as likely to offer himself to France as to Russia. It was advisable for Austria to move quickly and sell her modest wares in the Parisian market before Prussia got there with goods of a less neutral tint. Accordingly, Schwarzenberg was instructed to discuss the terms of Austrian intervention. It appeared that, in return for an Austrian army corps of forty to fifty thousand men forming the right wing of his army, Napoleon was ready to let Austria have both Serbia and the Danubian Principalities; to let her exchange, if she wished, Galicia against the Illyrian Provinces; and to let her recover Silesia at the Peace, if Prussia had done his bidding, for a territorial consideration, and, if not, then for nothing at all.

The negotiation of this scheme for the recovery of Silesia, just at the time when he was advising Scharnhorst that Prussia's place in the impending struggle was at the side of Russia, has not, of course, escaped the keen eyes of Metternich's critics. Yet his conduct was perhaps less cynical than at first sight appears; and Srbik has adduced more than one consideration in his defence. The kernel of his case is to be found in the fact that he regarded war as inevitable and Prussia as anyhow lost. In other words, he believed that for Prussia, now so greatly reduced in power and prestige, to ally herself with France meant a servitude as gross as had befallen the States of the Rhineland, and to ally herself with Russia a dissolution, if, as he was inclined to expect, Napoleon triumphed, as rude as that of Venice.[1] The latter policy, however, offered her the only possible hope of freedom and, which affected him probably more, was in line with the requirements of European liberation. If in these circumstances he recommended Prussia to take the bolder course, yet prepared in the expected subsequent scramble to seize again for Austria what was once her own, we may be more inclined to credit him with political astuteness than accuse him of moral obliquity. His policy must in any case be leniently viewed as the policy of a State that had been twice bit and had a right to be as many and more times shy. He never vacillated in his resolve to go no farther in supporting France than was necessary in saving Austria, and he watched and waited for the time when he might turn again and declare for the common cause of Europe.

It was not, however, in the circumstances too easy for Metternich to persuade his best ally in the struggle for freedom of his fidelity. The Peace of Schönbrunn, and still more the marriage of Marie Louise, had given the British Government some cause to doubt him, and, though in Hardenberg, who was Hanoverian Minister in Vienna and the main channel of his communications with England, he possessed an understanding friend and in the Anglo-Austrian Count Nugent a convenient emissary, Mr. Buckland's recent study[2] shows us in detail under what difficulties good relations between Austria and Great Britain were maintained in the critical years between 1809 and 1813. As reported by Johnson, perhaps the most reliable of the British agents, Metternich solemnly declared in 1811 that, whilst it was necessary, not only for France, but for the greater part of Europe to be deceived as to his principles and intentions, he would

[1] "Mémoires," II, p. 423.
[2] Buckland, "Metternich and the British Government from 1809 to 1813," p. 179.

never, so long as he was Minister, listen to any proposal of active co-operation between Austria and Napoleon. Action against England, indeed, he not only never took but expressly excluded from the terms of the subsequent Franco-Austrian alliance;[1] yet, even so, the pledge, if correctly given, was badly honoured. Necessity is said to know no law; and Metternich's necessity was doubtless beyond measure great.

It was in March 1812 that the Austrian Government signed a definitive treaty with Napoleon by which, in return for the right to compensation in Illyria in the event of losses in Galicia, for a guarantee of Turkish integrity which reversed the Erfurt policy of Turkish partition, and for certain more indefinite advantages, it placed at his disposal an army corps of thirty thousand men to act as the right wing of the Grand Army. This contingent was, however, to remain a unit under an Austrian commander taking general instructions only from Napoleon; and that commander was to be the experienced diplomatist, Prince Schwarzenberg, who for the last two years and more had been Austrian Ambassador in Paris.

The treaty was a secret, but a month later, through the indiscretion, calculated or otherwise, of the Count de Neipperg, at that time Austrian Ambassador at Stockholm and one day to succeed Napoleon as the husband of Marie Louise, the Russian Government became aware of it. The effect upon the mind of Alexander was immense; and the incident has been held by Vandal[2] with much plausibility to have determined the fate of the war. For the fear of an Austrian attack upon his flank induced the Tsar to abandon that projected stand in the region of the Vistula, where he might probably have suffered irreparable defeat, and to let the Grand Army advance unopposed across the Niemen and so on into a country whose features afforded a grim setting for a "six-months shooting-party," as the Golden Youth of the Faubourg Saint-Germain, now beginning to appear as staff-officers in the French armies,[3] were content to call the coming campaign during the gay Paris-season of the preceding winter.

Under the menace of the Franco-Austrian treaty, then, Alexander fell back on the defensive, but Metternich was not long in letting him know that from Austria at any rate he had nothing to fear. Before setting out for Dresden, where Napoleon was holding his Court, Metternich in secret gave Alexander assurances that the Austrians

[1] Demelitsch, "Metternich und seine auswärtige Politik," p. 517.
[2] Vandal, "Nap. et Alex.," III, p. 375.   [3] *Ibid*. p. 339

I

would do as the Russians had done in 1809—would afford, that is, the least possible assistance, advance to the least possible degree, and commit the least possible injury. Similar pledges were given by Russia. Metternich had thus in effect secured Austrian soil from invasion by either combatant.

At Dresden the Napoleonic pageant was being given for the last time, yet with no foreboding of finality. Once again an assortment of sovereigns and satellites of smaller significance revolved around a new *roi soleil*, still more grandly named; whilst the presence of two Empresses raised the standard of splendour and caused even the memories of Erfurt to be eclipsed. If the Russian Emperor was wanting, the Austrian Emperor was there—the placid, imperturbable Francis, walking delicately beside his only half-domesticated son-in-law, at once the pawn and patron of a deeper game than Napoleon knew. Pale kings followed behind—poor Frederick Augustus of Saxony, devout and pacific, both faithfully and fatally attached to the man of blood and iron who was in name his guest; poor Frederick William of Prussia bending and bowing that stiff sergeant's soul of his before the throne of his conqueror, all his long hesitations resolved at last into a base submission to one who had just violated his territory anew, occupied his capital, and to all intents and purposes impressed his troops. Of the lesser princes and smaller influences who were swept into the Napoleonic constellation there is neither space nor occasion to treat.

Metternich had come up to Dresden with his master and saw much of Napoleon in those interesting weeks that preceded the Russian campaign. They talked mostly of things indifferent but a little of politics; and thirty years later the survivor had occasion to recollect and record certain features of the other's conversation. The Emperor, he remembered, had talked of France and the French, observing that their wit, as he put it, runs the streets (*court les rues*), but that it was wit only with nothing behind it of character and still less of principle. Everyone, he declared, wanted applause and notice, no matter whether it came from above or below. For these reasons, he thought, France lent itself less to representative government than a number of other countries; yet he professed himself no despot and favourable to chambers that were more than dummies.

Far more interesting, however, at the moment than these excursions into psychology were Napoleon's observations upon the coming campaign. Metternich, as we have seen, had inclined to think that the French would win with the aid of the Polish Nationalists;

but he was unfavourably impressed by the Emperor's illusions, and particularly by his belief that the Russians would advance instead of retreating. All might, however, yet have gone well with the campaign had Napoleon but adhered to the programme he foreshadowed in talking to Metternich—an advance in 1812 no farther than Smolensk, attended by the merciless economic pressure of an army upon the occupied districts, and then, if this failed to bring Alexander to account, by a fresh advance with a more extended pressure in 1813. "We shall see," he observed, "which of us will first get tired; I of feeding my army at Russia's expense or Alexander of feeding it at that of his country. . . . The affair, as I have told you, is a question of time."[1] There is no sign of failing grasp or fading genius in the tenor of these observations. So conceived and so promoted, the Russian campaign, more especially if it had been inaugurated by a declaration in favour of Polish independence, should have justified Metternich's belief that the French held the winning cards. But Napoleon forsook his plan, and Fortune her favourite.

With the closing of the merry month of May the high pomps and pageantries of Dresden came likewise to a conclusion, and the high personages there assembled went their different ways, Metternich and Napoleon amongst them. Pausing in some manner of recollection, as the pious Saxons noticed, at a shrine[2] and passing, as one has put on record,[3] through Thorn with the now misplaced menace of the Chant du Départ upon his lips, the Emperor moved on through Poland and Prussia until, within reach of the Niemen, at the very gate of Russia, his horse, startled by a fleeting hare, stumbled and ominously threw him. The gloom of the incident was dispelled next day by the splendour of June sunshine and the spectacle of a myriad bayonets gleaming above the refulgent waters. Crossing the Rubicon of his adventure with that vast host beside him, Napoleon vanished into the mists—the mysterious mists of Muscovy—whilst all Europe waited, expectant, for the unknown event.

[1] "Mémoires," I, p. 122.
[2] Vandal, "Nap. et Alex.," III, p. 428.
[3] Brandt, "Souvenirs d'un Officier Polonais" (ed. Ernouf), p. 232.

VII

THE NEMESIS OF NAPOLEON

It was "drear-nighted December" when Napoleon reappeared, a swiftly moving figure hurrying across Europe to reach Paris before Christmas. The Grand Army followed him still, but at a distance, and seemingly without much about it to justify its name. Ragged, starving, its guns, its horses, its baggage, its very discipline for the most part gone, its numbers reduced to perhaps one hundred thousand from the original six, it struggled back—all that was left of it—to tell the tale of a disaster to which History could offer no parallel in magnitude and horror. Thanks to Metternich's diplomacy, the Austrian army corps which had formed the tip of its right wing had avoided active operations and returned to Galicia, when the retreat was over, practically intact. The cadres of which the corps consisted admitted of expansion into a larger army, but for the moment it suited the Austrian Government to disclaim the possession of resources.

Metternich, was in, fact, characteristically intent upon peace. The failure of the Russian campaign, he argued, had changed the position of Napoleon; and to bring peace became the real work of Austria.[1] It was work, however, that had to be carried on under peculiar and difficult conditions. We ought never to forget, what Metternich had constantly to remember, that the Emperor of the French was the son-in-law of the Emperor of Austria, and that the Emperor of Austria was by no means devoid of conscience. Any change of Austrian associates, any shifting from a French to a Russian alliance must be effected without discredit. Metternich had not only to see that his moves were safe but that his master's moral sense was satisfied.[2] He envisaged these embarrassments with his usual coolness and resolved them with his usual resource. It did not, in fact, at all conflict with his faith in the doctrine of the balance of power as the corner-stone of international wisdom that the French Empire should stand possessed of the Rhine frontier, for he never forgot that to weaken the French was to strengthen the Russians.

[1] "Mémoires," I, p. 127.
[2] This seems to me the obvious answer to the complaint of the hypercritical Bibl, who investigates Metternich's whole career all too much like a meticulous schoolmaster correcting an exercise, that the Austrian Government did not declare war at the close of the Russian campaign (see Bibl, "Metternich in neuer Beleuchtung", pp. 77-8). But it is not the only answer.

Accordingly, he instructed the Austrian Ambassador in Paris to offer Austrian mediation on the basis of the so-called natural boundaries of France. Napoleon retorted with a demand for a closer alliance; but it was obvious that what he had really in mind was to deal with his various opponents singly. Metternich eluded the trap and tripped up the trapper. He was looking for a way to pass from the status of an unwilling ally to that of an armed neutral. He had now a pretext. Napoleon, he declared, by proposing new ties had severed old obligations, and Austria was no longer bound.

This was in April (1813). In May military developments enabled the Austrian Government to pass a stage further—from armed neutrality to armed mediation. Napoleon had by then proved a match for the two Eastern allies, had thrown them both back across the Elbe and beaten them at Lützen and Bautzen.[1] The news of his victory reached Metternich a week later. It was just such a victory as to cause the pressure upon the Austrian Government to declare war to increase—and not from one side only. The position was, in fact, as dangerous for Austria as it was flattering to her consequence.

Metternich recognised that the hour for which he had been waiting—the hour of decisive intervention—had arrived. Before the Powers in conflict should require him to make war, he resolved to require them to make peace. They had agreed, though only from exhaustion, to an armistice at Pläswitz; and he seized his opportunity. Hurrying the placid Francis off to the centre of operations, he negotiated simultaneously with Napoleon and Alexander. To the former he addressed a proposal of mediation; to the latter he gave an undertaking that, if mediation failed, Austria would join the Coalition. Of success in his capacity as mediator he had little or no expectation; the point, as he told Alexander, was to show that Napoleon was neither wise nor just.[2]

The terms that Metternich offered were such as a wise, if not a just man might well have agreed to—the suppression of the duchy of Warsaw and its partition among the intermediary Powers; the restitution of the Illyrian Provinces to Austria; the renunciation by France of German territory beyond the Rhine[3]—and, at Napoleon's invitation, he went to Dresden to discuss them. But no rational discussion was intended; and the interest of the famous encounter at the Marcolini Palace between the chief heir of the Revolution and the rising champion of historic Europe is derived from other considerations. Had Metternich quailed, had Austria been frightened

[1] May 21.   [2] "Mémoires," I, p. 144.   [3] Ibid., p. 250.

out of a policy of armed mediation and back into one of alliance
with France, the impending battle of the nations might never have
been fought at all or, if fought, might have been charged with
consequences of a very different character. Speculation as to what
would have followed from some imaginable change of current in
the vast stream of circumstance can, of course, never be carried to
conclusive demonstration, at any rate by beings with such limited
grasp and vision as ourselves, yet diplomatic studies desiderate it
more than most, for without it an art that instinctively hides itself
is doubly concealed. Without its assistance we might fail to see that
the diplomatic Waterloo was won in the presence-chamber of the
Marcolini Palace and Europe potentially rescued as Metternich
passed outside its doors. It is quite possible that the passage of Time
a little enriched in his Memoirs the dramatic quality of a scene,
which is none the less contemporaneously depicted in his
Despatches as "a series of demonstrations of friendship alternating
with outbursts of the most violent character." Yet even so it would
be hard measure to damn a witness, all too painfully addicted, as
Srbik shrewdly notices,[1] to elaborate documentation, with the
character of a romancer. Vitzthum, who heard Metternich himself
tell the story forty-five years later and in Dresden, comments, not
only upon the Shakespearean power shown by the narrator in rendering the scene, but upon his seeming vigour of memory for detail
and upon the relatively, at any rate, romantic version of Thiers.[2]
Let the naked truth be as it may, that midsummer day of 1813—
it was, to be precise, the 26th June—must still stand out for remembrance in the high annals of diplomacy. The fate of Europe was in
play and both men knew it. "Thirteen times" during that nine hours[3]
conference, so Napoleon told his suite the same evening, "I threw
down my glove, and thirteen times M. de Metternich picked it
up."[4] It was a duel between two conceptions of society, the one
based upon force, the other upon the justice that law gives rise to.
At no moment of his life was Metternich greater.

The Austrian Minister, as he passed in to the interview, had been
stopped by one of a crowd of staff officers, whose grave disquiet was
ill-concealed beneath the brilliant liveries of war. It was Berthier.
"Do not forget," the Marshal pleaded, "that Europe requires peace,
and especially France, which will have nothing but peace." Metternich passed on without a word, his hands, however, so much the

[1] Srbik, II, p. 437.
[2] Vitzthum, "St. Petersburg and London," I, pp. 246, 247.
[3] 8¾ hours to be accurate.   [4] "Mémoires," I, p. 154.

stronger for the knowledge that the schism, of which Talleyrand and Fouché had apprised him as much as four years before, between France and Napoleon had spread even to the Emperor's very chief-of-the-staff. His policy, not Napoleon's, was that of the French people. He went forward into the presence-chamber.

Napoleon had everything in readiness for the intended scene. His hat in his hand, his sword at his side—the one a missile, the other a menace—he made the customary inquiries after his father-in-law's health, then frowned and began the engagement. "So you, too, want war; well, you shall have it! I have annihilated the Prussian army at Lützen; I have beaten the Russians at Bautzen; now you wish your turn to come. Be it so; we shall meet in Vienna." Then with an unerring appreciation, not yet of the consequences, but of the calamity of his second marriage, he added, "Men are incorrigible: experience is lost upon you. Three times have I replaced the Emperor Francis on his throne. I have promised always to live in peace with him; I have married his daughter. At the time I said to myself, 'You are perpetrating folly'; but it was done, and to-day I repent of it!"

Metternich tells us that, as he listened to this fierce invective, his spirit rose; that he felt himself to be the spokesman of Europe and that, if this could be said without conceit, he felt Napoleon "small." It was under the influence of these emotions that he replied. His master, he said, was governed by higher than family considerations. The world was intent upon tranquillity, but Napoleon had hitherto embodied the spirit of war. There was here an absolute opposition; and the Emperor, if he pursued the struggle, would fall in the conflict. "Today," he concluded, "you can make peace; to-morrow it may be too late. My master only allows himself to be guided by conscience; you in turn have now to consult yours."

The appeal was well calculated to tear away the last rags which veiled Napoleon's selfishness; and it did so. He spoke of peace as if it were dishonour, of negotiation as if it were degrading. Though the Austrian mediation would, in fact, have left him, in addition to the France of the Bourbon Monarchy, the Netherlands, what he could hold of Spain, what he held of Italy, even—so far was Francis prepared to go for the sake of peace—the Illyrian Provinces, he professed that it would be an outrage upon the French people and consequently incompatible with honour and conscience. But his speech contained a truer account of his reasons. He did not dare to defy those elemental forces from whose hands he had received his kingdom. "Your sovereigns, born to the throne, may be beaten twenty times, and still go back to their palaces," he confessed; "that cannot I—the child of fortune; my reign will not outlast the day when I have ceased to be strong, and therefore to be feared. I have committed one great fault in forgetting what this army has cost me—the most splendid army that ever existed. I may defy man, but not the elements; the cold ruined me." Then, swiftly exchanging the chill memory of the Russian snows for a comfortable confidence in the enduring *élan* and devotion of the French people, he added the assurance: "I have made up for the losses of the past year; only look at the army after the battles I have just won! I will hold a review for you to see."

It was obvious for Metternich, with Berthier's words still ringing in his ears, to say that it was precisely the army which desired peace. Napoleon interjected that the generals were the pacifists, not the soldiers. Metternich did not stop to argue the question; all that seemed to him to be required was to drive home the central fact that the Emperor had become impossible. "In all that Your Majesty has just said to me," he observed, "I see a fresh proof that Europe and Your Majesty cannot come to an understanding. Your peace is no more than a truce. Misfortune like success hurries you to war. The moment has arrived when you and Europe will exchange challenges; you will pick up the gauntlet, and Europe as well; and it will not be Europe that will be defeated." The Emperor fell back upon the terror of his name, not yet lost nor altogether to be lost before the Allies were in Paris. He spoke of 1809, contrasted the present strength of the rival armies, explained away the Russian disaster, strove by every lure to shift his opponent from the strong rock of an armed mediation to the quicksands of an armed neutrality. It was useless. "I have seen your soldiers," Metternich told him brutally, "they are mere children."

The climax of the conflict had been reached; and Napoleon flung his last reserves into the battle he was losing. His features torn with the semblance of passion, his lips alive with oaths and curses such as would not have shamed Malacoda and his crew of devils, the Emperor let fall the frightful sentence, which was no idle word, which does not wait to be recalled to memory by the accusing tongue of the Recording Angel but has been transmitted by outraged and indignant Humanity to the very text-books of history. "You are no soldier," he said to Metternich, "and you do not know what goes on in the mind of a soldier. I was brought up in the field, and a man such as I am does not concern himself much about the lives of a million of men." And with that he tossed his hat into the corner of the room.[1] Metternich left it to lie there; then, his habitual self-control exchanged only for the deeper calm of strong emotion, inquired why such words had been kept within the four walls of the room and asked that the doors might be thrown wide and the opinion proclaimed to all the listening world of France beyond. Upon that Napoleon, as if the exposure of himself were still incomplete, passed from the defiant bass of crime to a shriller note of self-excuse. "The French," he said, "cannot complain of me; to spare them, I have sacrificed the Germans and the Poles. I have lost in the campaign of Moscow three hundred thousand men, and there were not more than thirty thousand Frenchmen among them."

"You forget, Sire," cried Metternich, in words that disprove the charge against him of a deficient sense of nationality, "that you are speaking to a German."

Then at last Napoleon, seeing there was nothing to be gained either by cajolery or anger, returned with sure instinct to the irreparable error of his career, to the bait which Metternich had cast and he had swallowed. "I have perpetrated then," he said, "a very stupid piece of folly in marrying an Archduchess of Austria." "Since Your Majesty desires to know my opinion," replied the suave and ruthless voice, " I will candidly say that Napoleon the Conqueror made a mistake." And Metternich went on to add that the Emperor of Austria set the interests of his people before even the fate of his daughter. But Napoleon cut him short, epitomising in a few bitter phrases both the situation and the issue:—"What you say does not astonish me: everything confirms my idea that I have made an inexcusable mistake. When I married an Archduchess, I tried to weld the new with the old, Gothic prejudices with the institutions of my century: I deceived myself, and I, this day, feel the whole extent of my error. It may cost me my throne, but I will bury the world beneath its ruins."

Upon that sombre prophecy the discussion closed. The night had already fallen, and the two men could no longer clearly see each other's faces. Metternich made his way to the door; Napoleon followed him and laid his hand upon the handle. It was just possible, the Emperor thought, Metternich had been bluffing; the man was

[1] The Duchesse d'Abrantès, who takes occasion to describe Metternich as "une généreuse et noble créature, ayant une excellente bonté," gives a different version of the story. The hat in her account is Metternich's and Napoleon knocks it out of Metternich's hand (Abrantès, "Mémoires," Vol. XVI, pp. 173–75).

clever enough for that. "We shall see one another again," he said tentatively. Metternich replied that this was as the Emperor pleased, but that he for his part had no hope of accomplishing his mission. Napoleon tapped him on the shoulder. "Come, now," he said, "do you know what will happen? You will not make war on me?" "You are lost, Sire," the other retorted without a pause. "I had the presentiment of it when I came; now, in going, I have the certainty." He passed out into the anteroom. The same faces were there that he had recognised when he went in nearly nine hours before, but he moved through the staring crowd without giving a sign. Berthier followed him to his carriage, and ventured the inquiry whether the Emperor had satisfied him. "Yes! he has explained everything to me," was the reply. "He is lost."[1]

The play was over, but the epilogue had still to be spoken. Both sides thought that they stood to gain by delay; and to prolong the armistice, so that the rival armies might muster in full strength, it was necessary to go through the farce of a peace conference. Metternich was at pains to discover from Schwarzenberg exactly what space of time the Austrian military preparations desiderated. The answer was that twenty more days would enable the Commander of the Austrian army to add seventy-five thousand men to his troops, but that twenty-one days would be an embarrassment to him. It was, therefore, necessary to prolong the truce from July 20th to August 10th and to arrange meanwhile for the feeding of the destitute armies of Russia and Prussia by way of Bohemia without prejudice to Austrian neutrality. Maret, the French Foreign Minister, whom Napoleon had converted into the Duc de Bassano, had been left to toy with the tail-end of the negotiations. Metternich, however, finding Maret powerless even to meet the needs of procrastination, adopted the nowadays familiar expedient of making preparations for departure. Immediately he was invited to see the Emperor again. They met in the Marcolini Garden. Napoleon was all speed, as before he had been all delay. Without hesitation he signed the four brief articles which Metternich drew up and which committed him to accept Austrian armed mediation, a Conference at Prague between July 20th and August 10th, and a discontinuance of military operations between those dates. This was followed by a verbal guarantee on Metternich's side, of the assent of Russia and Prussia to the arrangement, and a verbal permission

---

[1] Vitzthum's narrative confines the answer to four words: "C'est un homme perdu." "The air of triumph," Vitzthum adds, "with which Metternich repeated this answer is not to be described."

on Napoleon's for the victualling of the Allied armies by Austria.

The conference, as has been said, had no substance behind it beyond a desire on both sides to strike, when all was ready, with better effect. The French Plenipotentiaries—Caulaincourt and Narbonne—came to Prague without credentials and were left to wait for them until the 12th August. But Metternich did not wait so long. On the night of August 10th the beacon-fires, which had been prepared between Prague and the frontier of Silesia, were set blazing; and the Austrian forces began to pour through the passes of the Riesengebirge. The decisive battle of the old dynasties with the new ideas had been joined.

It was the special character of this concluding phase of the conflict that monarchs and ministers moved in the wake of the contending armies, so that diplomacy may be said to have manœuvred in the closest conjunction with war. For this reason the choice of a generalissimo possessed something more than its usual consequence; and Metternich displayed his usual quick eye for position by obtaining the appointment of an Austrian, and that Austrian one who added to the abilities of a soldier the training and caution of a diplomatist. The nomination, upon which the Emperor of Austria insisted, of Prince Schwarzenberg to the supreme command was, however, far from being acceptable to the Emperor of Russia; and Alexander, who greatly wished to pose as the conqueror of Napoleon and had furnished his staff in the persons of Jomini and Moreau with military talent sufficient to supply any defect in his own, did not long delay to propose that the Prince should be supplanted by himself. Metternich warned him plainly that this arrangement would entail nothing less than the withdrawal of Austria from the Coalition. The Emperor rejoined with a petulant threat; he would, he declared, put the blame for any ill-success upon the continuation in office of the existing generalissimo. The affair might, in fact, have had the worst results if two days later Moreau had not been killed. This circumstance was enough to bring all Alexander's mysticism into play. "God," he told Metternich, "has uttered His judgment: He was of your opinion." Thus the Coalition came to enjoy, in so far as the presence of the three Sovereigns permitted, the advantage of an undivided command; and Metternich secured a hold over military operations, which Schwarzenberg strengthened by so intermingling the Russian with the Austrian forces that they could with difficulty be separated. This proved in due course of particular importance in regard to the passage of the advancing armies through Switzerland, which was effected against Alexander's wishes and promises under the compulsion both of military and political considerations.[1] As a violation of neutrality it reflects upon the Coalition and as a violation of a pledge upon Metternich. Yet the same sort of excuses can be made for it as for the occupation of Salonica by the French and English armies just over a century later, the truth being that it needs a saint as well as a statesman to keep inviolate faith in face of an unscrupulous enemy. But let that pass!

The diplomatic hand which secured for Austria the primacy in command proved not less competent to make her first amongst her equals in counsel. The secret of Metternich's ascendancy over the policy of the Coalition is to be found in his humanity, his disinterestedness and his common-sense. His views were distinguished from those of the Prussians by a politic desire, independent of any faith in success, for negotiation; and he might, perhaps, as in October after the great victory he passed across the stricken field of Leipzig, have made his own the poignant but little noticed words of the French king in Shakespeare's "Henry V", by virtue of which the everlasting case for pacifism of the nobler kind is suddenly slipped into a warrior's tale. He was too good a European to be "mangling the work of nature and defacing The patterns that by God and by French fathers Had twenty years been made"[2] without a qualm. This attitude of mind, finding as it did a certain measure of support in the humane sentiments of the Russian Emperor,[3] despite Alexander's eagerness to show himself a better man of war than Napoleon, facilitated the generous offer of a peace on the basis of a French Empire extending to the Rhine—a peace, that is, well calculated, not only to satisfy in principle the obligations of Francis towards Marie Louise, but to exploit in practice the widening breach between the honour of France and the ambition of Napoleon. There can be no doubt that the Austrian Minister understood the French people; and he was, in fact, complimented on the circumstance by an unexceptionable witness. "Only Metternich," Napoleon observed to Savary when one of the twenty thousand posters containing the Allied manifesto was brought to his notice, "only Metternich could have written this." But Metternich also under-

[1] Cp. Haüsser's article on Metternich, "Hist. Zeit.", III, p. 283.
[2] Act II, sc. iv.
[3] "The Emperor Alexander inclined to the view of the Austrian Cabinet that the way should never be closed against peaceful tendencies even in the hottest fight." ("Mémoires," I, p. 174.)

stood the Emperor of the French. Negotiation could strengthen the
case of the Coalition but could not shorten the campaign. For
Napoleon proved as good as his word at Dresden and would make
no concessions. The title of the old monarchies rested upon right
and was therefore patient of loss; his own depended upon might
and would not tolerate surrender. Though he had mastered the
Revolution outwardly, it was thus revenged upon him inwardly.
To the end his calculations were those of a revolutionary; and the
thought of justice as the interest of the stronger the last word of his
philosophy. The olive branch which had been extended from Frankfort in November was consequently allowed to wither, and when in
December Caulaincourt put out his hand to grasp it, he found it
shrunk and rotting. The Confederates had resolved to enter France;
and the Plain of Langres took the place of the Rhine as their
objective.

As military operations developed, the diplomatic relations of the
Coalition became more tense. Metternich, in order to avoid the
intrusion into the common counsel of the Confederates of particular
interests, had proposed that all the territories recovered from
Napoleon (with the exception of a few obvious restitutions, such
as Hanover, Hesse and the bulk of the States of the Church) should
be regarded as the common property of the Coalition until the
Peace Congress, when all claims could be considered and adjusted.
For this proposal no countenance was to be obtained from Russia
and Prussia, who, at the Treaty of Kalisch in the beginning of the
campaign, had exchanged guarantees for the acquisition, respectively,
of Poland and Saxony. Confronted by these mutual pledges for their
own self-aggrandisement on the part of the Eastern Powers, and
by Castlereagh's instructions to his ambassadors to get the Coalition
converted into an alliance as well for the protection of peace as for
prosecution of war and, with this end in view, to cause the aims of
the other Governments to be clearly defined whilst leaving England
uncommitted either as regards maritime right or colonial conquests,
Metternich was not a little embarrassed to hold his course. The more
France was reduced in size, the more the Coalition would have to
dispose of, and the more likely it became that Alexander would
propose to the Austrian Government the exchange of Galicia, which
he wished to add to his embryonic Kingdom of Poland, for Alsace,
which would be but a poor compensation for the increase of Russian
power in the East. The Prussian aims were quite as alarming.
Under the influence of Stein, Arndt and the rest, Prussia was doing

her best to infuse into the sleepy, contented little kingdoms of the old Germanic Empire that same strong wine of nationality which had already gone to the head of France with disastrous consequences for Europe, and which a hundred years later was to set the brains of modern Germany on fire. Metternich would have been something less than a statesman if, in those critical months of the Allied advance, he had not kept his eyes behind as well as before. There was no use in putting down one tyrant to set up another; and he did not lose sight of the political future under the excitement of the military present. "To finish, and that with glory;" he wrote to Schwarzenberg on Jan. 13th, 1814, "to obtain what is to be desired and what is of use without going to Paris to get it, or else to go to Paris if one can't get what is necessary. There is my whole policy."[1]

"Admit," Princess Bagration observed over a year later when all the difficulties of the resettlement of Europe became apparent, "that it cost far less to overthrow Napoleon than it costs now to divide his spoils." "It was for that reason," Metternich replied, "that I wished to preserve him. There is the key of my policy. I foresaw all that and I wished on that account to reduce but to keep him."[2] He had in truth rightly ceased to identify Napoleon with those forces of social chaos with which he was primarily at war. "Bonaparte," he told Alexander, "has mastered the Revolution."[3] It was a considered opinion and reappears again in his Memoirs. And Napoleon would have agreed with him. "Bonaparte often used to say," Mme. de Rémusat records, "that he alone held up the Revolution, that after him it would resume its advance."[4]

The plan of maintaining Napoleon on the throne, had Napoleon himself been content to accept the conditions attached to it, possessed therefore the first claim upon a mind at once coldly sensible of the difficulties that attended every conceivable solution and sincerely anxious to leave France sufficiently strong to act as a counterpoise to Russia;[5] and Metternich explored it in good faith though perhaps with no great expectation of success. "The sincere wish of the Austrian Cabinet," wrote Gentz, who was in a good position to speak, "was to make peace with Napoleon, to limit his power, to guarantee his neighbours against the projects of his restless ambition, but to preserve him and his family upon the throne

[1] Gentz, "Oesterreichs Theilnahme," p. 794.
[2] Weil, "Les Dessous du Congrès de Vienne," II, p. 146.
[3] "Mémoires," I, p. 184. Cf. "Mémoires," IV, p. 14.
[4] Mme. de Rémusat, "Mémoires," III, p. 225.
[5] Gentz, "Dép. Inéd.," I, p. 71.

of France. . . . M. de Metternich was convinced in his wisdom that the restoration of the Bourbons would serve much more the special interest of Russia and England than either that of Austria or the general interest of Europe."[1]

With the coming of the New Year and the passage of the old French frontier by the army of the Allies, Metternich recognised that circumstances had changed at least to an extent requiring the Emperor of the French, if he was still to reign at all, to consent, in accordance with Talleyrand's epigram, to become King of France.[2] The Allies would never restore the Empire; the Bourbon monarchy remained at the disposal of the Bonapartes until France had fully learnt that the Allies were reasonable and Napoleon impossible. Once this had been demonstrated the next choice in Metternich's view was easily Louis XVIII. A Minister less statesmanlike and more ambitious might have played with the idea of a regency under Marie Louise; and a year later, when the Bourbons had been driven out, he did, in fact, though reluctantly,[3] consider a project that would have made the influence of Austria paramount at the Court of France and have made of himself another and a greater Kaunitz. Yet even in 1815 he preferred the elevation to the throne of the Duc d'Orléans,[4] as being better policy; and his dispassionate view justified his claim to be a good European. There were, of course, other less promising possibilities before the world. There was Bernadotte; and there was the summons of a convention with a commission to choose the form of government and perhaps the sovereign prince. This last idea in particular commended itself to the wayward mind of Alexander, victim as he was of idealists and revolutionaries; and Metternich in the first weeks of 1814 resolved to crush it. He obtained his master's authority to tell the Russian Emperor that its adoption would mean the immediate withdrawal of the Austrian army and to add significantly that it appeared pointless since the legitimate king was there.

All this while Metternich had been countenancing Castlereagh's idea of a general alliance. Professor Webster would indeed have us suppose that in this matter he gulled the ingenuous Aberdeen with fair words and fickle promises.[5] Certainly, like many not wholly corrupt politicians both before and since, he seems to have promised more than he could perform. But there exist some remarks of Gentz's which have always to be remembered in relation to these kind of

[1] Gentz, "Dép. Inéd.," I, p. 70.
[2] See Metternich's letter to Schwarzenberg of Jan. 6, 1814 (Gentz, "Oesterr. Theil. " p. 787).   [3] "Mémoires," II, p. 515.   [4] Ibid.
[5] Webster, "Foreign Policy of Castlereagh," I, p. 174.

charges. Metternich, his henchman observes, would be sometimes accused of duplicity where a want of sequence and order in his habits and an excess of amiability and facility in his address were in reality to blame.[1] Doubtless he was anxious, perhaps over-anxious, to please Castlereagh and Castlereagh's representatives, but his frequent references in his correspondence with Schwarzenberg to the British Foreign Secretary's arrival in person at headquarters as an event of the greatest moment and assistance to him,[2] fit ill with any policy on his part of deliberate deception. He probably thought, if the turmoil around gave him a moment to think about the matter at all, that Castlereagh, if present, would quickly discover the immediate obstacles to a project by no means in its broad features inacceptable to himself. And in fact the treaty of alliance, when Castlereagh at length brought it into being at Chaumont, dealt only with the case of France and left the complex territorial aims of the Allies to be determined at a post-war Congress.

It was in the middle of January that the Minister from whom Metternich hoped so much and upon whom in the fullness of time history has learnt to confer so high a name, arrived at Basel. To men now alive there can scarcely be a higher recommendation of Metternich's policy than the fact that he and Castlereagh found themselves, broadly speaking, to be natural allies, both during the advance on Paris and afterwards. They discovered each other's qualities quickly; and on Metternich's side at least the recognition was generous:—"Castlereagh behaves like an angel," he wrote to Schwarzenberg.[3] And elsewhere: "I can't congratulate myself enough about Castlereagh. . . . I find that in no single case does he differ from us, and I can assure you that he is most peacefully inclined— peacefully in our sense."[4] And, as he looked back over life, he always saw in the English Foreign Secretary a noble, disinterested figure: "Absolutely straight, a stranger to all prejudice, as just as he is kind, Lord Castlereagh knew at a glance how to distinguish the truth in everything."[5] Professor Webster, on the other side, assures us that "Metternich's temperament was undoubtedly the most congenial to Castlereagh of all those with whom he had to deal."[6] Castlereagh's praise of his new colleague, was not, however, without

---

[1] Gentz, "Dép. Inéd.," I, p. 149. This passage should be borne in mind in reading such judgments upon Metternich as that of Professor Webster in "Transactions Royal Hist. Soc.," 3rd Series, Vol. VI, p. 77.
[2] See, for instance, Gentz, "Oesterr. Theil." p. 779.
[3] Gentz, "Oesterr. Theil.," p. 805.
[4] Fournier, "Congress von Châtillon," p. 252.   [5] "Mémoires," I, p. 181.
[6] Webster, "British Diplomacy, 1813–15," p. xxxviii.

CASTLEREAGH

From the portrait by Lawrence in the National Portrait Gallery.

THE EMPEROR FRANCIS I OF AUSTRIA ("KAISER FRANZ")

Reproduced from the portrait by Lawrence at Windsor Castle by gracious permission of His Majesty the King.

discrimination. "Metternich," he said, in his clumsy English, "is constitutionally temporising; he is charged with more faults than belong to him, but he has his full share, mixed up, however, with considerable means for carrying forward the machine, more than any other person I have met with at headquarters."[1]

To Metternich's considerable means for advancing the cumbrous machine of the Coalition, Castlereagh was in a position to contribute supplies of fuel for the engine and of grease for the wheels, whilst to the main principles of Metternich's design—unity of command, community of counsel, and pacific overtures—he took no exception. Schwarzenberg received fresh authority to continue military operations as he might think best; the Allies set to work at Langres to find another common measure of their views; and Caulaincourt was invited to enter upon peace negotiations at Châtillon. Metternich encouraged these negotiations the more perhaps that he felt sure they would not be successful. They were politic in so far as they served to detach the French army and people from the Emperor, but they did not in reality prejudice the cause of the Bourbons. Schwarzenberg's letter of January 26th to his wife, which is often cited, must be read in the light of this consideration. "We ought to make peace here; that is my advice," wrote the Generalissimo. "Our Emperor, also Stadion, Metternich, even Castlereagh, are fully of this opinion—but the Emperor Alexander!"[2]

Alexander was, in fact, as intent upon pressing on to Paris to blow up the Tuileries[3] as were the Prussians, with the honourable exception of Hardenberg, to blow up the Pont de Jéna. Castlereagh and Metternich, on the other hand, were less concerned to provide comparisons between the treatment of the Russian capital by the French and the French capital by the Russians, or between the atrocities of the school of Frederick and the atrocities of the school of Napoleon, as to restore the order of Europe by re-establishing its natural equilibrium. Castlereagh, indeed, informed his Cabinet quite firmly that he would be no party to the continuation of the war against Bonaparte, provided the essential aims of the British Government could be secured. Those aims were the liberation of Spain and Portugal and, what was much more important to England, the liberation of Holland and Antwerp; and they were fully satisfied

---

[1] Webster, in "Transactions Royal Hist. Soc.," 3rd Series, Vol. VI, pp. 75, 76.

[2] Fournier, "Der Congress von Châtillon," p. 58. Paul Bailleu (Sybel's "Historische Zeitschrift," Vol. 44, p. 260) omits "Castlereagh" and substitutes "even Metternich."

[3] Gentz, "Oesterr. Theil," p. 794. "L'Empereur Alexandre," writes Metternich on Jan. 13, 1814, ". . . croit devoir à Moscou de faire sauter les Tuileries. Elles ne sauteront pas."

by the offer of the Allies at Châtillon to leave Napoleon in possession of the France of 1792. But, though Castlereagh's contribution to the counsels of the Allies was a notable one, any notion that he gradually supplanted Metternich as the Minister of the Coalition would appear to be a piece of insular patriotism. His abortive attempt to improve upon Metternich's policy of postponing till the Congress the decision of the European questions upon which the Allies were divided by effecting at Langres, in the middle of the campaign, a hasty allotment of the recovered territories, suggests no commanding grasp of difficulties; for such questions could not be resolved in a moment and the discussion of them risked confounding the already existing confusion of purposes. Metternich was both wiser and cleverer. The undertaking which he extracted from the Langres Conference that the Peace Congress should be held at Vienna was as good as an assurance that his own influence would dominate the deliberations at the settlement. Meanwhile the Allied armies kept advancing.

January passed into February, and through February Napoleon, elated by the transient success of his own brilliant strategy, scorned the proposals to which the admirable Caulaincourt perceived the necessity of assenting. As March arrived, Metternich, pacific even to the end, made a final gesture by sending Prince Esterhazy to Caulaincourt to warn him that the Allies would give no better terms —no, not if they were driven once more across the Rhine. "Is there, then," his message ran, "no means to enlighten Napoleon as to his true situation, or to save him if he persists in destroying himself?"[1] It was a last friendly, futile gesture on the part of one who, as his Memoirs show, retained always a generous admiration for the greatest of his opponents. Rejected at Dresden, at Frankfort, and at Châtillon, conciliation had now spoken for the last time. At Chaumont the Allies pledged themselves to reduce France to her ancient limits, to accept no separate terms of peace, to provide each of them field armies of 150,000 men, and to make common cause offensively or defensively as the concord of Europe might require for twenty years to come. The Coalition had become a concert.

This was on March 9th, and the Congress of Châtillon was to have closed on the 10th. But Caulaincourt asked for another ten days' grace and obtained it from the good-will of the Allies. He might have spared himself the trouble. Napoleon was still seeking to

[1] Bignon, Vol. XIII, pp. 380-81. Caulaincourt to Napoleon, March 3rd.

readjust his tottering crown, but by means of war and not of diplomacy. In those early March days he made a last wild bid for fortune by marching his little army eastwards in the hope of rescuing some of the imprisoned French garrisons, rallying the peasantry of the Eastern frontiers to his standard by the cry of France, and cutting the communications of the Allies. It was then that Schwarzenberg, Fabian though he was both by temper and policy, pushed forward and struck home. On the 31st March the Allies were in possession of the French capital.

At that critical juncture, Metternich was absent from the scene of action; and it was thus from Alexander, guided by Talleyrand, that the Bourbons received back the crown of France. Yet the attitude of the Austrian Government was not in doubt. In his first conversations at Basel with Castlereagh, Metternich had pledged himself to the opinion that, if Napoleon proved impossible, the only course was to bring in the Bourbons. This was consistent with the common feeling of the two statesmen that the Revolution was always and everywhere the real enemy. A Regency would have been compelled to rest upon the support of the Liberal and Jacobin elements which had originally made the fortune of the Bonapartes, and the Revolution, in Napoleon's own phrase, would have resumed its advance. Only the Bourbons could be sure of the support of those conservative forces upon which Metternich supposed every stable society to rest. Consequently, a few days after the collapse of the negotiation at Châtillon, he consented to receive a French Royalist envoy—the Baron de Vitrolles—who was, in fact, acting quite contrary to the instructions of Talleyrand in visiting him,[1] and on March 28th he joined with Castlereagh and the Russian representatives at a public dinner at Dijon in toasting the Bourbon Princes. Something, however, seemed still to be due to the fact that the reigning Empress of the French was the Emperor of Austria's daughter; and to this, in the first place, is to be attributed the absence both of Francis and Metternich from the French capital until the lot had been definitely cast in favour of Louis XVIII. But in truth the unsettled state of the country was in itself sufficient excuse for delay, to say nothing of the fact that the end came more swiftly than had seemed probable. In fact, when he arrived on the scene ten days after the capitulation of Paris, Metternich found the treaty with Napoleon ready for him to sign. He was quick enough to detect the flaw that it contained, though too late to mend the

[1] See on this Mis. De Roux, "La Restauration," p. 55.

mischief. If the fallen Emperor was to live at Elba, the Allies, he foretold, would find themselves again in arms before two years were out.[1] Alexander, however, had already pledged his word, a practice which he followed frequently and with frequent inconvenience to himself and others; and in the circumstances Metternich consented to give way and put his name to the document. He was at no time revengeful, and of all the Allied statesmen he was, perhaps, the only one who retained some personal feeling for the conquered Titan. Austria, besides, could least of all the Powers afford an ungracious gesture in that direction. As Metternich, reviewing the vicissitudes of the long struggle, expressed it to Aberdeen, she had played the part of the oak when she had strength and power but had bent like the reed under pressure of imperious circumstance. Only, as he proudly added, resisting or yielding, she had kept in view "the good cause of Europe."[2]

[1] "Mémoires," I, p. 195.
[2] Lady F. Balfour, "Life of Aberdeen," I, p. 99.

VIII

THE CONGRESS AT PLAY

ABOUT the character of the Peace which followed the abdication of Napoleon there can be no two opinions. Its terms were the most generous, the most conciliatory that an enemy, long and terribly outraged but at last in triumphant occupation of the capital of the foe, has ever bestowed. And let no one suppose that the French had taken their fill of glory with kid gloves upon their hands or according to the precepts of chivalry. "A number of grands seigneurs and of Austrian princes," says Mme. de Rémusat speaking of the year 1805, "paid with the entire pillage of their castles the obligation they were in to lodge for a single night, or some hours only, a general officer. The soldiery was held in check, and in appearance good order seemed to be established, but this Marshal or that could not be stopped, at the moment of his departure, from carrying off what suited him from the castle he was leaving. I have seen, at the close of this war, la Maréchale . . . tell us, laughing, that her husband, knowing her taste for music, had sent her an enormous collection which he found at the house of some German prince or another, and inform us, with the same innocence, that he had forwarded to her so large a number of packing-cases full of chandeliers and of *cristaux de Vienne*, picked up all over the place, that she did not know where to put them."[1]

So it had been in the campaign lit by the sun of Austerlitz. And with this singular confession, one may compare a curious story retailed by Emma, Lady Brownlow, the companion of the Castlereaghs in Paris, from the table-talk of the hour. An old French couple at the entry of the Allies into the capital had been required to put up a young Prussian officer. They gave him every attention and supposed they had given him every satisfaction. Before he left, however, he took his opportunity to convert the furniture of his room into a mass of wreckage. His hosts inquired why, after all their kindness, he had treated them so cruelly. His reply was startling. "I asked," he said, "to be quartered in your house that I might let you see in one room what your son did to every room in my father's house in Berlin."[2]

[1] Madame de Rémusat, "Mémoires," II, p. 210.
[2] Emma, Lady Brownlow, "Slight Reminiscences of a Septuagenarian," pp. 172–74

Such forgotten incidents bring out as nothing else can the greatness of the Allied statesmen in 1814, the restraint of their conduct, the consideration with which they treated France. Talleyrand saw their virtue clearly. "To judge fairly the character of the Peace of 1814," he wrote to Louis XVIII, a year later, "one must take into account the impression it made upon the Allied peoples. The Emperor Alexander at St. Petersburg, the King of Prussia at Berlin, were not merely received coldly, but with discontent and murmurs, because the Treaty of May 30th did not fulfil the hopes of their subjects. France had raised everywhere huge contributions of war, and they had expected that the like would be levied from her; she had none at all to pay; she remained in possession of all the objects of art she had conquered; all her monuments were respected; and it is true to say that she was treated with a moderation of which no period of history furnishes examples in similar circumstances."[1]

The truth is that Alexander, perhaps from love of fine gestures, and Metternich, from a regard for good policy, were agreed upon a peace which should for once be a peace indeed. "The Peace itself," as Metternich says in his Memoirs,[2] "bore the stamp of the moderation of the monarchs and their Cabinets—a moderation which did not arise from weakness, but from the resolve to secure a lasting peace for Europe. The situation was one of those in which it is more dangerous to do too much than too little. Only a calculation resting on firm foundations can secure the success of an undertaking. The peace to be made with France could only be regarded from one of two standpoints; either it would be dictated by the desire of revenge or it would be inspired by the purpose of establishing as perfect a political equilibrium as possible between the Powers. The Emperor Francis entirely shared my conviction and sought to solve the great problem in the light only of the general interest; this being the logical effect of the terms upon which Austria had joined the Alliance."

The restoration of the Bourbons to the throne, we may notice in passing, though it failed to consolidate the domestic situation and to prove in Joseph de Maistre's phrase, not a counter-revolution, but the contrary of a revolution, greatly facilitated the restoration of France to its ancient place in the European comity. With them at least Europe had no quarrel, and towards them the Allied statesmen could justly be generous. If the old doctrine of the French monarchy,

---

[1] "Corresp. Inéd de Talleyrand et de Louis XVIII," pp. 439–40.
[2] "Mémoires," I, pp. 200–201.

that the State was in fact the King, still held good, then the returning descendant of Louis XIV might reasonably claim that the State had done no wrong, since the monarchy fell over twenty years before. Not unlike the patriarch in the wilderness of Paran, he stood between the dead legions that the France of the Revolution had slain and the living Frenchmen of a new generation, and caused punishment to be stayed. It was such a service as few men have the chance of rendering to their country.

History as it was written until lately has dealt hardly with the last Bourbon princes of the older line; and the tribute of Gambetta to the eighteenth Louis—that bold recognition of him as, after Henri Quatre, the greatest of the Kings of France—is still in the nature of a violent paradox, even though now supported by M. de Roux's recent study of his reign. For our present purpose, however, there is no need to regard "Louis," nicknamed, not without reason, "des Huîtres," with his majestic head and unsightly feet, his blue coat and red gaiters, and "Monsieur, frère du roi," with his fine manners and excellent deportment, as more than the best court-cards in that singular hand of the Allies which held, besides the fallen Emperor, the King of Rome, the Prince of Sweden, the Duke of Orleans and the son of Josephine. For our present purpose, indeed, we can afford to think of them as the antitype of the Stuart brothers in another and to us more familiar Restoration—the elder in each case shrewd and witty, superficially cynical but ultimately religious,[1] and, if no worker, yet still wise; the younger, industrious and efficient, interested in sea-power, devoted to the Church, and still faithful, after the party system had modified the Constitution, to the idea of a national government entrusted to the sovereign's friends.

The psychological effect produced by the advent of the two Princes was, however, at the moment less than that created by the sad, *gauche* woman who seemed to carry the memory of her parents' execution in her red and swollen eyes. If the daughter had inherited the beauty of the mother, if the duchesse d'Angoulême had shown the gaiety of Marie Antoinette, if the queen-apparent had exercised the fascination of the queen-deceased, the fortune of the Restoration might have been other than it was. Much of the psychology of this critical hour in French history is indeed to be read in the contemporary incident of Alexander's visit to Louis XVIII at Compiègne,

[1] Roux establishes against the usual opinion that Louis XVIII was a convinced and practising Catholic (Mis. de Roux, "La Restauration," pp. 388–89).

when, after passing through magnificent suites allocated to Monsieur and Monsieur's sons and reaching at length the modest accommodation provided for himself, the Russian Emperor, in reply to some attempt at excuse on the part of Pozzo di Borgo, took occasion to observe that the duchesse d'Angoulême looked housekeeper enough to have attended to the matter. To the Tsar of all the Russias, indeed, the unbending pride of the Bourbons was hardly less astonishing than their too lively memories; and he staggered his suite by condemning Monsieur's coldness to Caulaincourt, who was credited with responsibility for the murder of the duc d'Enghien, on the ground that he himself dined frequently with Ouvaroff—a Russian general suspected of having strangled his father with a pair of powerful thumbs.[1]

It was, then, with a full complement of spite, pique and general discontent that the Peace of Paris gave effect to the eloquent plea of Chateaubriand for the substitution for Bonaparte of the Bourbons. Under the style of "monarchy modified by charter" a French king, an English constitution, an administrative machine created by the Empire, and a society permeated by revolutionary ideas and perambulated by military aristocrats, had been thrown together; but in what relation these new associates stood to one another nobody knew perhaps even so well as the parties who six centuries earlier had composed their differences at Runnymede. Everything depended upon tact; and the tact possessed fell short of the tact required. Within ten months France had tired of the Bourbons and was ready to have the Bonapartes back.

The diplomatic centre, meanwhile, had shifted by August from Paris to London, where Metternich used his opportunity to confirm English official sympathies and Alexander no less to lose them, and then again, by the close of October, from London to Vienna. It says much for Metternich's shrewdness that, in planning his diplomatic moves, he was, as we have seen, in the habit of seizing all the available advantage of position. The choice of the Austrian capital as the place of assembly gave him the powerful assistance in negotiation of the virtual presidency, of local sentiment and of the army of police spies under Baron Hager's direction. He did not, of course, escape the machinations of his enemies, who were in fact both jealous and active, but the situation nevertheless afforded his peculiar talents the best of play. He was always in his element in society, and he knew how to make society an element in his success.

[1] The story is told in Mme. de Boigne's Memoirs.

At the Congress and in full possession of the field was the society
he liked best—that *beau-monde* which, after languishing for a quarter
of a century, had got the better at last of its enemies. Lost or forgotten species were once again visible. Like some gorgeous butterfly
that has lain concealed through a spell of foul weather, the Prince de
Ligne, a man of the Old Order both born and bred, fluttered back
into the diplomatic campaign and enjoyed a St. Luke's summer.
The shrewdness of his eye was not dimmed, nor the sharpness of
his tongue abated. As convinced of the need of the old French
culture to the social soil of Europe as was Talleyrand of the need of
France to its political landscape, he fell into temporary association
with that master-wit and emitted a masterly witticism. No other
jest at the Congress surpassed his jest about it; and none is better
remembered—"Le Congrès ne marche pas; il danse."

It danced indeed, for women were there, charming as ever,
powerful as before, Egerias or Venuses ready, if occasion should
offer, to resolve the fate of nations. Not without difficulty can the
historian draw aside the gossamer-web of their activities. It was,
some said, through the salon of his niece, Princess Dorothea of
Courland, that Talleyrand, with the fortunes of France in his
keeping, found his way into the counsels of the Congress. Prussian
interests were the especial concern of Queen Louisa's sister, Princess
Thérèse of Thurn and Taxis, whilst William von Humboldt was
alleged to have the ear of the two most influential women of all—
the Princess Bagration and the Duchesse de Sagan—in appearance
at least the respective leaders of the Russian and Austrian factions,
yet too untrustworthy in themselves to make appearances reliable.[1]
England had only Lady Castlereagh, a good soul, somewhat portly
in form and dowdy in mind, but in dress at least most dashing, with
all her husband's orders sparkling in her hair and his Garter en-
circling her forehead.[2]

The Congress laughed and loaded the ingenuous lady with gifts
of finery. It was, after all, a Congress, as Strobl von Ravelsberg
bids us observe,[3] consisting half of women, and it was fashioned not a
little to satisfy their wishes. All ordinary forms of luxurious pleasure
were to be found; and some also that were extraordinary. Money
flowed as if the River Pactolus had burst its banks. The city was full
of sights, the air of music. One figure, greater than the rest, seemed
as if he were present to remind Humanity that there are harmonies

[1] Weil, "Les Dessous du Congrès de Vienne," I, pp. 192 and 205; II, p. 64.
[2] The authority for these details is Mme. de Boigne.
[3] "Metternich und seine Zeit, 1773-1859", p. 37.

which excel the utmost unison of human counsels; and one incident, more glowing than its like, illuminates as Fyffe has observed, "the faded record of vanished pageants." Beethoven, himself the representative of a world invisible but real, is found inviting to the great assembly rooms, which had been placed at his disposal, the lords and masters of a world both visible and vain. For the rest, whilst the fine arts, of whose importance to the country Metternich in his capacity of Curator of the Viennese Academy had eloquently spoken some two years before,[1] were honoured and studied by the Duke of Saxe-Weimar and his associates, the light graces of the stage and the heavy science of gastronomy did not go neglected. The charming Mademoiselle Vigano came from Italy to dance, and the famous Mademoiselle Schultz from Germany to act, until as French influences grew, Mademoiselle Stéphanie, the *comédienne*, appeared from Paris to cut the latter out. Of the good cheer of Vienna there is no need to tell. In fact, as Varnhagen von Ense, who was acting as Hardenberg's secretary, discovered,[2] the Viennese forced their epicurean philosophy of life and manners "with a sort of gentle violence" upon their guests; and these, remembering perhaps the old instruction to do at Rome as the Romans did, behaved at Vienna after the manner of the Viennese.

In the midst of these gaieties moved Metternich, leading the revels, not without ulterior purpose. "His great art," so Talleyrand reported to Louis XVIII, "is to make us lose our time, for he believes that he gains by it." Not that he himself was ever any long time idle! As Stern remarks,[3] however great the charm that social pleasures and triumphs had for him, no reproach is with less justice addressed to this tireless author of instructions and memoranda than that of laziness. What then did it matter to him more, provided he reached his goal, to be called by his diplomatic colleagues "Le Ministre Papillon" than once to have been styled by his fellow-collegians, according to Stein's recollection, "fin, faux, et fanfaron"? His manners and methods invited, if they did not provoke, such criticism; yet he knew very well what he was about. He understood that the best drama, contrary indeed to some modern opinion, is never the worse for being well staged. He understood that, if Austria was to play the part in Europe that he designed, it would never do for Vienna to carry her poverty upon her face. Therefore he spent lavishly, and countenanced prodigality, and doubtless enjoyed him-

[1] "Mémoires," II, pp. 452–60. Address to the Academy of Fine Art.
[2] "Sketches of German Life," p. 300.
[3] Stern, "Gesch. Europas," I, pp. 224–25.

self prodigiously. His own entertaining was conspicuous. A gorgeous tournament that he organised in the Circus, with the most illustrious of his countrymen equipped as medieval knights, seemed to some spectators to surpass everything else in charm and splendour.

Such pageantry, if not particularly congruous with the cast of Metternich's own mind, was no bad symbol of a reviving faith in once familiar things. The world of thought was forsaking rationalism and returning to romance. Voltaire had grown spectral and the Encyclopædia dusty. Rousseau had been read; to say nothing of the fact that his works—to recall Carlyle's grim sarcasm—had in their latest edition been bound in aristocratic skins and blotched with noble blood. Something new was needed; and novelty—the novelty of old, forgotten things—was already there. Goethe, early conscious of commotion in the intellectual air, had long since mounted a witch's broomstick and exchanged the light of common day for a dark world of wonders; Scott, like some knight-errant with chivalry inscribed upon his banner, was rescuing ballad and chronicle from the cavernous prisons of Time; La Motte Fouqué, mail-clad and mystical, wandered past lake and forest, hunting adventures and discovering strange creatures neither of earth nor heaven; and Chateaubriand constituted himself an apostle of primitive civilisation, a professor of Christian æsthetics, and a champion of the Altar and the Throne. In the background Victor Hugo lay waiting. Thus, with men of letters haunting the old pilgrim-ways and witches floating in the upper air, with the horns of elfland faintly blowing in the woods and bards chanting ancient lays by the fireside and psalmists singing afresh the songs of Zion, a wonderful new world seemed to be preparing—a world whose mirage may perhaps be seen, or echo heard, as eye and ear are momentarily turned towards that high tournament of Metternich's devising in old Vienna.

There was an alternative provided to these courtly amusements of the *ancien régime*. Treitschke[1] has dwelt with characteristic satisfaction upon the number of military reviews by which the Congress of Vienna was enlivened, and has supposed that in them he detected the especial contribution of Prussia to the pleasures of the hour and an earnest of the coming triumph in Germany of Prussian over Austrian ideals. There is no need to contest his contention. To recognise that the Prussians were well satisfied to kill men and the Austrians better satisfied to kill time is to gain understanding of Metternich's labours. He was serving a dynasty that had grown

[1] " Deutsche Geschichte," I, p. 600.

great rather by marriage than conquest; and he sought to give it a new lease of power by diplomacy rather than by war. He worked accordingly upon lines that, not merely recommended themselves to his own temperament, but were agreeable to the tradition of his master's House and acceptable to the country of his adoption. The Austrians had little in common with the stern brood of Prussia or the melancholy hordes of Muscovy. They were light-hearted like the French, easy-going like the English. Their temperament favoured those diplomatic affinities which their interests in the coming Congress desiderated; and Metternich faithfully reflected the interior dispositions of the Viennese. He took politics seriously, but not too seriously. He was as little duped by William von Humboldt's professional attempt to re-fashion the spirit of Germany after the mind of the Great Frederick as by Alexander's shifting ideologies— autocratic liberalism in France, equivocal nationalism in Poland, evangelical counsels for Europe. He knew such fine sentiments and high aspirations to be no more than local and personal ambitions masquerading in better clothing than they possessed. His own affinities were of another kind, and drew him a little towards Talleyrand, the master of cynicism, and much towards Castlereagh, the man of sense. Though Pascal is almost the last man whose memory he calls up, he understood what Pascal meant by saying that truth is one thing on one side of the Pyrenees and another thing on the other, that custom is the essence of political justice, and that the art of troubling and upsetting States is to break up established customs by probing their sources in order to challenge their want of equity. "Il faut, dit-on," says that deep and penetrating voice, "recourir aux lois fondamentales et primitives de l'Etat qu'une coutume injuste a abolies; c'est un jeu sûr pour tout perdre; rien ne sera juste à cette balance. Cependant le peuple prête aisément l'oreille à ces discours."

Metternich knew all that, had seen it exemplified in the Revolution and after the Revolution, and had builded his own house, not on the shifting sand of philosophy, but, like many another wise man before and since, by laying the foundations in tradition, and flooring all the upper chambers with common-sense. Whilst others pleased the eye with symmetrical structures or tickled the fancy with sky-scraping elevations, a single strong idea had satisfied his architectural enterprise. "He saw," as Mazade observes,[1] "in external and internal peace a principle, a kind of dogma of which he

[1] Mazade, "Un Chancelier d'ancien régime," p. 213.

made himself the apostle and that he was resolute to defend against new enemies." This was his real system, and those things in his policy to which men gave that name—the diplomatic balance and the monarchical idea—were no more than the means by which he sought to fortify it. Not deeply interested in abstract ideas, like the philosopher, nor at all inclined to sacrifice the world for them like the romanticist, Metternich nevertheless appreciated the fact that plausible errors in a world like ours are best countered by plausible arguments. He had for some while been intimate with one whom he subsequently described as a "fantastic idealist"[1]; and it is not without interest or importance that he should have entered into so close an association with a man whose mind, as he must have quickly perceived, was rather complementary to than congenial with his own.

Disraeli, in that strange interlude in his Life of Lord George Bentinck devoted to the glorification of the Hebrew race, has instanced the choice of Friedrich von Gentz to be Secretary of the Vienna Congress as evidence of the lasting hold of the Jews upon the fortunes of mankind. It was certainly a remarkable selection; but then the whole career of this child of Israel seemed to his friends an astonishing surprise. "Gentz," says Varnhagen von Ense in a study of him which must always rank among his foremost memorials, "is a meteor in the political sky of our time. . . . A position such as his has no one had and will no one again attain. Never was German scholar whirled to greater height, nor the power of pedantry more lavishly asserted."[2] Led on by an insatiable love of pleasure, Gentz, according to Treitschke's bitter reading of his character, had foresworn "moral wrath and wealth of ideas," liberal opinions and German sentiments, to become the champion of conservatism and a prisoner in the Austrian camp. The little man—for little he was, "loving," so Metternich declared, "all that was small and fearing all that was not"[3]—may at least claim to have fulfilled all journalistic righteousness by adding both to the gaiety and gravity of nations. This amateur of chocolates and perfumes, this childish spender, this finished ladies'-man with his well-built figure, tender, shining eyes, elegant language and engaging enthusiasms, with his gift of nimble debate and whimsical inquiry, his feminine fancy for the Revolution in its early Rousseauesque phase, his illogical susceptibility to the music and mockery of Heine, and his elderly attachment

[1] Schmidt, "Weissenfels," II, p. 310.
[2] "Galerie von Bildnissen aus Rahel's Umgang."   [3] "Mémoires," III, p. 562.

to Fanny Elssler, had assimilated the wisdom as well of Kant as of Burke and was in a position to advise the world against rationalism either in morals or politics. Without rival as a publicist, he was of too volatile a mind to be of much use as a counsellor; and Metternich, whilst valuing his wits, made no mistake about his measure.[1] Afraid of everything with which he could not argue, Gentz fell, in fact, easily into extremes of hope and fear, and, absurdly enough, into a sentimental decline when he discovered that even the great Goethe was mortal. Yet Death, before which in imagination he so often trembled, found him at the close no longer fearful, so that the last terror which he experienced was perhaps the least.

Seventeen years and over of richly variegated life had, however, yet to run for Gentz at the dawn of the Congress of Vienna—years in which he figured not only as indisputably "the first of German publicists,"[2] but as the original intermediary between Metternich and the Rothschilds. The Napoleonic Wars, as all the world knows, had laid the foundation and the Battle of Waterloo had raised the financial house of the five famous brothers. The Restoration was as their garden, their park, their wide-spreading acres. All Europe needed money, and every government the facilities for transferring money. The Rothschilds were in a position to furnish both. It was four years after the Vienna Congress that Gentz got personally into touch with them at Aix. They had possessions that he liked and attributes that he disliked. They had the cash for which his palms were always itching,[3] the flagons and food which were his strength and stay, and, if he thought them "vulgar, ignorant Jews," he satisfied himself that they were at least "outwardly presentable."[4] He presented them in due course to Metternich. Both parties to this introduction had something to gain. The tolerance of the Frankfort Liberals did not extend to the Hebrew race,[5] so that the power of the German Confederation was necessary for its protection against the municipality. Metternich could give the Rothschilds this and more. He could get them a title; he could obtain for them permission to own real property within the Austrian Empire; he could even bring them into the best Austrian society. Little by little, as our period advances, he accomplished all these things. They were not forgetful of his favours; and he turned to them for financial assistance both public and private. They arranged the affairs of

---

[1] See "Mémoires," I, p. 249.   [2] Treitschke, "History of Germany," II, c. viii.
[3] Corti, "Rise of the House of Rothschild," p. 407: "Gentz was paid to supply the banking firm with political information."
[4] *Ibid.*, p. 226.   [5] *Ibid.*, p. 280.

Marie Louise; they facilitated strange monetary transactions between the two great German Powers and the German Confederation; they negotiated loans to Austria and refused a loan to Russia; they made advances, which he duly repaid, to Metternich himself; they rendered services, both small and great, to his wife. Though these financial intimacies bred political communications, there seems to be no more reason to suppose that they corrupted honest morals, so far as he was concerned, than to suppose, as was alleged after his downfall, that he had been in the pay of Russia. Both the Rothschilds and Metternich wanted and worked for peace;[1] but there the matter ended, and when, in 1841, the former attempted to introduce a clause, dealing with the eventuality of hostilities, in a loan-agreement, Metternich said firmly that as Foreign Minister he could allow the banks no influence over the issues of war and peace.[2]

We have then to reckon throughout the age of Metternich—and particularly, as he notes himself, in respect of France after the Revolution of 1830—with the hand of the House of Rothschild, but it is as hard perhaps to gauge its precise power as to gauge that of the secret societies in which both Metternich and Disraeli saw forces of subterranean consequence. We may attribute to it quite safely, as well in Austria as France, no small part in the great railroad developments of the time; we may conclude, with Stadion, that the existence of the Rothschild firms had "become most intimately bound up with that of the Austrian monarchy";[3] we may notice that, not Metternich only, but Kolowrat also[4] is to be found advocating the presence of a Rothschild in Vienna for reasons of state; yet we have still to remember that, even with the patron of Gentz, even with the master of Disraeli, there was a mark set which the Rothschilds might not pass—a line drawn always between *la haute politique* and *la haute finance*, and drawn more firmly after Gentz was dead. Only, so Solomon Rothschild declared, after Gentz's death had he fully realised himself "what inestimable services" that extravagant person had rendered to the whole House of Rothschild.[5]

This glance at the personality of the Secretary to the Congress of Vienna has led us far. We have now to look back at the Congress itself.

---

[1] Corti, "Rise of the House of Rothsch'ld," p. 211. [2] *Ibid.*, p. 228.
[3] *Ibid.*, p. 280.   [4] *Ibid.*, p. 251.   [5] *Ibid.*, p. 72.

IX

THE CONGRESS AT WORK

"I BELIEVE," Gentz wrote to Caradja, the Hospodar of Moldavia, whose delegate he was and with whom he had permission freely to correspond, "that I have sufficiently conveyed to you what one can expect from this Congress. It will be a miracle almost as great as that which produced the downfall of Napoleon if one can bring about the condition of complete and lasting peace in Europe, as a result of it."[1] This was written early in October 1814; and such opinions, as the Austrian police-reports show,[2] had become the common talk of Vienna by the beginning of November when the Congress opened. Metternich lost ground daily with the general public and was even supposed to be in the pay of Murat. By February Gentz was penning that classic criticism of the Vienna Congress, which Prince Richard Metternich rather unkindly included among his father's Memoirs. "Those," he wrote, "who, at the time of the assembling of the Congress at Vienna, had thoroughly understood its nature and objects, could hardly have been mistaken about its course, whatever might be their opinion about its results. The grand phrases of 'reconstruction of the social order,' 'regeneration of the political system of Europe,' 'a lasting peace, founded upon a just division of strength,' etc., etc., were uttered to tranquillise the people, and to give an air of dignity and grandeur to this solemn assembly; but the real purpose of the Congress was to divide among the conquerors the spoils taken from the vanquished. ... To understand ... why the hopes of so many men, enlightened but more or less ignorant of Cabinet secrets, have been so cruelly disappointed, one needs to know the dispositions in which the principal Powers were, when they appeared on this great battle-field, and the development which particular circumstances and personal relations have given to these dispositions."[3] And Gentz proceeds to discuss those qualities in the negotiators which, as he saw things, rendered the Congress a failure—the vanity and acquisitiveness of Alexander, the impotence of Hardenberg in face of the Prussian militarists, and, above all, the neutrality, "often astonishing," of Castlereagh, which resulted in a peace-at-any-price policy on the

---

[1] F. von Gentz, "Oesterr. Theil.," p. 447.
[2] Weil, "Les Dessous du Congrès de Vienne," I, pp. 445–46.
[3] "Mémoires," II, pp. 474–75.

part of England. It is interesting to notice that this fragment of criticism, which incidentally exhibits the contemporary effect of certain salient features of Castlereagh's mind, since then very differently rendered in Professor Webster's attractive and sympathetic studies, leaves the credit of *la grande morale* at the Congress precisely to those two persons, in whom the world as a rule supposed *la petite morale* to be conspicuously wanting—to Talleyrand and to Metternich. The political attainments of the former are imperfectly understood, if they are assumed to lie merely in the direction of diplomatic intrigue; his cleverness consisted in fixing upon and working a principle which promised solidarity to Europe as well as security to France. In standing out boldly for the Legitimist cause in Europe, he not only held with consistency to the policy already adopted of a Bourbon restoration, nor merely advocated a settlement calculated to obtain for France the greatest measure of European influence at the time attainable, but at the same time asserted the dignity of Europe against the policy of plunder which the Polish Partitions had initiated and both the French Revolution and the Napoleonic Empire pursued. The principle of Legitimism more truly, as he saw, than natural frontiers or arithmetical exchanges of population, fitted in with the current notions of justice; and France desired nothing better than to see the principles approved in her own case everywhere applied. The confiscation of a kingdom was, he argued, as odious as that of a cottage and in effect an assimilation of its inhabitants to the live-stock on a farm. The Restoration, on the other hand, signified the return of use and wont, the renunciation of ambition and injustice, the recognition of individual right and general repose. "Never," he wrote to Metternich, "was a more noble aim offered to the Governments of Europe."[1]

Metternich, however, had no such easy hand as Talleyrand to play. He was hampered at first by the old ties of the Grand Alliance against France, for long by Castlereagh's notion of making Prussia a bulwark against future French aggression, and constantly by the opposition of Alexander and the fear of another war, as well as in the case of Naples by a circumstance presently to be touched upon. He groped his way patiently towards an achievement that was no example of what might be accomplished with a clean slate or new broom or other instrument or implement which perhaps no statesman has ever possessed, but that secured the assent, if not the

---

[1] See Talleyrand's Memorandum of Dec. 12, 1814, printed in Metternich's "Mémoires," II, p. 510, (§ 194).

satisfaction of all the parties concerned in it, produced an equilibrium of forces, provided sanctions and gave promise of peace. The Vienna settlement has often been criticised and condemned. It is well, perhaps, before we examine it more closely, to recall the verdict upon its makers of a critic, possibly too generous but abundantly ● learned. "The results of the Congress actually attained. . . " observed the late Sir Adolphus Ward,[1] "could only have been accomplished by means of patient argument, resourceful diplomacy, and a judicious display of firmness. Thus, while much of its success was due to the toil of the Humboldts and the Wessenbergs and of their indefatigable subordinates, some of the credit should, in equity, also be given to the magnanimous impulses of Alexander, the fair-mindedness of the British plenipotentiaries, and, above all, to the tact of Metternich and his confidential adviser, Gentz."

This is the same voice that has repudiated Talleyrand's "low view" of Metternich's intellectual capacity and has declared him to have been "the right hand of the Congress," "its President in fact as well as in name."[2] President in name, however, he did not really allow himself to be called[3]—the more wisely, perhaps, that the Congress as such was never formally constituted except by its Final Act—though Gentz, for whom such distinctions had probably more value, styled himself its First Secretary. The two men were, in fact, President and Secretary respectively of the Assembly of the Eight Courts,[4] or, as it has been more familiarly called, the Committee of Eight, that is, of the Eight Powers who had been signatories of the Peace of Paris. In this capacity they exercised exceptional influence, by no means diminished in Metternich's case by the lapse of power into the hands of the less formal committee of the Five Great Powers which used to meet evening by evening in his study.

Austria, it is worth noticing, put herself in a strong position from the first by foregoing her claim upon the Netherlands. To abandon that last, rich remnant of the old Burgundian inheritance of the Habsburgs made indeed for strength rather than weakness in the case of a State aiming at compactness and turning its eyes definitely southwards; but sentiment counts in such surrenders, and Metternich showed courage in ignoring it. If he had not got rid of "the cockpit of Europe" he had at least cast aside for ever the great stone-of-

---

[1] Sir A. W. Ward, "Camb. Mod. Hist.," IX, p. 671.
[2] *Ibid.*, p. 583.
[3] C. K. Webster, "Congress of Vienna," p. 87.
[4] "Assemblée des Huits Cours," "Mémoires," I, p. 203. The Eight were: England, France, Austria, Russia and Prussia, with Spain, Sweden and Portugal.

stumbling in the relations between the Bourbons and the Habsburgs. The matter had another aspect. The transfer of the Flemish and Walloon provinces to Holland in compensation for the Cape, which Great Britain had seized and was retaining, gave Austria some claim upon English support.

The abandonment of the Netherlands was not, however, the only renunciation upon which Austria was resolved. Metternich went into the Congress with a firm determination to prevent any resurrection of the Holy Roman Empire. That ghostly entity from which life had now finally departed could, as he saw well enough, render no assistance in balancing the forces either of Europe or of Germany. The weights that had to be swung and steadied, if European civilisation was to regain its poise, were those great countries, inclusive of the restored France of the Bourbons, who were at one in their opposition to the thought of a super-state such as Napoleon had attempted to found. Agreed in this, the High Powers of Europe were agreed in little else. Russia coveted above all things Napoleon's Grand Duchy of Warsaw, and Prussia the whole kingdom of Saxony. English policy, just missing, through an exaggerated fear of Russia and a misplaced faith in Prussia, the judicial detachment and decision which its disinterestedness deserved, saw peace in any Prussian advance and peril in every Russian advantage. For the rest, Austria had her eye turned upon Northern, and France upon Southern Italy. In these dispositions, then, as the event was to show, the Great Powers approached the principal issues which faced them at Vienna—the reconstitution of Europe, the reorganisation of Germany and the redistribution of Italy.

Peace, if it is to be anything more than a name for the cessation of hostilities, must give to its makers some new cause for satisfaction or some new sense of security. It is remarkable that this had already been recognised, however modestly in the case of France. Not only did the Habsburgs refrain from asserting their claim to Alsace which had been filched from the Empire at a date sufficiently recent, perhaps, to allow of a demand for restitution; not only did the Papacy give up Avignon and the House of Nassau Orange; not only was the Louvre permitted to retain the pictures that Napoleon had seized and the French nation to escape the payment of any indemnity for Napoleon's manifold depredations; but at various points concessions of territory were given with a view to the improvement of the French frontier to the north and east. If a beaten enemy could secure such terms, what might not a victorious friend reasonably aspire to receive? Both Russia and Prussia, did, in fact, as we have just seen, look for a good deal; and there were consequently no more contentious problems at the Congress than those of Poland and Saxony.

It was at Kalisch, in February 1813, on the eve of the War of Liberation, that, as was noticed, the Russian and Prussian Governments exchanged secret guarantees for the surrender to Russia of part of the Prussian plunder in Poland and for the acquisition by Prussia of compensating territorial advantages at the expense of Germany. These latter might have been less easy to decide upon if the King of Saxony, tacking unskilfully in the blinding storm that raged between Napoleon's victory at Lützen and Napoleon's defeat at Leipzig, had not been caught between wind and water. His conduct furnished the Allies with a pretext for interference; and his country, lying as it did in convenient proximity to her scattered possessions in the west, furnished Prussia with a prey. Though Alexander was an idealist and Frederick William no cynic, it was obvious, as soon as the Congress met, that, if the representatives of the Great Catharine and the Great Frederick had their way, the fate of Saxony in the beginning of the nineteenth century would not differ appreciably from that of Poland at the close of the eighteenth. By an odd irony the restoration of the Poles to some sort of unity under the Russian Emperor had thus come to depend upon the reduction of the Saxons to some sort of servitude under the Prussian King, and even a modest reintegration of Polish territory to involve a corresponding disintegration of Saxony.

These projects of barter threatened to work out to Austrian prejudice. The changes proposed would cause not merely Russia to overhang the Austrian frontier on the north-east, but Prussia that on the north-west. And, to make matters worse, any effective resurrection of the Polish Kingdom must produce unrest amongst the unredeemed Austrian Poles of Galicia; whilst, on the other hand, the incorporation of Saxony in Prussia would upset the balance of power inside the German Confederation to the Prussian advantage. Now Austria had long repented the Polish partitions and was no longer ruled by one who, as Frederick the Great had brutally observed, both grieved and grabbed.[1] "Even those," Gentz wrote in August 1814,[2] "who have enjoyed or still enjoy the fruits of that crime characterise it as reprehensible." The old Poland had constituted a convenient buffer against Russia; and the advance of Russia,

---

[1] "Elle pleurait mais elle prenait toujours."   [2] "Oesterr. Theil," p. 389.

once Napoleon seemed to be disposed of, became the terror of the time. If Alexander wanted Poland to be free, so, perhaps, we may paraphrase in bold outline the Anglo-Austrian argument, let her be free indeed—the Poland of the past with her own sovereign and her proper boundaries. If, on the other hand, Russia must add to her dominions, let it be at least—so the Austrian Government would have added—without reviving the ancient name of the Polish Kingdom and shaking the allegiance of Poles still subject to Austria and Prussia. But Alexander cared nothing for the dilemma. He wanted both the credit of restitution and the proceeds of crime. To the Poles he intended to grant the semblance of freedom; for himself he intended to retain the realities of power. At all costs he meant to be himself the head of a reconstituted Polish Kingdom.

Castlereagh, not so much in the interest of the Poles as in the interest of peace, believed that this policy ought at all costs to be thwarted. Believing that in the close association of the Central Powers against Russia was to be found the true European guarantee against the mentality of Tilsit, he was ready to hand Saxony over to Prussia without reserve or limit in order to bring this association about. He extracted from the reluctant Metternich a provisional consent to the occupation and retention of Saxony by Prussia. The Austrian Government, however, made it clear that this dispossession of the House of Wettin by the Hohenzollerns was to be paid for by Prussian support for Austrian policy in dealing with Poland, not to speak of the abandonment of Prussian pretensions to Mainz. Castlereagh extracted these things also from a somewhat heated Hardenberg; and with a policy of Polish independence, or at the least of a Russian boundary at the Vistula with Warsaw added, the common front against Russia appeared to be complete. The British Foreign Secretary had reckoned, however, without the Prussian King.

There are two days of the Congress of Vienna to be much remembered. There is November 6th (1814), when Russia and Prussia came to a mutual agreement; and there is January 3rd (1815), when England, France and Austria made common cause against them. At a meeting of the Russian and Prussian Sovereigns on the former date, Alexander brought his blandishments to bear upon Frederick William, and, summoning the forces of aversion to supplement those of affection, alleged that Metternich had offered him concessions in Poland, provided he would assist in defeating Prussian ambitions in Saxony. There is no evidence that Metternich had done any such thing. He denied the story himself; and the fact that Alexander, in an interview not a week before, had quarelled with him violently, reduces the value of the Emperor's testimony by some points further. Frederick William was, however, persuaded of Metternich's double-dealing. In no uncertain terms he forbade Hardenberg to have further dealings with the perfidious Austrian —an instruction which had the incidental effects of putting a spoke in the wheel of Castlereagh's diplomacy and opening to France the door through which her representative had up to that time been no more than uneasily peeping.

On that same eventful 6th of November, Talleyrand reported to his master that Metternich regarded the Saxon question as of more consequence to Austria than the Polish. This was as much as to say that French and Austrian interests in Central Europe had once again met, and before the year was out the Grand Alliance had split and severed. On December 29th, Metternich proposed the inclusion of France in the Committee of the Four Great Powers; on January 3rd, 1815, the secret defensive alliance in opposition to Prussia's Saxon aspirations was concluded between England, France and Austria; and on January 11th, Talleyrand joined the Council of Four, or rather, as it became thenceforward, the Council of Five.

The diplomatic reverse which Castlereagh had suffered in respect of Poland had put Alexander in possession of the most part of the Grand Duchy of Warsaw. With the exception of Posen, indeed, which remained to Prussia, the Prussian spoil in the second and third Polish partitions was to all intents and purposes gone, though Thorn was regained later as compensation for disappointment in Saxony. So far, however, as Austria was concerned, the settlement, apart from the conversion of Cracow into a free city and the loss of the Circle of Zamosc to Russia, did not differ to any appreciable extent from that contemplated by Gentz in a memorandum written before the Congress began and endorsed by Metternich as a highly interesting presentation of the Polish Question;[1] and we may there-fore assume that no vital interest was sacrificed.

Metternich, of course, like every other Foreign Minister who knows his work, incurred the reproach of making graceful con-cessions; and his critics were consequently successful in preventing for the time his promotion to be Chancellor. In regard to Saxony at any rate this patriotic agitation had the effect of rather strengthen-ing his hands than otherwise; and Castlereagh had full scope for his

[1] Gentz, "Oesterr. Theil.," p. 398.

gifts of mediation between Austria, which, as Gentz assures us,[1] genuinely wished to maintain Saxony in its integrity and the royal family upon the throne, and Prussia, which, as he also observes, would have liked, if feasible, to incorporate the whole Saxon kingdom.

The diplomatic battle raged around Torgau and Erfurt, which the Prussians ultimately secured, and Leipzig, which the Austrians insisted that Saxony must retain; and eventually Frederick Augustus, protesting ineffectually with his people against their common spoliation, emerged from the mêlée with something less than half his former territories, but still master of Leipzig and Dresden. So far as Austria was concerned, the arrangement did well enough. Her north-western frontier was left covered by a buffer state, which, if it loved her no better than before, loved Prussia less, and might be regarded, should there ever be a struggle for supremacy in Germany, as a potential ally.

To avoid that struggle was, however, an object both with Hardenberg and Metternich; and the second great problem of the Congress —the organisation of Germany—was none the easier to solve for it. Gentz declares that the universal wish of the Germans, in 1814, was that the House of Habsburg should resume the Imperial crown and be endowed with a more extended and more genuine authority.[2] And, though this may be hyperbolical, there is some reason to suppose that at one moment even Prussia would have offered no opposition to such a solution.[3] But to the eyes of Metternich as well as of Gentz any restoration of the Holy Roman Empire would have been as little in the interest of Germany as of Europe. If it reappeared in its classic absurdity, there was little or nothing to recommend it; and if, on the other hand, it was reconstituted effectively, it must violate the principle that Metternich always and everywhere maintained—the principle of avoiding super-states and of balancing power. He had, in fact, already committed himself to another system. He had given specific undertakings both to Bavaria and Württemberg that their sovereign independence would be respected; and his pledge had been confirmed and amplified by a stipulation in the Peace of Paris that the States of Germany were to retain their freedom. There was no place left for the revival of such a suzerainty as the Holy Roman Emperor had exercised in the palmier days of his power.

[1] "Oesterr. Theil," p. 429. [2] *Ibid.*, p. 443.
[3] *Ibid.*, p. 554. And see Weil, "Les Dessous du Congrès de Vienne," I, p. 237. Cf., however, *Ibid.*, II, p. 334, "Tout le monde le désire à l'exception toutefois des Prussiens."

Austrian statesmanship, perhaps, had it seen its way to let the whole thankless task of German reorganisation slide, might have preferred to do so.[1] But the Austrian Emperor had made it little less than a condition of the Austrian entry into the war that a Germanic Confederation should emerge from the conflict; and it was, besides, an international conviction that the stability of Europe depended upon the security of Germany.[2] The intractable character of the problem is shown, however, by the fact that the sessions of the German Committee of the Congress lapsed for some five months from the end of November 1814, and, had it not been for the return of Napoleon from Elba, it is difficult to say by how much negotiation might not have been prolonged.

In May 1815—actually during the Hundred Days—Metternich revived some proposals which Austrian hands had drafted in December, and, on the eve of the signature of the Final Act of the Congress by the Great Powers of Europe, obtained the assent of thirty-six of the existing German Governments to the German Federal Act, for which he proceeded to secure a European guarantee by incorporating it in the Treaty of Vienna. The Constitution of Germany was to consist of a Diet, composed of the delegates of seventeen States which were to receive equal representative rights and to be required to avoid alliances inimical to one another or to the German Confederation as a whole. In this body was invested all ordinary authority. Organic constitutional changes and other matters of general consequence to the Federation were reserved for the consideration of a body of sixty-nine nominees, chosen on the basis of population but so as to give to each State at least one representative. The Federation, we have always to remember, included such possessions only of the Emperor of Austria and King of Prussia as had been formerly reckoned to fall within the limits of the Holy Roman Empire. Hungary, Croatia and the Italian provinces lay outside it; so did Prussia proper and Posen.

The plan lacked all the charm of strong political construction. The Federation, as was clearly explained at the first opening of the Diet, was no Bundesstaat but a Staatenbund—a federation, not a federal State. Metternich neither was nor sought to be a Bismarck; and admirers of Bismarck's type of statesmanship are justified on their theories in condemning him. He might have used the leading position of Austria to greater immediate effect; he might in due course, before Prussia grew too strong, have provoked a war for

---

[1] "Oesterr. Theil," p. 555.   [2] Sir A. W. Ward, "Germany," p. 39.

German hegemony. One, however, who had been as Gentz said,[1] not only the first Minister of Austria, but the first Minister of the Coalition, owed it to his reputation to seek a settlement on other lines. He had been ready in the last resort, as was shown by the secret Treaty of January 1815 with England and France, to oppose Prussian aggression by force of arms, but he had no wish to raise an issue which, even if ultimately unavoidable, was not in his time ripe for decision. He secured, therefore, for Austria what nobody would have denied that she might fairly claim—the Presidency of the Confederation. He tried, by proposing an exchange of Salzburg and the Quarter of the Inn for Mainz, Landau and the Palatinate, to secure in the work of German defence an equal share with Prussia, now just beginning her "watch upon the Rhine" in virtue of her new trans-Rhenish Province; but Schwarzenberg and the soldiers frustrated his attempt and the Emperor even menaced him with dismissal[2] if he persisted. And, finally, he showed the utmost regard for the susceptibilities of others, consulting Prussia separately about the form and detail of the Constitution and preserving to the smaller States the sovereign rights which had been promised to them. It was characteristic of his plan that the law of the Constitution hung loose and that much was left to be worked into custom as time went on. There have been worse principles and worse arrangements.

It remains to consider the settlement of Italy. The fate of Naples dominated all other difficulties, for there the Legitimist principle was in open conflict with treaty pledges and the Bourbons and the Bonapartes alike possessed an unanswerable case. A private episode seems further to have complicated the considerations of public policy. The reader may remember that among the ladies who had enjoyed Metternich's attentions in the days of his Paris embassy was Napoleon's sister, Caroline, subsequently as much Queen of Naples as marriage with Joachim Murat, on whom the Emperor had conferred that throne, could make her. The recollection of this intimacy and the fact that the two intimates were still in correspondence in 1814, raises a suspicion that in concluding in June of that year the secret treaty by which, in return for a pledge of neutrality on King Joachim's part, Metternich guaranteed King Joachim's kingdom, a private as well as a public motive was present. With Louis XVIII this was more than a suspicion. When Talleyrand advised him from Vienna of this secret agreement, he declared that it was the most disgusting piece of policy that had ever been heard of[3]

[1] "Oesterr. Theil," p. 387.   [2] Srbik, "Metternich," I, p. 203.   [3] "Corresp. Inéd.," p. 269.

In point of fact, however, the Austrian deal with Murat suited the Allies so well that it was perfectly defensible on its political merits, as indeed its acceptance by England makes plain; and the real charge against Metternich is, not that he concluded the secret treaty when it was convenient, but that he slipped out of it when it became embarrassing. Whether, as M. Weil seems to imply, we are to suppose that this latter event corresponded with some decline in Metternich's affectionate understanding with Queen Caroline, or whether, like Gentz, who admits that here his knowledge of the inner history of the Congress fails him,[1] we are to see in it just the successful culmination of an intrigue of Talleyrand's for the restoration of the Bourbon line in Naples, it is clear that by the middle of January 1815 the Austrian Government had exchanged the vague notion of ruling King Joachim through his wife, and Southern Italy through King Joachim, for the clear conviction that Murat must be king no more. Writing at that time to Bombelles, the Austrian Ambassador in Paris, through whose hands and those of Blacas, King Louis' domestic adviser, there passed behind the back of Talleyrand a thread of secret diplomacy, Metternich spoke of the similarity of French and Austrian interests in this affair of Murat's, of the need of circumspection, and of the avoidance of precipitancy.[2] A month later Castlereagh, passing through Paris on his way home to attend the meeting of Parliament, carried with him an offer from the Austrian Government to exchange the dethronement of Murat in Naples against the enthronement of Marie-Louise in Parma and Piacenza. But it is the despatch written after Castlereagh's departure and for Castlereagh's information that contains the conclusive evidence of Metternich's double-dealing. "We ought," he wrote on February 18th, "to take every care to cover all these transactions with a veil which shall be impenetrable until the time when it suits us to disclose our political and military resources against Naples. We shall try to find the former in the steps Joachim has recently taken against our will in the affairs of the Pope and in his agitation of the Jacobin question—circumstances which, far from bringing him into line with our policy, have alienated him from it. We need some time yet to assemble our military resources."[3]

[1] "Oesterr. Theil.," p. 620.   [2] Weil, "Le Roi Joachim," II, p. 335.

[3] Weil, "Le Roi Joachim," II, pp. 457–59. Cp. Croker ("Mems.," p. 228. Wellington to Croker, March 10, 1851) for the English view of the affair. "Designs were entertained to depose Murat and to restore the former Government. These were occasioned principally by Murat's eccentricities and his tormenting the Pope. The King of France was very anxious upon this subject."

Metternich had appealed to Time, and Time did not play him false. He told Consalvi confidently on Feb. 24th that Murat would commit more follies and give Austria the pretext for the rupture that he sought.[1] Almost as he spoke, the fool was rushing upon his fate. Intoxicated like any *grognard* by the last venture of his old commander, Murat gambled wildly in Napoleonic stocks, staked all his fortune upon the Hundred Days venture, lost the throw and paid a traitor's price upon the shores of Calabria. His actual treachery to the Allies obscured Metternich's intended deception, and, though one of Metternich's earliest biographers[2] declared that, so early as the autumn of 1814, the Austrian Minister had resolved to break his pledges, it was left for Weil to present the case for Murat with such strength as it possesses. That strength is not, however, remarkable, if we remember that Metternich had good ground for fearing Murat's defection. Not only had the man covered himself with infamy in the affair of the duc d'Enghien,[3] but, even before the Congress began,[4] the Austrian police reports were accusing him of playing a crooked game—a view borne out by Eugène Beauharnais's statement to Princess Bagration in November 1814, that he possessed letters showing "ce coquin-là," as he called him, to be deceiving Austria.[5] And as soon as Napoleon returned from Elba Wellington may be found writing to Castlereagh:—"If we do not destroy Murat, and that immediately, he will save Bonaparte."[6]

Metternich's treatment of Murat in fact resembles closely, as Srbik points out, his treatment of Murat's master. He did not hasten to dethrone him, but neither did he scruple to outwit him. Had Napoleon been reasonable, there is every reason to think that Metternich would have left him in possession of the throne of France; had Murat been honest, there is no reason to assume that Metternich would have deprived him of the throne of Naples. But in both cases the Austrian Minister rightly discerned that he had to do with men governed by an ambition incompatible with good faith. The kingdom of Italy was to the one as world-empire was to the other; but Europe had no more use at that time for a new Theodoric than a new Charlemagne. An effete Bourbon filled, in fact, the place that had to be filled better than an avid Bonapartist.

Beside all this, King Ferdinand satisfied the requirements of the

[1] Weil, "Le Roi Joachim," II, p. 446.
[2] Schmidt-Weissenfels, "Fürst Metternich," p. 214.
[3] See Mme. de Rémusat's "Mémoires," I, p. 318. "Murat se charge de tout. Il est odieux dans cette affaire."
[4] Weil, "Les Dessous de Congrès," I, p. 295. [5] *Ibid.*, p. 462.
[6] Desp. XII, March 28, 1815.

diplomatic situation in a way that King Joachim did not. His restoration was acceptable to his cousin, the King of France, and consonant, therefore, with the understanding between France and Austria which developed as the Congress proceeded. It was not less acceptable to England, for long the protector of the fugitive monarch in his sea-girt kingdom of Sicily. The reunion of the two Sicilies—of Sicily proper, that is, with Naples—was in itself a further argument on the same side. Without it there would be no state in Italy of sufficient size to balance the power of Austria. The influence of the Habsburgs extended from the Ligurian to the Adriatic Sea; and the Austrian Emperor might have boasted of his dominion with something of the terminology of David. Lombardy was his by ancestral right; Venice, lustrous as the glass it makes, had become his washpot; Modena and Tuscany might be as glad as they could of the return of his relatives to rule them; whilst over Parma and Piacenza his daughter had now cast out her Parisian shoe.

It would be an anachronism, then, to imagine that the fall of Murat was prejudicial to the cause of Italian unity. Though Maistre perceived that this dream must presently pass through the gate of horn, it was no time for it to be realised, nor was Murat the man to make it come true. Fifty years had to go by before the country was ready to turn from Greek to Roman models, and a full century before the young nation was capable of assimilating the new doctrine of its destiny. For the moment the old idea of the city-state and the picturesque plan of the local tyrant held the field. This is not, however, quite the whole case for Austria. Though in the light of subsequent events we think of the House of Savoy as Italian and the House of Habsburg as German, there was no particular reason to do so in 1814. The Duke of Savoy was as arguably a foreigner as the Emperor of Austria. Both alike had been long associated with the Peninsula, but a man no more became an Italian by calling himself King of Sardinia than by calling himself King of Lombardy and Venetia. The only indisputably Italian potentate was, in fact, the Pope; and it was towards the Papacy that the eyes of Italian patriots originally turned as the nucleus of a future federation. Metternich was not wholly unsympathetic. By his attempt to establish a Lega Italica—a vague confederation of States on the same lines as the German Staatenbund—he put himself in line with the tendency of the times, just as by his subsequent good dispositions towards the employment of Italian officials he put himself in touch with the spirit of the place. Austria, however—and there lay the inexorable fact in the case—was in possession of the fortresses of the Quadrilateral; and no other Power in Italy could match her in military strength or administrative capacity. An Austrian statesman, who in 1814 had attempted to effect the unity of Italy, might have shattered the unity of Europe but must have shattered the prestige of the Habsburgs.

The deliberations of the Congress respecting Germany and Italy had not been brought to a conclusion when in the March of 1815 the negotiators were suddenly surprised. Metternich, as the reader may recollect, had foreseen that Elba would not long be able to contain Napoleon; and it was appropriately enough to him, first among the assembled statesmen at Vienna, that the news of the escape from Elba came. The Council of Five, which met the evening before at his house, had, as it happened, worked on into the early hours of the morning; and he had enjoyed no more than two hours' rest when at 6 a.m. on the 7th an urgent despatch from the Consul-General at Genoa was brought to his room. Vexed at the interruption, he avenged himself for the unexpected annoyance by laying the document unread upon a table and folding his hands again to sleep. But sleep refused to come; and at half-past seven he surrendered to fate and opened the despatch. The contents were sufficiently exciting. Napoleon had disappeared from Elba; and inquiries at Genoa had been unable to elicit further information. Metternich dressed, and within half-an-hour was with his master. Francis received the news with his usual phlegm and told his Minister to announce to his fellow-sovereigns that he was ready to set his troops marching upon France and to intimate that he expected them to do no less. So far as the Emperor of Russia was concerned, the commission was not a little delicate. During the heat of the negotiations about Saxony, Alexander had conceived the idea that Metternich was misrepresenting his intentions to Hardenberg, who was deaf enough in all conscience to be accountable for any number of misunderstandings, and had impulsively declared his resolve to challenge the Austrian Minister to fight. The duel fell through, but not the quarrel; and for months the Emperor had declined all social intercourse with his intended adversary. Of all virtues, however, Alexander esteemed magnanimity the best. Responding immediately to the requirements of the new situation, and appealing to the claims of a common faith in Christianity, he proposed to his interlocutor that they should forgive one another's offences and forget one another's differences. Metternich, denying, with some economy of truth, that either had anything to forgive, agreed to forget; and harmony was restored. A cynic might have been excused for observing that hatred of Napoleon had at least as much to do with this result as the brotherly love of believers.

Talleyrand supposed, when he heard of the escape from Elba, that Napoleon would make for Switzerland. He was mistaken. Metternich told him at the time that the Emperor's immediate goal was France; and so it proved. To make for Paris was on the Emperor's part a direct challenge to Vienna. "The Congress is dissolved," Napoleon is said to have declared as he stepped on to French soil; and the Congress retorted by branding him an outlaw and describing him as "the enemy and disturber of the peace of the world." Neither the stigma nor the description was excessive. The Revolution had again become possessed of him and, though with the worst will in the world, he turned to the Jacobin element for support and placed Carnot at the Ministry of the Interior. Whilst the sovereigns and the soldiers hurried off from Vienna and the diplomatists set to work to cement the newly affirmed solidarity of the Powers, Metternich threw himself afresh into the business of the German Constitution— a matter, since the mutual hatred of France and Prussia was the dominant feature of the century, of as great moment to Europe as the character of the government in France. And we do Metternich wrong if, as we contemplate the gathering of armies for the crowning struggle at Waterloo, we forget that statecraft as well as generalship was still at work and that just a week before the battle, the Assembly of the Eight, reduced, but scarcely weakened by the absence of the Spanish plenipotentiary, set their initials[1] to a treaty, whose provisions assumed the effective defeat of the revolutionary spirit and the restoration of ancient order and time-honoured institutions.

The Treaty of Vienna, concluded perfunctorily in those anxious days without phrase or flourish, afforded, as was natural, but little satisfaction to such a mind as that of Gentz. Yet his lamentations in general over the failure of the Congress to inaugurate in set terms a reign of universal peace, and in particular over the refusal of England to incur the material obligations and of Russia to suffer the moral restraints of some international guarantee of security,[2] ought not to blind us to the fact that there was large and lucid thought behind the work of an assembly seemingly preoccupied with the fate and frontiers of Saxony and Poland.

---

[1] The treaty was not signed until June 19, and not by the Russians till June 26.
[2] "Oesterr. Theil," p. 548.

Nothing, despite Vitzthum's adverse criticism, is perhaps better calculated to dissipate the legend of Metternich's obscurantism and to raise the estimate of his statesmanship than his rejection of the idea, recommended to him for different reasons in various quarters— by the Roman Court, the British Government, the aristocracy of Vienna and the people of Germany—of redecorating his master with the shadow of a splendid name. A lesser man would in the circumstances have revived the Holy Roman Empire. The old student of Voltaire found, however, no place in his mind or in Europe for the famous institution which Voltaire had so famously mocked. It belonged to an age when community of religion was a realised ideal and when civilisation could therefore be securely poised upon the notions of Empire and Papacy. Doubtless to this day the political equilibrium which it set up corresponds more closely to the balance of our being between soul and body than any other that can well be imagined. Dante, who saw its practical defects, saw also its intellectual beauty; but not even Chateaubriand in the early nineteenth century was interested in a poet who perhaps of all poets saw deepest into political philosophy. Civilisation, as its barriers break down under the pressure of physical science, must search anew for organic spiritual unity, but all that Religion had to give to Politics in the actual hour of the Restoration was inevitably coloured by national sentiment and articulate in the association of the Altar and the Throne. An attempt in 1814 to poise Europe upon the thought of Charlemagne must have proved as futile as Napoleon's attempt in 1807 to reconstitute it upon the thought of Diocletian. Neither medieval nor pagan balances could at that time discover the equilibrium of a Continent swaying this way and that under gusts of revolutionary passion; nor was the divinity that had hedged the old Cæsarism or the new of the sort to suit the nation-worship of the new century. Religion and Politics had yet to enter into some new relationship with one another before they could enter again together into the life of Europe.

Alexander, indeed, thought otherwise and at Paris, where the Allied statesmen found themselves once more after the second fall of Napoleon, attempted to make good the religious defects of Vienna. Everyone has heard of the Holy Alliance; everyone knows that it was not particularly holy nor much of an alliance. Critics, Goethe making one notable exception, mocked it in its own time; historians mocked it when it had become a memory; yet the worst mockers were to be found among its first promoters. Frederick William and

Francis lent their names to it, not because they thought it holy, for apparently they regarded it as fantastical, nor because they took it to be an alliance, for they were careful to see that it committed them to nothing at all, but merely to please Alexander, who, persuaded by Madame de Krüdener that his imperial prayers were of peculiar efficacy in the ears of the Almighty, supposed that problems which had defied the Catholic organisation of the Middle Age would yield to his own evangelical counsels. Metternich's opinion of the whole affair was contemptuous to the last degree. It was "nothing more," as it seemed to him, "than a philanthropic aspiration, clad in a religious garb," "the overflow of the pietistic feeling of the Emperor Alexander," a "loud-sounding nothing."[1] And he pointed out, not however quite accurately, what ought nevertheless to be remembered by those who refer to it as a veiled instrument of autocracy, that it was not afterwards mentioned between the Cabinets concerned.[2]

The whole conception was indeed vague and high-flown enough to justify Castlereagh's characteristically English description of it as "a piece of sublime mysticism and nonsense"; and its prospects were not improved by the fact that two notable personages on the European stage remained outside its compass, the one by design, the other by desire. The exclusion of the Sultan from the benefit of the Christian precepts of "justice, charity and peace," to which the adherents of the Alliance were pledged alike in their domestic administration and their foreign relations, was not the less advisable that Alexander sometimes entertained views about the Turkish dominions incompatible certainly with peace, probably with charity and possibly with justice.[3] The Pope's refusal to participate in the counsels of the Holy Alliance was otherwise significant. The work begun at Westphalia was consummated at Vienna. The medieval Papacy, that outward and visible sign that Christendom, if united about nothing else, was at least one in its worship of Christ, found no place in Alexander's bodiless conception of the European soul; and, if Metternich had not given way to Consalvi, with whom in general he entertained good personal relations, the Temporal Power,

---

[1] "Mémoires," I, pp. 210–12.

[2] *Ibid.* It was, however, alluded to at the Conference of Aix-la-Chapelle in 1818, when France was admitted to it.

[3] It is only fair to Alexander to say that he was ready in February 1815 to include the Turkish dominions in a general guarantee, subject only to the settlement of points in dispute between Russia and Turkey by arbitration. The arbitrators were, however, to be the Powers allied with him, and the Porte refused. (See on this Webster in "Transactions Royal Hist. Soc." 3rd Series, Vol. VI, pp. 72–73.)

worn as it was already to a shadow, would have been still further reduced by the loss of the so-called Legations. Neither the Popes themselves nor perhaps anyone else suspected that, by losing temporalities beyond its capacity to govern or need to possess and by dwelling upon the deeper spiritual aspect of its powers, the Holy See was in the course of a century to gain a majesty and an influence, magnified so much the more by contrast with the downfall of the four great Continental Monarchies which had been signatories of the Holy Alliance. There were indeed more things in heaven and earth than had entered into Alexander's philosophy or that of his contemporaries.

Without niches in it, then, either for Pope or Sultan, the gaudy Muscovite temple of concord rose to such eminence as its design permitted of in the September of 1815. Before the end of the following month, however, Metternich, with Castlereagh at his side or, if we prefer to follow Professor Webster, Castlereagh with Metternich at his side, had provided a plainer, more serviceable structure for the cult of European peace. The Second Peace of Paris was negotiated in circumstances of peculiar difficulty. The French had given the Allies provocation without parallel. Neither appalled by the hideous carnage of the past twenty years, nor conciliated by the generous liberality of the settlement of 1814, they had once more fallen back into their Napoleonic idolatry. The cry for vengeance—or for what on such occasions appears to be much the same thing, justice—was loud amongst those they had wronged. Yet the Allied Powers, to their eternal merit, were not diverted from the policy of conciliation to which they had set their hands. For this, the greatest credit, perhaps, is due to the resolute will of Castlereagh and Wellington, whose immense services, as Gentz noticed,[1] enabled them to ignore the English populace, clamouring for revenge, and the First Gentleman in Europe, bursting with indignation. With them went the mind of Alexander, who, being more occupied by the affairs of the East than of the West, was less anxious to support Prussia in getting the frontier of Germany advanced than to be supported by France in getting that of Turkey reduced.[2] The Germans, on the other hand, not unnaturally felt that the hour of their revenge was come. Jena and Friedland rose again before their eyes. Elsass and Lothringen seemed once more within their grasp. Hardenberg, hard pressed by his compatriots, demanded at least the surrender of the fortresses of Saarlouis, Thionville and

---

[1] "Oesterr. Theil.," pp. 715, 716.   [2] "Camb. Mod. Hist.," IX, p. 665.

M

Luxemburg to Prussia, and of Landau to one or other of the German Powers; the demolition of the fortifications of Hüningen and, unless it became a free city, of Strasburg; an indemnity of twelve hundred million francs; and the occupation of France by an army of two hundred thousand men. He proposed, further, the surrender of Condé,-Valenciennes and some other strong places on the Belgian frontier to the newly-constituted Kingdom of the Netherlands, in compensation for the loss of Luxemburg. Metternich went some little way with these ambitions. "Austria," wrote Gentz, early in September, "concurs with Prussia in respect of the separation from France of Landau, of the razing of Hüningen, and of the necessity of finding some means of preventing Strasburg from threatening the right bank of the Rhine. As regards Saarlouis and Thionville, Austria thinks that one of these two fortresses cannot be refused to Prussia. Everything which concerns the exchange of Luxemburg for the French fortresses on the northern frontier it leaves to the English Government. It recognises the need that France should remain in military occupation during an indeterminate period. It is understood that Austria, without making any exact statement about the amount of the war indemnity to be demanded, will vote for an average between the proposals of the Prussians and the other Allies."[1]

Some measure of Metternich's influence may, perhaps, be found in the fact that these terms approximated to the final settlement. France lost the duchy of Bouillon and some part of the department of the Ardennes to the Netherlands, Saarlouis and Landau to Germany. Hüningen was demolished; and the State of Baden was put in possession of one half of the bridge between Strasburg and Kehl. The indemnity was fixed at 700,000,000 francs, the army of occupation at 150,000 men; and the period of occupation was to continue for five or perhaps only three years. Castlereagh and Wellington, contrary, there is some reason to think, to Metternich's inclinations,[2] were inexorable in requiring the restoration of the art treasures which France had plundered and which a too great liberality in 1814 had allowed her to keep; and the good-will of the Parisians, when the Duke caused everything that had ever belonged to Holland and Belgium to be removed from the Louvre, characteristically turned to hatred.[3] Nevertheless, as Metternich said, "the Second Peace of Paris," but for the lesson France received in the loss of some frontier places, in the compulsory restoration of stolen

[1] "Oesterr. Theil.," pp. 717, 718.   [2] Ibid., p. 728.   [3] Ibid., p. 729.

art treasures, in the imposition of an indemnity, and in the occupation, for a time, of some of her departments, was "the complement of the First."[1] It might even have been described in the contemptuous language of a more ferocious age as 'a compromise peace.' Yet on this very account it accomplished its purpose of pacification so much the more easily. France was left with no rankling grievance. Her frontiers differed by very little from those she had possessed before the Revolution; the burdens laid upon her were not beyond her capacity to bear; and, if her gallant colonels now and again rattled their sabres and celebrated the charms of warfare, the pleasures of peace, provided they did not become associated with the pains of boredom, proved sufficiently attractive to the mass of her people to encourage Louis-Napoleon, when in 1852 he resumed his uncle's crown, to assert with much economy of truth that "l'Empire c'est la paix."

Still precautions—and precautions of material other than that of which Alexander's dreams were made—had to be taken; and it was to these, which, as he pointed out,[2] saved France from subdivision, that Metternich gave his attention. November 20th, 1815, was more than the date of the Second Peace of Paris; it was the coming of age of the Concert of Europe. That idea, old in conception, had been brought to birth by Castlereagh at Chaumont in the midst of the first advance on the French capital, but it was rather Metternich who carried it to maturity. The Four Allied Powers pledged themselves not only to maintain the treaties they had concluded, but at fixed intervals "to hold meetings consecrated to great common objects and to the examination of such measures as at each one of these epochs shall be judged most salutary for the peace and prosperity of the nations and for the maintenance of the peace of Europe".

The words, as time was to show, were pregnant with possibilities. Gentz passed from dull despair to rosy hope and fancied that he had found in the Quadruple Alliance the realisation of his visions. "The negotiations of 1814," he wrote, "left much still to wish for, and much to fear. The negotiations of 1815 have completed the work. Now is the moment come when the prospect of a Golden Age in Europe no more belongs to empty dreams. The new Treaty between the Four Powers, subscribed on the very day of the conclusion of peace with France, is the key-stone of the whole building."

The exuberant enthusiasm of a professional publicist must be dismissed with a smile; yet, for all that, the conception of a European

---

[1] "Mémoires," I, p. 209.   [2] *Ibid.*, III, p. 167.

Concert—of a balanced harmony rather than a balanced discord of European Powers—must be recognised as a remarkable achievement. The old religious unity of the Middle Age, the agreement at the Peace of Westphalia dogmatically to differ, and at the Treaty of Utrecht dynastically to divide, were all superseded by an enlightened statesmanlike selfishness endorsing the golden rule. The basis of political science, so Metternich assures us in pages[1] of which there is no reason to doubt the sincerity, is to be sought in the Christian precept not to do to another what one would not wish done to oneself, and to be found, internationally speaking, in the single word "reciprocity." Translated into practice this signifies respect for established rights and treaties; and it is in this, as he holds, that the great human society formed under Christian influences differs from the abstract states of philosophers and the isolated states of the pagan world in whose external relations the principle of retaliation prevails. He goes on to distinguish his own diplomatic work from that of Richelieu and Mazarin, Talleyrand and Canning, who all looked at things from the national, not the international standpoint. Fortune, however, gave him as an associate Castlereagh; and in Castlereagh he found another man of the world, content, not so much on philosophic as on practical grounds, to play the part of a true European and to keep in view that essential condition of the modern world, "the society of states."[2]

It is, of course, obvious to comment that international morality like personal morality will not long survive the disappearance of the faith upon which it is based. If Christianity is felt to be a delusion and Christendom found to be a vain imagination, individuals and nations will presently discover that standards of conduct have insensibly adjusted themselves to the change. Morality, however, can generally be trusted to last for at least one generation after its foundation in faith is gone; and the Vienna settlement served Europe well until Austria and Russia in 1908 and Germany in 1914 forgot how considerable a place regard for treaty rights had occupied in the Vienna dispensation under which they had flourished for the best part of a century. It was in truth just such a dispensation as the Habsburgs with their central position in Europe, their long tradition of empire theoretically co-extensive with civilisation itself, and their strange genius for uniting divers peoples under a single civilising sway, might have been expected to recommend; and we may fancy, if we please, that "the ramshackle

[1] "Mémoires," I, pp. 30–32.   [2] See "Mémoires," I, p. 30, for the phrase.

Empire" formed in Metternich's eyes a sort of microcosm or model of the ramshackle Continent with which he had to deal. Such a sodality of States as, with Castlereagh's aid, he promoted, rests upon a common civilisation and, since forms of government are in the last analysis part of civilisation, it will operate best where no conflict of institutions aggravates the conflict of interests. We have seen in our own time the difficulty that beset the Assembly of Nations at Geneva in assimilating a plutocratic State like America or a communistic State like Russia. Great local eccentricities in fact are incompatible with strong cosmopolitan harmonies, and violent disparities of domestic vision communicate violent differences of international understanding. English opinion, with its strong faith in the virtue of leaving people to manage their own affairs, tends easily to minimise the effect of these considerations; and not even Castlereagh furnished an exception to this rule. But Metternich, with his acute sense of the interdependence of home and foreign affairs—not to speak of Talleyrand with his wholly unethical interest in principles —saw deeper and clearer. He knew that the acts of a nation are no more purely self-regarding than those of an individual, that no concordant building can rise from the juxtaposition of different styles of architecture, that a repose of ideas is as important to peace as a reconciliation of interests. For this reason the monarchical idea, representing as it did the victorious protest of the Five Great Powers of Europe against a revolutionary disintegration, formed a necessary feature, not so much of his science, as of his statecraft. The same effect was, of course, attempted a hundred years later with Democracy as the governing principle and States both great and small worked into the design. Who will make so bold as to assert that the result, though immeasurably more laboured, has been better? Metternich at all events seized upon the only forces available at the moment; and a statesman could have done no other.

With the Second Peace of Paris there closes the first part of Metternich's career. By craft, by resource, by judgment he had fought and defeated the Revolution in that first phase of its existence when, incarnate in the greatest of the gods of war, it trampled pitilessly upon the lives and liberties and loyalties of men. He had now to meet it in a more insidious form, to join issue with a force tireless as a flood advancing. He faced the conflict with calm and courage and for thirty years and more, until his strength failed him, he held his ground. Yet the contest was almost as if a man were in literal fact to take up arms against a sea of troubles; and the cold steel of intellectual criticism passed in vain through the liquid, formless, but nevertheless formidable agitation of democratic ideas. Napoleon was about to perish, but Marx was soon to be born.

Though on the field of Leipzig, as he passed amongst the dead and dying, Metternich had been profoundly moved by a feeling that "the hand of God was armed,"[1] mysticism had seldom place in his mind. Just, however, as the Napoleonic section of his career closes we catch a breath of subtler air. He had been dining with Blücher one summer's evening at St. Cloud in the very room where he had so often talked for hours with Napoleon and had afterwards stepped out upon the balcony of the Palace. Paris, all radiant in the evening sun of July, lay stretched before him; and its lavish beauty doubtless added point to the strictures that Blücher in his rough way had just been passing upon the madness of the man who had staked and lost it all for the sake of the mad dash to Moscow. There followed the reflection—all the more intense, perhaps, because, like the reflections in Grey's "Elegy," so obvious—that that sun and that city would be still embracing long after the traditions of Napoleon, of Blücher and still more of himself had passed from memory, and that in this sublime attraction, recurring day by day under the compulsion of immutable law, was to be found a criticism of human life which made all the labour of men to make a mark upon time appear as the wallowing of children in slime or sand. Only in the recollection of good deeds done could he take comfort; and in this respect he felt no desire to change places with Napoleon.[2]

Yet, when the sun of Austerlitz sank at last into the sea at St. Helena, there was for Metternich no gladness in the afterglow. "You will perhaps think," he observed to an English acquaintance, "that, when I heard of Napoleon's death, I felt a satisfaction at the removal of the great adversary of my country and my policy. It was just the reverse. I experienced only a sentiment of regret that I should no more converse with that great intelligence."[3] And, when he was sounded by Marmont to find out whether he had any objection to the Marshal's imparting reminiscences of Napoleon to Napoleon's son, he gave a reply that could hardly be bettered:— "I make one single condition—that you tell him the whole truth without disguising either the good or the evil."[4]

---

[1] "Mèmoires," III, p. 311.
[2] "Mémoires," II, p. 525. I have paraphrased here with some little freedom.
[3] Buckle, "Life of Disraeli," V, p. 498.
[4] Montbel, "Le Duc de Reichstadt," p. 264.

X

THE CONGRESS METHOD

THE Restoration had been accomplished, the Most Christian King once again seated upon his throne, the more illustrious Emperor finally incarcerated in a sea-girt island, and a Europe with pack re-balanced, set ambling in her ancient, half-forgotten ways. These things had been effected by the co-operation of British sea-power and British generalship with the military strength of the three great eastern Monarchies of the Continent and through the general application of the Legitimist principle by the leading diplomatists of the time. It seemed desirable to perpetuate the concert of Great Powers and the system of monarchy to which the world was indebted for international and domestic peace; and from this desire sprang those Congresses after which the period is named. The student of history if, then, he would breathe the air of that time, must march with knapsack and note-book from Vienna to Aix; from Aix, by way of Carlsbad, to Troppau; from Troppau to Laibach; from Laibach to Vienna. Only so can he hope to become a party to the counsels of the European Restoration.

Over the society of that epoch there hung four dominant perils —the plain menace of the Revolution, to which the fortunes of the Bonapartes were partly tied; the proved menace of France; the unproved menace of Russia; and the yet more menacing combination, as once at Tilsit, of these last two together. Castlereagh was not less alive than Metternich to these dangers, but viewed them with something of the detached insularity of his Irish origin and English traditions. He wanted, that is to say, to maintain monarchy everywhere without meddling anywhere—or at least anywhere outside France—and so far as possible to enjoy the advantages of common counsel without suffering the inconvenience of particular commitments.

Such an attitude of mind, though it gave him much, did not give Metternich all that he required to make the Vienna settlement sure. In one way or another he had to protect the new-made map of Europe as well from plague-spots of Revolutionary activity as from a revival of that close understanding between France and Russia from which the utmost resources of his diplomacy had but lately availed to save Europe, and which, if renewed, might be expected to bring the one to the Rhine, the other as far as, and even beyond the Danube. Alexander, in these anxious days—Alexander, that is, in the new evangelical mood resulting from the ministrations of Madame de Krudener[1]—was hardly less dangerous than the old orientally despotic, occidentally democratic Alexander of the Napoleonic period; nor had his mixed troop of cosmopolitan advisers as yet lost credit with him. Capodistrias, the Corfiot, at the Russian Foreign Office, Pozzo di Borgo, the Corsican at the Paris Embassy, Stakelberg, the Russian Ambassador at the Austrian Court, were all united in a so-called Liberal opposition to one whom they damned as the Dalai Lama of Vienna. The arm of Russia, as Metternich knew, was widely busy—pointing as always at the prospect in Turkey, fingering the pulse of Spain, poking the embers of revolution in Italy, seeking the hand-shake of France—not altogether without appearance of success. It was the pressure of the Russian Emperor that had brought the admirable Richelieu to the head of French affairs and displaced the cynical but understanding Talleyrand. A Minister of Anglo-Austrian sympathies, rationally reached, had in fact been exchanged for a Minister, alike in honesty, patriotism and pipe-smoking propensities curiously suggestive of a French Lord Baldwin, yet instinctively and naturally drawn towards a country where he had served as Governor of Odessa and towards an Emperor whom he could reckon as a personal friend. He was, indeed, as his predecessor characteristically phrased it, "the Frenchman who knew the Crimea best." Possibilities of further change held for Metternich no prospect of improvement. Behind the Charter King and the Russophil Duke rose the form of the Heir-apparent, of the Chambre Introuvable, and of those intransigent deputies of whom Richelieu, as if in revenge for Talleyrand's well-known epigram, publicly affirmed that, not having emigrated, they seemed to him sometimes, with their relentless hatreds and passions, to be mad.

Watching France thus nervously as the proved source of storm and trouble, Metternich was perhaps hard to please. Nor did Germany bring relief to his diplomatic perplexity. The Courts of Württemberg and Baden were already allied by marriage to the royal house of Russia; and the King of Prussia was in these anxious years engaged in marrying his daughter to a husband who was then indeed no more than one of Alexander's brothers, but whom

[1] "Mémoires," III, p. 52. "La tendance de cette femme est plus dangereuse que toutes les autres, parceque ses prédications ont toutes pour but d'exciter les classes indigentes contre les propriétaires."

circumstances were presently to set for a generation upon the Russian throne—the Grand Duke Nicholas. In the south Spain under the Bourbons was resuming its old relations with Bourbon France, whilst Italy presented various studies in uncertainty. The supersession of Bentinck's Sicilian Constitution by the King of Naples under Austrian advice did nothing to strengthen the good relations between England and Austria; and in general the attitude of Castlereagh towards Continental affairs became not exactly unsympathetic, yet increasingly reserved and insular. One might in those years have been pardoned for supposing that the machine that Metternich had set himself to drive was already falling out of gear, that the cunningly balanced mechanism was no longer playing true, and that an explosion would presently occur. Metternich, however, was equal to his occasion. Unable to draw England into any closer connection, he boldly turned to the very Powers whose projects he feared. His plan was, in fact, to bring the understanding between them once more within the scope of wider influences and broader conceptions. Tempting Richelieu with the prospect, supremely important at the moment to a French Premier, of clearing French soil of the Army of Occupation, tempting Alexander with the mirage—dear to the soul of more than one Romanoff—of a scheme of general disarmament, he persuaded them alike to a European Conference, and at the Conference he drew them once more within the compass of a system that had its pivot in Vienna.

It was not without craftsmanship, or as some may prefer to say, without craft, that this result was attained. A less skilful statesman would have allowed the Congress to meet at Basel, as Alexander's Liberal henchmen desired that it should do. But Metternich knew the importance of the surrounding climate to diplomatic negotiation. At Basel the moral atmosphere would have been congenial, not to his own ideas but rather to those of the mixed company of voluntary exiles or political refugees who had made the names of Ferney, of Coppet, of Les Charmettes famous and caused the lake-country about Geneva to be infested with the philosophy and romance of the now abhorred Revolution. He suggested instead as the place of meeting the Imperial city where the founder of the Holy Roman Empire had been born and lies buried; and he gained his point. It was to Aix-la-Chapelle, or if we will to Aachen, that in the autumn of 1818 the Princes and Ministers of the Great Powers of Europe took their road.

Metternich himself came on to Aix from taking a course of

German waters. Like other statesmen of those more festive and more spacious times he had not only occasion to seek but leisure to profit by the advantage of saline springs, and, probably under the charge of his physician, the despotic Staudenheim, and his valet, the faithful Giroux, he is to be found from time to time enjoying the amenities of their surroundings. A side of him that is apt to drop out of view in the pages of historians concerned exclusively with the political aspect of statesmen and circumscribed both by space and sympathy, appears in the agreeable and amusing letters that he writes to his wife from Lucca and Carlsbad. He submitted without complaint to the strange precepts of such places—the six o'clock start, the ten o'clock déjeuner, the dinner at three with no supper to follow—and enjoyed without reserve the charms of the adjoining country, the walks, the talks, the odd characters who were to be met with, the ignorances they betrayed, and the follies they perpetrated. Goethe was on one occasion among his guests and was introduced by him to Mme. Catalani, the Melba of the day, with the comment that the poet was a man of whom Germany was proud. Thereupon her husband inquired of him "Who is Goethe?" and obliged him to explain that Goethe was the creator of "Werther." Not long after—but the story shall be concluded in Metternich's own words! "The poor goose did not forget it; he must needs go to him a few days later and say: 'My dear Goethe, what a pity you could not see Potier in the part of Werther; you would have split with laughter."

It was whilst taking the waters in that August of 1818 that Metternich heard of the death of his father. The end was peaceful; for the old man's faculties had failed, and decay and death came unperceived. Metternich wrote kindly to his mother, but not without one curious, characteristic touch of self-esteem. "My poor father," he observed, "will at least carry away from this world the conso- lation that I have never caused him a moment of distress." His confidence in himself never faltered, neither in public business nor private trouble.

A fortnight later the Prince, for Prince he had now become, was off to Aix and dropping new plums of self-satisfaction—tasty, yet in the worst of taste—as he went upon his way. The apogee of his fortune had been reached. He was never, perhaps, less attractive or more powerful. "I came to Frankfurt," he wrote to his wife, "like the Messiah to free the sinners. The Diet took a new appearance as soon as I busied myself with its affairs; the seemingly impossible was accomplished. Never, I think did twelve days at so important a juncture bear more fruit."

Childish vanity becomes childlike delight in the next letter, for his possessions pleased him almost as well as his position. As he went on his way he was able to glance at the magnificent estate of Johannisberg, with which the Emperor had presented him. Standing on the balcony of the house in the softening light of a September evening, he saw spread out for his eyes to feast upon that famous Rhineland property which held so great promise for him and his descendants of abundance of wine and wealth. He lost no time in making the acquaintance of the administrator of these fruitful fields. This was none other than an elderly abbé with, as he observes, so little of the traditional primary weakness of a monk that he had a horror of tasting a bottle of wine and had made himself the greatest connoisseur in the district solely by the use of his nose. All delicacy of taste is said to be derived from smell; and, with no surer guide than sniffing, the Père Arnot could tell the year and the vintage of the grapes and even detect a mixture.

Less than a week later Metternich, as busy with the problems of Germany as with those of France and Italy, was entertaining a large batch of German notabilities in these new surroundings. Deaf old Hardenberg was the principal figure in the company, just as the affairs of Prussia were doubtless a principal concern in the discussions; but beside him there were to be seen persons of mark at least in German circles—Goltz, the Prussian Member, and Buol-Schauenstein, the Austrian President of the Diet; the industrious Wessenberg; the indispensable Gentz; Münster, who had been the spokesman of Hanover at the Vienna Congress, and Wintzingerode, a Russian who had in like manner assisted to represent Würrtemberg at that same assembly. We can picture them contemplating, with astonishment as Metternich notes contentedly, the marvellous view of the Rheingau and confronting with less satisfaction the infinite confusions of the German problem. Was it a time to introduce into Germany that constitutional government which the thirteenth article of the Federal Act had so lightly foreshadowed, not, it is true, as in the original draft, in the form of any absolute promise or by an appointed date, yet as an ultimate purpose which sovereigns might put into effect when they found it convenient? Not a year before, when the Jena University students had combined the commemoration of Luther with that of Leipzig, the Uhlan's corset, the Hessian pigtail, and the corporal's cane had—not altogether without professorial approval—been cast together into the flames, to symbolise the passing of the old order of things in which they had figured; and a pamphlet, written by one, Schmalz, from Metternich's angle of vision, and a history of Germany by the ill-fated Kotzebue followed after them. Was it the moment, then, to take risks, with society still in commotion? Above all it was essential in the Austrian Minister's view to prevent the King of Prussia from setting up a national parliament. Provincial estates were well enough, being both traditional and tractable; but a central assembly was anomalous and must confirm the bad example set only a few months before in Bavaria under Zentner's premiership and the bad influences flourishing, as the Jena outrages all too disastrously showed, under the authority of the Grand Duke of Saxe-Weimar, perhaps the most Liberal prince in Germany.

So or somewhat so they must have talked, having regard to the circumstances of the time, in those shortening September days of 1818; and then Metternich was off to Mainz to meet his master. Before the close of the month, however, he had returned to Johannisberg with a still more illustrious company, so that the visitors' book, which he had established, looked, as he says, like the protocol of a congress. In gorgeous weather, amidst an orgy of acclamations, with music playing and guns sounding and boats in great number attending, the Emperor made his way by water to his Minister's splendid residence. The view was admired; the dinner was approved; the preparations sufficed. Never, the host flattered himself, had the place received a more notable guest.

The imperial progress continued to fulfil the hopes of one whose policy desiderated a marked preponderance of popularity in favour of the Emperor as compared with the King of Prussia, the new sovereign of the country. At Cologne Metternich was mistaken for his master by the expectant crowd, which met his remonstrances by the retort: "We like our Emperor well enough to acclaim him twice over, if you are not he;" and on his arrival at his lodgings there were further demonstrations. He was, in fact, vigorously kissed by old and young alike. He implored his enthusiastic but unknown friends to be reasonable. They replied that they believed themselves to be so. Seeing that his case was hopeless, he submitted to the osculation. On emerging, he found that his valet, despite a beard of eight days' growth, had fared no better. The moral at least was satisfactory. The Rhinelanders, it was plain, greatly preferred the Austrians to the Prussians or the French. Metternich, a Rhinelander by birth, an Austrian only by adoption, could have received no more flattering tribute to his own career, no better assurance that at the coming Congress he would find himself among friends.

Monarch and Minister passed on to Aix, where the sovereigns of Prussia and Russia met them. A change was apparent in Alexander. "We found one another again," Metternich writes to his wife, "as in 1813." It was the best of auguries for the success of the Conference. For the rest familiar faces were everywhere in evidence. Capo d'Istria, the declining, Nesselrode, the rising star in Russian counsels; Wellington and Castlereagh with their cool British good sense; Hardenberg, with Bernstorff to help him to hear—and perhaps to understand; and finally Lady Castlereagh, giving parties from whose "inconceivable atmosphere of boredom" the company with common accord fled to Metternich's tiny *salon*.

The prominent new feature of the meeting was afforded by the presence of Richelieu, which was quite as it should be. He was there to speak for France; and it was primarily with France that the Congress was concerned. The issue here was simple. The occupation of the country by the Allied forces had become intolerable to the French people, and, though Prussia was not without her misgivings as to what might follow, the Powers were agreed that the burden, financially as well as sentimentally a grave one, must be lifted. Wellington, who was best qualified to speak, was in full agreement with this policy. It was, in fact, his persuasions which had paved its way by inducing the Allies to accept 240 million francs of indemnity instead of the agreed 800 and the financial house of Hope and Baring to furnish France with a loan.

A greater matter remained to be regulated. France had been retained as a great nation in the comity of European Powers; she had now, if she was not to be a continual source of disaffection, to be fully restored to their concert and counsels. It was not quite obvious in what manner this should be done. As things stood, the other four leading Governments were bound by the Treaty, concluded at Chaumont, renewed at Vienna, and subsequently enlarged at Paris in 1815, so as to afford, not only a guarantee against French aggression, but a pledge of common counsel at fixed intervals for the consideration of measures designed to secure the peace and prosperity of Europe. In deference to Castlereagh's wishes, France had not been mentioned as the particular target of these phrases, but France had been meant, for her policy as well internal as external remained of supreme interest and importance to Governments equally afraid of Revolutionary ideas and Napoleonic ambitions. This Treaty of the Quadruple Alliance Alexander proposed to leave unchanged; but he was ready to add a new and more definite guarantee for peace in which France should formally participate. The Five Great Powers were to pledge themselves to maintain the state of things both territorial and institutional approved by the Vienna Settlement. A general alliance, in other words, was to protect Europe—and Europe only was named—against any change of boundaries or of Governments.

The scheme had obvious attractions. It paralysed the hand of Russian ambition fishing in Eastern waters. It shut the mouth of Prussian militarism declaiming against the close of the Allied occupation. It charmed the ear of Metternich intent as ever upon international ideas and federal solutions. Its only obvious defect was that it failed to please the keen and watchful eye of the British Government. English opposition was based upon the fear of incurring material liabilities, upon the dislike of interfering with others and, of course, upon the determination not to be interfered with. Metternich was loth to lose the advantage of English co-operation. He set himself to find a means of seizing the convenient pledge that Russia tendered without parting with the moral support that England had long afforded. His plan was to substitute the idea of a diplomatic concert, with its pacific connotation, for that of a general military alliance, and thus to bring the proposed agreement into line with the pledges of peace exchanged at Chaumont. The older Four-Power Treaty would still embody the particular international sanctions desiderated by the affairs of France, whilst in the newer Concert of the Five Powers Europe would possess a permanent association, formed to preserve concord on the new territorial foundation, yet ostensibly bound not to extend its sphere of discussion to the particular concerns of other Governments without the express invitation of the parties interested.

In words as vague as these the Congress of Aix finally reduced to a common measure the ideal aspirations of Alexander, the prudent hesitations of Castlereagh, the consolidating internationalism of Metternich, the nervous anxiety of Frederick William and the penitential shriving of France. But, if we ask what precisely it all signified, it might be sufficient to reply that the Great Powers had taken to themselves authority to interfere with the Lesser whenever they conceived the general interest to be threatened. Doubtless this was

in one sense nothing new; doubtless there was room for gibes
and jeers at the assumption by the strong of an exalted purpose;
doubtless the interference, though in principle joint, proved in
practice to be often several. Yet, though the coming century saw
many cynical things done, there was none comparable to the seizure
of Silesia or the partition of Poland or the suppression by Napoleon
of the liberties of Spain and Venice. The equilibrium in the Concert
did act as a certain check upon the oppression of the weaker elements
of the world outside it. Wars were rarer; spoliation was less unblushing; community of civilisation was more emphasised. The ideas
of concert and congress, if they seemed at times to fade from view,
tended again to reassert themselves till the end of the century, and
the one gave countenance to international morality and the other
to international law. Metternich and Castlereagh as they left Aix
had reason to congratulate themselves that all the great nations
of Europe had taken counsel together, not merely as before in order
to liquidate the losses of war, but so as to enlarge the pledges of
peace. Faint effort after better things as it was, the Congress must
yet be reckoned to have saved Europe from lapsing anew into
hostile combinations of rival Powers.

Meanwhile Metternich had been watching Prussia with close
attention. He recognised that the King had almost reached the
parting of the ways and must soon declare himself for or against a
central parliament and that his decision would profoundly affect
the rest of Germany and Austria with it. In these circumstances he
addressed a memorandum of importance to Wittgenstein, the only
member of the Prussian Government in whom he recognised a
kindred spirit. It shows conclusively that he was no blind supporter
of arbitrary power. "The Government," he observes, "has made
promises and must keep them. The peoples, and especially the
Germans, warned by the example of the past, taught by the appalling
abuse of power of which many German princes, under the empire of
an exaggerated sentiment of their sovereignty, have been guilty
since the fatal year of 1806, wish for guarantees against pure despotism."[1] But these guarantees he wished to provide, not in the form
of a brand-new central assembly, but through the development of
the existing indigenous Estates of the heterogeneous Confederation.
The genius of Prussia was to be found, as it seemed to him, in its
monarchical and military institutions; and events were to justify this
opinion more fully indeed than he might have appreciated. With

[1] "Mémoires," III, p. 182.

similar insight he recognised that the fortunes of Prussia were in a quite especial way of importance to Austria; and again his words were, perhaps, even truer than he knew. If Democracy were to triumph there, the Old Order would be doomed in Germany; and the European House of Lords, as Talleyrand had wittily styled the Austrian Empire, would have suffered a heavy defeat at the hands of the Commons. It was essential that the two great Governments of Germany should envisage together the burning questions of University education, of press-censorship, and of those young men's associations which under the name of gymnasia were centres of political activity.

Revolving these issues, Metternich passed, in the spring of 1819, into Italy in the suite of the Emperor. Florence was an old friend. It was otherwise with Rome. There he had, as he says, such an experience as sometimes happens to one with people whom one has often pictured but never beheld. He found, in fact, the famous city utterly different from what he had expected. He had seen it old and gloomy; he beheld it superb, brilliant, smiling, eternally young for all its age. The Vatican staggered him by its size and the wealth of its treasures, and St. Peter's no less. And yet, after the living glories of the place had been extolled, he turned to the dead Rome beside it—to the Palace of the Cæsars, the Coliseum, the Baths of Caracalla—to find sights that for him surpassed in splendour all the other buildings that he knew. When it came to the religious aspect of his surroundings, however, his praises died away. The Holy Week ceremonies left him cold. For one thing the battle of the tourists for good places was even then in full swing and destroying all dignity and devotion. And, if the Papal benediction was impressive, the succeeding distribution of indulgences was the reverse. He describes the unedifying spectacle to his wife:—"A Cardinal comes forward and throws the indulgences written on leaves of paper to the crowd. All the ragamuffins collect, fall head over heels, and scramble to catch them. There are cries and laughter as when money is scattered in the street; the victors dart off at full speed and use their indulgences I don't know how. I confess that I don't understand how a Protestant becomes a Catholic in Rome.— Rome is like a most splendid theatre with very bad actors." "Keep my remark to yourself," he adds, "or it will be all over Vienna; and I love religion and its triumph too much to wish to attack it in any way. One sees in all this that Italian taste has greatly influenced the ceremonies; what pleases and makes for gaiety on one side of

criticism. The Liberals, at least according to Metternich,[1] despised it; the new king—Charles Felix—at Modena repudiated it; and the two Emperors at Laibach marshalled their forces to meet it. Eighty thousand Austrians were put under orders to cross the frontier into Italy and ninety thousand Russians to cross the frontier into Austria. At Novara Austrian troops in conjunction with the Italian troops of Charles Felix anticipated the better-remembered battle of twenty-eight years later, and, as at Rieti, the old order triumphed. Metternich had been brilliantly successful and effective.

An honour such as only once before and once afterwards fell to an Austrian subject was conferred upon the swift, effective statesman —conferred, so he declares, without his previous knowledge and without his cordial consent. At the close of May, when he returned to Vienna, he was proclaimed Chancellor of the Household, of the Court and of State. This signified not merely an extension of dignity, but an extension of labour. "I don't care," he told his intimates, "to undertake many things at the same time, because I prefer to stick closely to my proper job. . . . To-day there has fallen to me a prize sufficient to satisfy twenty ambitious subordinates. . . . At least my new employment does not involve wig or ermine; that would have been the summit of misfortune."[2] His policy was praised of all men; yet, as he noted cynically, all men by this time had foreseen from the first the impossibility of taking any other course and the simple certainty of his achievement. "It is exactly like my valet, Giroux," he told a correspondent, "who when one maintains the opposite of what he has just said, never fails to reply: 'That is what I was telling you.'" In fact "les héros d'occasion" sprang up like mushrooms. Amidst the turmoil of his success he snatched a look at his newly decorated villa with its carefully chosen legend, apparently recording some momentary reaction against spacious interiors— "Parva domus, magna quies"; the first part, he comments, perfectly true; the latter, pretty much of a lie.

There or elsewhere, however, as the summer advanced, he found time to read Mme. de Staël's "Dix Années d'Exil." He thought all her portraits stamped with truth and that of Fouché in particular excellent;[3] but her political judgments seemed to him as the work of one who should advise arsenic as the best prescription for health and recommend it by striking descriptions of the agony of its victims.

---

[1] "Mémoires," III, p. 463. [2] *Ibid.*, p. 470.
[3] "Fouché est le seul homme qui peut véritablement seconder Bonaparte, en portant, malheureusement pour le monde, une sorte de modération adroite dans un système sans bornes."

o

A mot of Talleyrand's came back to him as he read—"L'esprit sert à tout et ne mène à rien"—and, as that wet September of 1821 ran its course, he reflected that Mme. de Staël would not have found it difficult to show that, if the weather was bad, it was only because the English Constitution had not been everywhere introduced.[1]

In October Metternich set off to Hanover to meet its new King, who was of course no other than the Fourth of our English Georges. If profusion of compliments forms part of the outfit of a gentleman, the First Gentleman in Europe might fairly claim that in this respect at least he satisfied his too familiar name. The Austrian Chancellor, who had ingratiated himself with the Prince Regent during his stay in London in 1814, was tenderly received in the royal embrace and, after some honeyed phrases had passed about his master, was himself compared by the royal tongue to Minos and Cæsar, to Themistocles and Cato, to Gustavus and Marlborough, to Wellington and Pitt. Never, as he says, had he been told such pretty things. A subtler flattery then followed. The Prime Minister of Europe was made a party to the King's opinion about the Prime Minister of England. That opinion, which lashed, with a single exception, the whole body of British Ministers as well, though not so severely as Lord Liverpool, is described by Metternich as "an appalling outburst." The single exception was Londonderry, as Castlereagh had now become. Of him the King observed that he understood Metternich and was Metternich's friend, and that in these two statements everything was said.

It was precisely with Londonderry that Metternich had business The Greeks had chosen the spring of that fateful year of 1821—that earlier "year of revolution"—to begin settling their long score with the Turks, and, though at Laibach the Emperors had agreed to leave the insurrection to its fate,[2] Alexander wrote subsequently at some length to Francis to explain that he was finding it difficult to maintain his new-found faith in conservatism in the atmosphere of Petersburg.[3] He wrote also to Metternich and to the same effect. Turkey was not among the objects that the most conservative of societies wanted to conserve. The old ambition to reach the Straits combined with the claims of the Orthodox religion to make intervention popular amongst the Russian people. The spirit of Peter the Great seemed to point them forward to the city of Constantine, and from the city of Constantine the body of the murdered Patriarch Gregorios, whom the Sultan had taken and hung at Eastertide by

[1] "Mémoires," III, pp. 476–78.   [2] Ibid., p. 492.   [3] Ibid., pp. 474, 475.

way of reprisal for a massacre of Turks in the Morea, seemed to beckon them on. Over against this mass of feeling stood Metternich, calm as usual, reasonable as ever, resolved in the interest of Europe that the Vienna Settlement of 1815 should not be disturbed and in the interest of Austria that the Russian Empire should not be increased.

If there was one man who could help him more than another it was the Minister whom the King of England and Hanover had just affirmed to be his very good friend. Londonderry had always seen,in the aggrandisement of France or Russia the lasting peril of England and Europe. The Anglo-Austrian Entente, a little loosened by the proceedings at Troppau and Laibach, was therefore quickly re-knit; and the two Ministers agreed to act together in Eastern Europe. Peace was to be maintained, Russia advised of the far-reaching dangers of its breach, Turkey persuaded of the necessity of modera-tion and good faith. Tact had carried Metternich far; he hoped it might carry him even farther. He knew, as he told the Emperor, all the dangers of meddling with the domestic business of other States, but he knew also what Londonderry was worth to him and where Liverpool was lacking. In these circumstances he resolved to take advantage of the opening that the King had given to him to do what he could to substitute the one for the other as the head of the British Cabinet.

The Premier of Europe was interesting himself, indeed, in the Premiership in England. His interference, though he spoke frankly enough, appears to have given no offence to George, probably well satisfied to be told that public policy, subject only to the preservation of constitutional forms, required the retirement of a Prime Minister whom he detested. Metternich calculated that, if his intrigue matured, Londonderry would give him the credit for it and be more than ever his friend. No calculation could tell him that Londonderry had only nine months and ten days to live.

One thing, however, the new Anglo-Austrian understanding lasted long enough to effect. Though in England the Greek revolt grew into a pseudo-classical cause and Liverpool into a public institution, in Russia Metternich was able to dispose of an opponent whom he had lately compared to a devil struggling in a stoup of holy water.[1] The international history of the first months of 1822, which were the last of Castlereagh's life, is to be read in the frantic efforts of the hated Corfiot to snatch the Russian Emperor from the

[1] "Mémoires," III, p. 449.

grasp of Metternich and to send Russian armies to the aid of the Greeks. Capo d'Istria might plausibly argue that in serving the cause of Greek freedom he served also the tradition of Peter the Great. But Metternich, not eager to see Athens free or Constantinople fall, was besides fully alive to the advantage that the revolutionaries of the West might draw from the pre-occupation of Austrian and Russian forces in Turkey. It was this consideration above all, that made him urgent for the preservation of peace.[1] Confirmed in conservatism but embarrassed by circumstance, Alexander resorted to secret diplomacy. Tatistscheff was despatched to Vienna to confer with Metternich behind the back of a Russian Ambassador who was officially dependent upon Capo d'Istria; and this covert negotiation proved completely successful. Metternich represented that the Porte must be compelled to satisfy both its actual and moral obligations, or in other words the treaty rights of Russia and the natural rights of its Christian subjects, and that it would be in complete harmony with the principles of the Holy Alliance that these aims should be enforced by the European Concert assembled in Congress. Tatistscheff accordingly returned to Petersburg with suggestions to this effect, and Alexander approved them. The larger interests of Europe had prevailed against the narrow ambitions of Russia.

For the moment the Austrian Chancellor stood on a giddy pinnacle of diplomatic fame. To the political victories in Naples and Piedmont of the year before—victories which had made his journey through Germany something of a royal progress and brought, so he tells us, all the revolutionary rabble grovelling to his feet[2]—was now added the credit of a diplomatic achievement which his own Sovereign acclaimed as perhaps the most difficult and most brilliant of his career.[3] He had secured it by a personal influence over statesmen of as different a nature as Londonderry and Alexander, in relation to States at that time the strongest in the world, and in respect of a problem where the interests of those States notoriously differed. The Great Powers of Europe were once more bound for Vienna, for at Vienna the coming Congress was to be initiated. Once more Metternich would preside in deed, if not in name, over the proceedings. Once more he might count upon having Alexander and Londonderry as Austria's guests. Once more, and with no little complacency, he took the measure of his surest but, though he knew it not, then already mentally failing friend.

[1] "Mémoires," III, p. 568   [2] Ibid., pp. 481, 482.   [3] Ibid., p. 588.

"The difference between Londonderry and myself," he wrote in May, whilst the negotiation was at its tensest, "is that he doesn't know as I do what the Emperor Alexander wants and what Capo d'Istria does not want. . . . He will never understand the real knot of the issue, which is that the Emperor will not listen to the Greek question, whilst Capo d'Istria has a horror of the Spanish. Capo d'Istria seeks in the latter an instrument to force the Tsar to intervene in the affairs of the Porte. He advances therefore in all directions his thesis in the following curious form: 'You see the Emperor . . . is on the wrong line; he rushes ahead of his destruction and will drag you into his ruin. You have only the choice between two evils; let him then choose the lesser.' "[1]

Again, in June, when the diplomatic battle was over: "I can see Londonderry's face from here," he declared. "He ought to feel as happy as a man whom one has dragged from under an avalanche."[2] He saw the British Foreign Secretary indeed as less cool and patient than himself, as capable of writing a despatch full of fire and fury "to prove that what is absurd cannot be reasonable," where he would have been satisfied with sending "a tiny card of invitation" to talk things over;[3] yet he saw him always as a brother in diplomacy. "I want him here by the end of August," he wrote, with his eye on the discussion of preliminaries in September. But when the end of August came, Londonderry lay beneath the shadow of the famous Abbey which has enshrined for generations such dust as his. With the very hand that had worked so wisely for Europe he had dealt himself a deathblow.

[1] "Mémoires," III, p. 544.   [2] Ibid., p. 548.   [3] Ibid., p. 545.

XII

CHATEAUBRIAND AND CANNING

"No one," observed Chateaubriand, as in the evening of his days he cast an artist's eye back over his political career and set upon the stage of memory the figures in whose counsels he had shared at Verona and against whose will, for the most part at least, he had made the ensuing war in Spain, "no one remembers the speeches we delivered at Metternich's table." And then, stimulated by the mention of a city, not dependent only upon a congress for its fame, to contrast the ephemeral affairs of the statesman with the everlasting memorials of the creative artist, he adds the bold reflection that "no traveller will ever hear the singing of the lark in the fields of Verona without recalling Shakespeare."[1] The traveller may perhaps have been credited by Chateaubriand, like the schoolboy by Macaulay, with more than his just measure of memory, but at least, if Juliet was rightly taught to suppose that the lark made sweet division, we must hope that the eminent personages assembled at Verona in the late October of 1822 took occasion to recall the songs of a bird whose charms had drawn, not two years before, the sweetest music from Shelley's lyre.

For, indeed, there was occasion at the Verona Congress for the sweetness that corrects the acidities of division. So long as Castlereagh lived, it might have been said of the Great Powers of Europe that they went on their way, not disagreeing except in opinion. But during the year 1822 there came into office both in England and France Foreign Ministers of great mark whose influence contrasts with that of Metternich and Castlereagh and vitiates the intercourse of Europe. There lies between Chateaubriand and Canning as much difference as there well can be between a master of French sentiment and of English, between a supremely brilliant journalist and a supremely eloquent orator, between a mind flamboyantly romantic and a mind responsive to the colder charm of the classic muse; yet they were at one in their dislike of Metternich and in their opposition to Metternich's European mentality. Whilst Chateaubriand appropriated the international office of the Altar to the use of the Throne and endeavoured to nationalise the monarchy by virtue of a free press and a military adventure, Canning within six months of

[1] "Oeuvres Compl.," xii, p. 467.

his return to the Foreign Office was likewise professing nationalism, though in more pagan terms, and advising a new generation that things were, as he put it, getting back to a wholesome state again; that every nation was now for itself and God for them all; and that the time for Areopagus and its like was gone by.

Wellington's instructions, originally drafted by Bathurst, were sharply strengthened by a despatch from Canning stressing the British objection to any form of European intervention in Spain. On the other hand Chateaubriand was empowered to promote a policy designed to separate France from the other Powers just so far as would enable her to intervene in Spain without being herself interfered with by Europe. It was, in these circumstances, natural enough that, although other issues, such as the suppression of the slave-trade, the independence of Greece and the condition of Italy, were down for discussion, the problem of Spain became predominant at the Verona Congress. Canning saw in it an opportunity of enforcing the independence of British policy by taking up that attitude of non-interference in Spanish affairs which was ultimately to lead him to recognise the revolted Spanish colonies as separate states; and Chateaubriand equally saw an occasion for asserting a peculiar interest on the part of France, over and above that professed by the rest of the Continent, in the suppression of a revolutionary agitation that might cross the Pyrenees and prove infectious. Both standpoints were obnoxious to Metternich, the one because it seemed to challenge the Concert and countenance the Revolution, the other because it tended to substitute military for diplomatic intervention: and yet there was another point of view that he feared as much or more. Alexander, converted and repentant, was always ready to place his soldiers at the service of the Restoration. In principle this was well enough; in practice it signified the passage of Muscovite hordes across German territory. The old Rhinelander had no use for Russian armies, except as distant thunder. Austria, therefore, with Prussia at her side, stood for a policy of merely diplomatic pressure upon Madrid and was thus openly opposed to the two Powers with which she had been more particularly associated at Vienna in 1814. The Congress had in fact put the Concert out of tune.

Chateaubriand in later days maintained that he had been pitted against the two leading statesmen in Europe and had got the best of them both, and, though Dr. Temperley, whose opinion deserves full consideration, observes that "it is but too clear that Chateaubriand was no match for trained diplomats,"[1] French diplomacy, if judged by results, certainly showed no marks of inferiority. Not only did Chateaubriand gain an ascendancy over Alexander at the Congress itself, but, in conjunction with his colleague Montmorenci, emerged from it with undertakings, should France be drawn into war with Spain, of both moral and material help from Russia, of similar assistance, subject only to the exigencies of her own domestic situation, from Prussia, and of at any rate moral support from Austria. This was all he needed to enable him, in spite of Canning's eloquent objections, to prosecute, untrammelled, an enterprise calculated to satisfy the idea of glory which, as the observation of three decades had taught him, counted for more in a Frenchman's mind than love of liberty,[2] and to prepare, as he frankly confesses,[3] for that recovery of the Rhine frontier upon which the soul of France was set.

The sowings of the autumn at Verona came to sight in the spring at Madrid. Upon the indignant rejection by the Spanish, supposedly Liberal Government of a demand for the release of King Ferdinand and the abolition of the Spanish Constitution of 1812, the Four Great Continental Powers withdrew their Ambassadors from the capital, the French Ambassador lingering a little behind to make assurance sure. There followed that famous advance across Spain of the armies of France which seemed to combine the comforts of a military promenade with the merits of a paladin's adventure and flattered the vanity of the French without wounding the pride of the Spaniards. The latter wished indeed for nothing better than to see their tyrant restored. There was a battle—but mostly of flowers; and the fleur-de-lys met with no more resistance than was required to relieve the monotony of roses—roses almost all the way. Chateaubriand had brilliantly gauged the political as well as the diplomatic and military opportunity. Disregarding alike English solicitude for the constitutional liberties of the Peninsula and the less substantial alarm of Austria at the arbitration of one who in his day had been the advocate of "la monarchie selon la charte," he had revived by a simple dexterous stroke the memory of the Family Compact, the prestige of the French army, and the power of the House of Bourbon. Who could say that a Government which had so cheaply crossed the Pyrenees, taken its path to Cadiz, and set Spain in order might not in due season consolidate once more the influence of France on the lost frontier of the Rhine?

---

[1] "Foreign Policy of Canning," p. 61.
[2] "Oeuvres Compl.," xii, p. 49.   [3] *Ibid.*, p. 182.

The triumph was glorious, but its glitter was quickly gone. The King's restoration unfortunately left both his powers and his character unchanged. More secure than before, he ruled his country for the last decade of his life with just such a mixture of cruelty and intrigue as his soul delighted in, whilst his Court and counsels were torn by the struggles of his wife and brother and their respective adherents to secure control of the succession. Fortunately for Chateaubriand a facile pen lay ready to his hand to cover the failure of a too facile sword. "The sovereigns of our time," he wrote, "seem born to destroy a society doomed of itself to destruction."[1] Not only those who put their trust in princes have occasion to echo that exceeding bitter cry! It will be torn from all who make romances out of forms of government and forget that liberty is nothing but a perfect law in the soul whether of sovereign-kings or sovereign-peoples.

Chateaubriand fell from power within a year of his day of triumph; and we shall meet him no more. In the long life of Metternich he figures as a political episode just as in his own Metternich figures as a psychological enigma. Some years after his dismissal he took a fancy to live in Venice; and an approach was accordingly made to Metternich for the necessary permission. The answer was characteristic: "As M. de Chateaubriand calls himself my personal enemy," wrote the Austrian Chancellor, "I ask nothing better than to be avenged of him by doing him service."[2] Chateaubriand's revenge was differently conceived. "Authority," he wrote, "comes either from the genius of the governor or the mediocrity of the governed; this is the point that remains to be settled in the case of M. de Metternich."[3] But the last word of all lies with Sorel:— "At bottom both . . . held themselves, each after his manner, to be supreme, Metternich in the art of leading men, Chateaubriand in that of enchanting them."[4]

The duel between Metternich and Canning ranged over a far wider field than that between Metternich and Chateaubriand, though the principle at stake was again fully illustrated in the affairs of "the Peninsula." The questions upon which no conclusion had been reached at Verona were those of the Spanish Colonies and the Greek Insurrection. They resembled each other more than might at first sight appear. Being alike the direct concern of Powers whose title to deal with them was good enough but whose strength

[1] "Oeuvres Compl.," xii, p. 362. [2] "Mémoires," V, p. 137.
[3] "Congrès de Vérone," p. 38. [4] Sorel, "Essais d'histoire et de critique," p. 8.

to do so was insufficient, they promised to drag on indefinitely, and, being alike fruitful causes of piracy, they proved to be particularly embarrassing to an Empire, like the British, of which the maritime business was considerable both in the Near East and the Far West. Canning, as we have seen, began his term at the Foreign Office by asserting the principle of non-intervention, apart from treaty obligations, in the domestic affairs of other Powers, but was rapidly driven by the depredations of the pirates into a *de facto* recognition as belligerents both of certain self-styled South American Governments and of the Greek Insurrectionists. In each case he effectively challenged the principle of European solidarity.

Austria and Russia had so far held away from the struggle between Turk and Hellene. But, if the English meant to patronise the Greeks, the Russians could no longer be expected to remain indifferent and, if the Russians moved, then the Austrians were bound to reconsider their position. Metternich thought the time had come for the sovereigns of Russia and Austria to meet. Whilst Byron waited idly at Cephalonia, the two Emperors conferred at Czernowitz. Metternich himself was, however, absent, at least in the body. He had been taken dangerously ill with some rheumatic or catarrhal affection on the way and was held prisoner by it at what was in those days Lemberg. The Emperors between them nursed him back to life—Alexander, as he says, by keeping faith with him at Czernowitz and working towards the common end; Francis by charming attentions. Little vignettes inserted in his letters tell the tale admirably:—

"Imagine the situation . . . the only man of affairs in bed at Lemberg; the two emperors *tête-à-tête* at Czernowitz. As a result only two eventualities possible, either an immediate war between Russia and Turkey or an equally immediate peace. Myself, who hold peace in my hands and alone know the means of assuring it—myself in bed!

"When it was settled that I couldn't accompany His Majesty to Czernowitz and I had chosen Mercy as my substitute, I sent him to the Emperor to announce it. The Emperor with his usual good-humour then said to Mercy: 'Well! that won't do badly. I only know the business superficially; you only know it since yesterday; we two shall cut a sorry figure. If it won't work I shall drag the Emperor Alexander to see Metternich. The latter will be farther ahead in half-an-hour than we should be in a week.'

"I cannot praise enough the delicate kindnesses of the Emperor. He has not let a single day pass without coming to see me . . . he has stayed hours together sitting by my bedside—or, on his return from Czernowitz, in my salon—not to talk of business, but to distract me with gossip."

It is no wonder Francis was beloved of his Minister and well-liked by his people!

The memorandum, furnished by Metternich to the Austrian Emperor before the Czernowitz conversations began, contained the intelligence that, in respect of the points that Russia had insisted upon as preliminary to the re-establishment of diplomatic relations, the Porte had given way, or was, as Metternich fondly supposed, about to give way. Certain rights or privileges of Russian merchant-vessels in the Black Sea were, that is to say, to be safeguarded from Turkish encroachments; the passage of the Bosphorus was to remain open to ships of nations trading with Russian ports;[1] and the long overdue evacuation of the Danubian Principalities by the Turkish forces might be immediately expected. To the postponement of the Greek Question, until the Allied Powers could intervene with effect, Alexander had already agreed; and there was nothing, therefore, to prevent the despatch of a Russian representative to Constantinople, and the more reason for it that otherwise the intentions of Russia must continue suspect. The mission of Minciaky to the Porte represented accordingly the immediate gain of the Czernowitz meeting; and the suggestion of a conference at St. Petersburg to discuss the Greek affair its remoter advantage. Neither Turk nor Greek desired the intervention of the Concert; but Russian sympathy with Orthodox beliefs and English sympathy with Hellenic studies were from Metternich's point of view both of them forces requiring to be brought under European control.

A circular note from the Russian Government in the following January—the January of 1824[2]—kept the project of a conference alive. The scheme submitted of three autonomous Greek principalities under Turkish suzerainty was unwelcome both to England and Austria, who feared alike a Russian protectorate; and the discussions dragged on like the guerilla warfare which they were designed to end. A year later Metternich put forward an alternative, which says much for his insight and intelligence. A fine sense of realities had, in fact, led him to anticipate the real solution of the problem. Surrendering not, as he saw things, to right but to necessity,[3] he authorised the Austrian Ambassador at Constantinople, if the Porte refused the concessions demanded by the Powers, to propose the establishment of a single state of Greece, sovereign and independent. We might have expected to find British and Austrian policies working thenceforward towards a common end. But Canning was not Castlereagh.

[1] See Metternich, "Mémoires," IV, p. 81.   [2] See for date "Mémoires," IV, p. 215.
[3] See "Mémoires," IV, pp. 212, 213.

In that spring of 1825 the melancholy close of a long companion-ship took Metternich once more westwards. He had been anxious for some little while about the health of his wife, whose lung was affected; and in February a visit to Paris became imperative. He arrived in the French capital on the 14th March and five days later records "the irreparable loss" of one to whom in that hour of sorrow he ascribed much beauty of soul and whose dying breath had been spent in thanking him for, as he puts it, "all that he had done, and all that he had not done for her."

These griefs were not without diplomatic concomitants. All the five weeks that he spent in Paris Metternich was studying the French situation and getting into touch with French notabilities. He saw something both of the Princes and the Powers that were and of the Princes and the Powers that were to be. He dined with the reigning King of France; and he dined also with the coming King of the French. Charles X received him with the utmost civility, expressed complete approval of Austrian principles and policy, and conferred upon him the famous Order of the Holy Ghost. Such attentions must, he thought, promote the notion that the liberties of the French Press were being sacrificed to his conversation at the royal table,[1] though in point of fact Peyronnet's Press-Law had left little or nothing more for censorship to do. A dinner at the Palais Royal should, however, have redressed the balance of public opinion in his favour, and the more that he felt at home with the Duchesse d'Orléans in a manner that was impossible for him or anyone else with the shy Dauphin, the melancholy Dauphine or even the merry, widowed Duchesse de Berry. In Marie Amélie, indeed, he recognised, not only an old acquaintance, but a charming woman, and in Louis Philippe, not only an intelligent prince, but a patron of art. For the rest he gave interviews to people of various political complexions, dined in Talleyrand's company, saw much of Bonald, who attracted him in spite, he observes, of "a profound ignorance on many subjects such as one only finds in France,"[2] and pretty thoroughly explored Villèle, who was at the time Prime Minister. The Government, though in his opinion the best that France had enjoyed since the Restoration, was, as he soon saw, what is commonly described in these days, as a "one-man-show." But he formed, and rightly formed, a high opinion of the Premier, who, though brought into power by the murder of the Duc de Berry, had not gratified the ultras of his party. "The strength of M. de Villèle," the Austrian Chancellor

[1] "Mémoires," IV, p. 160.   [2] *Ibid.*, p. 159.

wrote to his master, "is contained in a phrase he used to me. When I asked him frankly: 'Will you last, or will you be upset?' he replied, 'I am resolved to last, and a resolute man is not easy to turn out.'"[1]

All the same Metternich thought the mentality of Paris profoundly disquieting and the political situation definitely worse than he had ever himself seen it either during the Empire or at the date of the Allied occupation. He was far from sharing Bonald's belief that religion, honour and royalty possessed in the France of the Restoration at once the force of age and the grace of novelty.[2] Among eight hundred thousand Parisians, he declares, only some eighty thousand women and ten thousand men could be credited with any sort of creed; a third part of them had not even been baptised; and amongst the dregs of the people no more than one *ménage* in twenty satisfied the requirements of marriage. Missions seemed to him to be, in fact, as much required as in a pagan country.

These social soundings did not prevent the pursuit of certain diplomatic purposes. Metternich obtained, in regard to the revolt in the Near East, some assurance of French co-operation at the impending conference at St. Petersburg, and, in regard to that in the Far West, some expectation of French assistance for his plan of separating the continental from the island dominions of Spain in the Western hemisphere and setting the former free while leaving the latter bound as before to the mother-country. Never, perhaps, had he more temptation than at this juncture to suppose himself Prime Minister of Europe. Chateaubriand, as we have seen, had passed from the international sky like a flashing meteor; Alexander and Frederick William seemed to have become his satellites; from London there reached him a pressing invitation, sent by George IV and backed by Wellington, to extend his orbit. His presence there, so the English King apparently supposed, must either effect a change in Canning's dispositions or else enable Canning's counsels to be dispensed with. He was, in fact, as is shown by his cordial intimacy with Hertford—Thackeray's egregious Lord Steyne—whom he met in Paris and invited to Johannisberg, an international favourite with English Tories, but he was too wise to meddle thus openly with English internal politics. "It is useless," he wrote to the Emperor, "to bring out what shallowness, I had almost said absurdity, lies in this way of looking at things."[3] The invitation was, therefore, declined: and he turned south from Paris. Stopping at

[1] "Mémoires," IV, p. 160.   [2] "Pensées Diverses," p. 28 (ed. 1817).
[3] "Mémoires," IV, p. 165.

Genoa as he passed, he heard the political confession of the peccant Prince of Carignano, satisfied himself of Charles Albert's contrition and gave the sinner absolution. "I was a dupe," the young man told him, "and completely so . . . I shall not be that again."[1] It was too facile an assurance.

As he travelled on through Italy, the widowed Chancellor met with a strange adventure. At Milan he chanced upon a certain Cardinal Albani with whom he had long entertained friendly relations. The Cardinal, observing with some solemnity that he had a question to put on behalf of the Pope, pulled out an autograph letter from the newly-elected Leo XII. The Pope, so it said, had heard with pleasure from the Cardinal that the Prince would like to enter the Sacred College; and the Prince had so many claims to the distinction that he had only to signify his concurrence for the appointment to be made forthwith. Metternich was beyond measure astonished and begged the Cardinal to read the riddle. The explanation was singular enough. It appeared that in the course of conversation with his eminent friend, the Austrian Chancellor had alluded to the colour red as one that pleased his fancy, and that out of this grain of poppy-seed the too subtle ecclesiastic had grown a Cardinal's hat.

From such levities of a wind blowing where it listeth we have now to return to the charged atmosphere of Eastern Europe. The spring of 1825, as Metternich subsequently recognised,[2] had coincided with or perhaps provoked one of the critical periods in the psychological career of the Russian Emperor. It is in truth arguable enough that whatever influence the Chancellor gained in Paris he more than lost at Petersburg, and if Metternich himself is to be believed,[3] had he spent March in Petersburg instead of Paris, Russian policy would in many respects have taken a different turn. As it was, Pozzo di Borgo, outmatched by Metternich at the Tuileries, to which Court he was accredited as Russian Ambassador, took occasion to advise his master that Austria had offered to ally herself with France against Russia.[4]

These things had the more consequence that the Near Eastern Question was entering simultaneously upon another phase. At some cost of dignity the Sultan had at length brought himself to solicit help to suppress the Greek Insurrection from his all too-powerful vassal, the Pasha of Egypt; and Mehemet Ali had responded by sending his son Ibrahim with an army and an armada to reconquer

---

[1] "Mémoires," IV, p. 179.   [2] Ibid., p. 279.   [3] Ibid., p. 279.   [4] Ibid., p. 330.

the Morea. The ruthless and disciplined Egyptians proved more than a match for the untutored and disputatious Greeks; little but Missolonghi remained before long to the rebels; and the end of the business seemed to be in sight unless the Great Powers intervened. It was in these circumstances that Alexander turned his eyes towards England, where he was represented with much brilliancy by the Lievens—or perhaps more accurately by Countess Lieven, who had developed during a long, though largely literary liaison with Metternich her full passion for diplomatic intrigue. Canning met the Russian advances half-way. He, who might once have joined forces with Metternich to promote the sovereign independence of Greece, preferred to seek a solution of the vexed issue on less drastic lines through an Anglo-Russian understanding. Christmas, however, arrived, before Alexander's new tutor was in full possession of his pupil's mind; and on Christmas Eve, as we reckon it in the West, Alexander died.

In the interval between the Roman and the Russian Christmas the momentous question which of the Emperor's two brothers should succeed him was settled. There lay here a conflict of policies as well as of personalities. Constantine, the elder of the two, temperamentally passionate, politically pacific, and for the rest sympathetically disposed towards Austria, was no friend to England or Prussia and not much interested in the Greeks.[1] Nicholas, on the other hand, was stern and warlike, patriotically Russian and fervently Orthodox, a hammer of the Turks in will, if not yet in deed, and, which also was of consequence in international affairs, the husband of a Prussian princess. The long hesitation of the two brothers terminated in Nicholas's favour; and a new character took Alexander's place in the centre of the European stage. Canning saw his opportunity and seized it. Having occasion to despatch a special Ambassador to Petersburg to congratulate the new Sovereign upon his accession, he chose one who was at once the most distinguished of the British people and the most congenial to the Russian Emperor. Wellington carried, together with the compliments of the English King, the proposals of the British Foreign Secretary for Anglo-Russian intervention in the affairs of Greece.

The soldierly sympathy between the Iron Duke and the more than iron Autocrat carried the negotiation without much difficulty to the point of a protocol inviting the Porte to give Greece the status of a tributary Power with full freedom of conscience and commerce;

[1] "Mémoires," IV, p. 259.

a status which young Stratford Canning, just starting upon his diplomatic career in the Near East, had first satisfied himself would be accepted by, if not exactly acceptable to the now desperate leaders of the Greek Insurrection. At this point, however, the elder Canning found his Oriental diplomacy becalmed by the same consideration as had becalmed that of Metternich before him. Not a whit more than the Austrian Chancellor did the British Foreign Secretary wish to see Russia taking active measures—and least of all single-handed measures—against the Turks. Pacific moderation, proceeding from an Anglo-Russian Entente, with himself in chief control of the negotiations, in place of pressure from a European concert with Metternich in command, was what he had intended; and he had perhaps intended little more. Yet, even whilst the Protocol was preparing, the Russian Government was making use of the new diplomatic formation to assert its special interests. With something less than the assent of England to what was doing and nothing more than an intimation to Europe of what was done, Nicholas gave the Porte warning that, unless the Danubian Principalities were finally cleared of Turkish troops and the other points in dispute between Russia and Turkey acceptably decided, he should commence hostilities. A revolt on the part of the Janissaries rendered the Sultan more than usually powerless to resist. In the Treaty of Akkerman he made the required concessions; and Russia's power to coerce the Porte was amply demonstrated. But the Greek Question —of which the supreme difficulty, as the Austrian Chancellor noted, lay in the fact that the religious sentiment of the Christian Powers was there in conflict with their political counter-revolutionary convictions—remained still for decision.

Metternich's criticism of what had occurred was exactly what might have been expected of a critic of Canning. He approved what Russia had done on her own account and disapproved what she was trying to do in co-operation with England. He was himself for firmness and against half-measures. He wished for nothing better, he declared, than a Greek Empire, free and independent,[1] though it was far from clear to him by what process of conjuring this was to be made out of a people who were in truth little better than a band of brigands. So far as the requirements of Austrian policy went, a powerful Christian State in the south-east of Europe would serve as well as the present Turkish Empire.[2] But for a polity, restricted both in freedom and in strength, such as Canning had in view, he

[1] "Mémoires," IV p. 282.   [2] *Ibid.*, pp. 314, 315.

had no use at all. The British Foreign Secretary, he declared, always did the opposite to himself.

There was much sense, as well, doubtless, as some spite, in these criticisms. The Anglo-Russian Protocol, recommending as it did nothing that could cause alarm, accomplished nothing that could be called achievement. More than a year later, after the Porte had indignantly spurned it, it became the basis of the Treaty of London, whose aims and sanctions alike fell short of the needs of the case. To that Treaty neither Austria nor Prussia were parties. In Metternich's view not only was the end proposed inadequate but the approved means for reaching it insufficient. Neither by closing diplomatic relations with the Turks, nor by opening them with the Greeks, nor yet by cutting Ibrahim's maritime communications with Egypt, did he believe that the Porte could be effectually coerced, though he thought that, if the Five Great Powers together had menaced Turkey with a complete rupture of intercourse, the Sultan would have yielded. All, however, as he knew, that the Treaty of London had really made sure of was the supersession of the Concert of Europe. European solidarity, for the time at least, seemed to be gone. Three of the Great Powers—for Canning had in his Oriental policy now secured the support of Villèle—were taking action, in face of the formal dissent of the other two. The British Foreign Secretary had got, the Austrian Chancellor might be said to have lost, his way. If anyone still doubted, he had only to turn his eyes from the south-east to the south-west of Europe.

After difficulties too long to detail, the little Kingdom of Portugal had in the year 1824, and largely through Canning's intervention as mediator, been finally separated from her gigantic colony of Brazil. The King remained king of the one; the Heir-Apparent became emperor of the other. It was clearly understood, though not formally provided, that there should be no reunion of the two crowns upon a single head; and the new Emperor openly acknowledged that he had abandoned his rights of succession in Portugal. But, when King John VI died in the March of 1826, Dom Pedro—to speak of the sovereign of Brazil in the familiar fashion of the peoples of the Peninsula—instead of allowing his brother, Dom Miguel, to ascend the throne of Portugal as the next male heir of his father and in accordance with the general desire and expectation of the Portuguese, gratified his political hobbies and his family feelings by presenting the country with a constitution and a queen. The Portuguese cared little enough for either the one or the other. They were better

P

satisfied to see, as they had seen for centuries, sovereign-power embodied in a person than embedded in a charter; and they had little use 'for Dom Pedro's seven-year-old daughter on the throne. Dom Pedro had, it is true, included in his programme a marriage in the fullness of time between little Doña Maria da Gloria and her uncle Dom Miguel, who was meanwhile to be invested with the Regency. But this arrangement was only calculated to produce in its acutest form the problem of a *reine fainéante* and a *maire du palais*, and was so much the less acceptable that it had been brought from Brazil by the hands of a British plenipotentiary. Metternich indeed, when he heard of Sir Charles Stuart's intervention, supposed that Stuart must either be mad or else bent from some personal motive of vengeance upon Canning's discomfiture.[1] In fact, however, Dom Pedro's plan when it reached Portugal found just enough military support to get it tried, though not enough to get it accepted. Canning, as the seizure of the Danish fleet in 1807 had long ago demonstrated, never shrank from strong measures. Before the end of the year, in spite of a nominal policy of non-intervention, he had despatched five thousand British soldiers to the Peninsula, to supress the party of Dom Miguel, to recommend the adoption of Dom Pedro's constitution and to compel the acceptance as sovereign of Dom Pedro's daughter. By March 1827 the English had Portugal well in hand. The Queen came into her own or her uncle's, and the Charter followed with her.

Metternich might, perhaps, have had more to say about all this, but for the fact that little Doña Maria da Gloria was the Emperor Francis's grand-daughter. Satisfied, however, on the best consideration that he could give to the matter, that she was the rightful heir, he suffered both the unauthorised British intervention and the uncongenial Petrine charter. Meanwhile, by the curious chance that Dom Miguel had been sent him to complete an education which can in truth hardly be said to have ever begun, he held for the moment under his hand the wild young hawk whose dizzy flight was soon to set the European Chancelleries gaping.

Thus then matters stood when in the August of 1827, a month after the Treaty of London had been signed, Canning's hundred-days premiership suddenly closed in the fateful house at Chiswick where Fox had already died. He had not lived to carry his European policy to any clear conclusion, but only long enough to indicate clearly the difference that divided it from Metternich's. The friction between

[1] "Mémoires," IV, p. 320.

the Austrian Chancellor and the British Foreign Secretary was not the friction between one who meddles and one who minds his business, though that might have seemed at a first glance a plausible account of it. The force of circumstance impelled both alike to admit the principle of intervention on the part of the Great Powers in the domestic concerns of the smaller; and the real issue between them was whether, when such intervention became necessary, the intervening Power should act as the mandatory of the armed Concert of Europe, with all the moral sanctions and safeguards behind it that common counsel can give, or merely as a party individually interested, with such a risk to equity as a title so dubious involves. Public right, if we like to put it so, was pitted against private judgment; European solidarity against national interest.

The duel had been desperate; the combatants were but little divided in age; and, though Canning's science and staying-power may alike be called in question, his talent beyond all doubt had been singularly damaging to his adversary. Metternich, while he may be said to have fenced in private with Talleyrand and to have fought in the bullring against Napoleon, crossed swords with no greater diplomatist in the whole course of his career; and his Memoirs bear witness as well to the fierceness of the contest as to the relief that he felt when he saw it close. "Canning flies," he observes, "I walk. He rises into a region uninhabited by men, I keep on the level of human things. The result of this difference is that Canning will have the romantics on his side, whereas I shall be left to the prose-writers. His part is brilliant like a flash of lightning, but as transient; mine does not dazzle, but conserves what the other consumes."[1]

[1] "Mémoires," IV, p. 289.

XIII

APHRODITE AND ARES

THE year that saw Canning dead saw Metternich once more wedded. In the early November of 1827 he was married to Antoinette von Leykam, the daughter of a diplomatist of no great importance and of a lady of no great reputation. To make the *mésalliance* less glaring the bride was considerably created by the Emperor Countess von Beilstein, and, when sneers and sarcasms had grown stale, the charming, tactful girl of twenty-one filled her place quite successfully as the wife of the illustrious minister and magnate of fifty-four.

This second marriage appears to mark a psychological, if not also a physiological climacteric in Metternich's life. The dread of loneliness—a sure proof of advancing age—was upon him,[1] and with it there had come to him a stronger desire for a home that should be a home indeed. Family life was already in his philosophy, his children having always played a large part in his happiness; and to all appearance he now brought to an end those illicit intimacies which, on the plea that his first marriage had been a *mariage de convenance*, he had carried on with a minimum of self-reproach.

This is, then, perhaps the place to pause and glance for a moment at an aspect of Metternich's private life which, as Sorel supposed, had weakened his public effort at certain critical moments. It is possible for once to speak with certain knowledge and little fear of injustice, for he has told himself the tale of his affections too frankly and fully to be disbelieved. That the love-letters addressed to his last and greatest mistress are wholly without charm need cause us no surprise. On the one hand, a middle-aged minister of dubious morals; on the other, a worldly woman clever enough to be also a woman of the world! When we reflect further that Countess Lieven was also an ambassadress, whom everyone took to be really the ambassador, it is almost as if Russia were setting her cap at Austria. But what the letters lack in charm for the reader of letters they make up in information for the student of life. In dealing with a flirt of large experience it was, perhaps, as engaging to confess as to conceal the truth, and Metternich, who boasted to Madame Lieven of his veracity,[2] did so without demur. Whilst warning her that his name had been coupled with that of many women to whom he had never

---

[1] "Mémoires," IV, p. 538.   [2] "Lettres à la Comtesse Lieven," p. 18.

given a thought,[1] he confessed to two definite liaisons,[2] in addition
to a number of affairs into which no serious feeling had entered.
It is interesting and psychologically significant that he does not give
the word *liaison* its usual significance. From what he says and from
what follows it is clear that complete, even if transient fidelity to the
tie, and not sexual intercourse between the parties, constituted for
him the essence of its meaning. "I have never been unfaithful"—
so it pleases him to put it—"the woman I love is the only one in
the world for me." And he goes on to refer to an intimacy hardly
suspected by the world with one who, he says, had "come down to
earth only as it were to spend the spring there," who had loved him
with all the affection of a celestial soul, and whose death had seemed
to him as the end of life.[3] There appears to be little or no doubt that
the allusion here is to Countess Charles Zichy—*née* Countess Julie
Festetics—a woman of great charm and of unbroken loyalty to a
husband for whom she had no love. The other affair to which he
found the term liaison applicable was probably less platonic; and
the reader is left with a wide selection of candidates amongst whom
to choose. There is Princess Bagration, by whom Metternich had a
daughter in 1802;[4] there is Caroline Murat, at the time Grand-Duchess
of Berg, to whom Metternich made love during his embassay in
Paris; there is the Duchesse d'Abrantès (Madame Junot), whose
affair with Metternich at the time of the marriage of Napoleon and
Marie Louise was exposed by the jealous Caroline and brought the
faithless wife a severe beating from her husband; there is the
Duchesse de Sagan, who, according to Metternich's perhaps not
dispassionate account, had thrown herself perpetually at his head[5]
and was at all events in power during the advance of the Allies
during 1814. And finally there is the long liaison with Madame
Lieven herself, which may, as well as or better than the other affairs,
be what he had in mind and which, dependent mainly upon correspondence, appears to have terminated about the time of his second
marriage and most probably on that account.

"Love is not love which alters when it alteration finds," says one
whose claim to insight can with difficulty be called in question and
who, writing under the stimulus of youth's resolve to get at the
whole truth of the mysterious business, added with full assurance
that "if this be error . . . no man ever loved."[6] Backed by so high
authority we may perhaps take our stand in the ranks of

---

[1] "Lettres à la Comtesse Lieven," p. 68.   [2] *Ibid.*, p. 45.   [3] *Ibid.*, pp. 45, 46.
[4] *Ibid.*, p. xxxiii.   [5] *Ibid.*, pp. 196-97.   [6] Sonnet 116.

"those many fools" of whom Metternich complained because they told him that he rationalised too much for a man who knew love's meaning.[1] But, however that may be, he was certainly more of a libertarian in love than became one who never tired of asserting the claims of order and stability in human affairs. Those who are interested enough to look back to his professions of endless fidelity to Madame Lieven, come what might to either in the way of counter-attractions, and then to look on to the hour when she denounced him as a rogue and he dismissed her as a restless *intrigante*, may in fact be pardoned if in their turn they discover him to have been that which Love, at least according to the young Shakespeare, is not—"Time's fool." What chance, indeed, had a *grande passion* with Dorothea Lieven to qualify for the second circle of Hell if even a *grande passion* with Anna Karénina does not bring one in sight of Paolo and Francesca? But these be toys; and it is time to put away our dolls and return to our soldiers!

The Chancellor's nuptials had not been celebrated before events in the Near East had produced a European crisis of the first magnitude. The Treaty of London, as had been agreed by the newly-formed Triple Alliance, was presented at Constantinople for acceptance; and at the same time the French and British Admirals in the Mediterranean were instructed to insist upon an armistice. The Sultan procrastinated; the sailors pursued their instructions; and the Greeks pursued their offensive. A more explosive situation can with difficulty be conceived; and Admiral Codrington may be excused if he mismanaged an affair that would have taxed an experienced diplomatist. Could reciprocal pledges have been obtained from the shifty negotiators with whom he had to deal, something might perhaps have been accomplished without resorting to blows; but mediation was hardly possible between parties so deeply embittered. Whilst the Greek was assenting to an armistice, the Egyptian would have none of it; and Codrington had no sooner induced the Moslem fleets under pressure to lie quiet—at least until orders arrived from Constantinople—than the Christians must needs let loose a flotilla and sink a Turkish squadron. To avoid the extension of hostilities which this action promised to provoke the English Admiral, his French colleague consenting, drove back to port and there held prisoner the allied fleets of Sultan and Pasha. The sight of burning villages, the ambiguity of their instructions, the arrival of a Russian contingent of vessels, meanwhile emboldened

[1] "Lettres à la Comtesse Lieven," p. 129.

the counsels of the Christian commanders. The Admirals resolved, if possible, to bluff Ibrahim into the evacuation of the Morea and the dismissal of his ships to their home stations. Their threats were, however, parried by evasions; and they were presently compelled to some kind of action. Thus, though not intending to make war, the Allied Admirals brought their ships, with the decks cleared for battle, into Navarino Bay. The five fleets—the British, French and Russian on the one hand, the Turkish and Egyptian on the other— now lay close together; and the moral tension exploded the guns. The demonstration turned into an engagement; the engagement into an overwhelming disaster for the Porte and the Pasha. On the 20th of October, 1827, there was thus unexpectedly fought a battle which the Austrian Chancellor declared at the time to be the inauguration of a new era[1] and which a great student of the period has not hesitated to characterise, both on account of its immediate and its ultimate consequences, as one of the decisive battles of the world.[2]

To the eye of vision there drifted that autumn morning into Navarino Bay alongside of the Allied fleets the ghostly bark of British Diplomacy; the phantom form of the transient and embarrassed Goderich like some ensign of incompetence at its prow, the dead hand of Canning upon its tiller, the slumbering image of Dudley recumbent in its stern. Whilst the Russians had reason to congratulate themselves upon fresh prospects of fishing in troubled waters and the French upon a little blaze of glory, the British Cabinet had nothing about which to be pleased. The policy of mediation between the belligerents, which they had preferred to Metternich's plan of pacification either by the establishment of Greek independence or, more wisely as it seemed to him, by bringing all the pressure of the Concert to bear upon the Porte to set its house in order, had produced a new crisis in the decline of the Turkish Empire, and this under conditions peculiarly calculated to entangle the cause of European peace in the aims of Russian policy. Before the year was out the Emperor Nicholas had proposed to march upon Constantinople in order to recommend the Treaty of London; the Allied Ambassadors had been recalled; and the Sultan for his part, after ineffectually demanding compensation and apology for the loss of his armada, had raised the banner of Islam and declared a holy war against the Infidel. It was no wonder that the ineffectual Goderich, with the supreme international question of the century staring him

[1] "Mémoires," IV, p. 403.   [2] Alison Phillips, "Camb. Mod. Hist.," X, p. 196.

full in the face, gave place as the New Year dawned to Wellington.

Metternich hailed the change of ministry in England with satisfaction. He had not ceased to represent to the Porte that the only sensible thing to do was to cease from hostilities with the Greeks and to institute in the Morea a new régime which, whilst leaving the Turks in military control, would place the civil administration under a governor or governors of rayah—that is, of non-Moslem —origin. Tribute was still, as he planned the settlement, to be paid to the Sultan; and the distinctive, racial term Greek was to be avoided. His advice, however, fell upon deaf ears, and in the winter of 1828 he turned hopefully to the Wellington Administration, in which, however, Dudley still officiated as Foreign Secretary, with the suggestion that, if the Sultan remained obstinate, the European Powers should recognise the independence of a Greece limited to the Morea and to certain islands of the Greek Archipelago and should afford to this State, as they could easily do, sufficient military protection to sustain it against Turkish aggression. Such defensive measures, as he indicated in his despatch, were greatly to be preferred to a direct declaration of war against Turkey, since an offensive might easily extend in a manner that no one could foresee and bring the whole shaky structure of the Turkish Empire crashing down upon the Vienna settlement.

These ideas, preferring as they did in the first instance a conservative treatment of the problem but, accepting, in the alternative, a nationalist solution, represented the conclusions of an open and judicious mind. Neither Wellington nor Nicholas, however, had any use for them. The Duke and the Emperor still clung to the plan that they had themselves negotiated at St. Petersburg in the spring of 1826, though there remained this vast practical difference between them—that Nicholas was ready, and Wellington was not, to impose it upon the Sultan by force of arms. A position had, therefore, at length been reached which the policies of Metternich and Canning had been alike interested in evading but for want of co-operation had failed disastrously to avoid. Russia was about to act and to act alone. Declaring that he coveted no conquests, that he sought no more than treaty rights and commercial facilities, that he abhorred the Greeks, and that he stood firmly by the principles of the Holy Alliance and would give no assent to Greek independence, Nicholas in the May of 1828 caused his armies to cross the Pruth and by so doing caused European diplomacy in the East to cross its Rubicon. The dissolution of Turkey had begun.

Not, of course, that either then or later, the process of dismemberment was to be as rapid as people supposed! Metternich, who
in 1828 had imagined that Nicholas would attain his goal without
difficulty and inflict, not perhaps, in view of his assurances, any
crippling loss of territory,[1] but the more deadly wound of a crushing
tribute or indemnity, was as much out in his calculations as others.
The Turks put up an excellent fight; the Russian giant, like so many
giants both in fact and fiction, proved less formidable than had been
expected; and the war dragged through two summers and was only
won in the end by a bold, not to say temerarious move on the part
of the Russian commander.

The European Chancelleries, meanwhile, watched the course of
hostilities with jealous eyes. Metternich, of course, ever since
Wellington came into power, had been working for that collaboration between Austria and England which the Canning Administration had unwisely abandoned; and the supersession of the
incapable Dudley at the British Foreign Office by his old friend
Aberdeen meant that the British Government was of the same mind
as himself. The new Foreign Secretary indeed assured the Austrian
Ambassador in so many words that at the root of his policy lay the
notion of a diplomatic accord with Austria and not with Russia, to
which country, he added, England was now only attached by "that
deplorable treaty."[2] Deplorable it might be, but Metternich was too
good a diplomatist to think that England could hastily disentangle
herself from the Triple Alliance without disadvantage or that her
hold upon the Russian Government could be safely and suddenly
relaxed.[3] And in fact, whilst Russia was pushing or trying to push
through the Balkans, the Western Powers, by means of a British
naval demonstration before Alexandria and a French landing in the
Gulf of Corinth, were busy clearing the Egyptians out of Greece
and making sure of the Morea. Time and circumstance, however,
were still needed for Metternich's alternative policy of Greek
independence to supersede the project of Greek autonomy under
Turkish suzerainty embodied in the Treaty of London and still
dominant in Wellington's less mobile mind. By slow degrees only
did practical considerations vindicate the justice of Metternich's
vision. In March 1829 the successes of General Church, commanding
the Greek forces, caused the adoption by the Powers of the famous
Arta-Volo line as the frontier of the projected autonomous State;

---

[1] See on this "Mémoires," IV, pp. 482, 483.
[2] Ibid., p. 489.   [3] Ibid., pp. 485, 486.

and in the September following, the collapse of the Turks and the ensuing dictated Peace of Adrianople, which included amongst its provisions the recognition by the Porte of a Greece thus delimited, gave all the honours to Russia. The only way, in these circumstances, of preventing a country still nominally part of the Turkish Empire from becoming a Russian protectorate was to give it complete independence under a sovereign prince. So at least Metternich argued and so Aberdeen agreed. By a new Protocol of February 1830 the extent of the proposed State was, however, reduced to balance its growth in status. But the Greeks themselves had still to be reckoned with. Dissatisfied now with the exiguity of the new Greece as before with the limitation of its authority, they rejected the one plan as they had rejected the other. Just at this point, however, the July Revolution in France struck in and for a time submerged the Greek Insurrection.

In this way, then, had Canning's policy worked out in south-eastern Europe. It proved hardly more fortunate in the south-west. There, as the reader will recall, Doña Maria da Gloria had in the spring of 1827 been set up as Queen by British bayonets. Her uncle remained to be reckoned with. Of that handsome young man Metternich had on the whole formed a favourable opinion. Yet, although he credited Dom Miguel with good parts and a good disposition, he took certain precautions, at the instance of the British Government, before he allowed him to leave Vienna to take up his duties as Regent. The Prince was not only sworn to the Portuguese Constitution but betrothed to Dom Pedro's daughter. Among the accomplishments that he had acquired in Austria was not, unfortunately, included the obligation to keep his word. He arrived in Portugal, assumed the Regency, repeated his oath and then, as soon as the British troops had been recalled by Wellington's Administration, allowed the force of public opinion to raise him, as in truth it passionately desired to do, to the throne. The old Cortes took the place of the new-fangled Chambers, and by that time-honoured assembly Dom Miguel was acclaimed as king. Better men than he was have done worse things of the kind; but the affair was nevertheless, as Metternich thought, discreditable, and the Austrian Minister was withdrawn from Lisbon. The new King's popularity was, however, indisputable; and Metternich tried to make the best of a bad job by suggesting that Dom Miguel should retain the crown for the present and share it with his niece in the future—as soon, that is, as she was old enough to become his wife.

This plan met with no success. Doña Maria returned to Brazil; only among the islands of the Azores were her claims to sovereignty seriously taken; and her cause appeared to be lost when the back-wash of the July Revolution raised her once again to the throne of Portugal.

XIV

THE GREAT STORM

IN the dawn of the same decade which saw the crescent-moon of Turkey begin to pale and the eastern sun, like a symbol of hope and freedom, wake again into intellectual beauty the dreaming hills of Hellas, Shelley, musing within reach of the Leaning Tower and the Mediterranean Sea, had seized his lute and sung almost his last, perhaps his loveliest song:—

> "The world's great age begins anew,
>   The golden years return,
> The earth doth like a snake renew
>   Her winter weeds outworn:
> Heaven smiles, and faiths and empires gleam
> Like wrecks of a dissolving dream."

The notes of Ariel's enchanted music found, however, no echo in Metternich's practical mind. There rose before him no vision of a dream-city, violet-crowned, above some new Ilissus; nor did his inward eye behold a golden age returning. If faith must fail and empires fall, he knew of no golden fleece that Humanity might still pursue. Darkness and sorrow, disintegration or decline bounded the horizon to west and east; and beyond the Pillars of Hercules, as between the Bosphorous and Dardanelles, his mind discovered no joyous Utopias, but rather Canning's new-formed Republics in restless revolution and the old theocracy of Mohammed in rapid decay. The world might be weary of its past; but hate and death would not be exorcised by a poet's cry to cease, nor men stay their hands from slaughter for all the fancies of an ineffectual angel.

Trying to see things as they really were, Metternich recognised before the decade closed that their revolutionary aspect had grown more formidable. His despatches and his correspondence alike bear witness to the fact that even as early as the summer of 1828 he was even more alarmed by the situation in France than by the situation in the Near East.[1] "God knows," he wrote to the promising son and heir, who was to fall a victim in the following year to consumption, "where France is going to. If it was only a matter of the direct interests of the country, the stranger need pay no attention;

---

[1] "Mémoires," IV, pp. 423, 481.

it is otherwise when one has to do with the influence which this kingdom exerts upon the whole body of society."

The Martignac Ministry was at that date in power; and Martignac was playing, as Villèle had played before him, a shrewd and cautious game which was as well calculated as anything could be to avoid the unresolved problem of the French Restoration—the unresolved problem whether King Charles, whose brother had been restored by Europe, reigned by the grace of God or the will of the French People. But, wisely as Martignac manœuvred and eloquently as Martignac charmed, the issue could not be shirked. Liberals and Clericals alike were profoundly dissatisfied with a Minister who held the middle way between them, and the King, himself none too well pleased, turned at last to one who was, if possible, "plus royaliste que le roi." Polignac became Premier in August 1829.

This man, who is remembered as an idiot yet whose brief Ministry laid the foundation of the French Colonial empire, was, as a French student has lately pointed out, not precisely a fool. As an ambassador distinguished, as an administrator capable, Polignac at another date might have made a different name for himself in the history of Europe. He showed, however, remarkable stupidity in challenging at this particular juncture the cleverest corporation in France. Talent, of which the Restoration possessed so much, was in that age of political faith, if we must not say political credulity, conspicuously evident in journalism. Polignac, not content with Ordinances to dismiss the Chamber and fake the elections, must needs also try to muzzle the Press. France was not Germany, nor the year 1830 the year 1819; yet the severity of the censorship exceeded in some respects that of the Carlsbad Decrees. Metternich's comment upon the work of this too zealous disciple, when he heard of it, is significant:—"The measure relating to newspapers and periodical publications can only be provisional; without some modification it would really be impossible to continue the publication of a paper."[1] The French Ministers, he told the Emperor, have courage, but between courage and capacity there is often a gulf fixed. We may perhaps suspect with his biographer[2] that the memory of the one entirely competent French administrator he had known still influenced his judgment of French affairs and that unlike Chateaubriand, he thought, as indeed the eventual advent of the Second Empire showed that he had some right to think, the Bonapartes better fitted to rule France after the Revolution than the Bourbons.

By a singular chance, when the news reached him of the days in

Paris that have passed into history by the name of "les Trois Glorieuses," Metternich found himself within reach of Carlsbad, where Nesselrode, latterly somewhat estranged from him but now again his friend, was residing. Thus it came about that, whilst the Revolution gathered strength in its ancient home, the Austrian Chancellor and the Russian Vice-Chancellor took counsel against it in a town already associated with counter-revolutionary deliberations. Nesselrode would have nothing to do with Metternich's larger project for a revival of the Old Quadruple Alliance,[1] but there was concocted between them a little entente which, memorised at the time upon a convenient scrap of paper, goes by the name of "the *chiffon* of Carlsbad." It was agreed that France should be left to manage her own affairs, provided she made no attack either upon the geographical settlement or the intellectual peace of Europe. The *chiffon* did not reflect the Russian Emperor's more combative attitude to the Revolution in France; and its importance lies rather in the fact that it represents the reluctant adoption by Metternich, as an alternative to his earlier and happier design of a concert with the Western Powers, of the idea of a close political co-operation between the three Great Monarchies of the East.

Meanwhile there had stepped to the front of the tumultuous scene in Paris a figure long familiar to the Austrian Chancellor —his adversary on the field of Jemappes, his correspondent in the days of the French emigration, his client for a place in the Austrian army in 1809, his host in the Paris of 1825—the figure of the "bourgeois" king. At that critical juncture, when Royalism and Radicalism were fighting for the soul of France, this stout, shrewd, elderly gentleman of fifty-six, with his thrifty habits, his matter-of-fact mind and his fine store of information, emerged from the Palais Royal, rode down to the Hôtel de Ville, exchanged embraces with the time-honoured Lafayette in sight of the crowd below and then quietly took charge of the Revolution, which indeed at the moment resembled nothing so much as a dangerous lunatic in need of a keeper. Within a fortnight he had reached a position for the sake of which one of his ancestors was supposed to have become a poisoner and another had incurred the shame of a regicide. With no better credentials than some Bourbon blood that was not quite indisputable and a character most happily adapted to the circumstance of the hour, the duc d'Orléans was called, as the phrase went, to the throne.

[1] "Mémoires," V, p. 196.

In Louis Philippe a king had at last been found to satisfy the
needs of the doctrinaires—of that heterogeneous band of political
opportunists whose leadership was then passing into the hands of
Guizot, of Casimir-Périer, of Molé and of Broglie, and whose
principles were strangely compounded of Jansenist theology,
Scottish philosophy, German poetry, the reflections of Madame de
Staël and the sentiments of Chateaubriand, to say nothing of
some ingredients derived from the past history of England and
supposed applicable to the present politics of France. These were
they who now gloriously triumphed and by whom the Republican
horse and the Royalist rider had alike been thrown into the sea.

Metternich never ceased to exhibit a deep-seated scepticism about
the results of "les Trois Glorieuses." "The partisans of the *juste
milieu*," he observed even two years later, "wished to reduce the
results of those days to the measure of a palace-revolution; they
were mistaken and would not be able to extricate themselves
without a counter-revolution."[1] And he declared with conviction
that the reign of Louis Philippe was an agony of uncertain length.[2]
It was a curiously clever forecast. For on the face of things there
seemed no reason why a Duke of Orleans in France should not be
able to build as successfully as a Prince of Orange in England. It
looked as if he only needed to be able; and he was, as it happened,
extremely able.

Within a few weeks of his accession the new sovereign had proved
himself, indeed, to be a considerable diplomatist. Throughout his
reign he was in reality his own Foreign Minister; and his diplomatic
moves from the first showed that he possessed high qualifications for
that office. From the autocracies of Eastern Europe he had little to
hope; his orientation or, if we choose to have it so, his occidentation
was towards England; and he quickly placed his ablest diplomatist at the point of the utmost consequence to his fortunes.
Within six days of his recognition by the British Government
Talleyrand was established at the French Embassy in London. There
arose consequently between the two great constitutional kingdoms
of Western Europe an understanding which was very apparent
whenever Aberdeen was at the British Foreign Office and the
complete loss of which in 1846 promoted the fall of the Orleans
Monarchy.

On the day that saw the rule of Louis Philippe recognised by
Wellington's Administration—on the 1st September, that is, of

---

[1] "Mémoires," V, p. 303.   [2] *Ibid.*, p. 310.

1830—Metternich sent Nesselrode a few lines that betrayed his inmost feelings and have become historic. "For the rest," he wrote, "my most secret thought is that the old Europe has come to the beginning of the end. Resolved to perish with it, I shall know how to do my duty; and this phrase is not mine alone but also that of the Emperor. From another point of view the new Europe is not yet begun; between the end and the beginning there lies chaos."[1] In spite of these forebodings, however, the Austrian Government a few days later followed the British example and took the practical step of recognising the new King of the French and the return of the Tricolour. .

Meantime the spirit of revolt, if not of chaos, had crossed the frontier between France and Belgium and become active in a country which liked its new Dutch masters ill and remembered its French ones kindly. The fusion of the Netherlands, with its varieties of race and religion, into a single state, although effected under English influence and with a single eye to defence against French aggression, had been, like the forced union between Norway and Sweden, a great error in the Vienna Settlement; and the summary expulsion of an autocratic sovereign from France inevitably encouraged in the discontented Flemings and Walloons the desire to get rid of a no less autocratic monarch. King William of the Netherlands, though a man of culture and ability, had unluckily belied the regard for nationality and public opinion popularly associated with the House of Orange. His kingdom was no doubt a composite structure in ill-assorted styles; yet a wise man, possessed as he was of prodigious powers under the Constitution, would have made a virtue of diversity. It was the misfortune of King William I that he must have everything fitted to the model of his mind and that this model had been made in Holland. Though his Belgian subjects were at least half as numerous again as his Dutch ones, he made the Hague the seat of government, the court of judicial appeal, and, in violation of the law, the sole place of assembly for the States-General. Dutch Ministers predominated by a great deal in the administration, Dutch officials in the departments of State, Dutch diplomatists in the legations, Dutch officers in the high places of the army. The Dutch language was made official in Belgium; the Dutch debt to an utterly unreasonable extent was shifted on to Belgian shoulders; and the predominantly Dutch Government devised taxes better calculated to affect the poorer classes of the Belgian than the

[1] "Mémoires," V, p. 23.

Dutch population. To make matters worse the King, armed with the weapons of fine, pillory and branding-iron, had long terrorised the Press on the plea of public necessity and in the very year of Revolution had countered an opposition vote on the Budget with a royal decree, depriving six deputies of their seats and salaries. It is, in fact, rather with King Charles I of England than with King Charles X of France that the good man invited comparison.

Religious differences, in which the King's point of view, to be just, deserved fuller and fairer consideration than it received, merely intensified these political disagreements; and at length the Belgians, baited beyond bearing, responded to the cry of "Down with the Dutchmen" and swept the Prince of Orange and his soldiers back from Brussels. Early in October a Provisional Government proclaimed the independence of the country.

It was a critical question for the Orleans Monarchy, still settling into the seat of power, what attitude it should adopt towards these events. Was France, as militant Republicans desired, to join forces with the national movement just beyond her boundaries, to press forward to her "natural" frontier on the Rhine and to regain the lost laurels of the Empire? Or was she to stand by existing treaties, stay within her gates and settle the affairs of Belgium in collaboration with England? Fortunately for her, fortunately for himself, Louis Philippe knew what spirit he was of. The apostle of moderation, of the middle way, of the middle class, decided for the second alternative. The high wind of disturbance dropped quickly in the West. A conference of the Great Powers was arranged and, according to Metternich's principle of locating the deliberations in the country from which the strongest action was to be expected,[1] assembled in London. An armistice was effected between the unimaginative Dutchmen and their inflammable neighbours; the mediation of the High Powers was accepted; and before the year was out the Conference had declared for a dissolution of the Kingdom of the Netherlands. The end of the business, however, was not yet.

Meanwhile the revolutionary storm had been spreading across Europe. The Russian Emperor, convinced believer as he was in legitimist doctrine, had no room in his philosophy for constitutional usurpers. Resolved not to recognise the King of the French, Nicholas prepared to suppress the Revolution by force of arms. With no little ingenuity he required his disaffected Polish subjects

[1] "Mémoires," V, p. 66.

Q

to bear the brunt of the battle. Secret orders were sent to the authorities in Warsaw to be ready for the campaign; and Prussian co-operation was solicited at Berlin. But the Poles, already plotting to throw off a ruler who had failed to satisfy their national expectations either of constitutional government or reunion with Lithuania, were too quick for Nicholas. The projected campaign in the West was planned for Christmas; the intended recruits rose on the vigil of St. Andrew. Thus, as the Emperor was preparing to move against the Revolution, the Revolution sprang upon him, and for the best part of a year his hands were fully occupied.

In the same month of November, which saw Nicholas held in play in Poland, another great Conservative force at the other end of Europe was put out of action. To an eye quick to welcome all that made for stability and all that made for peace, the Catholic Emancipation Act of 1829 had seemed to promise an increase of strength both to the country that approved and the Administration that carried it; and Metternich had written to his old friend, the British Prime Minister, in that sense. But to many English Conservatives, the Duke's *volte-face* on the question wore a very different appearance, and before the following year was out Wellington fell, largely as a result of it. There came into office Lord Grey; and with Lord Grey there followed Lord Palmerston. The one was the apostle of Reform, the other the disciple of Canning. From such as these Metternich had little to hope and something to fear. It may even be that a spite of vengeance had entered into these changes. Behind the appointment of the new Foreign Secretary some have supposed that they discerned the hand of Princess Lieven. It is not impossible; and the lady herself would have assured us that it was true. She had fallen, as we know, out of love with Metternich and was now a little in love with Lord Grey.

Metternich, who to his great grief had lost his second wife in 1829, became, as it happened, once more engaged about this time; and in the depth of that winter of 1830–31 Fifty-seven was wedded to Twenty-six. Apart from this difference of ages, Mélanie de Zichy-Ferraris was well suited to be his wife. Her lineage was unexceptionable, her beauty remarkable, her piety sincere. She represented much that her husband stood for in its fairer form, if not always in its greatest and most gracious ways. Time was to bring out the storm and passion of her nature, the moodier, more bizarre features of her character. Time was to assert that she could be, not only charming and lovable, but haughty and indiscreet.

Time was to accuse her of separating her husband from his less aristocratic friends and impairing by her restlessness the domestic serenity which in the autumn of his life he so earnestly longed for. Let this be as it may; still, with her lively intelligence, her deep affection, her anxious vigilance as his years began to tell upon him, and her great pride in his greatness, she did not come so far short of the recorded aspiration of her wedding-day:—"May God grant me all I have need of to make him happy!"[1] And after thirteen years of marriage he, who was after all the surest judge, felt able to assure her in the tenderest terms that she had never given him anything but happiness.[2] She must presumably have satisfied him to the point of certitude of what he once told Madame Lieven he felt an almost Insurmountable difficulty in believing[3]—that he was loved.

The young bride, at any rate in the first flush of matrimony, found married life agreeable enough, as she sat beside the great man in the little barouche that he loved to drive himself, or as she read Voltaire with him and, to save those troublesome, tired eyes of his, his despatches to him, or again as she did hostess for him when, after his manner of revenge, he invited some embittered political assailant to dine. The Journal of Princess Mélanie, which becomes from this time so great a source of information about Metternich, exhibits, in fact, in its opening passages, all the anxious admiration of the young wife suddenly admitted into the confidences of a world-famous husband. "To-day," she writes, "for the first time since my marriage, I breakfasted alone with Clément; he spoke to me at length of public affairs, initiated me into his ideas and projects; and I was astonished to see how extensive was my ignorance. I wanted to understand him at his first word, to help in all things, to follow his discussions, myself to discuss with him. . . . Gentz interrupted our talk."

That intruder was not, however, always unwelcome. At once a joker and a joke, Gentz was at least no bore; and his constant presence in the house provided comic relief in private life as well as tragic reflection upon public events. He could be impressed by Metternich to blow soap-bubbles to amuse the little motherless Richard, the innocent cause of Princess Antoinette's death in childbirth; he might be made the victim of facetious mystifications in which, to Princess Mélanie's amazement, the Austrian Chancellor found time to conspire with the Prussian King; more generally, however, he

[1] "Mémoires," V, p. 88.   [2] Ibid., VII, p. 3.
[3] "Lettres à la Comtesse Lieven," p. 30.

was engaged in improvising by no means acceptable responses to Metternich's litany of lamentation over that "painful agony of this sad world" which, as poor Mélanie discovered, formed the staple of their talk. At no time, however, had the faithful Achates been so greatly divided from his leader as in these last months of his life. His friends alienated, his fortunes impaired by speculation, his health wrecked by nerves, Gentz had lost his old fighting spirit, and in his latter days was for coming to terms with the Revolution at least as it showed itself in France. His views, as the Princess found, caused her husband no little annoyance, yet, when a year later he muddled his life away by neglecting his medicines, his old chief, who had been with him in his last hours, was crushed by the blow. But of the monument planned to Gentz's memory Metternich made a new milestone on the road of life. From that time Princess Mélanie thought that she noticed a change in his habits and conversation. He spoke to her of the loss of friends, of the loss of collaborators, and, much to her distress, of the advent of death. These premonitions, however, were more than premature.

The storm, which in 1830 had blown one or two worthless princelings out of power in Central Germany, was in 1831 blowing to a stronger gale in Baden and the Rhineland and in Italy had reached the force of a hurricane. Marie Louise, the Emperor's daughter, was swept out of Parma—that poor ducal substitute for the imperial throne of France; Duke Francis, the Emperor's first-cousin, was hurled from his sovereignty in Modena; and in the States of the Church there was enough disturbance to make the Catholic world tremble for the safety of all that was secular in the sovereignty of the Holy See. A savage outbreak of cholera in Hungary added a further touch of horror to the spectacle as from the windows of old Vienna the citizens of a rocking civilisation watched the elements at play. In the background of the storm heralds of revolt were to be seen advancing. It was in those days that Mazzini, released from the prison at Savona, where his only companions had been the Word of God, the sharp speech of Tacitus and the bitter-sweet songs of Byron, settled at Marseilles the better to excogitate, undisturbed, the gospel of the Risorgimento; that Heine, fearing the wrath to come from Prussian hands, fled to Paris, to mock in safety the crumbling structure of the German Reich; and that La Mennais, with the ardent vision before his eyes of a Pope who should proclaim in organ-notes the infallible mind of the People, passed from the closed offices of the *Avenir* to the Court of Rome, only to be repulsed, wisely enough, no doubt, by that newly-elected Pope of whom Metternich thought so much.[1]

France, as these things showed, was still the spring of intellectual not less than of political change; and Metternich did well to watch it. He could not hope, as he well knew, to stem the tide of revolution, should the flooded river one day burst its banks; but for the moment the waters were locked and the flood-gates holding, whilst in the lock-keeper was to be recognised that same astute person who had passed so bravely down from the Palais Royal to the Hôtel de Ville in the preceding July.

In that first year of his reign Louis Philippe, in order to retain his post, was obliged to seek some accommodation both with the Republicans in Paris who, when the Poles rose in insurrection, saw "July" again in December, and with the Great Powers of Eastern Europe, who were no less busy in rough-handling their revolutionary subjects than he was in smoothing down his. He faced in consequence now this way, now that; and, if his integrity suffered, his dexterity must be admitted. Planning his policy as he did, both within and without, upon English models, he inscribed the legend of non-intervention across his banner. Here was the old challenge of Canning to Metternich. The French Foreign Minister repeated it in the most explicit manner at the date of the Italian risings. If his words meant anything definite, it was that, if Austria moved to repress the Revolution in Italy, France would place herself at its head. Metternich was confronted by a critical dilemma. The principles of the Counter-Revolution and prestige of the Austrian Empire were alike deeply involved in re-settling the Habsburgs in Modena and Parma and making the Pope master in the States of the Church; yet, with Russia busy, England malevolently neutral and France prepared to fight, there was some danger that the Austrian armies might be unequal to the occasion. The sources of diplomacy were, however, not yet exhausted. He even saw in the international situation the chance of a brilliant diplomatic stroke. Against a Bourbon with a bad title it was fair enough to pit a Bonaparte with a good one.

The family and connections of Napoleon were already busily fishing in the troubled waters of Europe. The two real or reputed sons of Louis Bonaparte—one of them some day to rank as the Third Napoleon—had been active among the revolutionaries of Rome; in the West the son of Eugène Beauharnais—the duc de

[1] Gregory XVI. "Mémoires," V, p. 149.

Leuchtenberg—had appeared as a candidate for the throne of Belgium; and in addition Metternich had for some months possessed among his papers a letter from old King Joseph offering to collaborate with him in raising the duc de Reichstadt to the throne of France.[1] The Eaglet was caged at Schönbrunn—a frail bird, its life even then drawing to a close, and its history destined, as Rostand has taught us in plaintive numbers, to be no more than that of an unhappy child. Just, however, at this political juncture, in the spring of 1831, the shadow of the Second Napoleon like some ghostly presage flits across the tangled path of Louis Philippe. Metternich had raised his hand as if to unbar the door that held the Eaglet captive. "Our enemy," the Chancellor wrote to Apponyi, the Austrian Ambassador in Paris, "is anarchy; our friends those who repel it. The day that we are driven back into our entrenchments and that we are reduced to nothing but a choice between the evils with which anarchy threatens us, we ought to choose the one that least compromises our own existence. That one we hold in our hands."[2] The gesture was enough for Louis Philippe. As events still distant were to prove, the true peril of the Orleans Monarchy lay, neither in a Royal Restoration nor yet in a Girondin Republic, but in a democratic dictatorship with the Napoleonic legend behind it. Confronted by Metternich with the prospect of the duc de Leuchtenberg as a candidate for the throne of Belgium and the duc de Reichstadt for that of Italy or even France, the King of the French reduced the revolutionary tendencies of his Ministers to academic proportions. Lafitte was replaced by Casimir-Périer as President of the Council, and, though Sebastiani remained at the Foreign Office, it was with clipped wings and tempered pratings. Metternich had secured to all intents and purposes a free hand in Italy. Neither there nor elsewhere had the Revolution thenceforward anything substantial to hope from Louis Philippe. There remained only the question of saving the face of France.

Princess Metternich, if she understood the real purport of what she was hearing and reading, had thus seen her husband score one of his finest diplomatic successes within the first few weeks of her marriage. He had been pitted against the cleverest monarch in Europe, coached by the oldest of diplomatic hands; but he had proved a match both for Louis Philippe and Talleyrand. She had after all some excuse for the naïve entry made one day in her journal after she had watched her husband write his despatches and heard

[1] "Mémoires," V, p. 159.   [2] Ibid., p. 156.

him expound their significance:—"This man is admirable. May God preserve him to me and to the world." Devoted to him as she had grown, she could ill bear to see him run the dangers of the ensuing autumn with cholera rife in Vienna. Already she had begun to perceive the spectre that haunts all fond wives with much older husbands.

The great storm, meanwhile, was gradually subsiding; and it was now mainly a matter of sweeping up the wreckage. The Powers of East and West undertook by mutual consent the jobs that were nearest them or touched them most closely. To the Western Powers, on account of proximity, fell the regulation of the issue in Belgium and, on account of their maritime and oriental interests, a large share in the fate of Greece. Russia, with a voice in Greek affairs, exercised, in spite of some murmuring in France, all the rights of a conqueror in Poland. Austria, predominant in Italy, enjoyed in Germany the full support of Prussia, where Ancillon, the distinguished historian of political revolution and a convinced disciple of Metternich in politics, occupied from the date of the July Revolution the post of Minister of Foreign Affairs.

As a result of these diversities of operation the work of the Powers lacked all real cohesion. The liberation of Belgium from the grip of Holland and of Greece from the grasp of Turkey was balanced by the subjection of Poland to a closer hug on the part of the Russian Bear. The principle upon which Metternich had so perpetually insisted as the first principle of international order—the maintenance of the treaty rights of reigning sovereigns—had been openly flouted in reference to the Netherlands by the London Conference, which, not content with mediatorial powers, had gradually assumed coercive jurisdiction. Protocols had succeeded one another with a rapidity that did more credit to the industry than the intelligence of "Protocol Palmerston"—protocols of which the most notable were declared to be "fundamental and irrevocable" when the King of the Netherlands accepted them and were then found to be marvellously elastic and convertible so soon as the King of the Belgians refused them. During the course of these negotiations the Dutch took up arms and gave the Belgians a good beating; while the French slipped an army across the frontier to keep alive the embryo Kingdom for which, after the rejection by the Belgian Congress of the duc de Leuchtenberg and by the London Conference of the duc de Nemours, a king had been found in the sage Leopold of Coburg, the widowed husband of Princess Charlotte and once in a fair way to anticipate his nephew as Prince Consort of England. The Conference still kept pace with circumstance. In face of the Dutch victory a new protocol of twenty-four articles more favour-able to Holland took the place of the eighteen whose orientation had been towards Belgium. A treaty was produced which was once more declared to be final and irrevocable, but of which the terms did not appear to be based upon any other principle than expediency. To hold Europe together, however, the plenipotentiaries of the great Eastern Powers associated themselves with England and France in insisting that King William and King Leopold must agree. The King of the Belgians was wise and gave in; but not all the diplomatic authority of the Powers, nor the ships of the King of England blockading the mouth of the Scheldt, nor the soldiers of the King of the French besieging the city of Antwerp, could win the assent of the obstinate Dutchman. It took, in fact, no less than a decade to show him that he was beaten. He was doubtless an obstinate, fine fellow.

The Greek Insurrection was brought to a conclusion more easily than the Belgian. With the Turks helpless and tractable, the Russians engaged in Poland, the French politically in the pocket of England, and the Whigs in power at Westminster, the year 1831 presented conditions peculiarly favourable to the attainment of Greek aspira-tions. Palmerston wisely secured for the new Hellenes all they could reasonably require—the Arta-Volo line as a frontier and a sovereign-prince at the head of their State. The Prince selected had a fancy to be king; and that dignity also was added to him. Doubtless he needed all that could be done to increase his consequence—this Bavarian boy of eighteen suddenly set, by the common counsel of England, France and Russia, over a people somewhat ruthlessly described by a modern historian as at that date "a race of brigands and herdsmen."[1] Metternich for his part disclaimed all responsibility. "You are certainly not ignorant, M. le Baron," he wrote to the Foreign Minister of Bavaria, "that the Emperor has taken no part whatever in the transaction or the negotiations that led up to it."[2] But apart from the selection of the King, the Austrian Chancellor had no reason to regret the settlement. It had proceeded along lines that he had been the first to point out and incidentally had terminated for practical purposes the inconvenient association of the three Protecting Powers in Near-Eastern politics.

If affairs in Greece showed the constitutional monarchies of the

[1] Alison Philips, "Camb. Mod. Hist.," X, p. 204.   [2] "Mémoires," V, p. 382.

West working in association with Russian autocracy, affairs in Poland drove them apart. There the Revolution, momentarily successful, had ended in catastrophic defeat. Not only were the large liberties hoped for not acquired, but even the poor liberties possessed were lost. Metternich, as we have seen, had never approved the Polish Partitions, and the notion of a buffer state of Poland between Austria and Russia did not lie altogether outside his political philosophy. But in 1831, with half Europe, as we say, seeing red, all his diplomacy was directed towards tightening the understanding between the three Eastern Powers which he had knotted with Nesselrode at Carlsbad in 1830. His treatment of the Poles is not above reproach. Their attitude towards Nicholas was ambiguous, but his dealings with them were ambidexterous. He appears to have received their confidences, yet not to have considered himself precluded from giving away their plans. But, as his advice to them was always to negotiate and submit, they had no reason to suppose him to be more their friend than the friend of Russia.

Metternich at any time was the last man to appeal to in the hour of revolt and at this time as little so as ever. For Austria was at the moment pretty heavily engaged with the Revolution both in Italy and Germany. Austrian troops had barely replaced the dispossessed Habsburgs upon the thrones of Parma and Modena before their help was required in the Papal States. To enter the Romagna, to occupy Bologna, to suppress the insurgents and to reinstate the Pope was no great matter for disciplined forces, but to teach those to rule who had no gift for ruling was a more difficult affair. "The Papal Government," Metternich observes caustically in one of his despatches, "does not know how to govern; it does not even know how to administer a spoilt city like Bologna."[1] In that devastating defect, common at the time to most Italian Governments rather than characteristic of the ecclesiastical intellect, lay the essence of the problem. Time was, if we take the trouble to reflect, when Cardinals and Bishops had furnished the Courts of Europe with as competent statesmen as they have ever possessed; and besides, as Metternich pointed out for Palmerston's instruction, holy orders had never been necessary at Rome to fill the first posts in the administration. This point was worth making. Consalvi, perhaps the greatest Cardinal-Secretary of the nineteenth century, only took minor orders; the Prince of Belvedere, after twenty years in the Sacred

[1] "Mémoires," V, p. 343.

College, left it to become the father of a family;[1] the whole of the
prelatura, from among which officials were recruited, wore indeed,
as the members of the diplomatic corps had also been accustomed to
do within Metternich's recollection,[2] the ecclesiastical habit, but
were as much laymen for all their clothing as any civil servant of
to-day who has kept clear of the bonds of matrimony. What was
really needed to make the States of the Church into a sound working
concern was to arouse once more in its native home the political
genius of the Roman people—a genius not as a rule long contented
with democratic forms, but capable of satisfying the three crying
needs of sound finance, of incorrupt justice, and of civic education
as set out in Massimo d'Azeglio's contemporary commentary upon
Manzoni's visions.

The diplomatic representatives of the four great Continental
Powers in Rome put their heads together and, with such aid as the
British Agent in Tuscany was permitted by Palmerston to afford
them, produced a plan of reform in which the emphasis rested upon
an increase of the elective element in the local and of the lay element
in the central government of the Papal States. This scheme the
Cardinal-Secretary approved without show of enthusiasm and promulgated without desire of effect. The Austrian troops withdrew;
the Ambassadors ceased to deliberate; and the Administration went
on as before. But, whilst reformation tarried, revolution spurred
ahead. Once more outside help was appealed for by the Papal
Government; and this time Metternich, though without thought
of conquest, resolved to make an end. Bologna was reoccupied
and for an indefinite period.

The jealousy of the French was aroused. What the Austrians had
done by request, they resolved to do without it. Ancona was seized
and a French force installed there. Before this uncalled-for violation
of neutral rights Metternich, unprepared as he was to convert his
protests into hostilities, was at first helpless. The death of Casimir-
Périer, however, quickly eased the situation. The French who had
appeared in the light of Liberals assumed, with the gradual gravita-
tion to the right of the Orleans Monarchy, the colour of Conservatives. Their presence, meanwhile, was turned to account by the
Papacy. The Papal Government maintained that freedom was a
condition of reform and that, so long as the unsolicited occupation
continued, freedom was wanting. The argument made no impression
upon Louis Philippe or Guizot. For the six years that the Austrians

---

[1] "Mémoires," V, p. 377.   [2] *Ibid.*, p. 377.

remained in Bologna, the French were to be found in Ancona. Their continued presence and their lack of performance gave the precise measure of the French King's feeling for the Italian revolutionaries or in fact for revolutionaries of any kind.

A new year had come in whilst these various events were in progress, and in May 1832 the Revolution, which had been for some while sinuously moving through Germany, raised its head to strike. At the Castle of Hambach in the Bavarian Rhineland, where French influence was notoriously strong, an influential journalist, one Siebenpfeiffer, collected a vast crowd of persons, some of them doubtless, as usually in such cases, full of divine, but others of devilish discontent. The health of Lafayette was drunk, a German tricolour was displayed and the cause of armed revolt received the suffrages of the assembly. Metternich asked for nothing better. He was now not only ready to intervene but possessed of a reason for doing so. A month later almost to a day he persuaded the Federal Diet by a unanimous vote to pass Six Articles of which the broad effect was to enable the Confederation in its corporate capacity to intervene whenever a sovereign attempted to make constitutional concessions to his subjects or whenever his subjects attempted to extract constitutional concessions from him. The validity of this proceeding turned upon the interpretation of the Final Act of the Vienna Congress. By certain articles of that Act, as Metternich argued, the concentration of sovereignty in the hands of the head of the State had been required and the interference of the Confederation to maintain the domestic peace of each individual State had been approved. But, if the letter of the constitution was still preserved, there can be little question that its custom was changed and that, just as by the American Civil War the American States lost something of their original sovereignty to the Federal Government, so here the ultimate seat of sovereignty was shifted from the local to the central authority. It was a move that the Monarchs of Austria and Prussia, standing as they did in regard to some part of their dominions entirely outside the German Confederation and yet counting for so much more than most of their fellow-sovereigns within it, had no occasion to regret.

Palmerston, taking his stand in like manner upon the Final Act, raised objection to these developments. The Revolution of 1832 in Great Britain, preserved though it had been by the complementary efforts of William IV and Wellington from any overt violation of constitutional forms, had caused England once more to forge ahead of France in the work of political adjustment to new conditions; and the leadership of the popular movement in Europe had passed insensibly that year from the French King to the British Foreign Secretary. Partly doubtless on this account, partly by virtue of a constitutional tendency to meddle which perpetually overcame in his case the English tradition of non-intervention, 'Palmerston took upon him to interfere in an affair that another man, with all the accredited authorities in Germany agreed against him, might well have preferred to leave alone. Metternich's answer, however, to the British objector was temperate, thoughtful and interesting. He pointed out with much good sense that the interests of the great Sea-Power which Palmerston spoke for harmonised perfectly with those of the great Continental Power which he himself represented; that their differences arose, therefore, not from positions, but from principles and lay in the moral and not the political sphere; and that the conservative principle must lie at the base of Austrian policy both internal and external. He added, however, that this principle, like other sound principles, did not admit of being followed to excess; that they who accused Austria of wishing to march backwards or to follow "an absurd stationary system" either were unacquainted with or calumniated her; and that her influence both within and without the German Confederation, whilst eschewing what was chimerical, took account of the needs of the time. The distinction between the English and Austrian attitudes lay not, as was supposed in England, in the difference between concession and repression. On the contrary, the essence of Austrian policy was to be found in the adoption of a *preventive* system precisely to avoid a *repressive* one, just as the essence of sound government was to be found, not in concessions involving as they must the idea of some detraction from the established sovereign rights of the Crown, but in acts tending to a progressive amelioration and in conduct at once just, simple and sagacious. He deprecated, however, any purely theoretical discussions. It was with principles of government as with dogmas of religion; discussion was often dangerous and always futile. The talent of cabinets consisted in living in peace and harmony; and the surest way to accomplish this was by eliminating subjects of probable difference and pursuing objects of common interest. He did not, as he said, for a moment arrogate to himself the right to scrutinise British theories; and he asked that England should extend the same unrestricted freedom of motive to Austria. For practical purposes it was significant that the two countries were agreed in regarding repression as the hardest of necessities, in ensuing peace, and in maintaining all that could claim legal existence.[1]

The old statesman was prescribing for one who was yet young in diplomatic experience, whose distinctive character, as he saw, was a mixture of arrogance and naïveté, and with whom the aged Talleyrand, at that time winding up his long career as Ambassador at the Court of St. James's, was playing as with a tyro.[2] A few months later he wrote in something of the same sense for the benefit of another novice in the conduct of foreign affairs—the duc de Broglie, who had been made Foreign Minister in Soult's new Administration. Speaking with appreciative comprehension of the difficulties with which the French Government was confronted, he observed that from a consideration of the condition of things in France there emerged a truth which he had long preached upon the housetops. "It is," he continued, "that there exists between Governments of whatever sort these are, a solidarity of interests which cannot be ignored as a rule except to their cost or to the particular cost of the Government which is blind enough not to see the need of this solidarity and to behave accordingly."[3] He calls this his profession of belief; it is rather the first clause in the gospel of civilisation. The moment was opportune for recalling it. A proposal for a conference, from which Metternich had hoped greater things than the reduction of armaments that it was designed to bring about, had come to nothing; and the world was going on its way with the old leer on its lips and Palmerston contending with Metternich for that primacy in European counsels, of which the site of the conference had become the symbol.[4]

Meanwhile, though the face of Europe was scarred, the great storm had blown by. The lightnings and thunderings and voices of revolt died away in the distance; the cloudbursts ceased; yet the deluge had been drenching, the panic greater than is now remembered. Macaulay, writing only of its incidence on English soil, compared the conditions with those that had prevailed in 1679 and told how a "society . . . but a short time before . . . in a state of perfect repose" had "on a sudden" become "agitated" and had seemed to be "on the verge of dissolution"[5] Yet in England constitutional government was of long standing.

[1] "Mémoires," V, pp. 390–94.   [2] Ibid., pp. 457, 458.
[3] Ibid., p. 465.
[4] See on this C. K. Webster on "Palmerston, Metternich and the European System," (" Proc. of Brit. Acad.," 1934, p. 131).
[5] Essay on Sir William Temple, written in 1838. I think there can be no doubt that the reference, though not specific, is to 1832.

In the circumstances Metternich, as he lay sick in the dark December days of 1832, may have reasonably told himself that he had not over-estimated the perils and possibilities of revolution, and have as reasonably congratulated himself that on the whole Europe had weathered the storm so well. The gods had added yet sixteen years to the term of his political life, but he had looked the end full in the face, and, so far as his personal fortunes were concerned, without fear. Courage, as he had told Mme. Lieven, had never been a difficulty to him. On the field of battle[1] as in the field of affairs he had found that danger raised his spirits.

[1] "Lettres à la Comtesse Lieven," p. 256. Leipzig was perhaps the battle where he had been in peril.

XV

PALMERSTON

It has been said of Metternich that, like Bismarck and like Palmerston, he was no good judge of Eastern affairs.[1] If it was so, a statesman of his generation, bred amidst the commotions of Christian States and busied with the conflicts of first-class Powers, may be better excused for insufficient attention to the progressive decline and impending fall of the Turkish Empire than the great German Chancellor who in a later age recovered from France the hegemony in Europe which Austria lost to her in the 'fifties. The Turkish problem could hardly be a preoccupation so long as France was revolving at full speed through a whole cycle of governments and Germany and Italy were in labour with nationalism but unable to bring forth. Yet in fact a meeting, which took place at München-grätz in the autumn of 1833 between the Emperors of Austria and Russia and excited no little attention and no little alarm at the time, is evidence that the case of Turkey occupied no insignificant place in Metternich's thoughts.

Princess Metternich has left in her diary some incidental record of those not unimportant September days spent with her husband in a town which she characterises both as very small and very ugly. She has much to say of the charm and good-nature of the Emperor Francis; something to say of his preference for her company as against that of those "terrible creatures," the Grand-Duchess of Saxe-Weimar and the Grand-Duchess's old Mistress of the Robes; something to confess of the first icy effect upon her of contact with the Emperor Nicholas; and something more to add about the amiability and gaiety that she discovered in his conversation when subsequently he came to visit her in her tiny lodging and freely exchanged ideas about Louis Philippe—ideas which, there is every reason to suppose, were by no means complimentary to that astute but *parvenu* monarch. Amongst Mélanie's little items of gossip, however, there is nothing for the historian of equal interest with the words of Nicholas as he greeted her husband:—"I come here to put myself under the orders of my chief."[2] So much had feelings changed since Nicholas mounted the throne of Russia eight years before; so nearly did they now agree with those which his brother

[1] Srbik, I, p. 684.   [2] "Mémoires," V, p. 446.

Alexander had at one time entertained towards the Austrian Chancellor!

The principal, though not the only matter to be discussed between the two Sovereigns and the Crown Prince of Prussia, who also was of the company, was, as we have seen, the future of Turkey. That future had again become interesting owing to the recent activities of Mehemet Ali. The Pasha, first cheated by the Powers of the pashalik of the Morea and then cheated by the Sultan of the pashalik of Syria, had some two years before resolved to make war upon his suzerain, and all the more readily that, as he realised, his suzerain was only waiting an occasion to make war upon him. His arms, with Ibrahim again in command, were successful. The cities of Palestine were seized, and the cities of Syria after them. From Damascus the victor moved swiftly forward, the sympathy of the Arabs making his paths straight before him. The Turks were beaten at Homs and then at Hamah. Aleppo fell. The gates of Syria were reached. Again—at the pass of Beilan—the Sultan's forces suffered disastrous defeat. A suggestion of Metternich's (which, in Temperley's judgment,[1] might have "averted disaster") to the effect that French and British naval squadrons should intervene in the Levant was rejected. The Egyptians swept on over the mountains. Asia Minor was entered; Adana occupied. The Sultan began to tremble. Inspiring neither love as ruler nor reverence as caliph, he had reason enough to suppose that Islam was ready to turn against him. In his extremity he resolved to seek the help of the Christian Powers. It was a question which of them would save him at the cheapest cost and bully him to the least extent. He decided to appeal to England, whose representative, Stratford Canning, was to be the very good friend of his dynasty for the next quarter of a century. Accordingly the Ambassador transmitted and recommended proposals for an Anglo-Turkish alliance. But the disciple of the great Canning was not so bold as Canning's cousin. Palmerston refused the Turkish offer. The Egyptians struck hard again at Konieh; and the Sultan, more terrified than before, began to toy with the thought of Russian aid. With mocking ceremony the ever-advancing Ibrahim asked permission of his suzerain to lead his hundred thousand men forwards to Brusa. The old capital of the Turks lay but a little way inland across the Sea of Marmora. The Sultan saw that nothing but the proffered forces of the Ortho-dox Emperor could save the Commander of the Faithful from

[1] H. Temperley: "England and the Near East," p. 79, quoting F.O. 7/241.

defeat. He surrendered to necessity and appealed for Russian assistance.

The two Western Powers became aware that Russia, with Austria at her back, was on the eve of a momentous diplomatic victory. Too late Palmerston and Broglie exerted themselves to save the situation. In order to persuade the Porte to break off the negotiation with Russia the French Ambassador to the Sultan pledged his credit that Mehemet Ali would agree to Murad's terms. The Pasha's ambitions, however, proved to be far in excess of the Sultan's concessions; and, whilst the French and British agents proposed and parleyed, Russian troops and Russian ships gathered in the vicinity of Constantinople. Their presence was doubly decisive. If the Pasha was moved to agree with his adversary by the menace of war, the Sultan was similarly impelled by the menace of famine; for the Russians had imported their stomachs as well as their arms, and the customary supplies of food from Anatolia were unequal to the occasion. The Convention of Kiutayeh, which embodied the terms of peace, displayed a reluctant regard for realities. Mehemet Ali was made Pasha of Syria, but only upon an annually terminable tenure, whilst to his son, Ibrahim, was accorded no more than the style of collector of crown-revenue in Adana. These appointments, though thus modified to save the Sultan's face, conveyed in fact full titles of authority and, doubtless, full opportunities of plunder.

Russia had still to be reckoned with. Behind the closed doors of the Seraglio there was secretly negotiated between Prince Orloff and the Sultan a Russo-Turkish alliance with a secret clause. It was made known to the world that the Treaty of Unkiar Skelessi afforded pledges of mutual assistance to the contracting parties; it was known to the parties themselves that the Russian Government had privately bartered its share in the compact against a Turkish promise to close the Dardanelles to the warships of all nations, if required to do so by Russia. The actual phrase employed—"au besoin"—was indeed ambiguous, but in the corrupt atmosphere of Constantinople the real meaning was easily elicited from the Turkish Commander-in-Chief.

Orloff's able diplomacy left the Western Powers both furious and impotent. Palmerston buried his head in the sand and declared that the Treaty had no being, yet, none the less, in conjunction with Broglie, protested at Petersburg against its existence; whilst at Constantinople the British Ambassador, unable to get speech with the Sultan, consoled himself as best he might by gaining the ear of the Sultan's fool. Such manifestations of annoyance and evidences of discomfiture might have been wisely avoided by recognising a fact of which Metternich had given Broglie some months earlier something more than a hint.[1] Over three years before—at the close of the year 1829—the pundits of Russian diplomacy had sat in secret council to consider the policy of Russia in regard to Turkish affairs. They had found on examination that, contrary to the traditional idea, nothing would serve Russian interests so ill as the downfall of the Ottoman Empire; they had urged that the dismemberment of Turkey might result in the creation of independent states in the Balkan Peninsula not at all necessarily dependent upon the Russian Government; and they had obtained the assent, if not the approval of the Russian Emperor for their conclusions. The Sultan therefore had no occasion at the moment to fear the loss of his throne, nor the Powers the disruption of his Empire; and Austria framed her diplomacy upon this assurance. Like Russia, and even better than Russia it suited her to keep the Turkish Empire going both as a matter of principle and a condition of peace.

It was in the July of 1833 that the Treaty of Unkiar Skelessi was signed. Metternich's precise reaction is hard to define. According to the British Ambassador in Vienna he felt himself deceived and humiliated; according to Palmerston, he was delighted without cause; while according to Professor Temperley, though he had not been fully informed beforehand, he was "at least fully protected against any unpleasant results."[2] Anyhow, in the September following, as we have seen, a corresponding diplomatic movement, some day to be fully developed as the League of the Three Emperors, became manifest at Münchengrätz. The two Emperors of that time, with the Crown Prince of Prussia at their side, resolved in general that any independent sovereign might invoke the aid of another either against his internal or external enemies and that, if that other chose to respond, no Power had any right to intervene in a contrary sense. But also in particular the Sovereigns agreed—and the agreement was subsequently ratified by the King of Prussia in Berlin—that the three Powers should afford each other mutual support on these lines and should be allied, though secretly, against any outside opposition to the arrangement. As between the two Emperors,

---

[1] "Mémoires," V, p. 503.

[2] Professor Webster's conclusions ("Palmerston, Metternich and the European System," p. 136 of "Proc. of Brit. Acad.," 1934), deserve comparison with and discrimination from those of Professor Temperley in "England and the Near East," pp. 78–82.

the maintenance of the Turkish Empire and of the reigning dynasty in Turkey became an object of common policy, the possession of their Polish territories the subject of a mutual guarantee, and the observation of strict neutrality by the little Republic of Cracow, where the revolutionaries of Eastern Europe were in the habit of foregathering, a matter to be insisted upon, if necessary by force. The three great autocratic Powers had, in fact, effectively closed their ranks and stood at the close of the year 1833 like armed sentinels guarding the conservative tradition of Europe. The secrecy of their counsels, the silence surrounding their decisions, were misinterpreted. In France and England it was suspected that they had agreed, not upon the preservation, but the partition of Turkey.

Had Palmerston been less suspicious, the diplomatic tension might have been eased, as Metternich proposed, by the conclusion of a Four-Power Pact to ensure peace in Eastern Europe and Western Asia—a "statesmanlike idea"[1] which would have given Austria the position of "honest broker" in the busy dealings on the Levantine exchange. But the mind of Palmerston worked largely upon considerations—to borrow his own memorable phrase—of "tit for tat." To the conservative combination of Eastern Powers he desired to oppose a not less striking example of western and whig solidarity, and from the situation in the Peninsula he contrived to draw an alliance at least outwardly as imposing as that which had sprung armed from the situation at the other end of the Mediterranean. A disputed succession disfigured at that time both the politics of Spain and Portugal; and in each country a Queen with the Liberals behind her was opposed to a King embodying the absolutist theory of government. The reader will recollect that in Portugal Dom Miguel had successfully established his claim to the throne against that of his niece Doña Maria da Gloria. His Government, popular in the country principally concerned, was unpopular with the constitutionally-minded rulers of France and England; and, in spite of their non-interventionist principles, they afforded what surreptitious assistance they might to the girl Queen's pretensions. The French found a pretext for taking one fleet from King Miguel, but, which was more serious for him, an Englishman—Captain Napier—two years later decisively defeated another. Incompetent generalship did the rest; and by the end of 1833 both Lisbon and Oporto were in the hands of Queen Maria, though Miguel remained master of the rest of the country.

[1] Temperley, "England and the Near East," p. 81.

That same year saw the death in Spain of Ferdinand VII. As in Portugal the right to the succession was in dispute between the champions of his brother, Don Carlos, and those of his infant daughter, Isabella. The Cristinos—the party of the Queen-mother, Cristina—had the best of it; Isabella mounted the throne; and Don Carlos became a focus of rebellion.

It was in these circumstances that, in April 1834, Palmerston, in order to afford countenance to the young Queens of Portugal and Spain and so to the principles, most imperfectly apprehended by their parental Regents, of a Liberal administration, concluded with France and with the Courts of Lisbon and Madrid a Quadruple Alliance. In the absence of any effective assistance from the Eastern group of Powers the tottering throne of King Miguel collapsed under the pressure of this compact; but in Spain, thanks in some measure to the secret diplomacy of Louis Philippe, who to a large extent shared Metternich's sympathy with Don Carlos,[1] the Cristinos were left to defeat the Carlists as best they might.

A triumph of policy over principle, this veiled understanding between the French King and the Austrian Chancellor had come into existence not altogether without difficulty. It was but a year before that a diplomatic indiscretion had set all Europe talking. Though only the student is left to recall the fact now, there was probably no salon in France or Austria where, in the winter of 1834, one might not have heard of Princess Metternich's retort to the French Ambassador. Sainte-Aulaire, meeting her at a Court ball on New Year's Day, had incautiously remarked that the diamonds which she was wearing produced the effect of a crown. München-grätz, where the Russian Emperor had spoken to her so slightingly of the King of the French, was perhaps still in her memory; and Mélanie did not resist a rejoinder which could have but one meaning for the representative of Louis Philippe. "Why not?" she returned. "My crown belongs to me; if it was not my property, I should not wear it."[2] They were standing as she spoke in the middle of the room with ready listeners around them. The point of the remark was unmistakable; the story passed quickly from mouth to mouth; and the French Ambassador even complained to her that she herself was giving it currency. In due course the incident was reported in Paris, and Metternich was obliged to explain it away as best he might at Vienna. Louis Philippe was doubtless annoyed; yet, human nature being what it is, there would be nothing to feel

[1] See "Mémoires," V, p. 667.   [2] *Ibid.*, p. 557.

surprised at if, in true *parvenu* style, he became so much the more eager to establish his title to the best society. The approved method by which this is effected in all times and circles is marriage; and the best-approved method at that time in royal circles was marriage with the House of Habsburg. An Austrian Archduchess as a bride must silence even an Austrian Princess as a critic.

Whatever value may attach to this conjecture, there were more valid reasons for that new shifting of Louis Philippe's policy from west to east which marked the close of 1834. There was the increase of republican propaganda in France; there was the strongly conservative character of the French Elections; there was a certain growing sympathy, both temperamental and political, with Metternich, who after all, unlike his wife, envisaged monarchy rather as the rule of one than as the rule of the anointed one; and, not least nor last, there was a growing antipathy to Palmerston.

That astonishing person, whose praises are still paradoxically sung, but whose policy was tersely summarised by Wellington even in 1852 as "neither more nor less than the creation of confusion everywhere,"[1] was indeed under no illusion as to the impression he made upon more professional diplomatists. With the frankness of a schoolboy, he instructed Strangways not only to announce his resignation to Metternich but to vouchsafe further that the Chancellor, he felt sure, could experience no greater joy and had at no time found him more agreeable. Confronted with this extraordinary message, Metternich replied that reasonable men did not feel sentiments of joy except in the case of events of which they could calculate the bearing, but that, if the word "hope" were substituted for "joy," Lord Palmerston would not be mistaken.

Hope, however, at least so far as Peel's Ministry of 1834 was concerned, told its usual flattering tale. Some five months later Melbourne was back in power and Palmerston once more at the Foreign Office. But before that happened an important event had occurred in Austria.

[1] Lady Burghclere, "A Great Man's Friendship," p. 241. "I have had," Wellington adds, "some practical experience of the working of the system of the Foreign Office policy of this country in peace as well as in the operations of war . . . there is nothing so inconsistent with the interests and honour of this country as what is called Palmerstonian policy."

XVI

THE CHANGE OF EMPERORS

"THE passage from one reign to another is in the nature of the event itself an immense embarrassment if not a more or less actual danger. It seems as if there opened between two reigns a precipice that human will cannot succeed in filling up."[1] So wrote Metternich in a circular despatch to the Austrian diplomatic missions of the 12th March, 1835. Ten days before, the death of the Emperor Francis II from pneumonia had closed his own long and fortunate association with one whose lack of shining gifts had by no means prevented him from accomplishing the first and last word of kingly wisdom and making himself greatly beloved. In common with his far more famous son-in-law, Francis—if the contemporary conjecture of Macaulay[2] is correct—possessed to a greater degree than any ruler of his time a strong hold upon the affection of his subjects; and it is certainly true that he was capable of performing acts worth a whole posse of police to his ministers. Princess Mélanie records how one day, as he was walking near Schönbrunn, he came across a funeral of which the personnel consisted of no more than the priest, the bearers and the corpse. At once the Emperor was the father of his people. "Let us follow this poor fellow," he said to his aide-de-camp, "he is much too solitary."[3]

Metternich, as we have seen, had loved and lauded the man whom fortune had given him as a sovereign and had been beloved and belauded by him in return. It was indeed to the credit of both that each could hardly say enough in praise of the other; that Francis declared he would be lost without his Minister, and that Metternich rejoined that force would fail him to carry on without the steady support and unfailing good sense of his master.[4] To the Emperor who saw him at close quarters his Chancellor had been anything but the ruthless insensitive being of Liberal tradition. More than once in conversation with Mélanie he took occasion to comment on Metternich's utter freedom from rancour and revenge. "He is worth more than me," he told her," "he never gets angry and never harbours bitterness even in respect of his worst enemies; I am not as good as that."[5]

[1] "Mémoires," VI, p. 2.   [2] "Essays on Chatham," No. 2.
[3] "Mémoires," V, p. 262.   [4] Ibid., p. 261.
[5] Ibid., p. 443. Cf. p. 88.

These personal affections did not suffice to obliterate an important nuance of temperamental disagreement. The Emperor was of the same school of thought as that contemporary English Prime Minister out of whose store of good sense the world has appropriated but little beyond the immortal "Why can't you let it alone?" In the value of that generally tempting, sometimes excellent advice the Emperor Francis had been born a believer. "Darüber muss man schlafen," he would say; and he slept long.[1] It was consequently no more than two months before his death that for the second time in his life he formed a serious purpose to examine a memorandum, submitted to him by Metternich no less than seventeen years before and containing some modest suggestions for what was nevertheless organic constitutional change. The memorandum is now lost. Of its contents we know only what the Chancellor long afterwards recalled and recorded; but that little is enough to show that Metternich's mind was not of the same complexion as his master's and that, within two years of the close of the war with Napoleon, he had proposed the creation in the new imperial Austria of some faint image of a parliament—of, as he called it himself, "a Volkshaus,"[2] a council of empire, empowered to discuss budgets and laws of general interest, and formed from a kernel of imperial nominees—whether active officials or merely men of worth we do not know for certain[3]— but anyhow completed by the inclusion of delegates elected in the same way as those chosen for the Provincial Estates.

This was doubtless no revolutionary project; yet the mother of Parliaments can be traced back to beginnings as small, and it is enough to free Metternich from the charge of stagnant statesmanship and to place him, not indeed in the ranks of the reformers, yet in those of the evolutionists. But Francis was more conservative. The memorandum, though urgently pressed upon the Emperor's notice by his Minister, lay nine years idle upon the imperial writing-table.[4] A grave illness brought the recollection of it once more to the Emperor's conscientious but indolent mind. He would, he assured Metternich, not lose another day before he took action. "To-morrow and to-morrow and to-morrow!" Nine years more went by. Then in 1835 Francis thought once again of the memorandum and again resolved to act before the year was out. But Time had grown tired and waited for him no longer. The year was still

[1] Quoted by Bibl, "Der Zerfall Oesterreichs," I, p. 155 and by Springer, Geschichte Oesterr. I, p. 437.
[2] Hübner, "Une Année de ma vie," p. 16. [3] See on this Srbik, I, p. 465.
[4] Hübner, "Une Année de ma vie," p. 16.

young when the Emperor lay dead. The very modesty of Metternich's proposals must therefore be judged a mark of statesmanship. If indolence, reinforced doubtless both at the time of Kotzebue's murder and of the July Revolution by fear, had combined to block proposals so unalarming in themselves and derived from so safe a quarter, what chance would there have been for more drastic suggestions? Francis in truth made no secret of his dispositions. "So long as I live," he told Belliard, Louis Philippe's Ambassador at Vienna, "things will remain as they are."[1] Here was indeed crude conservatism framed in innocent egotism.

There were other changes, however, involving no constitutional concessions, that Metternich proposed and to some extent promoted in the hope of giving to the provinces of the Austrian Empire a moral unity independent of the personal bond afforded by a common sovereign.[2] His State paper on the subject is in truth a model of good sense. The exordium, invoking the glorious memories of Maria Theresa's reign, alluding to the less happy recollection of Joseph's ill-judged reforms and affording to Francis the opportune assurance that, in an empire so well-founded as his, reconstruction need only proceed along traditional lines, tactfully introduces the idea of greater decentralisation. His plan was to avoid the snare of symmetry into which the Emperor Joseph had fallen, to preserve all that was characteristic in each several state or province unchanged, yet to draw the Empire to an organic harmony of structure. The crux of the problem lay in the difficulty of adapting the strongly national and independent character of Hungary to the more or less feudal aspect of the rest. He proposed to deal with this, not seeking to alter the administrative architecture of that kingdom, but by introducing its salient features into the facade of the adjacent states. He conceived a comprehensive Ministry of the Interior whose supreme head should bear the title of first Chancellor and which should comprise within itself four Chanceries charged with the government of the Emperor's German, Slav and Italian subjects. There was to be a Chancellor of Bohemia, Moravia and Galicia, a Chancellor of Austria, a Chancellor of Illyria and a Chancellor of Italy; and these officials were each, so to speak, to face both ways, to think locally when they were in communication with the central administration and imperially when they were in communication with their administrative regions. Such a scheme would have had

---

[1] Vinet, "Mémoires du Comte Belliard," I, p. 354.
[2] See for a compact statement by himself of his idea, "Mémoires," II, p. 117

the effect of depriving the existing chanceries of Hungary and Tran-
sylvania of all singularity. The imperial pediment, as one might put
it, would have rested upon six parallel columns.

This façade, however, formed only part of Metternich's design.
As is indicated by some proposals which he made as early as 1811
for the establishment on the one hand of a purely consultative council
of state and on the other of a ministerial conference consisting of the
heads of departments, he had been impressed during his diplomatic
life in Paris by the separation of the advisory from the executive
functions of government in a constitution which he probably
and perhaps rightly regarded as the most efficient piece of political
machinery that the period had produced. And, though it may be
true that in the autumn of 1814, when some reorganisation of the
Austrian Imperial Council in Metternich's sense took place, the
ideas of Montesquieu rather than those of the dethroned Napoleon
were uppermost in his mind, the challenging logic of French
models still swayed his mind so that the leading aim of his recommendations was to effect a division between the broad—the "moral,"
as he calls it—business of government and the technical work of
administration. The nomination in 1816 of Stadion to be Minister
of Finance represented another step in this direction, but in order
to confine the office of the Crown to the control and co-ordination
of policy, the plan had to be carried farther still. Metternich's
memorandum of 1817 proposed, not only, as we have seen, the
creation of a Ministry of the Interior, but also of a Ministry of Justice.
Police and public accountancy he was content to leave to the management of the existing presidentially-controlled "chambers"; and the
idea of a war department under a ministerial head he reserved for
further consideration. He had suggested enough change for a
beginning of reconstruction on more efficient lines.

The scheme, we do well to notice in passing, bore little trace of
personal ambition. It countenanced no premiership, such as in effect
Count Wallis's alternative project of 1814 had recommended; it
left the Austrian Emperor, just as the French Constitution of the
Year XII had left Napoleon, the acting head of the state; it even
established a counterpoise to Metternich's position in regard to
foreign affairs by the creation of a chancellor with equal responsibility in the home department. If Metternich is identified with
Austria in all the period of his power, it is not because he ever
sought or ever held the post of Prime Minister, but because he
stood intellectually a head and shoulders above his fellows. The

Emperor, had he played the part assigned him, would have been a monarch in deed but no longer in detail. Francis, however, had, as we have seen, no use for change. Government appeared in his eyes to be no more than administration, and, though he consented to Metternich's reorganisation of the Council and the Departments of State he never appears to have treated it seriously. "He never dreamt," says a high authority,[1] "of changing from cabinet government to government in council." In other words, he continued to deal with public business in patriarchal style.

This is a fact that must not be forgotten in estimating Metternich's responsibility in regard to the affairs of Italy. The Emperor in his inmost being favoured the dispositions of his uncle and not of his grandmother; and in this difference between the Josephist and Theresian traditions lay a further nuance between his policy and that of his Chancellor. Francis, to borrow Kübeck's ingenious simile, wanted Lombardy fat and prosperous but as little virile as a eunuch; Metternich, as his appointment of Count Greppi—a Milanese, who lived actually into our own time[2]—to be his Italian *chef-de-cabinet* interestingly illustrates, was content to see Italy administered by Italians. The Emperor's lack of imagination lost him just the advantage that Napoleon had gained by covering an equally alien and autocratic domination with the magic name of Italy. In Confalonieri and in Silvio Pellico the Risorgimento, as all the world once knew, found respectively a martyr and a saint. Yet Francis was not without a common-sense reply to the romantic prisoners of the Spielberg and their associate "guelfi," "carbonari" and "federati." His administration, he might well observe, was as good as could be got in Italy[3] and no harder than Napoleon's; his sovereignty possessed all the added title that a European Congress, not ten years old, could give to it; and finally, his subjects had been fully warned that, if they conspired against him, the law of treason would be invoked. They did so conspire; they were tried by a mixed tribunal; and they suffered the rigour of the law. Mercy, however, was not utterly neglected. In the case of Confalonieri the death-penalty was commuted to one of lifelong imprisonment, and this again would have been reduced had the Senate at Milan requested it.[4] Andryane was similarly fortunate.

[1] Srbik, I, p. 461.   [2] See the account of him in Bülow's "Mémoires," III, p. 20.
[3] Mr. Woodward, no easy-going critic, endo̶ this opinion: "Outside the territory under Austrian rule good government ̶ly ̶ted."—("Studies in European Conservatism," p. 94).
[4] Srbik, I, p. 489.

Capital, however, could be made—and was made in particular by Silvio Pellico in "Le Mie Prigioni"—out of the duration and severity of the imprisonment suffered, although, so far as the Risorgimento was concerned, this was rather in the nature of un-earned increment. Like prisoners at most times and in most places, the captives of the Spielberg had their grievances, but it is as unreasonable to hold Metternich responsible for the unctuous exhortations and ugly instructions of the prison-chaplain as it would be to pillory a prime minister for the questionable practices of a prison-warder. The Emperor, however, and perhaps Münch-Bellinghausen, cannot be so easily exonerated on the main issue.

In the poetic version of the treatment of Confalonieri, however, much as in that of the treatment of the Second Napoleon, Metternich is commonly made to appear as the villain of the piece.[1] That the Eaglet's wings were clipped and the Patriot's feet kept shackled is not in dispute, but for the rest he gave to the King of Rome the honour owing to a prince in exile and to the Italian Count the con-sideration due to a gentleman in disgrace. Upon the death of the former he was the friend who inspired the compilation of a memoir, and at his visit to the latter at the Spielberg he appears to have sought merely the political information which Confalonieri had volunteered to give and not the personal informations which the Austrian Government had reason enough to desire.[2] Confalonieri's own statement, moreover, to Stratford Canning is there to show that he bore Metternich no grudge, but rightly or wrongly laid the whole blame for the length of his confinement upon the Emperor.[3]

As in the government of Italy so in that of Hungary a strife between the Josephist and Theresian traditions was to be discerned. The Emperor Joseph II was, according to abstract ideas, one of the most enlightened of rulers. He forced upon Hungary, as he had forced upon the Austrian Netherlands, reforms that appealed to his own symmetrical intelligence; yet he produced nothing but violent

[1] I see no reason to reject Montbel's evidence, derived largely from Prokesch-Osten and published in 1832, in favour of Mr. Herman's account of the relations between the duc de Reichstadt and the Austrian Government published in 1932. The Young Napoleon appears to have been devoted to his grandfather, defiant of his doctors, and all too fond of his soldiers for the state of his health. When leave to go abroad was applied for, Metternich's reply ran: "Tell the duc de Reichstadt that, apart from France, access to which does not depend upon me, he can go to whatever country suits him. The Emperor puts in the forefront the restoration of his grandson to health." (Montbel, "Le Duc de Reichstadt," p. 331.)

[2] See on this, Srbik, I, p. 486.

[3] Lane-Poole, "Life of Stratford Canning," I, pp. 350, 351. "I have it," wrote Canning, "on good authority that the Emperor kept the state-prisoners in the fortress of Spielberg under his own personal control."

resistance in his subjects and mortal disillusionment in himself. And the decade between 1780 and 1790, during which he reigned alone and when Liberalism was in vogue in Austrian counsels, was precisely the period to which Metternich could effectively point as the only one in which the destruction of the Hungarian Constitution had really been attempted by the Viennese Government. It was no wonder that he looked back behind Joseph to Joseph's greater mother and based his policy upon the wisdom of a Queen who, alone perhaps of all the long Habsburg line, had known how to convert the proudest patriotism into the purest loyalty, and to draw from Magyar throats that dramatic pledge of fealty which, should all else about her be forgotten, will still make the name of Maria Theresa a household word. Hungary, like England, lay, as he recognised, a little outside the usual political categories of government, and the discontent that existed was the easier to deal with that it arose, not from the absence, but from the abeyance of a constitution.

For twelve years—from 1812 to 1825—Francis had governed the country without summoning the Diet, which ought to have met once in every three. For nine years, in other words, he had raised taxes and recruits by unconstitutional means, to find at the end that he had roused the proud Magyar spirit. The first cause, in fact, of the friction that had become manifest was, as the rising young leader of the Opposition—Széchenyi—put it, the distrust of the Government felt by the Estates. Metternich agreed to this. "Confidence like distrust is," as he observes in some marginal notes made on a memorandum that Széchenyi submitted to him, "the result of experience."[1] But he argued that the unconstitutional irregularities complained of were sufficiently explained by the exigencies of the Napoleonic wars, and that the constitutional assurances required were implicit in the King's known principle of maintaining everything that had legal existence.

A resolution, nicely calculated for the purpose, had, meanwhile, driven a wedge between the adherents of the old traditional party of opposition in the Hungarian Diet and the adherents of the new revolutionary spirit of the age; and a Rescript, embodying what was in effect a royal apology for the past and a royal pledge for the future, effectively extended this breach amongst the Government's critics. Széchenyi, however, remained dissatisfied. Puzzled to say what spirit he was of but inclining still to the party of discontent, he accepted Metternich's invitation to discuss matters further in

[1] "Mémoires," IV, p. 251.

Vienna. At the interview the Chancellor read out his annotations to the young patriot's memorandum. The young man, rather clever but, as it seemed to Metternich, vain and shallow, found little or nothing to reply and appeared to admit the force of the elder statesman's observations. Upon that the Chancellor taxed him with vanity and ambition, with fostering trouble and finding no egress from it. Széchenyi was moved. He confessed that he belonged to that category of men who are urged forward by natural activity and honourable ambition; and he pleaded that, deploring the moral collapse and ineffectiveness of the Hungarian magnates, he had set himself to afford enthusiasm and guidance to the rising generation of his countrymen. To this end he had sought and secured some reputation as a patriot and a zealous servant of the good; and this reputation he was intending to place at the service of his sovereign. Metternich received these avowals with faint praise and put them at once to a test well calculated to sift cant from aspiration. Would Széchenyi, he asked, dare to confess the same sentiments to his friends? Széchenyi acknowledged that this could never be. Then, said the Chancellor, you are wanting in loyalty either to me or to your friends and are, in a word untrue to yourself. Warned for the second time that, if he held on the course he had chosen, he was politically lost, the young man went away sorrowful, for he had great commitments.

"Metternich," observes a modern authority, "had meditated more deeply upon the affairs of Hungary than any other representative of the Central Government and had attained in some questions to other conclusions than those which followed from the traditional conservative view."[1] But in truth we need turn to no modern student of his times to frame his apology, for Széchenyi himself—Széchenyi grown twenty years and more older, and taught by the very triumph of his cause—was presently to write it. In the patriot's journal during the Year of Revolution these words were found: — "There rings incessantly in my ears what Metternich said to me twenty or five-and-twenty years ago, 'Pull one stone out of the structure and the whole will crash.'"[2]

But to return to Kaiser Franz! The Emperor's interests, it is plain, revolved principally around the conduct of finance and foreign affairs—defences respectively as they appeared to him against his two dominant alarms, national bankruptcy or European

---

[1] Szekfü, "Der Staat Ungarn," p. 159.
[2] Quellen zur neuen Geschichte Ungarns. Der literarische Nachlass des Grafen Stephan Szechenyi (A. Karoly), I.S. 371. (I quote the reference from Srbik.)

revolution—and the Ministers concerned with those departments enjoyed in consequence a sort of priority over the rest and developed a certain rivalry with one another. So keen was their contention that from the year 1831, when the budget showed a promise of balancing,[1] Metternich is alleged to have lost influence over domestic affairs, though his influence as Chancellor was at no time executive.[2] Francis, if he liked his Foreign Minister much better than he liked his Finance Minister, liked very much indeed the unfamiliar prospect of a surplus revenue and took perhaps a little additional pleasure in that ancient capacity of his house for division and rule. He was shrewd enough to know which of his great officers of state was the better man of the two, but he was satisfied to see their power balanced so long as he himself was alive to hold the scales.

Kolowrat is still something of a mystery, but, if second-rate, was also formidable. "The powerful rival," Hübner[3] calls him, "of the Chancellor, the most influential Minister in home affairs, the unavowed but recognised chief of Liberal opinion in Vienna." A Bohemian by race, he appears something of a gipsy in the world of politics, shifting his tent as circumstances suggested, cutting now a few Liberal capers or again fiddling some bars of the old Vienna valse, trespassing a little upon the territory of the Ministerial Conference, over which Metternich as the senior head of a ministerial department presided, to steal an advantage for the State Council, and then again sacrificing the claims of the State Council to secure some exercise of the Emperor's direct personal authority. His financial ability must remain largely a matter of guess-work if only because, as Beer indicates, any exhaustive, detailed treatment of Austrian finance before 1848 is impossible for lack of figures.[4] It may be that, if pitted against some democratic financiers we have seen, Kolowrat and the departmental officials behind him—Nádasd and the more eminent Eichhoff and Kübeck—might have to be accepted as capable financiers, whilst, if compared with Gladstone, they would lapse to the level of a modest mediocrity. Kolowrat's true form was, perhaps that of George Grenville. Like Grenville he failed to rise to the large occasion of the greater statesman but worse financier at his side; and like Grenville, too, his activities proved disastrous to a dawning dream of empire. He was born—so Metternich wrote in 1837—to

---

[1] See on this Beer, "Die Finanzen Oesterreichs in XIX Jahrhundert," p. 141 (footnote 3). The July Revolution, however, upset financial calculations.
[2] See his statement to Hübner in "Une Année de ma vie," p. 18.
[3] "Une Année de ma vie," pp. 10, 11.   [4] Beer, "Die Finanzen Oesterreichs," p. 170.

be an instrument.[1] Circumstances made him both the agent and the tool of an Opposition.

As the reign ended the two men might, so far at least as official influence was concerned, have appeared not so unequally matched. But the moment the Emperor's testament was known it became clear that Kolowrat was nowhere. Francis bequeathed Metternich to his son as his own most faithful servant and friend, as the proved confidant of many years' standing, as the indispensable councillor without whom the new sovereign must take no decision either in regard to persons or problems. This mention of the Chancellor had all the force of a death-bed legacy behind it, since it seems to have been wanting to the original draft of the document, which was apparently drawn up some years earlier by Gentz, on Metternich's instructions, to reflect the ultra-conservative tendencies of the Emperor's own mind rather than the intelligent conservatism of his Minister. "Change nothing," runs the reiterated charge, "in the foundations of the structure of the State; govern and change nothing. Apply with an immovable resolution the principles of which the observance has enabled me to guide the Monarchy across the storms of a difficult period." It was clear advice, adapted to a simple understanding.

The understanding of the new sovereign was, in fact, of the most modest description. The offspring of two first-cousins, the inheritor through his maternal grandfather of the wretched blood of the Neapolitan Bourbons, the Emperor Ferdinand at the age of forty-two had, perhaps, reason to congratulate himself that he was no worse than a good-natured child. Some vague idea that he might with advantage be set aside had floated in the air and lodged in the mind of his sister-in-law, the Bavarian Princess Sophia, for her husband possessed some small intellectual advantage over his elder brother. The plan had, however, its obvious difficulties, since Ferdinand had been five years before crowned King of Hungary, and, though Kolowrat appears to have given it consideration, Metternich would have none of it. Legitimism was not, indeed, vital to his philosophy, but to break with it in Austria might have been to raise more problems than a breach could settle. It was unlucky perhaps that the ablest of the princes of the blood royal was the Archduke Charles, a great soldier, a popular man, an exponent in politics of the doctrine of the middle way, yet unlikely from ancient enmity to be able to work with Metternich and unable, owing to the

[1] "Mémoires," VI, p. 219.

existence of his nephew, Francis Charles, the husband of the Archduchess Sophia, to produce much in the way of a claim to the
succession, if, that is, primogeniture was still to count for anything
at all.

Primogeniture, no doubt, in its strict application, served Metternich ill even to the point of irony. All things considered and in
spite of Bibl's acid argument to the contrary,[1] he was probably wise
in circumstances so difficult to stand by the late Emperor's testa-
mentary dispositions. These, in effect, whilst handing on the crown
to the testator's eldest son, provided for the regency of the testator's
youngest brother, the Archduke Louis, a man honourable and well-
intentioned, but of small intelligence, some indolence and much
indecision. Metternich might perhaps, in the circumstances, have
made himself master in the State; and many doubtless would argue
that in the interest of the State he ought to have done so. To all
appearance he had only to seize the position that the testament gave
him and to leave Kolowrat in the position where the testament put
him, in order to exercise ubiquitous authority over the counsels of
the childish monarch and the ineffectual archduke. He was, perhaps,
too unambitious, or too old, or too much of a gentleman, or, as he
would himself have put it, too little of a Richelieu, to grasp his
opportunity. But he gave Hübner in 1848 an impersonal reason
which is also worth record. "Austria," he said, "precisely because
of the diversity of nations that compose it, is no place for mayors of
the palace."[2] Two months after Francis's death Kolowrat was permitted to resume his former office and recover much of his former
authority. The effect of this was to create a kind of triumvirate in
which the two Ministers battled for the ear of the presiding Prince.

Three such minds, or perhaps we ought to say three such temperaments, for, if Metternich is to be believed, Kolowrat was profoundly temperamental[3]—could not combine for common action.
While they saw eye to eye in refusing Archduke Charles's wish to
become generalissimo, they were by no means agreed about military
expenditure or ecclesiastical concerns. Metternich, not perhaps
entirely uninfluenced by his wife's sympathies, had during the
crisis of the succession allied himself more closely with the Church
than before and now passed with his critics for a clerical. Kolowrat,
on the other hand, was numbered amongst the children of Jansen,
Febronius and the Emperor Joseph. The question whether the

---

[1] "Metternich in neuer Beleuchtung," p. 64.
[2] Hübner, "Une Année de ma vie," p. 18.   [3] "Mémoires," VI, p. 119.

permission, accorded to the Jesuits, to reside in Galicia should be extended to include the rest of Austria was not, however, of a nature to provide a decisive engagement between Ministers whose desires in point of fact fell short of mutual destruction. A duller issue intervened. Not Jesuits, intriguing for the removal of restrictions upon residence, but beet-producers, infuriated by the reduction of duties upon imported sugar, brought Kolowrat down. The Minister of Finance had always been of a resigning disposition and might now have conveniently retired. The courtesy of Austrian custom, however, preferred to veil his failure by a grant of six months' sick-leave. This time was not wasted by Metternich. He took the opportunity to promote once more those ideas which he had consistently advocated for the co-ordination of the work of government by means of a clearer division between its consultative and executive functions; and he induced the Archduke Louis to agree to a lucid apportionment of business between the State Council and that which he now proposed to dignify by the name of the State Conference, or in other words between the assembly of the councillors of state and the assembly of the heads of departments. A decree promulgated on the last day of October 1836 introduced the change.

Metternich, as his wife intimates,[1] had been particularly anxious to modify the constitution without seeming to advance himself. But it was plain enough no doubt to everybody that, as chairman of the State Conference, he must necessarily become the fly-wheel of the new machine; and upon this fact his opponents fastened. They knew that they hated the thought of his ascendancy; and also they hated, although perhaps they knew it not, to be reformed. Under the pressure of these sentiments Kolowrat hurried down from his unwelcome villegiatura in Bohemia and Archduke John hurried up from his accustomed residence in Tirol. The former, whose control over internal affairs had passed almost unchallenged at the end of the late reign, found himself relegated to no more than the chairmanship of one of the four proposed sectional committees of the State Council or alternatively to the position of a Minister of Finance responsible to the State Conference. The latter, jealous for the honour of the Royal House, conceived that his brother Louis was about to surrender the last remnant of sovereign power under the Chancellor's new arrangements. It was easy to depict Metternich as a *maire du palais* intent upon usurping the functions of a *roi*

[1] "Mémoires," VI, p. 125.

fainéant, and as easy to cause Kolowrat to be represented as a monument of nobility and disinterestedness. A month sufficed to kill Metternich's plan.

The Chancellor, in truth, put up but little fight against his enemies. It was not in his character to care overmuch for power at any time, and least of all perhaps at a time when his physical condition was giving his wife much ground for anxiety. As if to show how little substance there was in the suspicions entertained of him and how little he himself entertained the ambitions of an autocrat, Metternich agreed to the Archduke John's amendment placing a prince of the blood-royal at the head of the State Conference. After the Emperor's name, therefore, and before his own there appeared on the presidential list the names of Archduke Louis and of the heir-apparent. The change, though in appearance trivial was actually decisive. The State Conference, exciting as it did no interest in its President, became inert; and the four permanent members of it—the two Archdukes, Louis and Francis Charles, Metternich and Kolowrat— walked once more in their ancient ways. Archduke Louis found it less trouble to decide things by himself or sometimes not to decide them at all. Archduke Francis Charles found that he counted for no more than he had counted for before or—which was much the same thing—than his wits allowed of. Kolowrat found that, thanks to the Archduke Louis's convenient omission to bring any matters of domestic concern before the Conference and no less convenient practice of substituting written opinions for verbal consultations, he was able to regain control of the internal administration. And Metternich, urged forward by his great friend, Clam-Martinitz, the efficient chief of the military section of the State Council, was left to make what stand his preoccupation with foreign affairs gave him time for against the disintegrating and centrifugal influence of his colleagues. Something indeed he came near to attaining, when Eichhoff was required to render an account of his stewardship and the national finances were thus brought under the review of the State Conference and the appropriate committee of the State Council; but in the Austrian economy there remained unfortunately a great gulf fixed between a resolution and the execution of it. Metternich had once had energy, drive and determination. In these qualities, however, he now seemed even to his friends to be falling off or failing.[1] That period of twenty years which he had marked out for himself in 1819 as the natural limit of his political effort—as the date

[1] "Mémoires," VI, p. 245.

when, as he puts it, he would possess an old man's right to repeat himself[1]—had been nearly reached. He was old; he was ill; he, who was once so calm, had become sometimes, as his wife's journal shows, nervous and agitated. He knew no better how to renew his strength than the Old Order how to regain its suppleness.

A little incident which Mélanie has recorded shows us as in a microcosm all the puzzle and pathos of a period not inaptly described by Metternich himself as a *regnistitium*. It was in the January of 1838, when they had been dining at the Palace, that the heir-presumptive drew Mélanie aside on the plea that his wife—the Archduchess Sophia—was anxious to speak to her. Passing together along a little staircase they reached in due course the Oratory of St. Joseph. There the Archduke stopped, saying that he must positively tell her something he had upon his mind. With tears in his eyes he then assured her at great length that she and her husband could always count on him. "No one," he said, "could turn him from the right path, and the right path was Prince Metternich."[2] Prompted by one woman and addressed to another, this assurance was in fact an appeal from a man who had never grown up to a man who had now grown old. In all probability it represented the beginning of an intrigue on the part of the Archduchess Sophia for the substitution of her husband for his uncle as head of the State Council or of the State Conference—an intrigue which later came to light. Metternich, at any rate, gave the idea no countenance, for there was no point in replacing an indolent by an incompetent member of the Royal House. He had, however, doubtless added to the political recollections of the Archduchess this insult to her despised counsels.

The year 1840 has some special importance in the story of the long-drawn-out and disastrous embroilment. An entry in Mélanie's journal gives us the measure of her husband's depression when that twelvemonth opened:—"He keeps well," she writes, "thank God! He is very busy with foreign affairs; he leaves internal questions alone for the moment as much as he possibly can, and he seems to me not to wish to deal with things where he finds only disagreeables and oppositions which wear him out. He has no strength to fight as he has done in the past. He does not disguise from himself the resulting inconveniences but he never says a word about them. He is troubled by all these things but avoids touching them, though he is sensible of the misfortune that this resolve will draw upon the

---

[1] "Mémoires," III, p. 314.   [2] *Ibid.*, VI, pp. 234, 235.

Monarchy."[1] By the end of the year, however, the situation had been sensibly modified both for the better and the worse. Though finance, a constant source of weakness, had been effectively brought under the review of Conference and Council, though Eichhoff at his own request had been retired, and though Kolowrat had simultaneously intimated his intention of abandoning his special concern with the exchequer, these gains were balanced by the loss of Clam-Martinitz, perhaps the best colleague that Metternich ever possessed. The presence of the sensible Kübeck who took Eichhoff's place and the recall of Ficquelmont, in whom Metternich had long fancied he perceived his proper successor and now found his coadjutor, tended, however, to strengthen the Chancellor's hands, yet not with much result beyond some further multiplication of counsels through the creation of a small preliminary conference to discuss what business should be laid before the State Conference. "In a word," observes a competent authority, "the central organisation of the State was already in the first years of the fifth decade in full decline. . . . Metternich played the part of Jeremiah, and no one listened to him. Nothing happened; life slid on; patience and strength wore out."[2]

"Woe to thee, O land," says a familiar voice, hardly less full of lamentation than Jeremiah's, "when thy king is a child, and thy princes eat in the morning." The words even after long centuries had not lost their application. In vain Metternich paraded the simple Sovereign through Northern Italy, had him crowned at Milan, and flattered himself that in the preceding twenty years the sentiment of Italy towards Austria had, as he put it, turned from black to grey and then again from grey to white. No such "poveretto" as Ferdinand seemed to Venetian eyes could hold his own, however imperially dressed, against a national movement in search of a monarch to lead it. Italy turned her eyes finally from the House of Habsburg to the House of Savoy.

The want of an emperor who was an emperor in deed was no less evident in Hungary. The Magyars are made for kingship but not so well-made to be the apostles of nationality. They find it hard to understand that what one claims of right one concedes in principle. They saw themselves, in the 'forties of the last century, as the equals of the Germans, but not the Slavs as the equals of themselves; and so perhaps they see the matter still. No real settlement of the Hungarian problem was in the circumstances to be had unless by

[1] "Mémoires," VI, p. 387.   [2] Srbik, II, p. 27.

means of the impartiality of the Crown or the disintegration of the kingdom.

With a king calculated to attract all that energy of sentiment without which sense has but little chance Metternich's programme for Hungary might have met with a different fate, for the popularity of the Palatine was enough to show what a prince might do and Metternich's handling of the Hungarian commotion was, according to the valuable witness of Jósika, lucid, practical and conciliatory. But Kossuth, denied permission to conduct an opposition journal, fought so much the harder against one whom he styled himself "the first statesman of Europe"; and under his guidance the charms of revolution grew.

Confessional disputes—that deplorable result of easy-going popes and conceited hot-gospellers—had meanwhile been adding something to the discontents of the Hungarian kingdom, the Austrian Empire and the Confederation of Germany. Feeling ran highest in the country about the Rhine, where the advance of Prussia had clashed with the old Catholic civilisation of the Ecclesiastical Electorates, and fixed upon the contentious conditions attaching to marriages between Catholics and Protestants. To a cool or even cynical observer the claim in such cases of the Catholic parent to have charge of the religious instruction of the child may appear more reasonable than is sometimes allowed. It is of the essence of childhood to be denied the right of private judgment and of the essence of Protestantism to inculcate it; and the Protestant party to the marriage may well in the circumstances hesitate to make use of parental authority in order to promote religious assent. To give the advantage of priority to one religion, it might be added, is only to leave the charm of novelty to another; and the Catholicism of the nursery, should it lack the firm support of maturing reason, may be fairly expected to collapse before the onset of logic and of life.

The Prussian Government was not, however, in reality so much interested in seeing children learn to decide for themselves as in seeing them decide as their fathers or forebears had done before them. A pacific gesture on the part of Pope Pius VIII in 1830, permitting the Catholic clergy, where no agreement could be reached about the education of the children, to assist, though not to officiate at the marriage ceremony, met with no response; and the controversy became keener in the pontificate of Gregory XVI. The Archbishop of Köln, who, though the nominee of Prussia, was no friend to compromise, was imprisoned by the Prussian authorities; and the

Catholics thus secured the advantage of persecution. To Metternich, more solicitous for peace in the State than good-will in the nursery, the Papal Brief of 1830 had seemed to afford the basis for a reasonable accommodation. The word marriage, as he told the Austrian representative at Berlin, inasmuch as the family is the foundation of civil society, had the highest importance for the legislator; but the adjective "mixed," on the other hand, raised a specifically ecclesiastical issue. The statesman was concerned to see that marriages both mixed and unmixed should be concluded, but the actual forms observed and conditions agreed upon lay in the domain of conscience and were no proper concern of the civil power. The Prussian Government ought not, therefore, in his view to prohibit promises relating to the education of the children of a mixed marriage, but neither ought the tribunals to entertain suits respecting the violation of such promises.[1]

The battle ended in 1838, as another more famous battle between the Catholic Church and the Prussian Government ended later, in the collapse of the civil power; but the sound and fury of the conflict had passed out into adjoining lands, and Metternich, seeking as he was at the time a closer understanding with the Church, was credited so much the more with clericalism. It was clericalism certainly of a very lukewarm kind, but another circumstance tended in these years to strengthen the popular impression. There is irony in the fact that, personally tolerant and considerate as he was towards the members of other confessions, Metternich should have promoted the expulsion of the unfortunate sectaries of Zillerthal. There was no doubt, as there generally is in such cases, some political excuse to be found in the fact that the presence of the so-called Inklinante was provocative to the population of Tirol— to those Bretons of Austria devoted by long tradition and heroic service to the claims both of the Altar and the Throne; and there was extenuation to be pleaded in the circumstance that all the rest of the Austrian Empire lay open to the unfortunate refugees. But, like the then recent ejection, in the interest of a union between the Evangelical Churches of Prussia, of the pastors of Silesia from their benefices and the resulting emigration of their flocks, the measure had its painful side and its unpleasing consequences. To Grillparzer, a poet with a dangerous predilection for political partisanship, it even appeared that Metternich was promoting a Catholic movement in Germany as a counterblast to the commercial union which under

"Mémoires," VI, pp. 303, 304.

Prussian leadership had begun to arouse a good deal of anxiety. The idea is not probable. Catholicism entered into Metternich's calculations as a counter-Revolutionary, not as an anti-Prussian factor. The real struggle for hegemony in the German Empire between the two great German Powers was, besides, remote. Frederick William III had been succeeded in 1840 by Frederick William IV; and the new King was a man of peace as his father had been before him, much interested in religion, and more interested still in art. Austria had as yet little to fear from her northern neighbour. Her immediate peril lay within and not without her territories.

XVII

LOUIS PHILIPPE

In foreign as well as in domestic affairs the devolution of the Austrian crown upon the head of a nincompoop inevitably resulted in some decline of power. Metternich had more or less foreseen that this would be so and had taken his measures accordingly. At München-grätz, when Francis was still alive and Ferdinand no more than shadow-king of Hungary, the Chancellor had arranged with Nicholas that, if the Austrian heir-apparent ever came to the throne, the Russian Emperor should stand Ferdinand's friend. At Teplitz, in 1835, some few months after the new reign began, this understanding was in effect confirmed. In conjunction with the King of Prussia, the two Emperors renewed their pledges to resist revolution; and Ferdinand, or Ferdinand's advisors, had thus an assurance, for whatever it might be worth, that, if his crown were in danger of falling from his head, the hand of Nicholas would be there to steady it.

In the diplomatic history of Europe during the next few years this circumstance must be reckoned a cardinal fact. It blocked incidentally the path of the presentable young man who appeared inopportunely in Vienna in 1836 to solicit the hand of Archduke Charles's daughter. Had he been no more than duc de Chartres, he would, as Metternich observed,[1] have made an unexceptionable *parti*; but, accredited as duc d'Orléans, he paraded the fact that his father was claiming to be King of the French, while the King of France was actually living on Austrian soil. Metternich had been able to find a place in his political philosophy for Napoleon, but there was no place in the Emperor Nicholas's philosophy for Louis Philippe. Thus it came about that the Archduchess Theresa, although she was a soldier's daughter, and that soldier the Archduke Charles, pretended to be too fearful of suffering the fate of Marie Antoinette to accept an amiable young man with a throne in prospect.

Not that Metternich for a moment thought the Orleans Monarchy secure! In the jungle of French politics there lurked always for him the beast of Revolution ready to spring out. None the less, his personal admiration for the King of the French was constantly extending. "King Louis Philippe," he wrote to Apponyi in 1837,

[1] "Mémoires," VI, p. 167.

"has positively a high intelligence. . . . On a field which had not been his and where he had attacked, whereas now he needs to defend, he has gained much experience."[1] Sagacity and circumstance had combined to draw the two men, in principle so greatly divided, near together. They had in common the knowledge that comes with years to all but the most foolish—the knowledge that patience and peace can do as much as anything to relieve the suffering and satisfy the needs of Humanity—and they had still the strength and the ability to delay for a little while, but for a little while only, the growing impatience and gathering pugnacity of a new generation imperfectly acquainted with the troubles of war or the perils of revolution. They had too a common interest in and common gift for foreign policy; and it was during these first years of the Emperor Ferdinand's reign that Louis Philippe, by discarding first Thiers and then Guizot, contrived to establish under the direction of the excellent Molé a Ministry which not only raised the standard of domestic prosperity in France to an unprecedented height and the standard of colonial administration in Algeria to a greater efficiency, but enabled the King to resist for a time the growing national demand for sensational and bellicose diplomacy. For a time, but not for long! Molé fell; Thiers forced his way into the Government; and in England the presence of Palmerston at the British Foreign Office between 1835 and 1841 made a boxing-match in the diplomatic ring as good as certain.

That last-named buoyant, not to say flamboyant personage was particularly concerned to wipe out the memory of the diplomatic defeat suffered at the Treaty of Unkiar Skelessi; and to this end he may reasonably be suspected of having fished in Eastern waters by the despatch to Petersburg as Ambassador Extraordinary and Minister Plenipotentiary of the remarkable man who passed in England by the name of "Radical Jack" yet made in Russia a fast friend of its Autocrat. The importance of Durham's mission to Muscovy in 1835 is overshadowed by the greater importance of Durham's mission to Canada in 1837, but it was nevertheless a diplomatic event of considerable consequence. The *rapprochement* that had taken place between France and Austria was in fact being countered by a more striking, more vigorous *rapprochement* between England and Russia. The British Foreign Secretary, rebuffed by France as regards intervention in Spain, had met half-way the advances of the Russian Ambassador; and Palmerston's patriotic

[1] "Mémoires," p. 185.

pique at the success of French policy embraced Nicholas's personal and political dislike of the King of the French. As a result Metternich lost and Palmerston took the lead in Europe.

The field over which the diplomatic battle was fought lay in and around the Eastern Mediterranean, where, in spite of the Convention of Kiutayeh, both land and water continued to be troubled by the contest of Pasha and Sultan. The Convention, giving to the Pasha of Egypt as it did no more than an insecure annual tenancy of the provinces of Syria and Adana, represented only a pause for breath in the prolonged struggle, and, though the Powers contrived to restrain the angry Sultan from falling upon his rebellious vassal during the Syrian revolt of 1834, the desire to try conclusions once again became too much for him some five years later. In view of the ruins of Babylon, yet with but a pale semblance of Babylonish power, the Turks assembled their forces for the invasion of Syria. At Nezib, where they were met by Ibrahim's army, they suffered as usual a prompt and thorough defeat; their camp was seized; and their conqueror pressed forward towards Constantinople. The Sultan died opportunely before tidings of the disaster could reach him, leaving it to Abdul-Medjid, his sixteen-year-old successor to learn the news and to learn besides that the Turkish fleet, basely surrendered to the Pasha at Alexandria, was as fully gone as the Turkish army. That the young Sultan would have to make and the old Pasha receive some further concession was now obvious enough; but the value of the concession depended upon the will of the European Concert.

That unstable corporation thought it advisable to feign to agree, though in fact they differed, and differed deeply. The French put their trust in the Egyptians, regarding them both as the accredited trustees of French culture in the Orient and the native executors of Napoleon's policy. Palmerston, on the other hand, confronted by the Decree of the Rose-Chamber, consented to act as if the Turkish Empire could be reformed and the Old Turk rejuvenated. The disposal of Syria became the prize of success for these rival diplomacies. Was that province to be reckoned, as the French desired, part and parcel of the hereditary dominions of Mehemet Ali or should it, as England and Russia were resolved, revert to the keeping of the Sultan?

Like competing jockeys urgent to gain a race, Thiers and Palmerston struggled for victory; the Frenchman on his Egyptian, the Englishman upon his Turkish mount. Their colours, more perhaps than their qualities, determined the sympathies of the Powers less directly interested. Whilst Egypt wore those of revolt, Turkey displayed the emblems of treaty rights and legitimate sovereignty. As a result Austria and Prussia put their money on the Turkish horse; and France was left to run her race without a backing. She had miscalculated the strength of Egypt; yet it was foul play, or something very like it, that finally wrecked her chances. Without consulting the Concert, she countenanced an attempt on the part of the Pasha to make terms with the Sultan behind the back of his supporters. The attempt failed, but it put Palmerston in a position to engage the other four Powers in a convention for the protection of Constantinople and the coercion of Mehemet Ali.

The proposed settlement tended to restore the prestige of Metternich. The terms, which in effect embodied a suggestion of his made some months before, represented a reasonable compromise. The Pasha was to become hereditary ruler of Egypt; the government of Southern Syria was to be his only for life; and Acre was to be included in this latter province. Ten days were given him to agree with his adversary, whilst for ten days more the offer of Egypt alone was to be open to him. The time passed; and the Pasha was formally deposed by his Suzerain. He had supposed quite reasonably that the French would come to his aid. Thiers, in fact, had raged furiously and caused the drums of war to sound so bravely that, as Metternich with justice observed, no State before had been in so little danger and raised so loud an outcry.[1] The French, however, were greater in word than in power. Thiers, the dashing young civilian, spent his strength and was replaced by Soult, the prudent old soldier. Quietly, amidst all the turmoil of the storm, Louis Philippe had been slipping his country into safety. The Pasha was abandoned; and the Powers had their way with him. Their mercies proved more tender than those of the Sultan. Egypt was left him as an hereditary government; Nubia, Darfour, Khordofan and Senaar were added for the term of his life. Meanwhile in Turkey the reforming decree had come to dust and was called no more Gulhané (Rose-Chamber) but Gulhan (dust-hole). It was not the first nor the last piece of political idealism to go the way of all flesh and flowers. There were at that time, as Temperley has pointed out,[2] Turks of the highest character who regarded the reforms pressed forward by Reschid Pasha under Stratford de Redcliffe's influence as hasty and impracticable; but there was among European statesmen, as Temperley has also

[1] "Mémoires," VI, pp. 486, 487. [2] "England and the Near East," pp. 245, 246.

pointed out, only one who saw the sense of what these Turks were saying—and that one was Metternich.

The tall talk of the French nation, the repeated mention of the Rhine frontier as the natural boundary of France, the re-birth under the auspiecs of Thiers of the Napoleonic legend, the return of the hero's body from St. Helena and its interment beneath the dome of the Invalides, were not without effect upon Germany. Guiltless as it had been of offering the faintest menace to the integrity of French possessions, the German Confederation found itself plainly threatened with assault as a result of the distant squabbles of the Sultan and the Pasha. Very naturally Austria and Prussia began to put their heads together and their common house in order. Military discussions were opened between Vienna and Berlin. The endless bickerings of the German States as to whether Ulm or Rastatt should be made the nucleus of defensive operations in Southern Germany were resolved, as Metternich wished, in favour of the former. The military organisation of the Confederation was reconstituted so that, a couple of years later, it was alleged at any rate to be up to the full standard of federal requirements. And thus as a result of his grotesque excitability Thiers had superimposed a dual alliance between the Central Powers against France upon the triple alliance already concluded against the Revolution by the three great Eastern Monarchies at Münchengrätz and Teplitz. English insularity and French truculence had in turn driven Metternich to anticipate the two fundamental conceptions of Bismarck's diplomacy. Yet for all that he was and remained a good European. Concert and Congress counted with him for more than any alliance or understanding. France was isolated. He resolved to bring her back once again into the comity of nations; and he succeeded in doing so.

The year 1840, meanwhile, had passed into the year 1841. Passion in France had cooled into common-sense; and in the seat of the so-called "Civil-Napoleon"[1] there sat the eminent, the ethical, the excellent Guizot, to whom, incongruously enough, Princess Lieven was now attached in the same capacity as once to Metternich. Upon the Orleans Monarchy there lay the urgent need to demonstrate to an unbelieving and perverse generation that peace could have her victories no less than war. A European issue of the first magnitude had been concealed behind the now terminating struggle of Sultan and Pasha. The question of the admission of foreign warships into the famous Straits that guard the Sea of Marmora on either hand

---

[1] Viz. Thiers.

—the question that the Treaty of Unkiar Skelessi had raised in so acute a form—had still to be resolved. It furnished France with a not ungraceful opportunity to re-enter the counsels of Europe; it enabled Metternich to indicate the gulf still fixed between English and Russian policy; and it illustrated once again the eternal need of a European sense overriding all national and local sentiment. Metternich tried, indeed, for a European Congress in London to settle the problem of the Straits without reference to Syria, as he also tried, in conjunction with Guizot, for a European guarantee to secure the integrity of the Turkish dominions; but in vain was the net spread in the sight of Nicholas and Palmerston. Those militant souls preferred pious opinions to rigid engagements and contented themselves with a declaration, affirmed by the Porte and approved by the Powers, that the passages of the Bosphorus and the Dardanelles were closed to foreign warships. For the principle involved in the so-called *Protocole de Clôture*, France, in association with the other Great Powers proclaimed her respect a few days later in the *Protocole des Détroits*; and Europe seemed to be once more at one with itself. Thirteen years later, however, when the French and British Fleets passed into the Sea of Marmora and out to the Euxine on their way to the Crimea it became clear that to respect a principle is not exactly the same thing as to observe a rule. The closed seagates of Constantinople were not without a wicket to admit a friend.

France, although through the diplomatic expedients of 1841 she had recovered her place in the comity of nations, continued to engage a full share of Metternich's attention. In the course of the preceding year, when Thiers was as busy brandishing the old umbrella of the Bourgeois Monarchy as if it had been the sword of Napoleon, the Austrian Chancellor had explained, not perhaps for the first time, to Apponyi what was the matter with her:—"The trouble of France is the Revolution."[1] "France," he wrote to Sainte Aulaire towards the close of 1841, "gives me the impression of being always very ill."[2] And eight months later, after the sudden death of the Duke of Orleans by a fall from his horse caused the French Government to be confronted in the shape of the Regency question with precisely the one difficulty that had not been provided for, he reflected despairingly that it was the misfortune of France to be ungovernable.[3]

These various remarks possessed as full a measure of truth as can be reasonably demanded of political observations. France was sick and continued to be sick; and her malady was revolution or, if we

---

[1] "Mémoires," VI, p. 438.   [2] *Ibid.*, p. 553.   [3] *Ibid.*, p. 618.

like it better, that feverish, ungovernable restlessness which results in upheaval. The seven-years administration of Guizot is a medical chart terminating in a death certificate. And yet the Orleans Monarchy was not old and, must have possessed, if its remains are any index, as solid a frame and as sound a constitution as a political anatomist could require. The form of polity suggests a perfect equipoise of strength and distribution of function. Neither a monarchy nor an aristocracy nor a democracy in the strictest acceptation of these terms, it seemed to have assembled the best credentials of each. The skeleton of the State, as we have it, discovers a backbone of the best, formed from the solid yet elastic substance of the middle-class; a brow not lacking in breadth; and a figure which, if not graceful, must have been fair and full-fleshed. Indeed, if sanity of body is any help to sanity of mind, then there should have been perfect mental balance springing from perfect health. And we have only to glance at that epitome of his labours which Guizot has appended to his Memoirs, with its impressive tale of reduced taxation, increased revenue, improved administrative efficiency, spreading railroads and a rising standard of public works to admit that the Orleans Monarchy did in fact faithfully pursue the golden mean and with a golden measure.

It was evidently from no organic trouble that this particular constitution perished. Consider, then, specifically its mind. Consider the King, sagacious, shrewd, even, since statecraft is sometimes said to admit it, a little sly; and in the next place the Prime Minister and his eminent rival—Guizot and Thiers, historians of great mark, the one leaning a little to philosophy, the other to romance, yet alike saturated with history sufficient to carry them, without loss of line, across deserts more trackless than Revolutionary France. Consider that at that time men of the most delicate political insight were to be found amongst practical politicians—such men as Alexis de Tocqueville and Duvergier de Hauranne. Consider that the Catholic Party, still a great power in the State, had under the influence of Montalembert largely forgotten its old association with the Legitimist throne and largely learnt to work under the new constitutional conditions. Consider that the Republican Party, clamouring for electoral reform, just as the Catholics clamoured for educational freedom, had abated something of its intransigence and taken to itself so Fabian a counsellor as the Lamennais of *Du Peuple*. Consider that it was the complaint of the greatest French poet of the time that the tribune was choked with Demostheneses, the platforms with

Ciceros, and the country with Mirabeaux,[1] and consider that, despite all the prose which he detected in the minds of his compatriots,[2] Hugo, not to speak of Béranger and Lamartine, contrived to sing well of matters that survive and surpass change and postulate peace—of love and family life and of these things seen through the lovely mist of reminiscence.[3] Consider, in short, that the Orleans Monarchy had thought in abundance and philosophers for politicians; consider that the people were intellectually brilliant as the Greeks and no less thrifty than the Dutch; and consider that the whole somehow concluded in a disillusionment so marked as to evoke from Lamartine the famous observation that France was bored. In the laboratory of political science the great experiment of the July Monarchy thus still "gives furiously to think." These pages, however, are neither a dissecting-room of human nature nor a workshop of constitutional philosophy nor a corridor between them. It is enough that the event vindicated the political acumen of a statesman who never took his eyes off France nor allowed his growing regard for the ability of Louis Philippe to delude him into a belief in the stability of the King of the French.

That patent extinguisher had done, in fact, no more than delay the spread of the revolutionary fire. Metternich felt in his bones that the great house of civilisation would burst again into flames and that the new outbreak would occur again in Paris; and he was right. Yet there was more evidently explosive material and less in the way of fire-escapes to be found in Italy, in Germany, in Hungary and above all in Spain. Between Spain and France, indeed, thanks to the old Family Compacts of the Bourbons, there lay half-hidden communications, and it is arguable enough that along this subterranean channel the revolutionary fire forced its way to Paris. Nowhere perhaps had the pacific foreign policy of Louis Philippe been felt by the Parisians to be more inglorious than in the Peninsula. The French had long been accustomed to meddle there. Louis XIV had meddled to the ultimate advantage of the Bourbons, and Napoleon to the final confusion of the Bonapartes. Even the Restoration, under the guidance of Chateaubriand, had as we have seen won there its solitary sparkling triumph. And in the closing days of the Orleans Monarchy there was a fine pretext for interference. The struggle between the Cristinos and the Carlists— between the Queen-Mother and the Legitimist King—was wearing

[1] "Feuilles d'Automne," Preface.   [2] Ibid.
[3] "À l'adolescent la poésie parle de l'amour, au père de la famille, au vieillard du passé."

the country out. French military intervention was not inconsistent with the Quadruple Alliance of 1834, would probably have been successful in eliminating either Isabella or Don Carlos, and must, if so successful, have cheaply furnished France with a new feat of arms. But Louis Philippe was so made as to prefer a victory in diplomacy to any victory in the field; and with the aid of Guizot he set himself to secure it.

In this manner there came to be played at the Court of Spain what to Metternich's eyes appeared to be "one of the saddest dramas ever enacted on our terrestrial stage."[1] Recognising that Austria had no vital concern with the affairs of the Peninsula, he watched it in the main as a spectator, though with sympathies fully engaged on the side of the agnate—or, to be lucidly redundant, male agnate— in the disputed succession, and with a conviction that the piece should terminate like a nineteenth-century novel in the union of the *de jure* Prince of the Asturias and the *de facto* Queen Isabella. In his time he had indeed styled the three-year-old girl "the Revolution incarnate in its most dangerous form,"[2] since her accession had violated the so-called Salic law of Spain, which, published at the close of the War of the Spanish Succession, represented something in the nature of a dynastic guarantee given to Europe. Provided, however, that the son of Don Carlos was enthroned as king-regnant and not merely as prince-consort,[3] he was from the first in favour of clearing up the situation by a compromise based upon a marriage between the contending claimants. He believed that upon this point Louis Philippe was originally in agreement with him,[4] and attributed to the strength of the King's family affections the divergence of view which appeared as Isabella grew to a marriageable age.

"Père de famille—capable de tout!" says the adage; and Louis Philippe did his utmost to vindicate the justice of the charge. He had a fine row of sons; and here were two eligible Spanish Princesses. It seemed a pity not to make something of so fair an opportunity, when the parties were closely, yet not perhaps too closely related, when the countries were neighbours, when the religion was identical, and when a throne or some prospect of a throne was there to bless the union.

England watched these fancies shaping—Aberdeen with anxious care, Palmerston with pugnacious hostility. There must be, it was felt, no revival under the Orleans dynasty of the old Family

---

[1] "Mémoires," VI, p. 689.
[2] *Ibid.*, V, p. 640.
[3] *Ibid.*, p. 672.
[4] *Ibid.*, p. 672.

Compacts of the eighteenth century. Plans were met with counter-plans. The Ambassadors of the two Powers at Madrid—the subtle Bulwer and the rough-handed Bresson—entered with zest into the negotiation and corrupted its commerce. To a son of France was opposed a scion of Coburg, whilst beyond the matrimonial market-place there were to be seen various Bourbon princelings, all of them in themselves unimportant and one of them—which was all-important—supposed to be impotent. Upon that supposition, as all the world knows, Louis Philippe hung his policy. Without regard for the welfare of Spain, without care for the happiness of his wife's great-niece, he prepared the espousals of Isabella and Don Francisco de Asis, Duke of Cadiz. He was not without excuse. An unmistakable understanding had been reached in the years 1843 and 1845 between the French and English Governments that Isabella should marry amongst the descendants of Philip V, and that, only if she were the mother of children, should her younger sister be permitted to marry a French prince. The effect of the agreement was to exclude both the House of Orleans and the House of Coburg from any candidature for the Queen's hand. When the Whigs returned to power in 1846, however, Palmerston in a despatch to Bulwer, the contents of which he himself communicated to the French Embassy, recommended the name of Leopold of Coburg as the most eligible of Isabella's suitors. The effect of this document, which incidentally condemned the actual "Moderado" Government of Spain as a grinding tyranny, was to infringe the Franco-British understanding and to precipitate a crisis. Queen Cristina had been given a good reason for making a compact with France; and King Louis Philippe a plausible one for breaking the compact with England. Before Palmerston had been four months in power Isabella had been married to the Duke of Cadiz and her sister, the Infanta Louisa, to the Duke of Montpensier.

As Louis Philippe's policy was disclosed and developed, Palmerston turned not unnaturally to England's old ally in the War of the Spanish Succession for support. Metternich, however, declined to be an alarmist for the benefit of the British Foreign Secretary. That the young Queen's younger sister should be married to the French King's youngest son did not suggest to his mind any strong probability that the crowns of France and Spain would coincide upon the heads of the Montpensiers and so offend the principles of the Peace of Utrecht.[1] As he rather maliciously pointed out to the

[1] "Mémoires," VII, p. 162.

T

British Ambassador, there would, in fact, never have been even the slightest danger of any such event if, instead of sustaining the claims of Isabella under the Pragmatic of 1789, the Western Powers had stood by the Pragmatic of 1713, which harmonised with the dynastic settlement at Utrecht and required the succession of Don Carlos.[1] To his eyes, in fact, British diplomacy had been characteristically clumsy. It had effected the Entente of 1830 with France in order to promote British influence in the Peninsula; but Louis Philippe had shown himself more than a match both for Aberdeen and Palmerston, and the Franco-British understanding had in the event provided a diplomatic triumph for France.

A diplomatic but not a domestic triumph! Upon the composite structure of the Orleans Monarchy French foreign policy was at this time exercising a disintegrating effect; and the British Foreign Secretary, worsted in Spain, had the less objection to see the French Government discomfited in Europe. It was to little purpose that towards the close of 1844 Thiers began to seek those personal relations with Palmerston that Guizot had long established with Aberdeen. Disintegration had set in. England was detaching herself from France just as Thiers had already detached himself from Guizot; and in these things was to be read the doom of the House of Orleans. In the composite building which in 1830 Louis Philippe had raised above the river of revolution, the imported English cement was giving way, the French pillars cracking. Only a flood, as Metternich had long foreseen, was needed to carry the whole structure away. And that flood was preparing.

[1] "Mémoires," VII, p. 275.

XVIII

THE TEMPEST

It was in the independent State of Switzerland and the free city of Cracow that the waters of discontent—both sweet and bitter—were accustomed to collect. Here there foregathered representative companies both of those who dream and of those who do, designers of new worlds and destroyers of old ones. All the rulers of the time had occasion to watch these central watersheds of change; but Metternich and Louis Philippe had most reason perhaps to watch them closely. Interference was not impossible, though perhaps inequitable. The guarantee of perpetual neutrality given to Switzerland by the Congress of Vienna implied some sort of reciprocal obligation to Europe; and it was plausible to construe this as affording the Great Powers a claim to insist both upon the maintenance of the Swiss Constitution as settled by the Swiss themselves at that time and upon the close supervision of foreign refugees who sought asylum upon Swiss soil during the revolutionary activity of the 'thirties. The former point was of especial concern to Conservatives, for Swiss Liberalism became identified with a movement to restrict the almost sovereign rights of the cantons and to extend the limited authority of the Federation. In the 'forties religious issues complicated the political outlook. In Aargau, contrary to the provisions of the Federal Pact, monasteries were suppressed; and in Lüzern, contrary to the wishes of the Liberals, the recall of the Jesuits was proposed. Upon the fortunes of that devoted Order contention was quickly concentrated. The Liberals of Lüzern resorted to arms and even to assassination[1] to supplement constitutional debate; and Protestants in general showed no more disposition to tolerate the Jesuits than they had lately shown to tolerate David Strauss. The Catholics of the Seven Catholic Cantons, not unnaturally, formed a league to defend themselves; and political confusion quickly turned to civil war in which the weakest went to the wall. But the Seven Cantons were no match for the opposing Ten.

Metternich, though not unfriendly, had no brief for the Jesuits. He did not, as he observes, identify them with religion or the Church or the foundations of society, and, to avoid offence and trouble, he had actually discouraged their introduction[2] into

[1] Leu in 1845.   [2] "Mémoires," VII, p. 114.

Lüzern; yet he saw no reason why a canton, if it chose, should not be free to put a few Jesuit professors on the teaching-staff of a seminary, and he detected, behind the fuss that was being made on so small account, the hand of the revolutionary agitator. The Swiss Federation in his view should be free to amend its constitution; but Europe, as he thought, was entitled, in return for its benevolent guarantee of Swiss neutrality, to insist upon the preservation of the individual sovereign status of the cantons. Guizot shared this opinion, but proposed to divide the responsibility of intervention in so far as the odium of it could be made to fall upon Austria and the credit of it redound to France. It was an old trick of French diplomacy, but neither in Switzerland nor in the Papal States would Metternich agree to the creation of a new diplomatic Ancona. He wanted France and Austria to act together, and Russia, Prussia and England to stand behind them. Russia of course detested revolution in general; and Prussia, with proprietary rights in Neuchâtel, had her own views about Swiss revolutionaries in particular; but the concurrence of England was a different matter. Palmerston, the greatest interventionist of the lot as Metternich knew him to be,[1] satisfied at once his national affinities and his international animosities by playing an astute game of dalliance. He had his doubts; he developed his hesitations; and whilst he parleyed and the Powers parleyed with him, the river of Revolution gathered strength, overflowed its banks and in the hour of flood swept away the Swiss Federal Pact of 1815 as effectively as the American Civil War blew to atoms the old State sovereignties of the American Confederation. Metternich had, indeed, at last, in conjunction with France and Prussia, concerted a Note which would have obliged the Swiss Diet to restore the old Swiss Constitution or else to suffer a commercial blockade or submit to a military occupation; but, before that Note could be put into effect, he had fallen from power. Thus, even in that fortunate country around which History curls but where she seldom plants her foot, the end of the Chancellor's long reign is coincident with the end of a chapter.

In dealing with the prime centre of Eastern discontent, Metternich moved with greater ease, expedition and result than in his dealings with Switzerland. He had, as the reader is aware, no sympathy with the partition of Poland, but he considered, as indeed statesmen even of the Liberal stamp still considered sixty and more years after he had passed off the stage, that the disruption of the Polish

[1] "Mémoires," VII, p. 358—"le plus intervenant des hommes d'État."

State had entered as an irreversible fact into the constitution of modern Europe. To make the best and not the worst of what had been done was in the circumstances no more than good sense. Not always to be chiding nor to keep one's anger for ever was, however, a principle that commended itself rather to the practical Galician peasantry than to the ideologues and refugees of Cracow. Suppressed in 1836, these rose afresh some ten years later; and this time Metternich, assured of Russian and Prussian countenance, struck hard. Whilst an Austrian officer, with a tragic fate before him —the luckless Benedek—took what Metternich describes as "a police measure" and annexed Cracow, the peasants of Galicia demonstrated their preference for their Austrian overlord as against their Polish landlords. The Austrian Chancellor was consequently in a good position to reply to French and English protests with flout and gibe. Why was middle-class democratic France championing the cause of the Polish nobility and Protestant England declaring for a nationality that wished to make of Catholicism a political flag?[1] Why, when Poles themselves saw that they could remain Polish without a Polish Government, was the suppression of the seat and centre of Polish agitation to be resented by the signatories of the Treaty of Vienna?

Yet, though the old man had little mind to acknowledge it, the condition of Switzerland and the annexation of Cracow were as an ugly rent and a tell-tale patch upon the well-worn cloth of the Vienna Settlement. It was plain that the once serviceable material was wearing thin, rubbed and jostled continually as it had been by the ideas of Nationality and Democracy and scratched from time to time by the beast of Revolution—a beast growing more evidently bold and omnipresent as the decade drew on to its close. The hot breath of the spectral monster was in truth to be felt not only in Switzerland, where the school of Mazzini taught killing to be no murder; not only in Cracow, where with plot and insurrection Mieroslavski maintained the indomitable hope of Poland; not only in Turin, where Charles Albert sat masking the face of confederate Italy; not only in Hungary, where Széchenyi and Eötvös were making the ways straight for Kossuth and Görgei, but in the corridors of the Vatican and the gardens of Sans Souci. It was in July 1846 that the Conclave of Cardinals decided to raise to the papal throne a member of their college who had not only been touched by the popular spirit of the time but had responded to its call.

[1] "Mémoires," VII, p. 360.

The elevation to the Chair of St. Peter, in that year of apprehension and anxiety, of a vaguely Liberal pope seemed, perhaps, less actually surprising than the appearance in the seat of Frederick the Great of a romantically Liberal king; and the medieval fancy of a "papa angelico," which encircled the figure of Pius IX, was a more hopeful venture in idealism than the medieval fact of a Holy Roman Emperor which inspired the policy of Frederick William IV. Yet neither from the standpoint of a long worldly experience promised well.

The old statesman at Vienna watched and warned. He was the victim neither of illusion nor enthusiasm. All the vast body of dogma which had been raised upon Rousseau's simple faith in the loosing of human nature left him cold and sceptical. The business of a government, he maintained, was to govern—to govern well, to govern wisely, to govern with due regard to the diversities of tradition among divers people, but always to govern. The Time-spirit, however, had tired of his words: and he, as Mélanie saw, was tiring of the Time. "Clément is admirable," she wrote as the last fateful year of his long administration opened, "fear has no hold on him, but he is sometimes much agitated."[1] Troubled by pre-monition or taught by experience, Metternich in that final January of 1848 cast the horoscope of the coming twelvemonth and con-cluded that the veil which had so long hid the future was now about to lift. The curtain of Liberalism would in other words disclose at last the Radicalism which lay behind it.[2] In his prophetic vision he saw Rome, as in the sixteenth century, the centre of the battle-field and the new Reform as no more than the renewed onset of the old Reformation. It was a picturesque presentment of the coming scene—no photograph, yet none the less instinct with poetry and truth.

The affairs of the Papacy during the preceding year had in fact exemplified the opinion that Liberalism is no continuing city but only the advance-camp of catastrophic change; and Pius IX, like his contemporary, Finality John, had experienced the fate of those who fondly suppose that they can say to the great tides of popular passion, "Thus far and no farther." "The Revolution," Metternich had written in 1847, "has taken hold of the person of Pius the Ninth and of public opinion by raising again the old banner of the Guelfs in the name of the Holy See."[3] From point to point the Pope was pushed, until the reputedly sympathetic student of Gioberti, Balbo and d'Azeglio found himself passing under the alternate pressure of benevolence and alarm from a political amnesty to an advisory council, from an advisory council to a constitutional government, from the Ministry of the liberal Rossi to the Ministry of the radical Muzzarelli, and finally into reaction of mind and flight of body. Before these developments were far advanced, however, Austria, despairing of the co-operation of Europe in the affairs of Italy, entered Ferrara in spite of Papal protests and held the fortifications in virtue of the Vienna settlement.[1] The whole situation was so much the more exacerbated.

For these things were not done in a corner. Though more than a year went by before all were accomplished, though Metternich had fled Vienna before the Pope left Rome, they were in their beginnings as the prelude to that high pageant of revolution which was carried from Rome to Naples, from Naples to Paris, and from Paris spread to half the capitals of Europe until the whole year stood out as one of dramatic excursions and alarms. It was in France and Austria that the force of circumstance—the sudden sequence upon small occasions of large events—received its most striking illustration. A banquet forbidden by the Paris police proved all that was needed to overturn the throne, to bring down a Premier instinct with philosophic moderation, a King naturally wise and now grown old in political experience, a Constitutional Monarchy framed and balanced with all the wisdom of English models. These vanished, indeed, not a jot more slowly than the last Legitimist monarch and the *ancien régime*, and with something less in the way of dignity. As the King of the French slipped away in disguise, Madame la République, somewhat older than when first we met her, but still capable of child-bearing and actually pregnant with empire, re-entered the capital in the car of Revolution and resumed her familiar seat at the Hôtel de Ville.

The things that had been done in Paris on February 24th were told in Vienna on February 29th. If Guizot falls, Princess Mélanie exclaimed, we are all of us lost.[2] She had judged rightly. Within a week there came the news that all Germany was in commotion. The tyranny of imitation had set in; and fashion moved swiftly from the west eastwards. The English models of 1688, reset with the French trimmings of 1830—parliaments, juries, a free press and religious equality—became the rage in Calrsruhe, in Mannheim, in Mainz, in Stuttgart, in Berlin—all over the German Confederation. People

---

[1] Article 103.
[2] Hübner, "Une Année de ma vie," p. 12.

seemed to suppose that they could make up for bad harvests and industrial depression, to say nothing of deeper deficiencies of character and conduct, by imports of political millinery from Paris and London. Led by Baden and the Rhineland, the German nation clamoured for costumes in the union-and-liberty style of the hour. The Sovereigns, with a single exception, managed to struggle into these new clothes without tumbling off their thrones. Only in Bavaria, where Lola Montez had been playing the Pompadour to King Ludwig's Louis XV, did the Monarch collapse, though even there the Monarchy remained. And only in Prussia did the romantic Sovereign's strange assortment of new-fangled robes and ancestral insignia excite deserved derision.

Before the Court of Prussia was thus transformed, there had occurred in Vienna an event which outstripped in sensation all the other fatalities of the time. On the 13th March, under pressure both from above and below, the Minister who for thirty-eight years had seemed to carry the burden of European society upon his shoulders as firmly as Atlas the earth had fallen from his place. Amidst threats of vengeance and shouts of triumph he fell, the embodiment for the blind millions and their too often blinder guides, of privilege and stagnation; and great was the fall of him. Yet there were those like Disraeli who saw that a stately column had been broken; that a beacon light had been quenched in smoke; that, for all the noise of brazen trumpets, a silver voice had ceased; that a watchman, grown old in the safeguarding of peace, kept vigil no more in the high places of Vienna.

It was on the 10th March that an official of the State Chancery came to warn Mélanie to put her jewels into security. A little later she knew that the fury of the mob was turned against her husband and the Archduke Louis. And presently she learnt from various signs—from the rain of threatening letters, from the dark hints of unfeeling friends, from the unfamiliar cecity of policemen in face of hostile manifestations and, finally, from the characteristic skill with which the Royal House withdrew into the background, leaving the Chancellor to face his foes alone—how insecure a claim upon consideration does even the longest service of the State bestow, how fleeting is the splendour of human power, analogue, as Dante warns us that it is, of a breath of wind, blowing now this way, now that, and changing name as it changes direction.[1]

The old man met the storm with a resolution born as we know.

[1] Purg. xi.

not of obstinacy, but of courage. Urged to action by such as in times of crisis usefully explain that something must be done without explaining exactly what that something is, he had at the beginning of March been reconsidering, as Hübner's diary shows,[1] some adaptation of his old scheme of 1817 for "a house of provinces" whose members, elected in the same manner as the representatives of the Provincial Estates, should possess deliberative, though not legislative powers. But in face of clamour he would yield nothing. On the fateful 13th he stood, calm and collected, before the Council, though he had but just passed through the scornful shouts of the angry mob without. Clad—for the scene deserves its detail—in green coat and grey trousers and with stick in hand, he urged the unwisdom, so lately demonstrated in France, of forced concessions, and stressed the obligation upon the Emperor to pass on such power to his successor as had been passed down to him. Dismissing the agitation as a hubbub of bakers, he advised that the rabble be dispersed by the police and the soldiery. Schmerling observed that the rabble was supported by the better classes, only to be met by the bland retort, "My friend, if you yourself—yes, if my own son were found amongst people who behave like that, they are rabble just the same." It must have been as if someone had suddenly said:

> Virtus, repulsæ nescia sordidæ,
> Intaminatis fulget honoribus,
> Nec sumit aut ponit secures
> Arbitrio popularis auræ.[2]

The conference closed; the agitation in the streets increased; life was lost; property destroyed; deputations to the Hofburg came and went; then in the evening Metternich returned and spoke again. His resignation had by this time been openly demanded; and at the hour appointed the mob was due to return and hear whether it had been conceded. There were members of the Royal House in full sympathy with the populace; Archduke John detested the Chancellor, Archduchess Sophia desired to set her son upon the throne. In the painful circumstances Archduke Louis, Regent in all but name, sought the opinion of the waiting crowd of courtiers in the ante-room and found it adverse. He came back, and, to his subsequent regret, for he had been over-persuaded, communicated the fact to Metternich. The Chancellor returned the only answer consonant with dignity and said that he was ready to retire. Then, for he was at no time concise, he began to set out with an old man's amplitude of

---

[1] "Une Année de ma vie," p. 16.   [2] Horace, "Odes," III, ii.

speech the dangers to the State involved in his withdrawal. The sands of the situation, meanwhile, were fast running out. At length Archduke John interjected the observation that in half-an-hour the populace would require an answer and that this answer had not yet been considered. Kolowrat was poor creature enough to seize the opportunity to pay off ancient scores. "Imperial Highness," he said, "five-and-twenty years have I sat with Prince Metternich in this conference, and always have I heard him speak without coming to the point in debate." "But to-day one must decide forthwith," rejoined the Archduke. "Are you aware," and he turned to Metternich, "that the People's leaders desire your resignation?"

The noble quarry, thus pitilessly used in the last extremity, lost nothing in distinction. In accordance with his old master's dying request he had sworn, he said, never to desert his present sovereign. He would consider himself released from his oath only if the Imperial Family wished for his retirement. The Archdukes gave him, apparently without demur, the assurance that he required; and he declared his resignation. There was but one touch, of equal worth as comedy or tragedy, left wanting to the drama; and this was not withheld. "In the last resort, however, it is I who am the sovereign and have to decide," observed a voice which had perhaps not yet been heard in the debate. "Tell the People that I agree to everything." It was the Emperor Ferdinand who spoke. His insufficiency was such that his wife had lately agreed with Metternich that, as soon as his promising young nephew came of age in August, he must vacate the throne in Francis Joseph's favour.[1] Necessity that respects no law of succession was soon to enforce their counsel.

Of Metternich's escape from Vienna there exists an authentic, contemporary account[2] from the pen of one whose son, marrying into a great English family and eventually naturalised as an English subject, became in our own time known and admired as a penetrating, if not always prudent, leader of religious thought in England. Baron Carl von Hügel had long been a familiar in Metternich's house, intimate as a son with the Prince and devoted passionately yet platonically to the Princess.[3] In the hour of trial—in the hour of that, as it seemed to his loyal and affectionate eyes, "most shameful persecution of the only great statesman in Europe"—he was faithful. Sacrificing a treasured villa near Schönbrunn, enriched

[1] Hübner, "Une Année de ma vie," p. 472.
[2] In the "National Review" for June 1883.
[3] The story was that his infatuation for Mélanie had driven him away to spend seven years in the East, where he had been a great collector.

as well by the spoils of travel as the toils of horticulture, and setting friendship before fortune, he became, together with his brother, the agent and companion of Metternich's flight. It was such a flight as a man may make without loss of dignity—a flight encouraged by the Government itself, necessitated by consideration for his wife and children, and carried through with what at the age of seventy-five is fairly entitled to the name of heroism.

ᐧThe fugitives, slipping with difficulty out of Vienna by a gate that a few hours later would have been closed against them, made for Felsburg, where Prince Liechtenstein afforded them momentary shelter. Thence on, amidst perils, discomforts and tribulations sufficient to remind all potential fugitives to pray that their flight be not in winter! At length, about a month after leaving Vienna, the Metternichs arrived in London, where, rather prosaically, they found a house, not too expensive for their embarrassed circumstances, in Eaton Square (No. 44). A generation had gone by since the Prince had known the swiftly spreading city; and it was as another Rip van Winkle that he walked its streets. A young Queen sat now upon her grandfather's throne; in Parliament power had passed from the Old Whigs to the New; outside Parliament the Middle Classes, enfranchised by the Reform Bill of 1832, were making their presence increasingly felt; and in the common-rooms of Oxford and wherever its influence penetrated, Newman's secession from the Church of England was causing men to review with various effect the almost forgotten problem of the Reformation in which Metternich, as we have seen, had perceived the old original of the Revolution. Only in Wellington's company at Stratfieldsaye did the old man recover for a day or two the feeling of a world that had almost passed away.

The Metternichs, as they took their walks or drives through those, as Metternich calls them, "interminable" streets, which yet left Kensington a country town and Kew a distant village, fancied themselves lost in the vast metropolis.[1] They were not, however, by any means lost to view by others. As soon as they were settled, their drawing-room was thronged with the celebrities of the time. Wellington came daily for all his seventy-nine years;[2] Aberdeen, another friend of those distant days when all Europe was in arms against the first Napoleon, renewed the ancient intimacy. And Conservatives like Lyndhurst and Londonderry were present to study a master in their school; nor Conservatives only. Brougham

[1] "Mémoires," VIII, p. 19.   [2] *Ibid.*, p. 176.

was to be seen in Metternich's drawing-room, and one more unexpected even than Brougham—the arch-enemy himself, the egregious Palmerston. The "Dalai Lama of Vienna" had become an English lion whom everybody who was anybody must stroke and everybody who was nobody must see. "Wherever one goes here," Metternich declares, "one finds oneself in what elsewhere one would call a crowd. Constantly I am recognised, surrounded, followed; and some orator or other comes up and makes me a speech containing always proofs of sympathy and tributes of respect to which I can only reply by these few words: 'I thank you sincerely.' "[1]

The prophet of Conservatism found himself in fact by no means without honour in a country where least of all perhaps he had reason to anticipate it, though in truth his strong sense of history had long taught him to recognise that the English are a peculiar people, not to be influenced by Continental prejudices nor governed by Continental methods.

[1] "Mémoires," V, p. 163.

XIX

THE RETROSPECT OF LIFE

THE consideration shown him in England does not furnish the main interest of the year and a half that Metternich spent in London and at Brighton. Without the episode the student of his life and mind might fail to grasp the breadth of his political sympathies or suspect the character of his ideal polity. Critical as he had been of the Englishman abroad, he found in the English of that time a people who, more truly perhaps than the Spartans in Plato's case, embodied a dream and satisfied a desire. "That," he cries almost as soon as he touches English soil, "which has always made the strength of this great people is the unshakeable conviction it has of the value of right, of order, and of the liberty which really to exist must rest upon these foundations."[1] Again, ten days later, he declares: "If I had passed my life in London, and if I were English, I could not see myself surrounded . . . by a greater number of friends. . . . I find myself here in the element in which alone I breathe freely, in an atmosphere where pure good sense predominates. This element is, by the force of things, the historic one, and, consequently, mine."[2] As the days go on he reiterates his belief in this at first sight strange correspondence between English mentality and his own. "My motto, 'La force dans le droit,' is wonderfully understood in this country."[3] "The English people are prodigiously sensible."[4] Nor was this just the figment of an old man's fancy—of an old man charmed by a hospitable reception and eager on his side to return a compliment. As formerly Metternich's ideas were said to have affected 'Athenian Aberdeen,' so quite certainly and considerably they now attracted and influenced the Hebrew genius who was soon to seek in a manner all his own to invest the English monarchy with the glory of empire, to combine "imperium" with "libertas," to attract the untutored sentiment of a now inevitable democracy to the interest of a "real throne." Nothing, perhaps, in his history is more curious than this meeting of Metternich's mind with Disraeli's. Whilst Princess Lieven—likewise a refugee as the result of her singular liaison with the fallen Guizot—was voting her old lover a bore,[5] Disraeli was proclaiming him to be an intellectual

[1] "Mémoires, VIII, p. 155.
[2] Ibid., p. 157.
[3] Ibid., p. 169.
[4] Ibid., p. 184.
[5] See the curious reminiscence in Crewe's "Life of Lord Rosebery," p. 190.

angel. "I shall come and see you," wrote the leader of the New Conservatism to the leader of the Old, "not merely because you are the only philosophical statesman I ever encountered, not merely because I catch wisdom from your lips and inspiration from your example, but because I feel for you the most tender and respectful affection."[1] He came, saw and was completely conquered. "I never heard such divine talk," he declared to Mrs. Disraeli; "he gave me the most masterly exposition of the present state of European affairs and said a greater number of wise and witty things than I ever recollected hearing from him on the same day. He was indeed quite brilliant, and his eyes sometimes laughed with sunny sympathy with his shining thoughts."[2]

There is no greater glamour than that of international diplomacy, or at least there was none for Disraeli. The future maker of the Congress of Berlin was now sitting at the feet of the past master of the Congress of Vienna. In that circumstance we can think, if we choose, that there lay matter of consequence for Europe in general and Turkey in particular,[3] and not the less perhaps that ten years later we find Metternich writing to Disraeli of the constant agreement of policy, both as regards general questions and particular interests, that existed between "the Continental and Central Power which is not maritime" and "the Great Maritime Empire which in Europe is not Continental."[4] Yet, in all likelihood, it was less of the Anglo-Austrian interest in the conservation of treaty-rights and Turkish territories that the two statesmen talked in 1848 than of those unseen foundations of society which at the time seemed everywhere rocking. Nothing, perhaps, is better calculated to dispel the popular notion of Metternich as a kind of Austrian Eldon than his intercourse with Disraeli; through whom, indeed, he might plausibly lay claim to be considered the political grandfather of Lord Baldwin. The static quality, the heedlessness of time, which gave a passing strength to Eldon's politics, was in fact precisely the thing that Metternich in his inmost being repudiated. "All spirit of reaction," he says in so many words, "is necessarily false and unjust."[5] As we have seen already he pitied himself as the victim of a period of transition, born either too early or too late. It is of a piece with this that we find him maintaining to his daughter that "time consisted of two elements only, the past and the future, to which the present served only as a hyphen," and that "to live in the present is a fact

[1] Buckle, "Life of Disraeli," III, p. 191.   [2] *Ibid.*, p. 130.
[3] Cp. Buckle, "Life of Disraeli," III, pp. 194, 195.
[4] "Mémoires," VIII, p. 435.   [5] *Ibid.*, III, p. 51.

METTERNICH IN THE INSIGNIA OF THE ORDER OF THE
GOLDEN FLEECE, 1835

From the picture by Johann Ender in the Vienna State Collections.
Reproduced by the kind permission of the Director of the Vienna State Collections and
Messrs. F. Bruckmann of Munich.

BENJAMIN DISRAELI

Reproduced from the portrait by Sir Francis Grant, P.R.A., at Hughenden by the kind permission of Coningsby Disraeli, Esq.

materially true but morally chimerical."[1] To Ticknor, as Rosebery took occasion in a sketch of Pitt to remind us, he declared that the present day had no value for him except as the eve of the morrow; that it was always with the morrow that his spirit wrestled.[2] He was, in fact, in line with Goethe, whose saying he somewhere makes his own, in believing that "deep natures are driven to live in the past and future."

By some such metaphysical magnetism, then, rather perhaps than by any raw belief in conservation were Metternich's sympathies drawn towards Disraeli's. Both men were for ever turning the pages of the past to elicit as from some mystic numbers the legend of the future, for both believed that, if human will is a variable, human nature is a constant and gives itself no lie. There lay between them, however, all the space of a generation; and what is to a man in the 'seventies a subject for speculation is to a man in the 'forties a call to action. Disraeli in those dark hours, when the old Europe seemed to be crumbling, afforded to Metternich, we may safely guess, not merely the compliment of discipleship but the interest of purpose and vision. Here was a thinker who sought to invest the certitudes of old time with new conviction. Here was a poet who, not five years before, had sat in spirit amongst the ruins of Marney Abbey and bewailed the lost music of the monks—the unsung hymn in the Lady Chapel, the unlit candles on the Altar, the gate for ever closed to the appeal of poverty, the wanderer turning away from a door no longer open[3]. Here was a churchman whom one mysterious mentor had reminded that the monasteries represented the cause of right as much as that of religion, that in their downfall had perished the heritage of the poor,[4] and whom another, appealing to "the eternal principles of human nature," had admonished that "man was made to adore and obey."[5] Here was a statesman who had satisfied himself that a real throne must appeal to an understanding people. And here was a rising politician who championed, as against Venetian oligarchs and convert free-traders, that old English "squire-Conservatism" which Metternich, after long contact with the Austrian nobility, found so entirely sympathetic.

The nature of aristocracy in England was, as the refugee explained to his daughter, misconceived on the Continent. "The English aristocracy is not the nobility; it consists in Conservative principles and the spirit that corresponds with them—a spirit that animates all

[1] "Mémoires," VIII, p. 195.   [2] "Pitt," p. 30. Ticknor, "Mémoires," II, p. 17.
[3] "Sybil," c. 4   [4] Ibid., c. 5.   [5] "Coningsby," c. 13.

classes. . . . The most emphatic aristocrats are the country gentlemen who have nothing in common with 'la noblesse', for everyone who has an independent position is a gentleman. . . . Titles are the equivalent of functions and everyone can by personal merit cut his way through to them. There is here an equality useful in its results—an equality that raises, instead of lowering like that of misery."[1]

In this appreciation of England as a country where discharge of duty constituted the true title to distinction, where privilege merely provided for the more efficient discharge of public business, and where liberty seemed in love with order and all the people in line with common-sense, we have the gospel of Conservatism according to Metternich. It agrees well enough with that rather idealised notion of Austria which, thirty years before, he had penned for the private eye of Countess Lieven.[2] One who had breathed an atmosphere first swept by Voltaire's icy rationalism and subsequently agitated by the tropical dust-storm of Rousseau's sentiment could not indeed be expected to entertain any vigorous belief in popular government. "The People," he told himself—and, in an age which had seen first a Revolutionary Terror and then a Military Empire enthroned by "the general will," the reflection must be reckoned charitable enough—"the People is everywhere good, but childish."[3] A bolder faith was doubtless possible if not profitable among nations of Anglo-Saxon origin; and he was not perhaps so far from confessing it. "The true character of our time," he told Guizot, "is that of an age of transition. . . . I made myself a conservative socialist. . . . Conservative principles are applicable to the most divers situations."[4] But it remained for Disraeli to proclaim the creed of Tory-Democracy, just as it remained for Abraham Lincoln to enrich democratic dogma both with cynicism and with grace. There is the consolation of this world to be had in the fact that you cannot fool all the people all the time, and perhaps the reflection of another in the thought that God would not have created so many common people unless He loved them best.

Though he might have claimed with as much reason as Disraeli that he was on the side of the angels, Metternich had not in fact much in the way of wings. His feet were well-planted on the earth; his eyes fulfilled that part of Christian theory which consists in

---

[1] "Mémoires," VIII, pp. 187, 188. Cp. his estimate of Kübeck (ibid., p. 282), a bourgeois ennobled by service but whom he took as a model of true aristocracy.
[2] Hanoteau, "Lettres du Prince de Metternich à la Comtesse de Lieven," p. 180.
[3] "Mémoires," III, p. 482.
[4] Ibid., p. 402.

seeing things as they are, recognising their probable consequences and not desiring to be deceived; and his mind had no use for all the tribe of visionaries, both interested and disinterested, who cry "Lo! here" and "Lo! there" and discover fleshly angels ascending or descending the moving stairway of political circumvolution. Is the same twelvemonth in which he exchanged ideas with Disraeli at Brighton, the Provisional Government in Paris, which had included Louis Blanc among its secretaries, was endeavouring to promote the advent of a new heaven and a new earth by the creation of *ateliers nationaux*. Metternich's comment on this proceeding and its accompaniments, although in a fully educated society it might constitute too heavy a platitude to record, may perhaps allow of repetition in our own. "Work," he observes, "is the natural result of industry, as this is the result of prosperity, as credit is born of order and quiet, which, no less, are impossible in the midst of agitation. To ruin those who possess something is not to come to the aid of those who possess nothing; it is only to render misery general. It is the consumers who bring gain to the producers, and both live off what the former dispose of. To misunderstand this truth is to rise against good sense, of which the roots are to be found in quite another soil than the poetical genius of Lamartine or the false humanitarianism of the socialist school."[1] It would have been well for the Revolution if it had preferred these digestible, if unpalatable sentences to the ponderous and poisonous fare that Karl Marx was just then busy serving up for the consumption of ignorance. For prominent amongst Marx's economic errors was, as Lecky has pointed out, the treatment of the question of wages as if it depended only on two parties—the manufacturer and the labourer—and the omission to state that "a third party—the consumer—must come upon the scene," and that "wages, profits and employment will alike fluctuate according to his demand."[2]

So much as this Guizot had known and all that "grande société saine et tranquille"[3] which Lamartine and Louis Blanc had thrown into wild perturbation by their hopes and fancies. But there were also things that Guizot and his friends never knew, yet that entered into the social philosophy of Metternich and Disraeli. "It is not mere fancy," Mr. Woodward observes in an admirable passage, "to take some account of Guizot's Protestantism. Like Bismarck he failed to see that the close and continual co-operation of every

---

[1] "Mémoires," VIII, p. 175.   [2] Lecky, "Democracy and Liberty," I, p. 325.
[3] Quoted by E. L. Woodward, "Three Studies in European Conservatism," p. 205.

U

element in society can alone lead to the attainment of the good life. He lacked the feeling for a commonwealth wherein inequality of condition was no barrier to the positive contribution of all the citizens to a common cause. He never attained to the catholic conception of the Church. . . . He was not free from that spiritual pride which saw liberty only in individual action and religion only in the right development of personal holiness. He would not understand the solidarity of human life, the common responsibility of men for the common weaknesses of men, the greater corporate responsibility of the strong for the failures of the weak."[1] It is an interesting commentary on the fall of the Orleans Monarchy, and all the more interesting that it comes from a quarter by no means favourable to Catholic influences. Incidentally it helps to explain a circumstance that puzzled Macaulay—the failure of Protestantism, after its first fervour was past, to extend its empire. The spirit of association, not the spirit of individuality, is, as indeed the words themselves proclaim, the essence of society; and the Reformation, emasculated by its own principle of private judgment, betrayed more and more in the region of human relationships its want of cohesive power. The quarrel with the visible Church, which at the first had inspired it with all the energy of which hatred is capable, passed, as the obligations of Christian charity were better perceived, into the keeping of a world content to worship the old Pagan gods under new titles, or perhaps no gods at all, and charged with a talent for mockery far more controversially effective than the substantial, though not unanswerable, arguments upon which the Reformers had relied. The fall of Guizot's Ministry has thus the incidental interest of marking the failure of the Protestant interest to intervene successfully in the great debate between the champions—to choose the metaphor that would have approved itself to Metternich— of a natural and of a supernatural chemistry in political life. In the great centre of European thought the solution recommended by English experience had been tried and, as Metternich had anticipated, found wanting. The problem of the Revolution required a deeper analysis than England or than Guizot knew.

One who was neither Catholic nor Protestant, one who claimed to have what none may really possess—a *tabula rasa* of a mind—one who to the alert intellect of adolescence added the trained, discriminating eye of the historical analyst, was at this time surveying on the spot this same momentous Paris Revolution which Metternich watched

[1] E. L. Woodward, "Three Studies in European Conservatism," pp. 218, 219.

from English shores. The science of the brilliant young Frenchman lacked nothing in cool detachment. We may gain something from a comparison of it with the reflections of the calm old German who for fifty years had dodged the storm only at last to be caught in a cloud-burst.

"In 1849," Taine records, "being twenty-one years of age, I was an elector and a very embarrassed one; for I had to name fifteen or twenty deputies, and further, according to the French usage, I was bound not only to choose men but to make a selection amongst theories. It was proposed to me to be a royalist or a republican, a democrat or a conservative, a socialist or a Bonapartist: I was nothing of that sort, nothing actually at all, but all the same I envied the conviction of so many people who had the good fortune to be something. . . . My affirmative friends constructed a constitution like a house . . . and there were many plans to be studied, plans for a marquis's residence, the house of a bourgeois, a workman's dwelling, a soldiers' barrack, a socialist's phalanstery, and even for an encampment of savages. . . . Each man affirmed of his model: 'There is the true habitation of man, the only one that a man of sense can live in.' In my view the argument was poor; personal tastes did not appear to me authoritative. I thought that a house ought not to be built for the architect, nor for itself, but for the proprietor who was to inhabit it. To ask the advice of the proprietor to submit to the French people the plans of its future residence was too plainly affectation or dupery: in a case of that kind the question always furnishes the answer, and besides, even had the answer been free, France was hardly more in a condition to give it than myself."

And then there follows the memorable sentence which, once heard will not allow itself to be forgotten: "Dix millions d'ignorances ne font pas un savoir."

"Ten million ignorances do not make up one knowledge. A people called into counsel can under pressure say what form of government pleases it, but not what form of government suits it. It will find out that only by trial: it needs time to test whether its political residence is convenient, solid, weather-proof, suited to its customs, business, character, peculiarities, angularities. . . . If abroad many political dwellings are solid and last indefinitely, it is because they have been built in a particular manner, around an original massive nucleus, and lean upon some old central building, many times repaired, but always preserved, gradually enlarged, and adapted by probing and lengthening to the requirements of its inhabitants. . . . The social and political fabric where a people can enter and abide is not left to caprice but settled by its character and its past."[1]

Taine had expressed with much of the majesty of the historian the answer of the *ancien régime* to the rude challenge of the Revolution. It was the same reply that Metternich had been giving or

[1] Taine, "L'Ancien Régime," Preface.

trying to give for forty years—the reply that violent measures are the folly of ignorant children, that constitutions are not made but grow, that the statesman seeks not to destroy but to fulfil, that the course of a nation's life must slowly broaden out from precedent to precedent.

The France of that date was, on the contrary, moving with darts and dashes. As Louis Blanc had dispossessed Louis Philippe, so in due course did Louis Napoléon displace Louis Blanc. The cleverest people in Europe had failed to discern the simple truth that Government is no variety entertainment on kaleidoscopic principles but the everlasting bond of that humane association between the dead, the living and their remote posterity which the supreme exponent of this thought has styled "a partnership in all science . . . in all art . . . in every virtue and in all perfection,"[1] and without which a polity dissolves into the mood of a generation. We misunderstand Metternich, however, if we imagine that he attached some sort of magic to monarchy; and despotism, as he plainly states,[2] represented in his view "a symptom of weakness." Monarchy, however, with all its obvious defects, had the merit in that age of entailing a minimum of political disturbance, as it has in every age the merit of supplying a model of corporate union. But Metternich was well aware that positive sweetness and light come of other things than forms of government and might have echoed the cry of Landor's Demosthenes, that politics, even when stigmatised as the "sad refuge of restless minds, averse from business and from study," were still too little damned.[3] He had the statesmanship to see that science can do more for the welfare of the human body, art for that of the human mind, and religion for that of the human spirit than all the politics in the world; and he welcomed them alike. But of these three, that to which his idiosyncrasy inclined was the first.

Nothing, indeed, is so damaging to the popular idea of Metternich as an obscurantist as his intense interest in science, both abstract and applied. One who appears in turn as a vigorous promoter of railways, as a fascinated student of the work of Daguerre, as an excellent amateur doctor, as a friend from whose scientific attainment Justus von Liebig could infer high talent and to whom Alexander von Humboldt could write, "Each of your letters repeats to me that nothing escapes you, that you grasp all with that beneficent zeal which quickens and encourages talent,"[4] was no champion of dark-

[1] Burke, "Reflections."　　　　　　　　　[2] "Mémoires," VIII, p. 637.
[3] "Imag. Conv.": "Demosthenes and Eubulides," II.
[4] Quoted by Srbik, I, pp. 297–99.

ness but a lover of lucidity and light. In him as in Frederick William IV of Prussia the old virtue of the Aufklärung lived on—that same conviction which seeks the improvement of human conditions, not in any curtailment of the rewards of industry and intelligence but in the expansion of human knowledge.

So far as Natural Science was concerned, Metternich, eager in this regard to see and hear every new thing, was in step with the spirit of the time. It was otherwise in regard to matters of sentiment and religion, for in both these directions the Eighteenth Century embarrassed his view. A lover of beautiful things to so great a degree that his room in the Vienna Chancery is said to have resembled the studio of a fastidious and wealthy artist rather than the study of a statesman, he found in classical art his dominant pleasure. It is so much the more an irony that he should be thought of as the foe of Italy, for Italy was of all countries that which gave him the richest hours of sensuous life. He luxuriated in that land of olive and myrtle, in its sunshine, its music, its monuments and its memories. But the poetry which he found there was not the poetry of the incoming age. The Italy that he loved, danced and sang indeed, but to more stately measures than could be derived from Marsellaise or Carmagnole. The mind of the mid-century, the magic of the Risorgimento, was hidden from his eyes. It might perhaps have been said of him that, as befitted so regular a student of Livy, he looked through all "the roaring and the wreaths" towards that older Rome, which, after the manner of a great artist, sits ever patient, surveying the balanced beauty of her buildings, listening to the frozen song of her statuary, seeing all things steadily and whole, thinking ever imperially, and resolving all strife of tongues and peoples by the immortal precept of the Pax Romana. Modern Italy has in our own day turned back from the poetry of its first Liberal romance to glance again at that graver and greater tradition. It is possible that Metternich might have worked more easily with a regime, intent at first upon restoring order and resisting Bolshevism, and, until seduced and terrorised by Nazi power, friendly to the pollarded Austria of the Treaty of St. Germain. But, as things were, he was confronted by a nation of poets whose songs before sunrise made prose indeed of the Austrian administration—of its new roads, canals and bridges, of the returning prosperity of Venice and the widening wealth of Milan. Though probably as good as any in Italy, the government of Lombardy and Venetia was as fatally prejudiced by the principle of nationality as that of the English in

Ireland. Its difficulties and its defects were similar; its defence was the same.

The good servant of Kaiser Franz entrusted with the care of his master's possessions in Italy and his master's allegiance in ecclesiastical affairs had in truth no title to perceive in the middle distance the flag of United Italy floating above the Quirinal or to raise upon a far horizon the walls of the Vatican City. In these matters all the honours of foresight pass to another. Between the one time representative at Petersburg of the poor Court of Sardinia and the powerful Chancellor of the Austrian Empire there lay differences as deep as ever separated allied commanders in a military coalition. For the Savoyard had discerned, not only the part that the House of Savoy might play in the re-integration of Italy, but the part that the Papacy must play in the re-integration of Christendom. Among the masters of the Counter-Revolution there is found none greater than Joseph de Maistre. The very dimness of natural sight in that lonely sentinel upon the Neva seemed to intensify his piercing and prophetic vision. With the same penetration that enabled him to display the public executioner as the ultimate sanction of civil society Maistre pointed to the Pope as its indispensable guide. In the great seminaries of France, the Eagle of Chambéry gradually ousted the Eagle of Meaux. French Catholicism ceased to be Gallican and became Ultramontane; and the acute national intelligence perceived that in Rome lay, if only it could be elicited, not merely the negative but the positive reply to the Revolution. It was a reply of gathering volume. As Chateaubriand met Rousseau's sentimentalism with a more radiant flow of kindred feeling, as Maistre, in contrast to Voltaire's sparkling mockery and fire-fly mirth, bathed the whole structure of society in lurid flame and kindled anew the old beacon-light of the Papacy upon the eternal hills, so did Lamennais, with the aid of his two best disciples, flash the brilliance of the Roman candle before the eyes of a people sitting, as Metternich had perceived, in great spiritual darkness. The challenge as well of a golden age as of a complex civilisation, as well of an education on liberal lines as of the sordid conditions of manual labour, was thus gradually taken up by champions, using indeed French armour, but bearing the arms of Rome.

To this resilient energy of Catholic life which, though after Metternich's time, was consummated in the definitive presentation of the Pope in his essential aspect of infallible doctor, in the lapsing of his medieval functions as international arbitrator, in the stripping from the Papacy of its temporal power and in the issue of the Leonine Encyclicals. Metternich remained as unresponsive as to the complementary German movement represented by Görres, Windischmann, Walter and the Swabian school generally. Its full significance, for one thing, did not immediately appear; his eyes, for another, were probably held by the eighteenth-century idea that the Papacy had fallen politically into a hopeless decline; and there was besides enough to give pause to a man of his antecedents in the operations of apologists who showed an incomparable talent for reforging the exact weapons of the Revolution in the interest of Catholic thought. Only perhaps in Newman's contemporary attempt to supply ecclesiastical biology with a doctrine of historic evolution would he have found something congenial, for he liked history and scientific method and English good sense. But of Newman perhaps he hardly knew.

For all that, Metternich passed almost insensibly from the Febronian influence which had pervaded the Austrian Court since the days of Joseph II towards that more generous appreciation of the Papacy as a force in the world which Von Müller's "Travels of the Popes" had first opened to a younger generation. The change was facilitated and attended by a development in his own personal life. Starting so far as religious conviction was concerned from little more than the deism of Voltaire, he had come as time went on to accept a more humane position. "Twenty years ago," he told Nesselrode in 1817, "a thorough investigation of the Scriptures would have made me an atheist like d'Alembert or a Christian like Chateaubriand; to-day I believe and scrutinise no more. I have read too much and seen too much not to know that it does not suffice to read in order to understand, not to know that it would be bold in myself to condemn what I can ill understand from ignorance or insufficiency of the studies essential to a profound and above all impartial criticism; in a word, I believe and dispute no more. Accustomed as I am to the consideration of hard questions of morals, what must I not have done or have allowed to be effected by the mere process of nature in order to reach the point where the Pope and my curé themselves would beg me to accept from them the most portable version of the Bible?"[1]

This childlike mind was not quite the completed story. Some-where about 1830, as a result of Mélanie's influence or, as his biographer suggests, of the reviving Revolutionary alarms of

[1] "Mémoires," III, p. 59.

1830 or, maybe, of the not unexampled discovery that positive religion is essential to the full development of character, Metternich became definitely more devout. He added a private chapel to his Vienna house, found an oracle in St. Paul, and read the Bible daily—one or two chapters in the version of Luther, which he declared to be the best of all translations.[1] "I am a Churchman," he declared, "a free and strong Catholic."[2] Thus by the close of life his title was complete to the moving and majestic rites of a Church which, perhaps, could alone have satisfied his sense of history and, perhaps, can alone supply the final logic of his international ideas. This full-fledged faith of his, although there was nothing of ultramontanism in the matter of it, and something perhaps of "the religion of all sensible men" in the manner of it, found expression during the last decade of his life, not only in some modification of his old eighteenth-century distrust of the Jesuits, but more noticeably in the welcome that he gave to the Austrian Concordat of 1855 with Rome—an agreement calculated to sweep away the secularities of "Josephism" and substitute the principle of co-operation between Church and State for the old, uneasy antagonism.

The Concordat of 1855 formed a mild feature in that severe and autocratic régime which, following immediately upon the abortive revolution of 1848, derived its name, as it derived its energy, from Alexander von Bach. This is, then, perhaps the occasion to point out that to a discerning eye Metternich's domestic apologia may well seem to rest securely on the fact that he was succeeded in power and for ten years far surpassed in arbitrary rule by the very leader of the Revolution, a Liberal, suddenly converted to the uses of auto-cracy and cynically ruthless, to Metternich's distress, in their applica-tion to Hungary. The study of the Bach System will help to steady a mind, if such there is, disturbed by Bibl's all too facile criticism of the Metternich System. Forms of government are in the last resort determined by how much or how little the mass of the people understand of the facts of life. From his house—his "Winter-palais" on the Rennweg—whither in the September of 1851 he had been permitted to return, the old statesman, almost as much a patriarch to the young Emperor, who asked but did not honour his counsels, as to the great-grandchild, who convinced him that his true vocation had been that of a nurse, had thus the opportunity of watching a curious vindication by his foremost critic of his own much-abused administration. As if to make his case complete, in the

[1] "Mémoires," V, p. 242.   [2] Ibid., VII, p. 424.

foremost centre of European ideas, Despotism, embodied in the Third Napoleon, had likewise displaced the milder forms of Monarchy; and that by virtue of a plebiscite. Democracy then did not believe in itself, even though plainly pleased to parade its power. As Metternich had always supposed, the hour—the inexorable hour—of its responsibility had not yet fully struck.

Whilst Bach in Austria and Hungary was thus converting Metternich's conservative reverence for monarchical tradition into a strong, centralised tyranny, Schwarzenberg was doing his best in Germany to substitute a definite Austrian hegemony for the Austro-Prussian diarchy which had hitherto operated under cover of an Austrian primacy of honour. He had doubtless his excuses, since Radowitz was aiming at a German union under Prussian control, but the move which culminated in 1851 in the so-called Punctuation of Olmütz was nevertheless a disastrous one, destroying as it eventually did the tacit co-operation of the two great German Powers and subordinating in the end the idea of a loose-knit federation, with many gleaming centres of cultural life after Austrian models, to the ruder charm of a compact military Bundesstaat in the style of Prussia. Metternich would never have manœuvred on these lines nor with these consequences. He understood the limitations of Austrian strength and the claims of Prussian power. He understood, as Bismarck informed Karolyi in 1862, that the support of Prussia, which Austria counted upon in her foreign policy, must be paid for by giving to Prussia a fairly free hand in the German Confederation.[1] And, as he apparently told Bismarck during their historic meeting at Johannisberg in the critical summer of 1851, it was in the Austrian interest that Prussia should become, what Austria already was, a "saturated state."[2]

The phrase was good metal and remained in Bismarck's storehouse of memory to be recoined by him, with a new stamp upon it, for Salisbury's edification in 1887.[3] It was not the only thing he had learned from Metternich. "The form of the living, the shade of the dead Metternich," observes Srbik, "accompanied Bismarck from his political beginnings to his departure."[4] Different as the great German Chancellor was from the Austrian—different as the air of Berlin is different from the air of Vienna, as the education of the nineteenth century is from that of the eighteenth, as the tradition of a National Protestant is from that of a Catholic Humanist—they

[1] See Srbik, II, p. 538.
[2] Ibid., p. 414.
[3] Ibid., p. 545.
[4] Ibid., p. 558.

drew, as at that first meeting, so in their final outlook, near together. It was not merely that, as men of the world, they saw in the Revolution a deadly reef and in Monarchy a fairer haven for order and continuity than Democracy was in any case to supply, but that, upon the stretch of international waters which it was peculiarly their business to navigate, they came in the end to select much the same anchorage, Metternich receding under the pressure of contrary winds from the congress and concert system of his more hopeful years towards a kind of hypostatic union between the three Eastern Monarchies, and Bismarck passing, by way of Dreikaiserbündniss and Reinsurance Treaty, from a policy cynically bellicose to one at least cryptically pacific.

There was this further resemblance. In both cases the pilots were dropped, and their charts discarded by captains confident with all the confidence of youth. It took no more, in fact, than a decade for Austria to lose the great diplomatic position that she had held in Europe since the fall of Napoleon as well as that primacy in German counsels which it needed, as we have just seen, a dexterous but not a miraculous diplomacy to maintain. The young Emperor—Francis Joseph—neither eager to be advised nor fortunate in the possession among his official counsellors of any first-rate adviser, defied all the tradition of the elders. The Austrian Government with an energy wholly beyond its strength became both active and odious on every front. Prussia was humbled in the manner already described; Russia, which in accordance with Metternich's far-sighted arrangement at Münchengrätz had come to the rescue of the Austrian Empire and suppressed the revolt in Hungary, was alienated by the absence of support, either moral or military, in her Near Eastern —her Crimean—conflict with the Western Powers; Turkey was coerced into the liberation and the loss of Montenegro; Italy—the idea, that is, of a united Italy, championed by Sardinia and backed by France—was openly challenged. This last mistake was the most immediately disastrous. Metternich lived just long enough to see it made, and in the final glimpse that we have of him as a statesman he stands as if desperately waving the young Emperor back from the perilous turning that led to Solferino. A grandchild long lived to relate how in the spring of 1859 Francis Joseph came to visit the old man in the house on the Rennweg:—"Grandpapa said to the Emperor: 'Only for God's sake no ultimatum to Italy.' Upon which the Emperor replied, 'It went yesterday.' "[1]

[1] Srbik, II.

Not many weeks after, the Austrian Empire had definitely entered upon the long decline of which we ourselves have seen the final end. Nothing, therefore, could have been more dramatically appropriate than that the Minister, who had raised the State so high, should have died between Magenta and Solferino. It ,seemed, indeed, almost as if he had waited to see if his work was doomed, until the knell was really sounding. Those who had made the pleasure and the drama of his days had with little exception passed from the stage. Mélanie, once so fearful of being left a widow, had herself been five years gone; and of the major statesmen who had figured with him at the Vienna Congress, Nesselrode alone remained. The poetry of old age had in the end found out one who had been exceptionally loyal to the prose of middle life. Few vales of memory have been richer in splendid shadows than his, or offer finer dissolving views to painters of the school of Lytton Strachey. Napoleon, Alexander, Nicholas, Talleyrand, Castlereagh, Chateaubriand, Canning—these and so many more moved for him behind the mists of time; and he might have borrowed the words of his great contemporary and compatriot to salute them:—

> Ye wavering shapes, again ye do enfold me,
> As erst upon my troubled sight ye stole;
> Shall I this time attempt to clasp, to hold ye?
> Still for the fond illusion yearns my soul?
> Ye press around! Come then, your captive hold me. . . .[1]

But, except for these shadowy existences, Metternich was alone with a new generation; and at that midday hour of a midsummer's day—it was the eleventh of June, 1859—upon which he died, an epoch, already somewhile dead, was buried.

There are those who will linger, as when a tale is told, to frame an epilogue or phrase a moral. What manner of man, they may say, was this, or with whom shall he be compared? A representative man, one must reply, for the half-century to which he belonged kept him forty years and more in power and the half-century that followed held him all that time and more in hatred; an able statesman, for his country at no date enjoyed a greater prestige; a good diplomatist, for his ways were ways of pleasantness and peace; a

---

[1] Tr. Swanwick.
> Ihr naht euch wieder, schwankende Gestalten,
> Die früh sich einst dem trüben Blick gezeigt.
> Versuch ich wohl euch diesmal fest zu halten?
> Fühl ich mein Herz noch jenem Wahn geneigt?
> Ihr drängt euch zu! Nun gut, so mögt ihr walten. . . .

great European, for a tired Continent had rest for a full generation. More than any man of his period he stood for that international solidarity which is admitted on all hands to be our own urgent need; and in this respect, if in no other, he looked beyond his own age into ours. As for comparison there is Kaunitz before him and Bismarck after him; and both are compeers who offer interesting points both of contrast and resemblance. Yet Metternich is more amiable than either and of a nobler nature. There is no blot upon his career like the Partition of Poland, no stain like the Ems telegram. Napoleon and Talleyrand, it is true, accused him of lying, the latter affirming that he lied but lied in vain. These are strange witnesses, however, to sustain this particular charge. Doubtless Metternich did not show his hand in play, but there is no evidence that he violated the rules, etiquette or conversation of the diplomatic game. His own account indeed of his diplomatic methods anticipates Bismarck's:—"Ma politique à moi c'est de tromper en disant la vérité."[1] Cynical comment as this is upon human nature, it is hardly open to moral stricture.

Englishmen—and this is more valuable testimony than Napoleon's or Talleyrand's—liked him well and found him honourable. "I must do him the justice to say," wrote Cowley to Aberdeen from Vienna in 1829, "that during a residence here of nearly six years I have never been able to discover any just grounds for the doubts and suspicions entertained at St. Petersburg and more or less at Berlin and Paris, respecting the proceedings of Austria at Constantinople."[2] Escott in his "Story of British Diplomacy" calls in evidence, somewhat to the same effect, a passage in the unpublished papers of Lord Rokeby, who frequented "the set presided over by the fourth Lord Aberdeen. Metternich belonged to it and showed himself there exactly as he was—not (wrote Rokeby) the Machiavellian genius some have described, but the pleasantest and most equal-tempered man I ever knew. He never lost his temper in his life, nor had a mean thought or said a mean word about anyone. But he wanted peace."[3] This is not so different from the character of a gentleman as Newman drew it in the famous half-critical, half-admiring, wholly subtle passage. "What a different man Metternich really was," wrote Disraeli to Stanhope, "to what those fancied him who formed their judgment in the glitter of Vienna.

[1] Quoted by Srbik, II, p. 529.
[2] Aberdeen Correspondence (unpublished), 1828-30, p. 252. (Lent me by Lord Stanmore.)
[3] T. H. S. Escott, "Story of British Diplomacy," p 268.

A profound head and an affectionate heart."[1] There was certainly something in his policy that corresponded with this notion of his personality—some strain of nobler effort befitting a great gentleman. Neither in the work of Kaunitz nor of Bismarck is there a good will to have done with animosities, to carry civilisation to the point of contentment, to weld Europe into a harmonious whole. But Metternich was a good neighbour and no way ambitious to remove established landmarks. Doubtless, as Mr. Woodward warns us, he lacked "final nobility." His was no soul like that of Thomas More, so richly endowed both with public virtue and with private grace as to shine brightest in the constellation of his time and at the last to set in radiant splendour. He was no more than a man of parts above the average and of merits reminiscent sometimes of the complacent equanimity of Aristotle's Megalopsychos. Doubtless, too, he was intellectually incomplete, as every ecclesiastical or political champion is bound at least to appear ever since the Reformation and the Revolution confused the great natural unities of Church and State by introducing the idea of the nation into the one and of party into the other. Yet it was surely high thinking that caused him to see all local aims in the light of a larger and more lofty purpose; to urge mankind to study to be quiet; to press the nations continually into council, not for the liquidation of war, but, as had hardly been attempted since the days of Constance, for the organisation of peace.

Nationality and Democracy hated Metternich, for they were the nurslings of the Revolution and he suspected those defects in their upbringing which Time has made plain to all but the blindest. We can imagine with what urbane satisfaction he would have pointed to the statement of one acute American observer of our own time that "Nationalism . . . must be accounted one of the major underlying causes of the (World) War," and of another that "the attempt of 1919 to reorganise the European Continent on the basis of race and in accordance with the principle of self-determination produced utter and unimaginable ruin."[2] Not, however, that he spoke or thought of Nationality in the manner to which we might nowadays be tempted, who have beheld her as the mother of the Furies, rousing the worst passions from Dublin to Calcutta and rendering insoluble a whole chain of political and economic problems from the Baltic to the Balkans. He was too statesmanlike for that. "I am not of those," he wrote to Apponyi, "who make no account

[1] Buckle, "Life of Disraeli," III, p. 194.
[2] Fay, "Origins of the World War," I, p. 44; F. H. Simonds, "Can Europe keep the Peace?" p. 348.

of the sentiment of nationality; I not only conceive this sentiment but respect it."[1] Yet subconsciously, if not in set terms, he recognised the truth, which Acton later emphasised in a penetrating essay, that Nationality forms too narrow a foundation for a state, and that commonwealths, raised like the British and Austrian Empires upon a diversity of racial genius, possess the rationale of a higher civilisation. Egoism makes no man noble, nor any nation; and the desire to be quit of the Habsburg Empire in 1918 was stronger evidence of intellectual limitation than of spiritual progress. Civilisation has but little cause to be interested in racial feelings except in so far as they blend to issue again in richer and more abundant life.

As in the case of Nationality, so in that of Democracy Metternich's criticism was tempered by judicious thought. He told Ticknor[2] that only Democracy could have carried America forward with such speed, for only Democracy created the necessary momentum of competition; and he added that Democracy, though a falsehood in Europe, was natural to the States. But he added that he agreed with Tocqueville that it was the most complicated form of government, involving "un tour de force perpetuel," that as a system it wore out fast, and that, whatever the end might be, it contained at least no promise of peaceful, mature old age. It was, in fact, to his eye a decomposing force, impatient and incapable of that united effort of a society towards a higher standard of civilisation to which Monarchy pre-eminently ministered.

Nearly a century has gone by since the conversation with Ticknor took place, and a man may reasonably wonder whether Metternich's reputation is not now better served by the enmity of the Revolution than it could have been by Revolutionary praise. To east and west of us that portentous agitation has raised its temples to Communism and Plutocracy, and from the Union of Soviet Republics and the United States of America[3] we may infer its final meaning. Was Metternich wrong who feared these gods, or obscurantist who fought this darkness? He rises in truth to his proper stature only when we remember that, disdaining that betrayal of our rational unity to national or secular prejudice which has been well stigmatised under the title of "la trahison des clercs," he carried in his hands for the short space of a man's life the torch of Latin civilisation—that ancient torch which seems to assemble in one steady, single flame

[1] "Mémoires," VII, p. 197.   [2] Ticknor, "Life, Letters and Journals," II, p. 14.
[3] If this judgment seems to anyone hard, I invite them to look at Mr. Allen's "Only Yesterday."

all the true lights of the world, the dry light of Greece, the trans-
cendent light of Palestine, the austere, vestal fire of Rome. Like a
pillar of flame it moves before the path of Humanity, not agitated
by wind of words, not flickering nor failing; and in its glow Liberty
is seen to be nothing but a perfect law, Equality to blush to a quaint
confusion before the face of chivalry, and all the harsh vermilion of
Fraternity to be toned to the deep colour of love. The *ancien régime*,
as much recent research seems to establish, failed indeed less at the
close in these high courtesies of citizenship than was once believed,
but, be that as it may, they represented at least its characteristic,
instinctive contribution to the science of government. As we pass
through some *salle des pas perdus*,[1] where the echo of historic
footsteps has died away, its spectral memories are brought again to
view until, as maybe at Versailles when we reach the Galerie des
Glaces, the charmed reflection of its meaning bursts upon our inward eye and we seem to see its incommunicable grace almost as
Burke once beheld it with bodily vision.

"Courtesy," says one whose words have found their way into
Matthew Arnold's Notebooks, " is the bond of all society, and there
is no society that can last without it." To Metternich also the true
significance of the old society, in whose penultimate act an Austrian
Princess had played precisely the rôle of tragedy-queen, was dramatically clear. Perceiving rightly enough that it contained much
sweetness and light of which Democracy was not, or at least not
yet worthy, he sought to keep it alive, not merely on account of that
"Little Public" of thinkers which Voltaire, roughly excluding the
rest of mankind as the vulgar, had boldly affirmed to be the Public
itself,[2] but in the broader interest of civilisation. His political
philosophy is not patently at fault. Natural science, poetic insight,
the wisdom of the world—all are ranged behind it; and his realism
rests upon the facts of life. Nature, not only by virtue of her infinite
inequality of function, but also of her endless insistence upon
sacrifice, is profoundly hierarchical. Order and Degree, as a man
need look no further than his Shakespeare or his Milton to learn,
satisfy the æsthetic requirements not less than the practical conditions of human society. And, for the rest, the truth of the aphorisms
that it is always the world of fashion which governs the world and
that the greater the change, the more marked the resemblance
reasserts itself continually after divers manners. These things

[1] The room in which the Congress of Vienna met was, in fact, so called. (Hübner,
"Une Année de ma vie," p. 407.)
[2] Voltaire to Helvétius (Œuvr. Compl. XLI, p. 296. Corresp. 4543).

Metternich knew; and because of them, his expectation that the Body Politic after much walking (*après avoir beaucoup marché*) would with surprise discover that it had returned to its starting-point,[1] may prove correct enough.

Yet, for all this, the Torch of Latin Civilisation is not stayed but, beckoning, as it does continually, to a greater seemliness, order and peace in the relationships of men and separating with its radiance the fair things of life from those that are foul and foolish, seems to light up the pageant of the Past only that it may point us, the wiser, upon our way.

[1] "Mémoires," VII, p. 402.

BIBLIOGRAPHY

I

THE general history of Metternich's period offers, of course, inexhaustible opportunities to the student. The Cambridge Modern History, with its bibliographies of the Revolutionary, Napoleonic, Restoration and Growth of Nationalities epochs, supplies the English reader with a convenient chart of European studies. Those who wish to pay special attention to Austria and Germany will find their needs sufficiently met by consulting—

A. Springer: *Geschichte Oesterreichs seit dem Wiener Frieden.*
A. Stern: *Geschichte Europas 1815-71.*
V. Bibl: *Der Zerfall Österreichs.*
H. von Treitschke: *Deutsche Geschichte im neunzehnten Jahrhundert* (which is also available in a translation by E. and C. Paul).

II

Metternich's personality and policy are to be sought primarily in his *Memoirs and Despatches.* The French edition in 8 vols. has been used for reference in this book. Only 5 vols. have appeared in English.

J. Hanoteau's *Lettres du Prince de Metternich à la Comtesse Lieven* and the *Correspondance du Cardinal Consalvi avec le Prince de Metternich* afford further first-hand information, and more may be unearthed almost indefinitely by hunting up Srbik's references and browsing amongst the memoirs of the time.

III

H. von Srbik's huge two-volume life of Metternich is not likely to be displaced for many years, if ever, as the leading biographical and critical authority on the subject. There are, however, numerous other studies of Metternich or of aspects of Metternich, among which mention should be made at any rate of the following:

V. Bibl: *Metternich in neuer Beleuchtung.*
F. von Demelitsch: *Metternich und seine auswärtige Politik.*
E. Molden: *Die Orientpolitik des Fuersten Metternich.*
A. Sorel: *Essais d'histoire et de Critique.*
C. de Mazade: *Un Chancelier d'ancien régime.*
M. Paléologue: *Talleyrand, Metternich, Chateaubriand.*
E. L. Woodward: *Three Studies in European Conservatism.*
Harman: *Metternich* and C. S. B. Buckland: *Metternich and the British Government from 1809 to 1813.*

W

INDEX